Simon Gray Unbound

Simon Gray Unbound

The Journey of a Dramatist

PETER WOLFE

McFarland & Company, Inc., Publishers
Jefferson, North Carolina, and London

LIBRARY OF CONGRESS CATALOGUING-IN-PUBLICATION DATA

Wolfe, Peter, 1933–
    Simon Gray unbound : the journey of a dramatist / Peter Wolfe.
        p.   cm.
    Includes bibliographical references and index.

    ISBN 978-0-7864-6299-5
    softcover : 50# alkaline paper ∞

    1. Gray, Simon, 1936–2008—Criticism and interpretation.
I. Title.
PR6057.R33Z96   2011
822'.914—dc22   2011002056

BRITISH LIBRARY CATALOGUING DATA ARE AVAILABLE

© 2011 Peter Wolfe. All rights reserved

No part of this book may be reproduced or transmitted in any form or by any means, electronic or mechanical, including photocopying or recording, or by any information storage and retrieval system, without permission in writing from the publisher.

Cover image: Simon Gray, ca. 1970s (Photofest)

Manufactured in the United States of America

McFarland & Company, Inc., Publishers
  Box 611, Jefferson, North Carolina 28640
    www.mcfarlandpub.com

To
Sam Latragna
(aka Sammy Ballgame)
the great-hearted one
whose expertise swathes James Joyce's
epiphanies and the bull-dogging headlock
of Cowboy Bob Evans

Acknowledgments

I would like to thank those people whose time and energy went into the preparation of this book: Mark Burkholder, who, as Dean of the University of Missouri-St Louis's Dean of Arts and Science, reduced my teaching load, an act of kindness that sped the book's composition; Katherine H. Burkman, the world's leading expert on Simon Gray, whose willingness to share her expertise bettered my treatment of the canon; Tim Nelson and Mary Zettwoch of UMSL's Thomas Jefferson Library, who tracked down vital research materials for me; and Retta Cardwell, whose computer savvy lowered my anxiety level at those fraught moments when this word processor stopped processing.

The combined help of the following people amounts to a major contribution: Myron Kove, Terry Weiss, Marva Scott, Ethel Johnson, Robert Feit, Kurt Schreyer, Moses Horowitz, Bron Brennan, Lawrence Lenke, and Norvelle Brown.

Table of Contents

Acknowledgments	vi
Abbreviations	viii
Preface	1
One Up from Bundling	3
Two Bundling Alchemized	24
Three The Labors of the Thrice-Born	42
Four Exit Wounds	58
Five Nodes on a Grid	105
Six The Death of Education	136
Seven Coercive Connections	170
Conclusion: Stranded	208
Bibliography	239
Index	245

Abbreviations

Throughout the text, parenthetical references to Gray's work will use the following abbreviations.

B	*Butley*	OM	*Old Masters*
BH	*Breaking Hearts*	RC	*The Rear Column and Other Plays*; includes *The Rear Column*, *Molly*, and *Man in a Side-Car*
C	*Colmain*		
CM	*Cell Mates*		
CODA	*Coda*		
CP	*Close of Play*	SD	*Simply Disconnected*
CS	*A Comeback for Stark*	SD	*The Smoking Diaries*
DD	*Dog Days*	SG1	*The Definitive Simon Gray I*; includes *Wise Child*, *Dutch Uncle*, *Spoiled*, *The Caramel Crisis*, and *Sleeping Dog*
FC	*Fat Chance*		
Four	*Four Plays*; includes *The Pig Trade*, *Japes Too*, *Michael*, and *The Holy Terror*		
		SG2	*The Definitive Simon Gray II*; includes *Pig in a Poke* and *Two Sundays*
Fox	*Enter a Fox*		
I	*The Idiot*		
J	*Japes*	SG3	*The Definitive Simon Gray III*; includes *Quartermaine's Terms*, *Stage Struck*, *Tartuffe: An Adaptation*, and *A Month in the Country*
J3U	*Just the Three of Us*		
Lady	*How's That for Telling 'Em, Fat Lady?*		
LC	*The Last Cigarette*		
LMC	*The Late Middle Class*	SG4	*The Definitive Simon Gray IV*; includes *Hidden Laughter*, *The Common Pursuit*, *After Pilkington*, *Old Flames*, and *They Never Slept*
LN	*Little Nell*		
LP	*Little Portia*		
LS	*Life Support*		
M	*Melon*		
OE	*Otherwise Engaged and Other Plays*; includes *Otherwise Engaged*, *Two Sundays* and *Plaintiffs and Defendants*	SP	*Simple People*
		UP	*An Unnatural Pursuit and Other Pieces*
		YJ	*The Year of the Jouncer*

Preface

Outliers and anomalies often magnetize us. What first drew me to Simon Gray was the dearth of magnetism he has generated beyond the box office. Although he ranks artistically alongside contemporaries of the English stage like John Osborne, Harold Pinter, and Alan Bennett, he lags far behind these worthies in attracting critical commentary. This neglect is surprising. Gray's first stage hit, *Butley* (1971), had such a long, happy run that the American Film Theater Series of 1973–74 slotted it into its first and only season together with classics like Chekhov's *Three Sisters* and O'Neill's *The Iceman Cometh*. Then academics like Sophia B. Blaydes (1977), Rüdiger Imhof (1981), and David M. Bergeron (1984) joined a conversation that peaked in the 1992 appearance of Katherine M. Burkman's *Simon Gray: A Casebook*.

Besides including an important essay on *Butley*, the Burkman volume offered fresh views of Gray's collaborations with Harold Pinter and the artistry of stage gems like *Otherwise Engaged*, *The Rear Column*, and *Hidden Laughter*. But critiques on Gray since the *Casebook*, though sharp, have also lagged. Only the onset of the official memorial website (<http://simongray.org.uk>), soon after Gray's 2008 death, has moved him from the wings. It hasn't moved him far. Though many of the blogs found on the website have value, they're mostly impressions and reminiscences.

Gray calls for an extended, systematic discussion of the growth and formation of his art. No easy job; nothing as dogged as a theme explains Simon Gray. Too wily and inventive to be contained by ideologies and -isms, his work lacks a commanding subject or "figure in the carpet" that tells all. On the other hand, the canon takes life from persistences, even obsessions. These continuities, which he delivers with grace and fluency, probe the particular and the personal. Memory here is key. His eight volumes of diaries and memoirs, mainly *The Smoking Diaries* (2004) and *The Year of the Jouncer* (2006), describe him moving both closer to his family of origin and as far away as he can get.

This feat takes root in the woes heaped on him by being evacuated to his Montreal grandparents at age four; returning home five years later, when German bombs had stopped falling on the UK, clueless about both his family of origin and English manners; and, finally, becoming aware of what he'd call many decades later "the sapping logistics of adultery" *(Little Nell*, x). He never outgrew his deep-seated resentment and, to his grief, his later envy of his philandering dad. Such a grip did this deadlock put on him that, besides losing his own marriage to adultery, he drove himself as a writer with the fury of a self-hater. Yet, following a tendency to treat others more kindly than he did himself, he tempered this anger with a refusal to ask too much from his characters. The festering emotions he dredged up from their psyches gauges the heartbreaking gap between life as it is and as it ought to be. Rather than merely recycling his materials, this self-referential artist kept mining them for their thematic heft. As well he might have. He built most of his work around the male psyche in extremis because, though raised in a tradition that prized pedigree, provenance, and heritage, he spent his life battling disruption and waste.

But he didn't go overboard challenging the moral authority of the state. His sentences have grace, his scenes, drama, and his people, depth. Another sign of the excellence of his plays: he doesn't make clear whose side he's on. To show a couple in each other's arms at final curtain would be to play his sensibility false. Love doesn't conquer all. Instead, when his people aren't alone onstage at play's end, they're caught in the amber of the bittersweet ambiguity they've concocted. A good move on Gray's part. Better at describing than explaining, he has left the fun of connecting the dots to us.

The dots spread out. He doles out the contradictions of personality in small hints, building conflict slowly till it gains terrific mass and might. This relentlessness, though, doesn't swamp his sense of humor. His plays shake our sides with laughter. What's more, his audiences and readers will also nod or sigh in recognition at certain lines in the plays. These lines provoke laughs, not necessarily because they're funny, but, rather, because they strike a chord in us. They voice a shared secret between us and Gray. Finally, their universality makes the rootlessness of his people less urgent, less desperate, but more tragic. A Ben Butley will only face the truth of his inner impoverishment in fleeting, painful moments. But these moments needn't define him. The plays traffic in diminishing male potency, aging, and mortality. Tempering this intransigence, Gray neither demonizes his people nor sugarcoats their flaws.

The immanence they glimpse both rarely and patchily also fuels their odd sorties into spiritual growth. These hints of spirit infusing the ordinary, even the seedy and rundown, show his people processing time and thus giving it meaning. They have become implicated in their evolving fate. They also show Gray to be more about continuity than change, a blow for freedom that reimagines the heretofore irreparable and the inescapable. Though his work tilts mainly toward the darkness, there's something in it both tender and subtly dangerous that also steers it fitfully toward redemption. Look closely, and you might spot a hint of it. Gray's late-life discovery of reality as regards *it*self, not *one*self, makes him the enemy of closed doors.

One

Up from Bundling

The subject of only one book of essays and a dash of articles and book chapters, Simon Gray qualifies as England's most neglected major playwright of the past 40 years. In her *Guardian* obituary, Lyn Gardner rightly said of him that he "barely figures in most books about postwar British theatre" (1). Readers, theater audiences, and critics have been content to assume that a play written by him must be good because he wrote it. Perhaps matters could rest there.

Despite having created a dead end, this assumption rests on solid footing. *Otherwise Engaged* (1975) was voted the Best Play of the 1976–77 theater season by the New York Drama Critics Circle; *Quartermaine's Terms* (1981) won eight Obie awards; a revival of *Butley*, named by the (London) *Evening Standard* the best new play of 1971, became Broadway's hottest ticket in the fall of 2006 with Nathan Lane in the title role. Nor has Lane been the only big-name actor to work in a Simon Gray play. From the start of his stage career, Gray attracted headliners. Alec Guinness had the lead role in Gray's West End debut, *Wise Child* (1967), with later plays including in their casts Nigel Hawthorne, Michael Gambon, and Jeremy Irons. It gets better for the theater buff. Gray's 1991 television play *They Never Slept* featured Pete Postlethwaite, Imelda Staunton, and Edward Fox, who later starred in Gray's 2004 hit, *The Old Masters*. Finally, 11 of the plays Gray wrote for both television and the stage from *Butley* to *Life Support* (1997) featured Alan Bates.

Many of these same plays, together with *Otherwise Engaged* and several others by Gray, were directed by Harold Pinter, whose statement about Gray, "He shows himself no mercy" (15), provides a good entry point for a discussion of Gray's work. First, it invites Freud's concept of the artist as a battlefield. The concept fits Gray. This "curious mix of mischief and irritability" (Gardner 2) who denied in 2008 that he has any wisdom to impart (CODA 62), parades his faults both often and openly in his non-fictional work. For instance, besides subtitling *Enter a Fox*, his 2001 memoir, *Further Adventures of a Paranoid*, he called himself in *An Unnatural Pursuit* "a liar" (216, 223) who nearly did jail time for stealing from the London Underground. This perpetrator of a "machine swindle" (SD 121) — dropping a coin no longer in currency into a ticket machine and receiving, along with his ticket to ride, a handful of change — had earlier broken into lockers at his Montreal grade school to pinch books for resale (SD 128–29). Later, in his student days at Cambridge, he would cheat at poker. Ever brutal with himself as Pinter noted, he said of his cheating, "I not only caught myself doing it but also caught myself pretending that I wasn't" (SD 121), thus branding himself a coward and a cheat in the same sentence (he'd confess to being *both* a coward and a bully in his posthumously published memoir, *Coda* [149]). He continued to berate himself, Josa Young finding in his diaries numerous references to "his self-disgust, his lack of certainty about anything, his low self-esteem" (1).

Gray's alleged paranoia? No fear of persecution by others influenced his disdain, voiced during rehearsals of *Common Pursuit*, for the play: "As these [the cast members] are all very good actors, the fault must be entirely mine. Either I've written a whole clutch of bad parts, or good parts that don't mesh" (UP 113). A further example of what he calls his "defects as a playwright" (UP 118) shows in both the play's "badly written" Epilogue (UP 113) and dialogue he mockingly calls "some of the dreariest I've heard on the stage" (UP 115). Fortunately, his insights into the flaws of his play, rather than crushing him, prodded him to fix them. Were he less honest, he'd not have fixed the passages that affronted his gimlet eye.

Nor do paranoia or masochism shape his fulminations about getting old, a repeated theme in his last four memoirs, *The Smoking Diaries* (2004), *The Year of the Jouncer* (2006), *The Last Cigarette* (2008) and *Coda* (2008). The aging process taints everything. All that's wrong with his life, like both his claustrophobia (SD 151) and his having allegedly sagged into "a shapeless and pendulous sack, with scary brown modules growing on his arms and chest" (LC 128), stems from aging. True enough; but did he forget that his sagging, mottled body housed a sharp, inventive mind with a gift for self-renewal? After turning 60, Simon Gray (1936–2008) wrote five full-length memoirs, a short novel, and seven plays, all of which, in Gardner's words, brought "a new emotional intensity to his work" (3).

Other signs of vitality show him staving off the clinkers of age. Along with his 1997 marriage to Victoria Katherine Rothschild, *Who's Who 2007* mentions "watching cricket and soccer, tennis, swimming" as his favorite pastimes (n.p.; Bloomsbury, NY, 2007: 906). He loved swimming to the end (SD 31, 128, 209); even as a dying man, he'd sometimes swim six times a day (CODA 112). His 1986 statement that he watches soccer and cricket "incessantly" (UP 232) rings true, as well. A technical term for cricket supplies the title of his 1979 work *Close of Play*; *Old Flames* (1990) opens during a cricket match; and the first subject he discusses in *The Last Cigarette* after his beloved house pets and his failure to quit smoking is England's soccer team.

Which, in a telling moment, he names "My team, my country" (LC 9), a designation that falls just short of being misapplied. Having called himself 13 years before "quarter-Welsh, quarter-English, half-Scots but temperamentally totally Welsh" (FC 67), he's talking about an intensity and impulsiveness that thwarts the vital process of setting down roots; *Enter a Fox* equates being Welsh with an "eager[ness] to take offense" (37). Stability, rootedness, and belonging eluded this "sort of alien with a distastefully complicated background" (UP 224). His Englishness is an act of loyalty prompted from without. When England's soccer team takes the field, his patriotism stirs.

One can see why it takes a sporting event to rouse his love of country. In a deed that may have saved his life, his parents evacuated him in 1940 from England to his paternal grandparents' home in Montreal (his physician-father took his M.D. degree at McGill University). The disconnectedness that plagued him in a Montreal childhood marked by "smoking, pilfering ... and general thuggery" (UP 231) followed him to both the Hayling Island girls' school he attended and Westminster College (1945–51). It persisted into his adult life, feeding his practice of identifying with some of his nastiest characters, like the treacherous Martin of *Common Pursuit*. The semi-outsider Martin also shows why, as in Chekhov and Tennessee Williams, energy in Gray's work often comes from those who feel excluded and oppressed. The nine years Gray would spend pursuing his Ph.D. at Cambridge left him feeling as rootless as ever without any compensating scholarly achievement to take pride in. He needed to set down roots. Having taken a B.A. at Dalhousie University in Halifax, Nova Scotia, and taught English as a second language in France, he interrupted his doctoral work in 1964 to lecture for a year at the University of British Columbia (Burkman, ed. xvii). Perhaps most notably, this self-styled "overeducated but not especially well-taught man" (LC 164) changed his dissertation topic so often that, what with his near-chronic movie-going and card playing (Hamilton 39), he left Cambridge no closer to his Ph.D. than he was when he arrived there nearly a decade before.

On the credit side, the rootlessness and the "distastefully complicated background" (UP 224) that left Gray's Ph.D. hanging fire also awakened in him a cosmopolitan sensibility that led him to adapt both Dostoyevsky's *The Idiot* (1970) and Molière's *Tartuffe* (1982). This cosmopolitanism extends further. The shock waves put out by the late 1960s' enthusiasm for sexual freedom, rock-and-roll music, and Hindu–flavored spirituality pulsated in Gray's early plays. Writing in *Commentary*, Peter Shaw saw in *Butley* contempt for the dull conformity and tameness that engulfed Britain after the fervor and idealism of the Swinging Sixties (88). But Gray's social criticism doesn't stop here. It also targets the casual brutality and the horror of Britain's imperial past. The Africa of both *Sleeping Dog* (1967) and *Rear Column* (1978), two plays set some 80 years apart in time, is a dreamlike, threatening place, hostile to the rule of reason and love.

Discreetly preventing background detail from swamping foreground action, these works unfold as romantic adventure tales gone wrong. Deceit and bribery, dirty deals and moral guilt, focus both of them. Harking to John le Carré's novels *The Constant Gardener* (2000) and *The Mission Song* (2004) as well as to the movies *Hotel Rwanda* (2004) and *Blood Diamond* (2006), they also forecast the civil wars, ethnic cleansing, and western plundering that continue to claw sub-Saharan Africa. To clinch this point, Gray materialized H.M. Stanley in the last scene of *Rear Column*. The play's earlier action had reminded us indirectly that the violence and cruelty perpetrated in the name of furthering the ideals of Christian civilization by Africa's greatest explorer would thwart his greatest wish, being buried in Westminster Cathedral (Porter 9). At play's end, the self-righteous Stanley reveals how little he learned from his mistakes.

Gray's interest in today's Africa reflects his schooling in literary history. No surprise here; he lectured at Queen Mary College of the University of London from 1966–84. The literary references in his published work put his area of expertise in the period swathing the Romantic poets and T.S. Eliot. A stage direction in *Melon* (1991) tells a character to let out "a little laugh of unremembered pleasure" (40), a phrase mined 17 years later in the following passage from *The Last Cigarette*: "I should put it here that I've heard some very nice things ... but compliments ... become generalized in the memory, as pleasant experiences tend to do, while unpleasant experiences never seem to slip their particularity" (237).

Both of these passages paraphrase lines 33–34 of William Wordsworth's "Tintern Abbey," viz., "Little, nameless, unremembered acts/ Of kindness and of love." Logan Bester, hero of Gray's second novel, *Simple People* (1965), followed his author by taking his Nova Scotia B.A. to Cambridge's graduate program in English. Again like Gray, poor study habits distracted Logan from his research, in his case, Wordsworth. A New World innocent who sees the truth more clearly than the home-counties-bred students (though he usually fails to act on what he sees), Logan enacts the theme, from Wordsworth's "Intimation" ode, of the child being father to the man; innocence perceives truths lost on the shrewd and the savvy.

Another prominent Wordsworthian chord sounds in *Hidden Laughter*. The action of this 1991 play unfolds in a cottage, the adjoining garden of which is its great, and perhaps only, enticement. Charmed by its lovely garden, the Pertwee family overcome their misgivings about the dilapidated house to buy it. They might have been more prudent. Intended as a refuge from London, the Devonshire cottage will host many business and romantic intrigues traceable to the same city buzz the family wanted to flee. When the house goes up for sale at play's end, the Pertwees' marriage perhaps having gone smash, as well, the local vicar is tending the nearby garden, as he was doing in Act One, scene one, before the Pertwees arrived there. Besides belonging to itself alone, nature has set man an ideal his captivity by the fret and hurry of modern life has put beyond his reach.

Another Wordsworthian moment comes forth in Act One, scene one, of *Japes* (2000) when a teacher reads aloud a student's term paper that quotes the remarkable Lucy poem, "Strange Fits of Passion Have I Known" (32). The eroticism developed in the play, two brothers bedding the same woman (who marries one of them) is both strange and *un*fit according to their society's standards. The "fond and wayward" (line 15) thoughts voiced at poem's end, i.e., that Lucy might be dead, shock the narrator with their obscure power. But Lucy, a dweller of untrodden ways, is obscure herself. This means that her death, which Wordsworth records in "A Slumber Did My Spirit Seal" (quoted in *Coda* [99]) and "I Traveled Among Unknown Men," will pass unnoticed and thus unmourned in the world at large.

But the genius of Wordsworth's expression of grief will keep Lucy's legacy fresh for posterity. Plays like Gray's *Otherwise Engaged*, *Quartermaine's Terms*, and *The Late Middle Classes* also remind us that every life has supreme value. In a motif that could owe more to Thomas Hardy than to Wordsworth (Hardy's "After a Journey," which also addresses the pangs of lost love, is quoted in *The Smoking Diaries* [167]), these three plays endorse the idea that history's great events both count less and reveal less than the agonies heaped on supposed nobodies. In Gray, an apparently forgettable moment, like one schoolboy taunting another, can take on moral resonance. Herein lies one of Gray's main gifts. Wordsworth's milkmaids and idiot boys return in Gray as young nobodies who later flop at their jobs and, if they marry, as husbands, yet all the same get the last laugh on their more successful contemporaries.

Logan Bester of *Simple People* chooses Cambridge over Oxford or Edinburgh when he sails from Nova Scotia to continue his education because of the alleged superiority of Cambridge's English Department. And Cambridge in the 1950s for an English major meant the great D.H. Lawrence scholar, F.R. Leavis, the "only great man" (UP 213) Gray claims to have met. (Graham Hough, who wrote a book about Lawrence, *The Dark Sun* [1957], was also teaching at Cambridge at the time.) In 1977, Gray told Ian Hamilton that his attending Leavis's lectures and seminars gave him a heavy dose of Lawrence (41). The dosage affected him in at least two ways. The judgmental reading of fiction that grew out of Leavis's strenuous practical criticism finds spokesmen in *Simple People* (1965) and *Little Portia* (1967) in the knee-jerk pronouncements of scruffy, self-promoting Cantabs who call Lawrence England's only life-affirming novelist and the only English novelist worth reading. To their credit, these draggle-tailed Leavisites have read their master accurately. Leavis's 1965 *D.H. Lawrence: Novelist* claims, "The affirmation of life was always strong in [Lawrence]" (29), having sprung from the "intensity and profound seriousness of [his] interest in human life" (275).

Lawrence's vitalism also charges Gray's work, with Leavis again the conduit. Leavis's belief that "the climax [of "The Daughters of the Vicar"] affects us as a heroic triumph of life" (95) finds parallels in plays like *Pig in a Poke* (1969), *Butley* (1971), and *Otherwise Engaged* (1975), where empty wives enact the Lawrencean imperatives that feelings trump logic and that nature governs human conduct. Each of these plays shows unfulfilled wives taking lovers who may be physically unattractive, professionally unsuccessful, and even dangerous.

What prods these women to risk security, comfort, and physical safety is their withholding husbands. Characters in *Stage Struck*, *Little Nell* and *After Pilkington*, where the withholding leads to death, unconsciously play the Lawrencean class game of erotic maneuvering. Like most of Lawrence's important characters, they're married. But unlike them, they sleep around. Their rutting, a sin against the Holy Ghost in Lawrence, builds in them a sense of guilt that the public acclaim they win as actors, publishers, and academics can't soothe. These archetypal figures express the moral and spiritual emptiness of the clever, witty celebrity whose shiny public image hides a deep agony.

Other influences? The poster of T.S. Eliot that adorns the wall of the room in which *Butley* develops resonates powerfully in the play, the last scene of which quotes passages from Eliot's *Four Quartets* (76), and "Prufrock" (77). The vibes given off here permeate the canon. "Prufrock" is quoted in *Jouncer* (106) and *The Last Cigarette* (59), which also reprints the same passages from the "East Coker" section of *Four Quartets* (184) used in *Butley* (76). Eliot's prominence in Gray's work can be explained. First of all, the 1948 Nobel laureate for literature was so popular during Gray's college and university years that any fictional description of the Humanities branch of academe during this time (1953–65) would lose accuracy *unless* it fore-grounded him. No worries on this front; Gray heard Eliot's name often. Although Ben Butley may never write his book about Eliot, Gray's brother, Piers Gray (1947–96) (MacCabe 2), did publish the acclaimed *T.S. Eliot's Intellectual and Poetic Development* (1982) despite being an alcoholic like his brother Simon and Simon's Ben Butley.

Much of the light shed by Eliot's poetry on Simon's life and work stems from the passage in "East Coker" that appears in both *Butley* and *The Last Cigarette*. It's about the sanctity of marriage, an imperative that many of Gray's people flout, including the taken-from-life Bernard Berenson of *Old Masters* and Charles Dickens of *Little Nell*. The phrase from Gray's introduction to *Nell*, the "sapping logistics of adultery" (x), indicates the electrical charge that womanizing had for Gray, whose father had at least two girlfriends during much of his marriage (SD 75).

Womanizing says a great deal about the second son of James Davidson Gray, M.D. "[My] father ... was prone to bouts of depression, from spending too much time in the company of ... women not his wife," said his playwright-son in 2006 (Intro, LN xiii). This perpetrator of "eight years of dogged, day-by-day ... onerous adultery" (SD 145) did more than write about wife-cheating. In 1997 he both divorced his wife of 32 years and remarried quickly. He had also been writing about adultery his whole adult life. The married middle-aged hero of *The Late Middle Classes* (1999) returns to his childhood home from Australia to tell his former piano teacher, in the play's closing words, that he has a "bit on the side" (88). Gray also built his two late plays, *Old Masters* and *Nell*, around real-life adulterers whose adulteries sparked his imagination. A wise choice; besides redirecting these energies, his decision to write plays about the private lives of Bernard Berenson and Charles Dickens helped foster his strongest work in decades, if not his whole career.

But at what price? That stabbing phrase from Gray's introduction to *Nell*, the "sapping logistics of adultery" (x), invokes the aftershocks of the one-night stands of Simon Tench of *Otherwise Engaged* and Terri Green of *Just the Three of Us*. These tremors run deep. Like Ibsen's main figure in *The Pillars of Society* (1879), himself an adulterer, Berenson and Dickens suffer crises at the moments when their fame has crested. In *Nell*, the crisis is sexual. In fact, Dickens, named Dick in the play to call forth his engulfment by illicit sex, probably killed himself by reading aloud, just hours before his death, to a spellbound audience, his descriptions of the gruesome deaths of Bill Sikes and his girlfriend Nancy. At the least, he connived with suicide. By describing these fervid passages from *Oliver Twist*, Dickens "murdered" (LN 53), breaking his promise to his friend and biographer John Forster, fellow novelist Wilkie Collins, and, above all, Ellen Ternan, or Nelly, his mistress for 13 years. Sapped by adultery's iron logistics, this married father of nine tried to meld into his persona of public orator to stop the pain gouging him from within. Gray told Claire Tomalin (whose 1991 biography, *The Invisible Woman: The Story of Nelly Ternan and Charles Dickens*, inspired *Nell*), "Dickens died of adultery" (Gould 3).

The recent English novelist who wrote most memorably about adultery has to be Graham Greene. Like the faithless hero of Greene's *A Burnt-Out Case*, the womanizing Simon Hench of *Otherwise Engaged* wonders if God hasn't punished him by having excused him from life's heartaches. Gray would often conjure up Greene, whose name turns up in *Man in a Side-Car* (RC 156), *Otherwise Engaged* (OE 156), and *Michael* (Four 203). *Dog Days* (1976) follows *Engaged* in having as its main figure a publisher who, like the anti-heroes of Greene's *The End of the Affair* (1951) and *A Burnt-Out Case* (1961), wonders if success hasn't dehumanized him. "I deserve punishing" (DD 85), says the well-heeled Peter when he hears about his wife's paltry, ill-favored lover. That lover's name, George Green (DD 89), looks ahead to that of Terri Green, who not only slept with her publisher-boss in *Just the Three of Us* (1997) but is also misnamed Toni *Gray* (J3U 11; emphasis mine) by her captors.

This misnaming merits a close look. Gray had already shored up the captivity motif in *Cell Mates* (1995) by layering into it Greene's celebrated Judas complex, i.e., the belief that betrayal is the bedrock of human nature. A professional spy tells his victim, the friend who had helped him flee prison, "Spies betray people.... That's what we do. It becomes a habit. Difficult to break — even when it's not particularly necessary" (CM 53).

Betrayal had already tainted the spy's politics. The nobler the goal, the uglier the tactics used to realize it, history tells us. As Greene noted in *Monsignor Quixote* (1982), using Torquemada and Stalin as his examples (most of *Cell Mates* takes place in Moscow), the pursuit of God's kingdom on earth has always caused atrocities (FC 71) like "maiming, torturing, starving, killing" (LC 12). Back in the sphere of sex, which interests Gray more than public politics, *Japes* (2000) lifts a plotting device whole cloth from *The End of the Affair* when a wife tells her lover that she "made a deal with God" (J 56) to sacrifice her dearest possession if He let her dying lover live.

Greene's influence perhaps runs the strongest in *Nell*, which shows Charles Dickens, England's great champion of family morality, using *Oliver Twist*, as Henry Scobie did his heart medicine in *The Heart of the Matter* (1948), to turn the emotional death he was living into an actual one. Both men also die to quiet the pain of women who love them. The legacy sharpens. In another convergence that shows the force of Greene's influence, Greene based his famous 1950 essay, "The Young Dickens" (Graham Greene, *Collected Essays*, New York: Viking, 1969, 101–10), on *Oliver Twist*. But Gray's womanizing pelted him harder than Greene's did *him*. No Roman Catholic, Gray lacked a theological template for that oddball view of salvation George Orwell called "the cult of the sanctified sinner" that Greene used to justify his own disloyalty as well as that of his people.

While passing through the realm of mysticism, we might ask if the spirit of Dickens had been working through Dr. James Gray to snag Simon's. In her excellent introduction to *Simon Gray: A Casebook* (1992), Katherine H. Burkman said that Dickens was Simon's academic specialty during his teaching career (xv). The Dickens work closest to Simon's heart was *Great Expectations*, which he called, in his introduction to *Nell*, the "greatest novel in the English language" (xvi). Dickens's 1861 masterpiece had been on his mind for a long time. Beggar My Neighbor, the game Pip and Estella play in Satis House, is mentioned in the 1997 plays *Life Support* (40) and *Just the Three of Us* (40). The memorable phrase from Part 9, Chapter 15, of the novel, a "clear impossibility" (Charles Dickens, *Great Expectations*, ed. Janice Carlyle [Boston: Bedford: Case Studies in Contemporary Criticism, 1996], 118), turns up in both *Enter a Fox* (60) and *The Year of the Jouncer* (12). Helen Twiscombe, the shambling narrator of *Breaking Hearts* (1997), specialized in Dickens while teaching at Queen Mary College, where Gray also "lectured ... frequently on Dickens" (Fox 11). Twiskers's drinking and her bloated body invoke the self-disgust registered in Gray's later diaries (e.g., SD 47, YJ 12). Her alcoholism was also a possible direction for Gray, who, in the 1980s and early 1990s drank three or four bottles of champagne and several shots of whisky almost every day before going into detox.

But the Gray who inspired *Breaking Hearts* was the playwright's younger brother, Piers, who died around the time Simon was writing it. A description of Piers's sad last months at the Hong Kong university where he taught business English would echo novelistically in *Breaking Hearts* (SD 133) and theatrically in *Michael* (2004), where Jason Cartt's boozing both costs him his teaching job and gets him barred from campus (Four 78). Piers may have crept into these works because, like Dickens's Pip, who left England for Cairo, he pursued a career away from his homeland. Simon's junior by nine years, he always admired his accomplished elder brother. This admiration wasn't taken for granted. The love Simon felt for Piers, suggested by both his frequent visits to Piers's grave (LC 311) and a picture of the Gray boys in which a smiling Simon is holding his infant brother on his lap (SD 243), recalls one of Dickens's greatest gifts—his love for children and with it, an extraordinary insight into the terror that the adult world can rouse in the young.

An act of adult terror opens *Great Expectations*, Pip being spun upside down by an escaped convict. The young Gray had his own burdens, too, even if they were less shocking. Having spent his first four years on Hayling Island, off of England's southern coast (Burkham, ed., xvii) and going, parentless, to Montreal, to escape German bombs, deepened his sense of separation. The ensuing challenges of coming to consciousness in a strange city, where his native English was a second language, during a war made danger a constant threat. Petty crime became a natural outlet for anxieties in him that never let up. His boyhood sorties into "pilfering ... and general thuggery" (UP 231) also chimed with the deep structure of Dickens's life and work.

Tuned up and running, Gray sought expression in the stage play, rather than the novel of Dickens or Greene or the poetry of Eliot. And how well Harold Pinter's "favorite living playwright" (Fraser 273) took to writing for the stage. In 1984, David M. Bergeron praised the skill in which he used Shakespeare to illuminate *Butley* ("'Butley' and Shakespeare," *Rocky Mountain Review of Language and Literature*, 38 [1984], 4: 179–88), as did another early critic, Sophia B. Blaydes, seven years earlier, when she hailed Gray's 1971 play's thematic use of Beatrix Potter's nursery rhymes ("Literary Allusions as Satire in Simon Gray's *Butley*, *Midwest Quarterly*, 18 [1977], 374–81). The canon brims with examples of Gray's creative use of stage tradition, too. The synchronized entrances and exits of characters in *Dutch Uncle* (1969), *Close of Play* (1979), and *Simply Disconnected* (1996) all show his mastery of a stock convention of the well-made play. This mastery was no fluke. His rehearsal notes to the 1986 Los Angeles production of *Common Pursuit* describes it as a function of theatrical know-how, instincts, and training. Re-blocking brought "normality, playfulness, and sexual tension" (Lady 63) to a scene languishing in dullness. In defense of the well-made play, which is often dismissed nowadays as lightweight commercial fluff, Gray said in 1984, "Anyone who does *anything* has an obligation to do it well" (UP 128), even if it means, besides re-blocking and re-writing individual scenes, shifting furniture, changing lights, and making costume changes.

Gray studied his art carefully. A split stage helps him link different aspects of the life of the eponym of *Melon* (1991). The play's 1991 sequel, *Holy Terror*, has Mark Melon looking away from his fellow cast members to address the audience (Four, 236, 250). Another example in the play of Bertolt Brecht's influence comes when Melon, realizing that he's lecturing, pauses to consult his note cards. Brecht's insistence that theater audiences understand that they're witnessing a play, or an artifice, rather than a slice of reality, comes forth when two characters finish each other's sentences in the play's last scene (Four 284–85). Collage, the time glide, and juxtaposition in *Little Nell* also show Gray rejecting a simple, continuous, empirically describable stage reality.

Man in a Side-Car (1971) unfolds four years after a young ne'er-do-well has moved in with a married couple, one of whom has been wanting him out. Like Ibsen's *Hedda Gabler* (1890) and Edward Albee's *Who's Afraid of Virginia Woolf* (1962), it's a drama of ripe condition. Using the device of delayed exposition, its present-tense action portrays strains and anxieties vexing to the characters long before curtain's rise. Gray's 1997 play, *Life Support*, takes place in a London hospital six months after a bee sting, inflicted in Guadeloupe, made comatose a woman who's in view throughout the action. The "vegetative" (LS 2) Gwen Golding's constant presence onstage helps build to a climax both shocking and inevitable in the eyes of her husband, who has been both fearing and hoping that she'll be removed from life support.

The benefits gained by matching ends to beginnings occupied Gray his whole career. Ben Butley holds both his first and last onstage dialogues with students, one male and one female. And just as Wagner's *Parsifal* fills the house at both the start and end of *Otherwise Engaged*, Handel's "Paradise Duet" plays at curtain's rise and fall of *Hidden Laughter*. Gray's instinct for symmetry expresses itself in other ways. Both the first and last words of *Close of Play* come from Daisy Blightworth while she's standing near the French windows of her brother's house. A revolving set rolls back time 20 years to open the last scene of *Common Pursuit*, which unfolds 15 minutes in time after the ending of Act One, scene one, Wagner's music triumphant in both cases. And if a play had to move to a different theater during the run of its production, as did *Dog Days*, Gray made sure that the director adjusted, along with the blocking, both the volume and speed with which the actors spoke. This happened too when *Common Pursuit* moved in July 1984 from Guildford's "compact" stage (UP 167) to the wider, deeper one at Hammersmith's Lyric Theatre.

The characters in *Common Pursuit* who work in publishing call to mind those in *Otherwise Engaged, Melon, Holy Terror, Simply Disconnected*, and, as an offstage presence, *Quartermaine's Terms*. Gray discussed his practice of recycling characters as well as plotting devices in his "Author's Note" to *Dog Days* (1975), whose leading figure also works for a publisher. Even one of the two leads in *Cell Mates* (1995) is editing a prison newspaper in the play's first section. Doing this modest job, its editor learns, invites the discovery that *all* writing is both a mask and an unveiling. Though Gray never worked in publishing, the recurrence of editors and publishers in his corpus is but one of many that gives insight into his way of thinking. There's also the run-of-the-mill English public school Ampleforth. Appearing as Amplesides in plays as different from each other as *Otherwise Engaged, Plaintiffs and Defendants, Dog Days*, and *Old Flames*, it's the sort of place that promising youths like Simon Gray and Simon Hench, both graduates of Westminster, would have disregarded when applying for prep school or college.

The Westminster education, shared first name, and one-syllable last name Hench shares with his creator, set a pattern. Important characters in *Wise Child* (1967) and *A Comeback for Stark* (1968), and another in Edith Dunlop's novel-in-progress in *Side-Car* (1971), whom Edith calls "a fraud" (RC 142), also go by Simon. The pattern reinforces itself. References to the real-life Simon Callow, Simon Williams, and Simon Raven inside of three pages of *An Unnatural Pursuit* (142–44) show in Gray a concern with his first name that resurfaces as Peter, another name for Simon in the Bible as well as a variant form of Piers, in *Plaintiffs and Defendants* (1975), *Dog Days*, and *Common Pursuit*. In each case, the name applies to a scoundrel who works in the publishing trade. (Like Gray, *Dog Days*' Peter has a smoker's cough and a paunch [33] and didn't drive a car [DD 31, LC 71]).

In still another reference that strikes close to home, as did the misnaming of a woman as Toni Gray in *Just the Three of Us*, are characters named Ben (after Gray's son), Nigel (his elder brother), and Louise (his daughter Lucy) in *Hidden Laughter* (1990). There's no telling either how or in what form a family member will pop up in a work by Gray. Academics anxious about promotion and tenure in works extending from *Little Portia* (1967) to *Japes Too* (2004) could hark to Piers Gray, in view of his career as a university don.

Such motifs occur in familiar surroundings. The French windows seen in *Little Portia* (1967), *Close of Play* (1979), and *Simply Disconnected* (1996) that lead out to gardens alive with sunshine, fresh scents, and the laughter of children at play often clash in spirit with the adult disputes taking place indoors. These disputes prompted Gray to re-map the marriage bond, using the love triangle or versions of the *ménage à trios* in *Stage Struck*, the *Japes* plays, and *Just the Three of Us*, each of which displays a set of French windows at curtain rise.

Marital problems differ in Gray. In *Common Pursuit*, a married father of four has an affair with the wife of the Oxford theologian who helped him write a book. *Stage Struck* (1979), one of Gray's "dark comedies of bad manners" (Burkman, Burkman ed., *Casebook*, xvi), includes the onstage death of an Australian graduate student who, like Gray, was writing a Ph.D. dissertation on Henry James (UP 219). Herman's Germanic first name evokes Dr. Boris Heinz of *After Pilkington* (1986), another murder victim of a neurotic wife.

Another portent in the Gray canon is the figure of the orphan. Martin Musgrave, the deceitful careerist in *Common Pursuit*, is an orphan (UP 22) as are two of the three speaking roles in *Just the Three of Us* (32). In this group also belong the Thwaite sibs in *Little Portia*, Peter and a pair of brothers whose last name isn't given in *Dog Days*, and the Cartts brothers of the *Japes* plays, all of whose parents died in car crashes when their kids were small. Like them, *Common Pursuit*'s Martin prospers, but at the cost of his inner peace; the backstabbing that brought Martin success has left him feeling "ruefully" (UP 22) empty. He has nobody to share his fun with.

Once again, a development in Gray stands as a surface manifestation of a piercing home truth. Perhaps he adapted Dostoyevsky's *Idiot* to the English-speaking stage in 1971 because two of the play's most put-upon characters, the eponymous Prince Myshkin and Natasha Fillipova, are orphans. In his discussion of *Common Pursuit* in *An Unnatural Pursuit*, he admits having felt like an outsider at Westminster, as did Martin. His reason? He was "an evacuee during the War, coming back to a middle-class education as a ... nasal-accented Canadian" (23).

Dickens redux? Are we looking at an update of a morally outraged Dickens, who was sent to work at a London blacking warehouse at about the same age of Gray when his parents packed him off to Montreal? Orphans feel abandoned and unwanted. Dealing with this affliction hammers them with a set of woes that those of us raised in our families of origin can't imagine. Standing behind the loss that induced the misery is the indifference of the adult world. Lacking supervising elders who bond psychologically with them, orphans must invent themselves without the love and guidance of a nuclear family. Gray's smothered parenthood conjured up a greater danger in 1940, one of the years of the Blitz, when he was the same age of the orphaned children in *Little Portia*, *The Three of Us*, and the *Japes* plays, all of whose parents died violently; German bombs could have left *him* without parents to come back to. A child who can't look to his/her parents for protection feels lost.

Lyn Gardner's observation that the five years Gray spent in Montreal as a child "may have developed his outsider's eye" (1) comes into play here. This process, no simple blessing, contained some unexpected drawbacks. The self-invention that would later profit Gray as an artist continued to plague him as a person. His speaking like an outsider in environments where he felt displaced to begin with, after each of his ocean crossings in 1940, '45, '53, and '58, put him through an identical string of ordeals. It follows that his people often feel unwanted and lonely, a plight that can leave them staring in the middle distance at nothing. The title figure of *Quartermaine's Terms* loses his only tie to other people when he loses his job. A woman in *Stage Struck* shocks her husband with the news that she's ending their marriage. Bombshells like these can explode any time. It's no wonder that Simon Hench of *Otherwise Engaged* hangs up the phone before finding out if the man he was talking to will commit suicide, as he was threatening to do.

These men and others like them in the canon bear the marks of Gray's upbringing. For even had Gray's father become a solid presence in the home, he'd have confused his three boys. Despite having qualified as a pathologist, Dr. James Gray either forfeited the honor of serving as a role model or redefined himself in his sons' eyes in terms that yoked the jungle allure of sex with the sin of betrayal. James was engaged to Barbara's sister until Barbara decided she wanted him for herself (CODA 7). And this was just one of many of his father's disloyalties that left Simon reeling. In his dismay, he attributed his Casanova father's success with women to his modesty, charm, and "for all I know, enormous cock" (SD 123).

A small boy living in the shadow of his over-endowed father's cock is not to be envied. *Side-Car*, *Two Sundays*, and *Dog Days* air Gray's disquiet by pairing off slack, dithering womanizers with high-octane wives. The alcoholic husband of a successful writer in *Close of Play* calls himself "weak. Feeble. Gutless. A moral no-hoper" (12). His wife, in her own eyes a "nurse, surrogate mother, victim, and tart on demand" (46), agrees with Benedict's disparaging self-assessment, rating him so low that two years earlier she aborted his child (12). Men continue to get the dirty end. The libido of Richard Howarth, a gay French schoolmaster in *Spoiled* (1971), also vexes *his* wife, a point Gray underscores by time-setting the play late in Joanna's pregnancy. As a father (to-be) and a teacher, Howarth twice exemplifies male authority, an ambiguity typical of Gray when his imagination conjures up his father. The disconnect infusing this ambiguity makes Howarth's betrayal of Joanna all the more painful. While supposedly prepping a male student for his upcoming A-level exams, Howarth seduces him — with a sleeping Joanna in the next room.

Overeating, which he does in view of *us*, has made Howarth fat, like several other food junkies in Gay's work. The list includes Graham Thwaite of *Little Portia* (1967), the "distinctly overweight" (SG4 214) Oxford don, James Westgate, in *After Pilkington* (1986), a womanizer who shares a first name with Gray's father, and the wanton lawyer and father-to-be Daniel Davenport of *Old Flames* (1990). Despite their upstanding public images, these men are all childish and self-indulgent. Howarth, in the words of his wife, always "seems to grab a small, but plum, part for himself" (SG1 255) in the student plays he directs. The face-stuffing eponym of Gray's first play, the BBC film script, *Caramel Crisis* (1967), whose name coincides with that of a junk food, loves éclairs. Tommy, who goes by his childish nickname throughout *Side-Car*, only stops eating when he's swilling booze. In Act One, scene 17, of this BBC play script (RC 151–52), he's playing the juvenile game of tiddly-winks with his married lover, Gerald Dunlop, whom he calls "Gerrie" (e.g., RC 150).

Gray began conflating plumpness with illicit sex, to him another destructive form of self-indulgence, early in his career. He also did it with exceptional skill. Ted Spill, the head of an English language school, who's mockingly called "the old virgin" (253) in *Little Portia*, plays the "plum" role of Santa Claus in a Christmas party he's giving his students. Resorting to an odd — but attention-getting — choice of words, Gray has Ted say, just before the party, that his assistant has packed his tunic with a pillow "to plumpen me and make sure nothing sticks out" (253). Gray will include the words "plumpen" (256) and "plumply" (255) in his description of the party's preparations. Then, in a jolt to the reader, Ted careens "plumply" (262) into some barbed wire while blundering "plumply" (265) through a night of darkness and rain. Sustaining the motif, Gray then shows a bleeding, dripping Ted limping "marshily" (264) across the room where the party is being held.

This orchestration of the plumpness conceit reveals such expertise that it makes us wonder about the heights Gray might have scaled had he stuck to prose fiction. Despite his last name, Spill, Ted is neither effeminate nor chaste, as Grahame implied to his sister Dianah when he called her boss "the old virgin" (253). In a revelation that makes us rethink the meaning of nearly everything that has happened up to this point, Graham learns that Ted and Dianah are lovers. She was also, in a wry touch, the assistant who arranged Ted's costume "to make sure nothing sticks out" (253). Sticking out, indeed, we discover in a single stroke both what Ted Spill has been spilling and where he has been spilling it. Plumpness will serve as a conceit elsewhere in Gray's early work. When Grahame reunites with his ex-girlfriend and bed-mate, after an absence of several months, he's told, "You're so big. Fatter than I ever thought, even" (LP 297).

Grahame's thickening jowls and waistline invoke the Lawrence of *Sons and Lovers* (1913), in which the health of three men, Walter Morel, his son Paul, and Baxter Dawes, plummet after going womanless. No shock, this development shows the enduring influence upon Gray of Cambridge's F.R. Leavis. Lawrence's stated contempt for homosexuality surges forth in the first paragraph of *A Comeback for Stark* (1968). Less tolerant of gays than he'd be in *The Common Pursuit* (1984), the moral exemplar of which is a gay professor of moral philosophy, Gray uses the electrically charged word "plump" (9) three times in the first paragraph of *Comeback*. The word describes the porn addict William Booter, who, at paragraph's end, is about to fit his "pink, damp lips" (9) around an iced coffee. In *Caramel Crisis*, "A very plump hand" (SG1 322) belonging to a woman appears on the television screen to pass a cup of coffee to her husband. The cup invokes the dinner that the flabby, caffeinated William Booter eats in a trattoria after watching a bondage-and-domination movie early in *Comeback*.

Booter's actions in the early going of *Comeback* have deep roots. The mosaic comprising food, drink, plumpness, and "the confusion of desire and thrilled shame" began taking shape for Gray with his "roly-poly playful laughing" grandmother in Montreal, who would cuddle him in a romp he called "bundling" (SD 38). The bundling would continue until his howls of laughter stopped his breath and brought him to the verge of tears. Gray became a quick study in the art of bundling but without recognizing its link to erotic excitement. He later speaks of tickling his baby brother Piers senseless (SD 132).

Role reversal would suffuse his writing. His remark in his Author's Note to *Dog Days* (1976), "Characters from one play would step into another ... before either slipping into yet another play or go back to the first" (DD 5), gives us pause. Do these repetitions denote a failure of imagination or an overtaxing of his creative powers? Had fatigue duped him into lazy writing? These questions are valid. The year 1971 saw the staging of four of his plays, including the immensely challenging *Butley*. A comment by him later in the Note addresses artistic burnout: "Within two or three months [in 1975] I'd finished two television plays ... and a stage play" (7). On the other hand, the repetitions he mentions form part of a larger blueprint, which, like a good crime story, unfurls elegantly. Formula writing isn't bad writing when the pieces of the puzzle have been given the right foreshadowing and come before us at in the right time.

Dog Days itself, as can be inferred by Gray's self-admitted tendency to recycle material, contains several staples of his theater. The woman writer who offers sex to a publisher to persuade him to accept her book returns from *Otherwise Engaged*. The fictional prep school of Amplesides both comes back from *Otherwise Engaged* and *Plaintiffs and Defendants* and will recur in *Old Flames* and *Simply Disconnected*. A five-year-old son of a candidate for the assistant headmastership at Amplesides in *Dog Days* was 16 in *Otherwise Engaged*. Elsewhere, the reprocessed element can exert thematic force despite being small. The lone sock that Ben Butley, from Gray's 1971 play, takes out of his briefcase serves as a more eloquent symbol of pathos and desolation when it turns up on the foot of an otherwise naked Humphry after his murder at the hands of a pickup in *Common Pursuit*.

This small touch, expressive of Gray's outstanding economy of means, is not unusual. Recycled elements in Gray always look better with use. The passage of years between *Spoiled* (1971) and *Old Flames* (1990) shows him restoring a motif with new confidence and creative vigor. Like *Plaintiffs and Defendants*, *Dog Days*, and *Two Sundays* after it, *Spoiled* puts onstage the heavily pregnant wife of an expectation-defeating Baudelaire-quoting schoolmaster. The slack husband in *Old Flames* is a lawyer, but his wife, setting Gray a greater artistic challenge, gives birth (to twins) during the play's present-tense action (in *Plaintiffs*, the expectant mother delivers a boy at the very end).

Sometimes Gray will restore a piece of dialogue, as he does a motif or a character, because it conveys an idea or attitude that stayed on his mind after its first occurrence. Charles, for instance, speaks the following words near the end of *Two Sundays* (1975): "Oh, I don't know. Old friends are like old habits. There comes a point where it doesn't matter any more whether you like them, they're what you've got" (OE 98). Roughly the same words come from the chain-smoking lawyer Peter in *Plaintiffs* (1975) after his having just confessed that he has been cheating on his wife for the past decade (OE 117): "I don't know. Old friends are like old habits. Once you've got them it's too late to wonder whether you actually want them" (OE 120). Still another Peter who smokes too much and deceives a wife called Hillary utters a comparable maxim in *Dog Days* that came from both Charles in *Two Sundays* and Peter in *Plaintiffs*: "Old friends are like old habits. It doesn't matter whether you like them, they're what you've got" (DD 48). These repetitions, which make friendship a form of entrapment, reflect Gray's growing belief that character is fixed and also, perhaps, that his people fight change because they're afraid of it.

In a lighter vein, the schoolmaster Charles of *Two Sundays* both acts the same way with and gets the same evasive response from his publisher friend Peter as an adult as he did twenty years earlier. Whereas Peter declines to read Charles's schoolboy poem, rightly suspecting that the love it expresses has targeted *him*, so does he, as an equally cautious adult, reject for publication the gay-themed novel that Charles has recently finished. Like Martin of *Common Pursuit*, Simon Hench of *Otherwise Engaged*, and the passively aggressive Peter of *Dog Days*, Martin of *Two Sundays* prefers what John M. Clum calls "an uncluttered life" (Burkman, ed., 68), an option that has skewed his friendship with Charles. The motif recurs and spreads. Unbalanced relationships, always a sign of cowardice in Gray, swarm the canon. They also point up Gray's belief, voiced to his friend, Tony Gould, that "the balance of a relationship is always set at the beginning and never really changes" (Gould 2). A fear of the consequences of straight sex, viz., marriage and children, has led Ben Butley to dabble in homosexuality. It follows that the emotional cowards in Gray who resemble Ben are calculating, sometimes ruthless, publishers in contrast to the complex, ambiguous creative types who court their favor. Unrequited love brings the sensitive and the vulnerable to grief in *Little Portia*, *Side-Car*, and *Two Sundays*. In *Stage Struck* and *After Pilkington* it leads to murder.

These events grip us. Gray has injected incident and implication into the somewhat soft, elitist lives he writes about. And he does it without force-feeding his dialogue with background information. He undersold himself when he carped in *An Unnatural Pursuit*, "My characters live within a precise, probably over-precise world" (41). Being human means facing need and loneliness. Specifically, the failure of Gray's educated professionals to connect finds them at loose ends, both socially and emotionally. Though the formula is recycled, it still rocks. Gray is a process artist rather than a peddler of theatrical fare for popular consumption. He plays it straight with his muse. The grit and attitude connected with scrappy guys with a blue-collar truculence rarely win out in his work. But selection affects dramatic form as well as character portrayal. Gray's concern with the professional class adapts smoothly to the comedy of manners, which, in writers like Oscar Wilde, Philip Barry, and the later Harold Pinter, describes social values and conventions influencing personal conduct.

One of these conventions is speech, always a marker of social class in England. The Cantab Grahame Thwaite of *Little Portia* balks at calling his girlfriend's shopkeeper-dad "sir" (220). Gray displays his responsiveness to spoken language in his reference to the "Scots undercurrent" of his elder brother Nigel's speech, which flows "underneath the Canadian accent which ... [runs] below the English one" (J 26). But it's received English, i.e., BBC or Oxbridge English, that sets the standard for him. He gave himself an extra reason to dislike George Blake, the KGB spy whose betrayal of the UK earned him a co-starring role in *Cell Mates*, because "despite his great gift for languages" (FC 13), Blake spoke English like an Afrikaner.

This barb isn't Gray's only whack at political correctness. In 1977, 18 years before the London production of *Cell Mates*, he told Ian Hamilton, "I think we're a less civilized country than we were. It seems to me that as the ostensible gaps between classes disappear, the gap between educated people and uneducated people increases because of some fraudulent idea of democratization"(46). *The Smoking Diaries*, published in 2004, ascribes democracy's alleged fraudulence to the lower classes not knowing their place. "Half a century ago ... there *really* were visibly defined classes, working/lower, lower middle, upper middle, and upper" (SD 16, emphasis mine). The logical upshot of this belief is the claim that, in his parents' time, his social inferiors wouldn't have dreamt of taking the liberties they believe themselves entitled to now. But he shrinks from the challenge of developing this idea. In a different vein, Gray, who spoke Canadian English as a child, endows some of his characters with a Henry-Higgins–like gift for placing a person socially on the basis of his/her speech. This gift declared itself often, with variations, in his early fiction. The Nova Scotian Logan Bester in *Simple People* (1965), for example, cringes every time a Brit assumes that he's American. Janice Trullope's pronunciation in *Little Portia* might always stop Grahame Thwaite from loving her or her family ("Mr. Trullope's accent was functionally worse than his daughter's" [220]). The north-country twang of one of Grahame's teaching colleagues blocks his permanent appointment to the faculty, the merits of his classroom performance notwithstanding (LP 244).

As this turn of events implies, Gray's attitude toward England's obsessive class distinctions can recoil upon itself. In *Coda* (2008), he calls Essex "the sort of accent deployed to conceal an expensive education" (20). He had also grumbled about "the BBC's diktat against middle-class English accents in the theater, even when the parts call for middle-class accents" (Fox 9), a trend started in the UK by folk heroes like the Beatles, Irish footballer Georgie Best, and the cockney-speaking Michael Caine in movies like *The Ipcress File* (1965) and *Alfie* (1966). In the same paragraph of *Fox* where he frets over BBC's "diktat," Gray also hails the American Gwyneth Paltrow as "one of the ... only [movie] actresses who speaks clear English" (9). But he has more to say on the topic. Later in *Fox*, he complains about the "middle-class accent" of a sales agent, which was he adds, was "OK in its time but ghastly now" (103).

Perhaps his crankiness stems from a problem defining the middle class, which, throughout his work, swathes degree holders from Cambridge and Oxford who later thrive as doctors, university dons, and lawyers. In *An Unnatural Pursuit*, he calls *Common Pursuit* "a play about ... English, middle-class, Cambridge-educated friendship" (21). Setting aside the difficulty North Americans would have accepting his definition of the middle class, we can nonetheless credit Gray's uneasiness with that class's addiction to conspicuous understatement. *Little Portia*'s Grahame Thwaite sees English politeness as a poor substitute for vital interaction. In *Two Sundays*, Peter claims to have sex with his wife out of "politeness" (OE 82). England's middle class is disappearing in *The Late Middle Classes* (1999) because its constituents have learned to distrust strong feelings to the point where they are rarely expressed and almost never felt.

Cricket helped form the collective psyche of the middle-class Gray family. Because Barbara, the boys' mother, had put cricket "at the heart of England, of being English" (J 204), she made sure that the curriculum she drew up to repatriate her sons, after their 1945 return to England, included trips to Lords. Her schooling stuck. Cricket remained a benchmark of Englishness for Simon. Like his grandfather, an avid follower of the game, this viewer of cricket matches on television published essays on the sport in both the *Wisden Cricket Monthly* and *Summer Days: Writers on Cricket* (UP, 13, rpt. 231–39). In *Last Cigarette*, while acknowledging that the best cricketers on England's national team come from South Africa and Australia, he hopes "passionately" that the team wins all its games because, foreigners and all, it represents "England, and therefore me" (LC 9). This identification doesn't confer total approval. Late in the book, he'll call England "educationally, morally, socially, the most backward ... among the advanced countries" (114). But his regional loyalties usually silenced these moans. With the fervor of a religious convert, he had a firm hold on the conventions and codes by which he defined himself.

It's likely that this hold would have loosened had he never left England. A fever of necessity infuses his self-definition. Several causes might be at work here. Gray was born on Hayling Island, which was joined to the mainland during his childhood by a single bridge. Besides leaving England to teach in Canada and France, he also spent five years away from his homeland during both of his first trips away from home, undertaken at ages four and 17 (Burkman, ed., xvii). Each of his returns home forced him to redo his hair, table manners, and speech to meet local standards. His mother's use of cricket to Anglicize him suggests that he was treated like an alien in his own home. Going outside the house brought no relief, especially at school, where his classmates made him feel like an impostor. His worries grew. The anxiety of feeling more English in Canada than he did in England and vice-versa not only creeps into his writing, where he demonstrated the benefits of avoiding self-pity. His genius for putting to creative use what might have been a disabling identity crisis also shows, to his surpassing credit, the strength of his artistic resolve.

The subtitle of *Enter a Fox, Further Adventures of a Paranoid*, resurrects slights and insults, real or imagined, that vexed Gray after his trans–Atlantic voyages. In his imaginative work, his paranoia takes the form of a character's either misnaming another character or pretending not to know the character's name. The theoretical source of this put-down lies in the unpaged acknowledgment to his memory play, *Melon*, where he credits N.S. Sutherland's *Breakdown* with having inspired the play. The parts of *Breakdown* where Sutherland discusses slips of the tongue might have hit Gray with the force of a mirror meeting. Here, according to Sutherland, is the core of Freud's response to a question about the subject: "Freud's answer was to suggest that the form mistakes [like misnaming] take ... are dictated by our unconscious wishes" (92–93).

Misnaming as a plotting device in Gray's work began years before the appearance of Sutherland's 1987 book. Doris Waterly, a small-fry member of a women's club in *Colmain* (1963), Gray's first novel, hears her opinions on several topics dismissed, if not altogether ignored. Likewise, she's called "that Carol Waterly" and "Carla Waterly" (C 60). Her club-mates aren't merely telling Doris that she doesn't deserve the courtesy or effort needed to learn her name. By inventing new names for her — which calls for more effort — they're going an extra step to show their contempt for her.

Simple People (1965) might have come closer to the knuckle of Gray's distress as a newcomer in Cambridge in 1959 after having spent five years in Halifax, Nova Scotia. Logan Bester, like Gray, went to Cambridge to further his education. But he comes from the town of Worthington, not Worthyville, as some of his new academic acquaintances think (SP 56). Even his advisor misspeaks by putting Worthington, which he had just called Wellington, in New Brunswick (35) rather than in its fellow maritime province of Nova Scotia, where it belongs.

Otherwise Engaged (1975) varies the technique when its main figure Simon Hench misnames the former wife of an old friend (OE 51). So bound up is Simon with his own issues that he had earlier misnamed his brother Stephen's main rival for a job Stephen had applied for, despite having heard that rival's name, MacGregor, just a minute before (OE 15, 16). But in the next act, Gray does a stunning reversal on the motif while sustaining psychological consistency. Here, Stephen, who had corrected Simon when Simon called MacGregor

"MacDonald," needs correcting himself. By why shouldn't he switch places with Simon on the matter of MacGregor's name? Stephen's defeat of MacGregor in a race for the same prize has pushed his ex-rival into the shadows. Another academic, James Westgate of *After Pilkington*, mangles names, too, but for a different reason. He's trying his hand at behavior modification. Edward, the student who's taking a tutorial with him, he calls "Edmond." Coming to James's office for the third straight time without an essay for James to critique has cost Edward his identity as a student in good standing.

Gray's most famous, or notorious, character has a darker motive in mind for misnaming the new boyfriend of Joey Keyston, his office mate, flat mate, and ex-lover. Reg becomes "Ted" when Ben mentions him because he's being written off as but one in a series; as Reg knows, Ted was Joey's lover before he, Reg, came into the picture. The Gray of *Little Nell* (2006) finds a new context for the misnaming motif when the words of a dying Charles Dickens become garbled, but without sinking into gibberish. The disjointedness of Dick's words creates a rhythm that mirrors the confusion and fragmentation brought on by a stroke. The dyslexic pattern taken by these words also graze meanings redolent of James Joyce's verbal games. Defying ordinary sentence logic and causal consequence, Gray's unsettling leaps of language reveal a fearless grasp of his subject matter. Dick is addressing Nelly: "Dread and dread are dood, stepfoots and I fog my dreet and swearest have pitle litty on her monkey. (*Pause. Stares at her bewildered.*) Mell? Nouse?" (63).

Nelly, or Ellen Ternan, is his "Mouse," or Muse, as well as his sweetheart, or honey, the *Mel* prefix beginning the word, honey, in several Romance and Slavic languages. "Dread" suggests Edwin Drood, the eponym of the novel Dickens was writing when he died, as well as naming the terror he faced every day lest his affair with Ellen be discovered and made public. "Nouse" could refer to the metaphoric noose he put around his neck by reading aloud the most *mel*odramatic passages from *Oliver Twist* just hours before visiting Nell, his mouse. Pronounced to rhyme with mouse, *nouse*, the Greek word for reason and intellect, targets the common sense Dickens defied by ignoring the words of those intimates who forbade him to read those passages. The "step foots and I fog" cluster might represent a crisis that has invaded the fogged thoughts of the dying author of *Bleak House*, the governing metaphor of which is fog.

Fog had kept bedeviling Dickens. A train carrying him, Nelly, and her mother five years earlier, in June 1865 from Paris to London, crashed in the fog near Staplehurst, England. At risk along with the lives of the three passengers was Dickens's reputation as Great Britain's icon of family values. His actions immediately following the crash, in fact, reflect his belief that his reputation, faced by "dood," i.e., death or, along with "pittle," waste, *was* his life. Rather than freeing Ellen and her mother from their derailed coach, thus showing little pity, i.e., "pittle itty" for them," he stepped outside and asked some station attendants to help the badly shaken strangers.

These meanderings spell out artistic growth. Their full impact can't register unless one notes the great imaginative distance between them and their prototypes, viz., the satirical misnaming motifs found 40 years earlier in the fledgling *Colmain* and *Simple People*. Only a sure-footed artist totally committed to his materials could have spanned the great distance between social satire and the ruminations of a dying genius.

Two

Bundling Alchemized

The uprooting suffered by Gray, if not exactly caused by education, took place in education's shadow. Within a year after his childhood voyage to Canada in 1940, he had his first dose of the classroom, an upheaval that left him in "a state of terror" (SD 107). *An Unnatural Pursuit* (215), *The Smoking Diaries* (107), and *Coda* (154–55) all discuss his bushwhacking by older boys en route home from school — a torment tempered only slightly by his bushwhacking newcomers to the school the following year. A ghastly homecoming followed. Soon after German bombs stopped falling and he returned to his parents for a classic English education, the trials of displacement dogging him were aggravated by sexual abuse. He was fondled and beaten at a Portsmouth prep school after leaving the safety of a girls' school on Hayling Island.

More grief followed. His father, now a pathologist (whose job resembles that of a coroner or medical examiner in the U.S.), was having trouble earning a living. The Gray family's 1953 move to Halifax matched the time when Simon was ready to enter university. Which he did; while acquiring a "harsh North American speech" (UP 215) in the process, he spent the next five years taking his B.A. at Dalhousie, which qualified him to study at Cambridge University. More movement followed his graduation, with temporary teaching stints at Clermont-Ferrand in France and Vancouver, British Columbia, after which he spent the next 18 years lecturing in the English department of Queen Mary College of the University of London (Burkman, ed. xvii, xix).

These years taught him a great deal about the leisure and politics of academe. He remained fascinated by the academy's moods, tensions, and endless give-and-take, much of which focused on status rather than money. At the secondary level, status anxiety all too often swamped classroom duties. Prep schools in *Little Portia, Otherwise Engaged, Two Sundays,* and *Old Flames,* far from being the strongholds of scholarship and tradition their headmasters claimed them to be, show the same cliquishness, backbiting, and homosexuality found in Lindsay Anderson's 1969 movie, *If...* and the two Alan Bennett plays, *Forty Years On* (1968) and *The History Boys* (2004). Sports rank higher with Gray's collegians, though. Even the bookworms, to protect themselves from their classmates' gibes, should play sports. Jocks like Graham Thwaite of *Little Portia* and Gray himself, who later give up sports in favor of their studies, can do as they please.

All this has a subtext. The colleges Gray depicts are theoretically governed by the concepts of duty, *noblesse oblige*, and the furtherance of the social class to which the boys' parents belong. Inside school walls, though, away from their masters, pubescent high-jinks, rivalries, and tests of face-saving hold way. Gray has added his mite to the classic Kipling, Evelyn Waugh, and Hogwarts social brew in which pranks can turn deadly and the death of a reputation rivals the real thing. When a literal death does occur, it sparks the same shock, pathos, and sense of injustice that perturbs A.E. Housman's Shropshire folk (Barbara Gray attended school in Shropshire [CODA 7]).

The 15-year-old Lopez, a "precocious expert bowler" (UP 235) who impressed Gray more than any cricketer he ever faced, killed himself soon after leaving Westminster. (In "Memories of Lopez," Gray says that the futility of facing this magnificent bowler "marked a change in my life" [UP 236], viz., never playing cricket again.) Most of Gray's Westminster curriculum included premature death. His best friend at Westminster, who was "more clever and daring" (UP 217) than Gray, died as an Oxford student. This tragic figure's vitality shaped itself as a love of both bullfighting and the poetry of Lorca in the figure of Michael Cranton of *Little Portia*, who also dies young — but not before transforming the life of Grahame Thwaite.

The gloom thickens. The two suicides that occurred during Gray's time at Cambridge carry darker messages than those associated with his time at Westminster. Analogously, university education in the UK fared no better at transmitting the values of democracy and intellectual attainment than did Westminster. The institution of higher learning Gray knew best, Queen Mary's College, in East London's Mile High Road, seems to laugh at these values. Far from being distinguished, it's barely mediocre and respectable at the academic level. Despite having dedicated *Butley* to "all the staff and students, past, present, and future, ever connected to" QMC, Gray portrays it as a dreary but logical next step for graduates of academic third-raters like Amplesides.

Yes, Ben's colleague Edna has her book on Byron accepted for publication after working on it for 20 years, the same amount of time Ben and his young colleague Joey Keyston say they'll need to finish *their* books. But Joey's work is an edition, not a work of original scholarship, and Edna's book, though accepted, has not yet appeared in print. Ben's chances of finishing his Eliot monograph? They're so tiny that they needn't be mentioned. A QMC graduate who makes it to Oxford in *After Pilkington* is, advisedly, a classicist, not an English major. He judges well to call the place "a dump down in the East End" (4SG 216); longtime QMC professor of English Helen Twiscombe of *Breaking Hearts will* call it "the Dump" (18), a term embellished upon in *Old Flames*, where the corpse of a QMC lecturer in social studies is literally dumped on QMC property (4SG 337).

This stroke of black comedy makes thematic sense. Judging from Ben Butley and the two English dons we meet in *Breaking Hearts*, there's as little interest in teaching among the English faculty as there is in research. One don commits suicide in Gray's 1997 novella. The other, Helena, the narrator, is so dazed by the gin she gulps that she forgets that she took mandatory retirement the year before, an agreement that also barred her from the staff common room. But the virus of discord that infects members of QMC's English faculty has spread beyond East London. Even the redoubtable F.R. Leavis, the "only great man" (UP 213) Gray says he ever met, was hated by his Cambridge colleagues.

Based on the belief that becoming a teacher is a good way to throw away your life, Gray's delvings into academic tribal lore energizes his work. As it should; during the 20-odd years he worked and lived among academics, he saw them — and saw through them. Mostly, his colleagues sought both self-knowledge and self-worth in the realm of their peers, a circumscribed society, as in C.P. Snow. But power means less to these underperformers than it does to Snow's more politically minded dons. Gray's academics are so busy protecting or burnishing their images that they have no time for academic politics, let alone exploring the dark hidden places in their hearts. His cynical take on the teaching profession — whether or not it stems from his having bogged down at the lecturer's rank during his 18-year stay at QMC (Lady 4) — remains one of the chief attractions of his work.

Beyond the academy, Gray often describes the heartaches his people get from trying to balance professional goals with family commitments. Striking this balance is particularly thorny for writers. Their priorities lie elsewhere. The selfishness of the serious writer comes forth in *Side-Car*, *Hidden Laughter*, *Life Support*, and *Little Nell*. *Stage Struck* (1979) uses a professional actress to convey the same dedication, and in Gray's second play, *Sleeping Dog*, a free-hand caricaturist introduces into the canon the plight of the archetypal figure.

In keeping with Freud's concept of the artist as misfit, Claud, a bartender in a posh South Kensington hotel, already feels cut off from his fellow Londoners. He's gay and a Trinidadian black, attributes underscored by both the soundtrack and the camera in this 1967 television script. In fact, rather than settling down in London, he has been saving money to go to New York, where he once spent five years. Gray uses the close-up camera to disclose the artistic skill that helps Claud pass the time before packing his bags. The following stage direction shows Claud exaggerating the most pronounced characteristics of a visitor to his bar; as is appropriate, exaggeration being the caricaturist's stock-in-trade: "*Claud is drawing in his pad — a thin elderly face caricatured into a corrupt effeminacy, suggestions of eye make-up and lipstick and a blouse and skirt*" (1SG 364).

With disarming accuracy, the sketch has conflated her withered ugliness and coquettishness into the torture of having sex with her. Claud's artistic economy of means, though, soon upends him. Sir Hubert, having sneaked a look at the sketch Claud did of his wife, vowing revenge, baits and goads him while pretending to befriend him. But not without suffering himself; more obsessive than he realizes, this former colonial sahib in Africa conjures up visions of Claud's black hands multiplying themselves and then darting inside Lady Caroline's clothes.

Claud doesn't make it to New York. He may never even return to London after Sir Hubert locks him in the cellar of his country estate. Like Joyce's Stephen Dedalus in *A Portrait*, Claud, the dissident artist, is punished by the establishment. It counts in Gray's favor that Claud's art has brought about this punishment by the symbolic father. The artist suffers for having shown his audience more than that audience wanted to see. Claud's sketch hit too close to the bone to be laughed off. Also, as a gay man, Claude holds no sexual truck with women. And even if a woman *could* excite him, it wouldn't be the wilted alcoholic, Lady Caroline, as her fuming, vengeful husband knows all too well.

Claud stands as little chance of joining his friend in New York as many of his straight artist-counterparts in the canon do of achieving family harmony. Reviewing a March 2007 revival of *Quartermaine's Terms* at Centenary College in Hackettstown, New Jersey, Bob Rendell called the play's Mark Sackling "an untalented incipient novelist whose wife has left him, taking their son with her, because of his single-minded obsession with his writing" (Rendell 2). Sackling's losing his family to his writing again references Joyce's concept of the artist as a suffering outsider. Sackling must renounce writing before his wife and son return to him. Count him lucky. He learned early enough in the game to drop his novel-in-progress in favor of reclaiming his home.

What if he didn't learn this lesson? His estranged wife thinks that being an artist means distancing, even excluding, everybody else (3SG 9). She speaks home. The artist-as-loner theme always gripped Gray. When a publisher warns his aspiring novelist-wife in *Hidden Laughter* that she'll have to cut herself off from her loved ones, all for the sake of headaches, insomnia, and the fear of having her work rejected, she tells him, "I have to, darling. I have to *try*, at least" (4SG 7). She has misjudged the cost of her resolve. Besides feeling like a criminal, Nietzsche's artist can't shake off the sickness to which his art is indebted. The chains that keep Claud in Sir Hubert's cellar symbolize this dehumanization of the artist. Louise Pertwee of *Hidden Laughter* will find self-expression so hard and selfish that it consumes everything. It's a cruel lesson. At the end, the artist may discover that she has no self to express.

Works by Gray as distant from each other in time as *Side-Car* (1971) and

Life Support (1997) include in their casts writers whose work has eaten away parts of their sanity and soul. *Life Support*'s Jeff Golding sees *his* home life collapse when a bee sting puts his wife in a coma during a research trip to Guadeloupe. The titles of Jeff's travel books, *Bananas in Borneo*, *A Chump in China*, and *Pootering through Portugal* (SD 16), describe him as a popular, rather than a serious, author. But because *all* writing is a painful, irrational process, as both Edith Dunlop of *Side-Car* and Chekhov's Trigorin in *The Sea Gull* learn, popularity may be a lean payoff for the hours of toil and self-denial a writer must undergo. The end of *Side-Car* shows Edith making a virtual pact with Satan. She'll let the boyfriend of her gay or bisexual husband, himself a defaulted novelist, continue living with them if the husband promises not to thwart her career. It's apt that the *"cell-like room"* in which Edith writes has a *"distinctly nun-like effect"* (OE 141).

The Jamesian theme of sacrificing life for art takes a new turn in *Just the Three of Us*. The denial and deprivation featured in this 1997 work portray a different side of art's obduracy. Writing under the ironic name of Lizzie Heartbourne, the best-selling novelist Enid Parkhurst kidnaps, in Terri Green, a young woman because she believes that Terri will provide Enid material for her next book. But in a second-act switch that spells out Gray's commitment to *his* art, the two women either reverse roles of captor and captive or Terri sheds her shackles so utterly that she gives Enid, or Lizzie Heartbourne, more than she had dared to wish for — the heart knowledge she needs to write the serious novel she had always aspired to.

A younger author who uses sex (unsuccessfully, it turns out) to coax a publisher into accepting her book in *Otherwise Engaged* conveys in a different form the ruthlessness of the artist in Gray. When told by a demurring Simon Hench that he'll gladly accept her book, edit it to her advantage, and get the best available American rights on it — providing it's any good — Davina Saunders replies, "That means more to me than being sucked at and fucked by the likes of you" (OE 32). She'd identify with the claim of the great art critic Bernard Berenson in *Old Masters* that he'd gladly forgo money for prestige in the community of scholars. This proposed sacrifice resonates in the canon. Gray's academics must also weigh the benefits of *their* dedication. Hillary, a university lecturer in *Plaintiffs and Defendants*, asks her husband if the daily demands of her job have reduced his interest in her. Her question has passed its use-by date. By the time she spots the warning signs in Peter's behavior around her (here in scene 21 of Gray's 1975 television play), her marriage is already at risk. The play's third scene had shown Peter in a Turkish bath, washing off the signs of a recently concluded rut.

Another Peter in *Two Sundays* (which also aired on TV in 1975), hears his friend Charles discuss some of the surprises that came from his having written a novel that began as a short story. "Even now I can scarcely believe I finished it" (OE 85), says Charles, recounting one of the shocks caused by the act of writing. A more seasoned author wouldn't have been surprised. A believer in the strenuous life, Charles runs four miles each day and coaches two sports besides teaching full time. All this has served as a distraction. He has suddenly found himself in deep waters. The suspicion that art menaces everybody close to the artist makes Charles feel relieved that his wife hasn't read his book. Charles had told Alison that he was working on a Molière translation while writing the novel. He practiced his art as if it were a vice, adopting the same stealth and deceit that Joyce's Stephen Dedalus did in *A Portrait*. Working in secrecy, Charles based his novel on a painful, unrequited, because undeclared, love he felt for one of his students. Now any emotional issue in Gray has at least two sides. Charles says that, despite the pain it brought him, the psychic demands of writing the novel "in a sense saved my life" (OE 85). Intriguingly, he tells this to Peter, a man who dropped his own novel-in-progress and who's portrayed in Charles's novel as a suicide. Peter, who needs to be asked three times if he loves his wife, has to wonder if Charles, like the suffering artists in Joyce, Mann, and Patrick White, has unearthed in himself a visionary streak.

Margaret Spencer of *Close of Play* has shut out the future. With the callousness that defines all serious artists, she refused to let the baby she conceived with her weak-willed alcoholic husband Benedict "muck up [her] creative processes" (CP 41). She has also stopped humoring Ben. Even if its rewards are ambiguous, providing that they can be realized at all, she has vowed to direct all her wits to the challenges posed by her book-writing, and that's that. Even a more upstanding husband than Ben would be looking at a childless marriage with her as his wife.

Usually in Gray's work, it's the husband who neglects the wife, sometimes from the start of the marriage. Act One of *Dutch Uncle* (1969) ends with May Godboy's calling herself a "warm woman ... [whose] fire's going out" (1SG 194). She sees that she's failing in her effort to lure her husband Perkin to bed for the first time in their two-year-long marriage. She doesn't suffer alone. Joanna in *Spoiled* (1971) asks *her* husband, "When did you last kiss me properly? When I was three months gone" (1SG 301). Hilary complains to Peter in *Dog Days*: "Love-making? You haven't made love to me for months. You just use me as a stage towards one of your post-coital cigarettes" (36). Husbands in Gray stay cold and impassive But their wives in the later work voice their frustrations less politely than Hilary or Joanna. "The hell for me is that we haven't fucked since you went sober to begin your first baby [i.e., book]," bawls Gwendoline Golding to her husband Jeff in *Simply Disconnected* (1996), adding, "Not a fuck in all these years. Just for your babies.... Separate beds" (23). Perhaps the Canadian-English background of the famous Rattenbury murder case of 1935 led Gray to base *Molly* (1977) on it. More likely, though, what attracted him most about the case was the husband whose sexual coldness set the murder plot going.

Though that husband probably never taught a class, John Louis DiGaetani may have hit the mark with his comment that Gray often writes about "people who happen to be teachers" (90). These teachers also happen to be flawed human beings. The eroticism infusing the teacher-student relationship brings to the fore tendencies and drives that might have otherwise stayed dormant. Helena Twiscombe of *Breaking Hearts* describes an American transfer student at QMC named Joey (Logan Bester has sex with a woman named Joey in *Simple People*): "I thought she was pretty cute. And cutely pretty. I could imagine belting her and chaining *her*, in her naked dread" (BH 20–21).

Helena's bondage fantasy will return in *Just the Three of Us* and elsewhere in Gray's work. A thwarted lust for power drives it. Harking to Ionesco's *The Lesson* (1951) and Genet's *The Balcony* (1956), the student-teacher bond in Gray, like any other server-servee relationship, is *based* on power, an engine always capable of unleashing danger and disarray. But it contains its own braking system. Though power incites lust, its enactment brings grief, which is why Ben Butley and Helena restrain themselves around the QMC students who attract them. Richard Howarth of *Spoiled* is less discreet. Gray's belief in the erotic underpinnings of the teacher-student tie makes us ask whether Howarth planned to seduce Donald Clenham from the start. He invites Donald to overnight with him and his wife to help Donald cram for an impending exam. The seduction can also stem from Howarth's being swept along by a field of force that took on an inexorable life of its own. Like the teacher in David Mamet's *Oleanna*, he should have checked the feelings brewing between him and young Donald. His weakness of will causes more damage than occurs in Mamet's 1992 play because Donald is another male.

This forbidden eroticism coexists with the gender confusion that has always stalked Gray. In *Enter a Fox* (2001), for instance, he speaks of the "two female cats and the female dog" in his home who "go about under male names" (41). *The Year of the Jouncer*, published five years after *Fox*, takes the idea forward: "George (spayed bitch) will mount Errol (neutered tom) and simulate fornication" (165). Also coming under question is the act of jouncing, the rocking movement Gray performed on his knees while facing down in his crib. It attributes a form of nascent sexual activity to the infant Gray that the adult Gray is asking us to ponder. This ongoing interest in the dubious and the disconcerting covers a broad range. The briefcase Ben Butley carries into his office at QMC contains an empty Scotch bottle, a crumpled newspaper, and a smelly sock, none of which refers to his job. The one academically relevant item he takes from his briefcase, an M.A. thesis on Henry James he's supervising, means more to Gray than it does to Butley, who never thinks of reading it during the course of the play. This self-referential motif conveys regret. Not only did Gray fail to finish *his* doctorate on James (UP 221, 226), the Australian Ph.D. student who gets murdered in *Stage Struck* (1979) had also come to the

UK to research James. Was his murder a function of his Australian blood? The comparison of Herman to a convict (3SG 210) indirectly voices another of Gray's aches, his feeling like a permanent outsider after the seven ocean crossings of his childhood and youth.

Until the 1990s, when homosexuality became a viable lifestyle in the West, male gays in Gray's work often wore masks. The repressed homosexual Charles in *Two Sundays* (1975), who writes his novel covertly, is doubly closeted. The noble Humphry outs himself long enough, in *Common Pursuit* (1984), to get murdered by a lout he might have met in a men's room. This act of violence shook Gray. Perhaps his oft-used conceit of the suffering, or even tragic, gay man explains the chapter subtitle in *Jouncer*, "Well, Am I Gay or Not?" (J 209). Does the conceit earn him a gold star for bravery? On the one hand, he answers the question in the negative. On the other, consider his statement, "The thought of having sex with any of my men friends is actually revolting" (J 209). The chapter in which this statement appears, one of the book's shortest, as if its dangerous subject matter had to be dispatched quickly, ends coyly: "They say that everybody in the world has a doppelgänger" (209).

The coyness persists. Immediately following the subchapter in which Gray asks if he's gay comes the six-part "Love Story" (210–220) which treats his bond with his "first true love, Richard Symonds" (213), whom he "loved ... more freshly than [he'd] loved any human being before" (219). Gray had spoken of this "passionate friendship, which never quite became an affair" in *An Unnatural Pursuit* (217). The meaning of the qualifier, quite, remains dark. As is intended; in the more candid and forthcoming *Jouncer*, the "rectal virgin" Gray (SD 169) withholds all signs that his "tangled and intimate relationship" (J 219) with Robert Symonds ever advanced physically beyond holding hands. Gray's stance here reminds us that D.H. Lawrence's warning to trust the novel and distrust the novelist applies more strictly to Lawrence himself than to any other writer of his time. Didn't Gray give the pedophilic Richard Howarth of *Spoiled* a first name similar to that of his best boyhood friend? And doesn't the bi-syllabic surname, Symonds, begin and end with the same letter, as did Howarth's?

The naked wrestling scene in *Women in Love* and the one in *Aaron's Rod* that shows one man oiling by hand the entire body of another (a moment that impressed Gray [4SG 353]) both imply in Lawrence a belief that men can act at a deeply physical level that is not sexual. Say what? Lawrence's theoretical loathing of homosexuality notwithstanding, he wrote in these two scenes graphic descriptions of gay sex. In this vein, his early (1927) biographer Richard Aldington called Lawrence 20 percent gay. Cynthia Nixon, in *Lawrence's Leadership Politics and the Turn Against Women* (1986), would disagree. Contrasting the abundance of buttocks, flanks, and thighs with the paucity of women's breasts and genitilia displayed in Lawrence's work, she rated Aldington's figure far too low.

Gray might have disagreed with her. His most autobiographical work, *Little Portia*, besides mentioning Lawrence often, devotes many pages and much care to a fictional version of his tie to Robert Symonds. Perhaps most revealingly, the epilogue, if not the finale, of Grahame Thwaite's loss of his virginity to the boyish and then nameless Janice Trullope, who later calls herself "Dick," begins when Grahame opens his eyes to "the swell of her buttocks" (LP 185). It had already been noted in *Colmain* that a male character "rolled his eyes around [the] buttocks" (164) of a woman he later credits with having "an eloquent rump" (168). Rüdiger Imhof wasn't trying to shock us when he called the pattern of male friendship in Gray "more profound and far-reaching than maternal bonds" (226). He might have even been too timid. We can credit Joanna Howarth's belief that Richard has been avoiding her; a heavily pregnant wife could easily put off a gay father-to-be, particularly if he's her husband. The introduction to *Little Nell* finds Gray ignoring the deep probe of his own imaginative art, to return, instead, to the double-talk he used to discuss his tie to Robert Symonds in *Jouncer*. He calls the feeling David Copperfield directs to Steerforth "a heterosexual's crush" (LN xvii). Will the final word ever be spoken on this subject? Yoking David's love for his "adored hero" to the adolescent passions in Sir Walter Scott and Robert Louis Stevenson, Allan Massie called these bonds in 2009 "matter ... for some aspiring Ph.D. student" (76).

Did the ideal of asexual male intimacy dupe Gray into protesting too much? He wrote it into *Cell Mates*, a play based on a true story. Alluding to the teamwork they must practice to trick the police, a man tells the convict he helped escape from jail, "We're going to be living together closer than — closer than a husband and wife" (CM 18). The marriage conceit holds. In the following act of *Cell Mates*, which unfolds six months later in faraway Moscow, the escaped con, a father of three whose wife has recently divorced him, says of his early days with his rescuer, "I needed you as a man needs a wife," explaining, "you were looking after me as if you were my wife. Or as if I were your wife" (35). Forecasting his author's view of David Copperfield's crush on Steerforth, the fugitive is describing chaste same-sex love, a bond that hasn't yet found a name. To Gray's disquiet; in *Fat Chance* (1995), while discussing the staging of *Cell Mates*, he notes the "instinctive alliance" swathing the cheap Irish crook Robert Bourke and the KGB spy George Blake. But then he takes a safer stance: "I think Bourke loved Blake from the beginning, *but didn't have enough experience of the emotional life to acknowledge it*" (FC 13; emphasis mine).

Lawrence's dark gods have gained control; what's most deeply felt bypasses the mind. Both Gray's inability to back his assertion with evidence and the words he chose in which to frame it hew to Lawrencean writ. They also give helpful new slants on the key event of *Spoiled*, Richard Howarth's seduction of Donald Clenham. How clean are Donald's hams? Did Donald, perhaps unconsciously, abet the growth of a harmless flirtation into a force that overwhelmed him and Howarth? Their having sex together knits with Gray's belief that academics rarely get anything right. The emotional immaturity Gray ascribes to George Blake stopped Howarth from diverting the course of a weekend already made "nervous" (1SG 24) or anxious by Donald's having twice flunked his O-level French exam.

The point can be added that Howarth not only planned to seduce Donald from the start but that he also chose the seduction site. Joanna's sleeping in the room next to the one where Howarth was groping and mouthing Donald maximized her opportunity both to discover what was going on and to use her discovery to start a divorce action. This outcome would have pleased Howarth, whose name roughly rhymes with the word, "coward," and who's as ill suited to the roles of husband and father as is the eponym of *Butley*, a play staged the same year as *Spoiled*. The shoal of possibilities stirred by the ending of *Spoiled*, no act of authorial evasiveness, strengthens the play. The same may be said about a possible source for the play. In Strindberg's *Miss Julia*, subtitled *A Tragedy*, a man and a woman, charmed by the sights and scents of Midsummer's Eve, also make the mistake of following their sexual impulses. Now Joseph Conrad said that tragedy must convey inevitability. The pairing of Donald and Howarth rivals in volatility that of the two leads in Strindberg's 1887 gem. It also raises as many issues—which it treats with the same candor. Credit Gray's judgment. Instead of trying to resolve the sexual ambiguities roiling his psyche, he funneled them into what would become a first-rate play.

Was he playing his art false when he called Freud "the biggest bore and the biggest fraud of the last two centuries" (DiGaetani 104)? Many of his people are driven by sexual desires that flout the great western virtues of duty, discipline, and self-denial. Also, most of the teacher-student links in the canon trace the curve of Oedipal sex, despite unfolding in a gay context. The classic Oedipal paradigm that looms over the action has skipped a generation. As well it might; the adored Montreal grandmother who, Gray remembered, would "tickle me until I nearly fainted [and] bundled me about the bed and held me to her breast" (SD 78) played surrogate mother to him between 1940–45, those highly impressionable years between four and nine. The crippling, aching, dissolving laughter that made him gag also taught him an indelible lesson: pleasure at its keenest point can cause intense pain.

A later physical depredation wreaked upon Gray gave this lesson an alarming new urgency. Like the one taught by his grandmother, it, too, stuck. Mr. John Burn, the "pederastic maths teacher" who inflicted "unendurable attentions" (Fox 15) upon a 12-year-old Simon made such a mighty impact on his victim that his fictional surrogate, Lindsay Burnlow, nicknames Grahame Thwaite—Gray's own stand-in—Little Portia. That the title of Gray's 1967 novel freezes Gray at the most desperate time of his life tallies the force of this psychological earthquake. It also reminds us how hard it is to think of one of

Gray's teacher-student relationships that's *not* painful. Gray says much more about these relationships than he does about parent-child bonding. And what he says usually strikes a jarring chord with this bombshell from *Fat Lady* (1988): "A swine of a prep-school master named Mr. Brown ... used to beat me savagely and regularly" (124).

Perhaps Brown had fallen in love with young Gray, demonstrating to him again the fusion of love and cruelty. This fusion infiltrated Gray's writing from the very start. In the autobiographical *Little Portia*, Lindsay Burnlow applies a bear hug to Grahame while also fondling him, his finger exploring a frightened Grahame's "naked bummy" (50). Then he purrs, "I must punish you, but only because I adore you" (51). Although Brownlow is caught groping Grahame and fired on the spot, his abusiveness caused irreversible damage. Years later at Cambridge, Grahame dreams about a girl "tied to the post of his bed" (127). Then Grahame's dream moves in a direction we might have expected. Presaging Donald Clenham's possible complicity with Howarth in *Spoiled*, as well as his own with Burnlow, Grahame fantasizes, in reference to his bed-bound victim, "She begged him to let her go, although deeply she wanted to stay chained to the bed, being loved and punished" (167).

This fantasy owes as much to the stifling, collapsing laughter that burst from Gray in his bundling sessions with his grandmother as it does to the perversities heaped on him by Messrs. Burn and Brown. What's more, they build a pattern. A bright five-year-old didn't have to gasp for air to realize that his busty grandmother's expressions of love violated propriety. His memory of these bedtime romps stoked his descriptions, years later, of the panic gripping Grahame Thwaite while wrapped up by a panting, predatory Brownlow. Gray had discovered early that love, no unmitigated joy, always includes a stab of pain. The stab kept digging at him. His fascination with the forbidden, unsavory aspects of sexual love floods his treatment of marriage. Reasonably contented married couples he marginalizes, using them as either foils or as comic relief. Children occupy much less of Gray's attention than they do his hero, Dickens. The parents of the main figures of *Little Portia* and the *Japes* plays having died when their kids were small, the chores of child-raising occupy Gray only in *Late Middle Classes*.

And here both of the young protagonists' parents are either having or have had affairs, as was said about those of the Thwaite sibs in *Little Portia*. A domestic realist like Chekhov, Lawrence, or Updike, Gray is not. John M. Clum notes shrewdly the absence of marital happiness in the canon. The only happy marriage in Gray, Clum adds, is that of Eddie and Thomas, the elderly gay couple in *Quartermaine's Terms* (1981), with Eddie the only partner of the union who shows his face onstage (Burkman, ed., 79). Both Thomas's nonappearance and his death, which happens during the play's present-tense action, express either Gray's indifference to or ignorance of sexual love that lacks the gleam of what's prohibited and illicit. The great marital virtues of patience and sacrifice have slid past his mind's eye. Judging from the examples of the elegant cricketer Lopez, the fictional Humphry from *Common Pursuit*, the Bernard Berenson of *Old Masters*, and the Charles Dickens of *Little Nell*, Gray's paragons, regardless of their fields of endeavor, have all been dying on the inside by the time they come before us. Was Gray punishing them for their success? Robert Gordon's 1992 statement, "Gray's presentation of the human personality is a complex and contradictory manifestation of an ultimately mysterious psychology" (Burkman, ed. 8), presupposes Eros's overthrow of pious moral certainties. A prudent fear of sex's backlash stopped both Charles, the Alan Bates role in the opening run of *Two Sundays*, and Ronnie Chambers of *Hidden Laughter* from indulging their love for teenaged boys. If their prudence has reduced them to half-lifers, it also gives them brighter outlooks for the future than what looms over Richard Haworth of *Spoiled*, whose eroticized mentoring of Donald Clenham unleashed the havoc of sex.

Even in the straight community, Gray's estranged wives will choose men who are safe and steady after having been run dizzy by mercurial mates or exmates. Anne, Ben Butley's wife, never denies Ben's allegations that his replacement in Anne's bed is the most boring man in London. Like Masha in Chekhov's *Three Sisters*, Simon Hench's wife in *Otherwise Engaged* didn't choose her new lover for his good looks, charm, or brilliance, either. In fact, if Beth marries her prosaic ho-hum colleague, Ned, both of them will have to deal with the guilt caused by his deserting both an autistic daughter and a wife who has been under psychiatric care for years. Edith Dunlop of *Side-Car*, herself a reader of Jane Austen, takes Austen's preference for sense (sound judgment) over sensibility to perhaps its ultimate limit by renouncing the fret and frenzy of marital closeness for celibacy.

Gray shows the dangers of sex uncoiling in different ways. All of them hark to his boyhood discovery of the violence, rage, and hatred skulking beneath the thin skin of civilization. This proximity has been noticed. Writing in 1984, Imhof spoke of Gray's fascination with "people endeavoring to dominate and possess each other" (225). Imhof judged well. The information garnered from reading the 20-odd plays Gray wrote after Imhof's notation proves that the domination-possession Gestalt *always* fascinated Gray. Sharpening the one etched into his psyche by his grandmother and Messrs. Burn and Brown is Hank Janson, author of soft-porn novels with titles like *Torment for Trixy* and *Skirts Bring Me Sorrow*. The chains, ropes, and gags binding Janson's heroines in such books, Gray recalled in *The Smoking Diaries*, supplied "what I had for a sex life" (12) at age 12.

Because Janson, though a major force in the growth of Gray's sensibility and a publishing powerhouse in his day, is virtually unknown in ours, let's back up. Under the name of Hank Janson, Stephen Frances (1917–89) wrote some 50 lurid thrillers featuring gangsters and their molls. Using as plotting devices kidnapping, extortion, and sadism, these works of "neurotic anxiety"

(Holland 9) sold eight million copies, making Frances/Janson Britain's top-selling paperback novelist. This success came about in part from an unexpected boost. In 1954, the books were banned by court order and both their publishers and distributors were jailed. The books' bawdy, violent covers were seized, too, on the grounds that they could corrupt and even deprave readers. Whether they deranged Gray can't be said. They did shock him. The deep tremors they caused in him persisted, as well, the cover art of a Hank Janson novel adorning the jacket of his bondage-themed play, *Just the Three of Us*.

The embryonic playwright Gray had been psychologically readied for the Hank Janson books, which reach us from the standpoint of a tough reporter for the Chicago *Chronicle* named Hank Janson. Let *Kill Her If You Can* demonstrate for us both their ambience and their subject matter. This story of violence, betrayal, and sadism pivots on Hank's bond with Beryl Pinder, a headstrong, hot-tempered daredevil airplane pilot Hank feels compelled to tame and besmirch. Sadists will relish the book's description of Hank's obligatory act of sex with her, the foreshadowing of which also provides a sadist's delight. Hank won't deign to fuck Beryl until he has put her through a forced march of 30 miles under a blazing sun. And even then, a compliant Beryl is so raw and blistered that she can barely endure his attentions. Her agony, though, thrills Hank. (If this brief account whets your interest in Hank, please note that you're not alone. Starting in 2003, Telos Publishers in the UK began reissuing the Jansons, sleazy covers and all.)

A circuit has formed. The scene from *Kill Her* we just looked at conjures up the excessive violence Pip foists upon Miss Havisham when he rescues her from the fire in Gray's favorite novel, *Great Expectations*. It also raises the possibility that the title of Janson's 1952 novel only came to him while he was writing the scene. On view here is the meld of sex and anguish so vital to Gray even when he's the victim who connives his overthrow. In *Smoking Diaries*, the most revealing of the memoirs, he said that Thomas Hardy, whom he had quoted in *Life Support* (33), had "a spirit that nourished itself on pain, most of it inflicted by himself, much of it on himself" (107). Gray's judgment of a kindred spirit calls to mind the deviant sexuality in his own work. Alfred Hitchcock's linkage of food and sex attains both a new urgency and a degree of humiliation for this familiar of "desire and thrilled shame" (SD 106). The sexually transgressive Richard Haworth of *Spoiled* and Daniel Davenport of *Old Flames* both gobble junk food in view of the audience.

The overweight Gray's sexual anxiety can cast shadows—and emit auras so pungent that they smell. Somebody in Act One, scene one, of *Common Pursuit* says of a Cambridge student's room, in which an offer of sex was recently rejected, "This room reeks of passion" (4SG 94). Another character in the next scene, which takes place nine years later, says the same thing about a room *he* has just entered (4SG 105). Again, no sexual act took place on the premises. In fact, Gray will depict a sexual naughting or undoing. Marigold, whose sexual advance was rebuffed in Act One, scene one, announces that she has just had an abortion in the later scene (4SG 107). Sex, an act undertaken to promote life, keeps serving death when it happens at all in this uncommonly chaste play. Before Humphry's death at the hands of a putative lover, Nick claims that he's a virgin (4SG 94). And so was the undergraduate Simon Gray at his age, claiming that he didn't have sex with a woman till age 25 (LC 101). The "overtly ambitious" Nick and Gray also resemble each other in their enslavement to tobacco (UP 23), a substance that curbs lust.

Which of the Cantabs in *Common Pursuit* Gray most resembles can't be known, but different forms of bondage, the slave's nightmare if not his/her deepest wish, turns up often in the work. Sometimes the motif discloses the masochism that Gray saw his doppelgänger Thomas Hardy conjure up either to defeat or to re-route his joy. A character in the second act of *Dutch Uncle*, for instance, goes to see the 1959 movie, *The Flame and the Arrow*, which depicts the liberation of an Italian village by the movie's rescuer-hero, played by Burt Lancaster. But Eric, who hasn't seen the movie, cites a scene in which the hero kidnaps his beloved, played by Virginia Mayo "and keeps her chained by a chain around her neck" (1SG 211). Both the homicidal Eric's word choice and imagery are characteristic. S&M devotees have always snapped to the image of a chained virgin(ia), particularly when the chains are applied as an affirmation of love.

Such well-judged tropes show Gray's artistry outpacing that of Janson/Frances. But is Gray dwelling on S&M to bask in it? Or, following Jean Genet, is he using it as the destructive element in which he has immersed himself in order to purge it from his psyche? *Dutch Uncle* finds him splashing around in it. In an effort to coax her asexual (or gay) husband into bed, May Godboy speaks endearingly about a beating his predecessor gave her: "If you were like Number One, you'd learn how to handle me. Once he gave me a tanning, and I loved him all the more for it" (1SG 168).

Pig in a Poke nods in the direction of Genet's sordid religiosity. In this 1969 television play, Wendy, a pampered rich man's daughter who has enjoyed luxury her whole life, says of her sitting tenant, "He's utterly filthy. He contaminates the whole house" (2SG. 173). Yet her job in a used-clothes charity shop invokes the self-division and self-hatred riding Strindberg's Miss Julia, a disorder that Gray's play develops. Guilty because of the privilege they have always enjoyed, both women want to dirty themselves. Wendy, though, who lacks Miss Julia's social conscience, is simply excited by the animal rankness of her tenant Grieg.

Her instinct clashes with the accepted rules of conduct set forth by her social class, putting her at odds with herself. When an acquaintance refers offhandedly to wife-beating, she responds, after licking her lips, always a sign of nerves in Gray, as it is in Raymond Chandler, "Wrong class, I believe" (2SG 191). The "tanning," to use the underclass May Godboy's word in *Dutch Uncle*, she secretly craves from Grieg, stands as an act of defiance as well as a sexual breakthrough. Bidding for Grieg's attention, she walks down the stairs clad in only a bra and panties at a time when she suspects he's at home (2SG 182).

A superb authorial stoke shows her later wearing dark glasses to cover the black eye she allegedly got walking into a bedroom door. Bedrooms and beds have been preoccupying Wendy. She is soon seen wearing sacrificial white in Grieg's basement bedsitter, where she has come for sex. Carrying her masochism forward, Gray shows Grieg brewing some post-coital tea, of which Grieg, planning to take his alone, says *"with the very faintest touch of self-righteousness"* (2SG 198), that he has work to do. (Advisedly, in the play's opening scene, he invited Wendy to have tea *with* him.) Gray continues to deploy his materials with flair. Wendy's next onstage appearance shows her hair pulled back, marking a return of her sexual apathy. When the source of that apathy, her husband Stephen, asks her about her eye, her answer, "Blacker" (2SG 199), cites the origin of both her black eye and her recklessness; she already skipped work that day.

Wendy is reveling in surrender. After she lures Stephen into bed, the camera shows his clothes *"folded into a neat pile, hers scattered everywhere"* (2SG 209). She's wilder than he. But her wildness, rather than dulling her wit, has honed it. Grieg, whom she keeps calling a pig (e.g., 2SG 196, 202), has created in her a grunting, wheezing pig of her own. Besides living in a poke, he tups, or pokes, her to conclude every beating she can coax out of him.

The sex she had with Stephen couldn't have thrilled her, because the scene immediately following it begins with a close-up of her face while she's *"seated on Grieg's bed, hands folded in her lap"* (2SG 203), like a docile student, acolyte, or postulant. Her need to keep returning to Grieg has totally degraded her if it hasn't hammered her into a puzzling new form. Her world revolves around the psychic electricity flying between them. She hates him and herself. She's dying to sleep with him. She's obsessed. Her sunglasses track her willingness to forfeit normal sight for an inner vision borne of pain and humiliation. After her well-bred husband finally loses patience and beats her up, he hears her say, "Oh Stephen … he does *much* worse" (2SG 207). The secaturs that Grieg brandishes throughout the play (e.g., 2SG 173, 207) symbolize Stephen's unmanning by him. In the last scene of this television play, Grieg has the screen to himself. Anything in the house is his for the taking.

Wendy doesn't know why she has been whoring herself out to this thug. *Pig in a Poke* is a free-standing work of imaginative art rather than a rehash of Lawrence's "The Virgin and the Gypsy," "The Fox," or *Lady Chatterley's Lover*, in which sad, suppressed women are brought to life by sleeping with a social inferior. The used clothing Wendy sorts out at her job are spun gold compared to the rags worn by Grieg (*Little Portia* contains a nasty little boy called Greg, and a drunken Greg in *Simply Disconnected* goes to jail for fighting at a soccer match). But has she sorted out feelings that leapt to the fore during her time away from work? The mood of resigned sorrow put forth by her and Stephen's final onstage appearance together, in the presence of her parents, suggests that, rather than sinking her foundering marriage, Grieg's roughneck interventions might have righted it. This optimism is validated by the play's careful orchestration of mood. Knowing that the technical resources of the television camera could overwhelm the viewers of a work as anarchic as *Pig*, Gray inserts an ironically witty scene just before screening his relentless finale. Stephen's statement to Wendy, "The time's come to do something about our friend downstairs," means that steps have to be taken soon to evict their resident squatter. Then Stephen says of the squatter, "He somehow gets into everything," to which Wendy replies (to greatest effect in a flat, noncommittal voice), "I know." She also has an unassuming comeback to Stephen's complaint that Grieg could be "up and down, in and out all day long." When she's asked, "Know what I mean?" her answer, "Yes, I do" (2SG 200), besides voicing agreement that Grieg has upset the routine of the home, gives this grim, disturbing play a couple of laugh lines when they're most needed.

Gray already used physical violence to move a script in *Wise Child*, where the sexual dynamics were more psychologically complex. But then, Gray always covers his tracks when dealing with gay subject matter. Young Jerry deliberately loses the games of "paper, scissors, stone" that he begs Mrs. Artminster to play with him. Understanding Jerry's needs, Artminster gives his eager palm a hard whack to crown each game. The play's first act ends with Jerry begging for another and, after he's denied, rubbing Artminster's feet. But the cigar-smoking Artminster is a crook in his fifties who wears women's garb to fox the police. He's not the only one in hiding. Jerry has connived at physical pain in order to mask a deeper kind. Displaying again his instinct for the dramatic climax, Gray ends the play's second act with Jerry calling Artminster "Mum" as he "*cuddles himself*" into her (1SG 126). So fragile and lost is he that he'll go to any lengths to get the cozy, anchoring warmth of a maternal security, even if it's administered (or Artministered) by a man.

The motif of the child's game which one of the players deliberately loses returns, masochistic echoes and all, in *Side-Car*. This time the game is tiddly-winks, and it's being played by two men whose same-sex antics have taken the form of a master-slave relationship. Gerald Dunlop throws the game soon after bribing the infantile Tommy to play with him. But before giving Tommy his winner's prize, he wants to make sure Tommy has earned it. Like the cuddling that ended Act Two of *Wise Child*, *Side-Car* features the romping of the two men "*crashing about, clutching at each other, half-laughing, half-gasping till they roll on the floor*" (RC 150), points directly to the aching hilarity that overwhelmed Gray at the tickling, probing hands of his grandmother, who was probably Mrs. Artminster's age during their bundling bouts.

This early influence had been steering Gray toward sexual bonds both conflictive and unorthodox. Because his knowledge of sex came to him in terror rather than fact, he's not motivated by a schoolboy's desire to shock his audiences. This detractor of Freud carried with him his whole life the signs of his charged encounters with his grandmother, Messrs. Burn and Brown, and the Hank Janson books. Signs, not stains; his belief in the horrific and the humiliating as promoters of vision in *Pig in a Poke* shows him writing from his naked self. To succeed, any writer must stick to what he/she knows. Gray's descriptions of sexual pathologies veer far from Lawrence's star polarities because they're based on childhood experience, not literature.

Graham Greene's 1950 essay, "The Burden of Childhood," contrasted the adult responses to the wrongs heaped on Dickens and Rudyard Kipling in early childhood: "Dickens learned sympathy, Kipling cruelty" (127), Greene said. Perhaps Dickens interested Gray more than Kipling because his rational, civilized self perceived the need for sympathy in a world rife with malice. Kipling's thirst for revenge, though natural enough, slighted harmony and happiness. But what does it matter? Gray makes us ask. The Dickens of his *Little Nell*, though gentle and loving, makes mistakes that foul three generations. Greene's *Collected Essays* (1969), one of the 20th century's great non-fiction books by a fiction writer, continues to teach us about Gray. Let's go to the essay on Walter de la Mare's short stories, in which Greene said famously, "Every creative writer worth our consideration ... is a victim: a man given over to an obsession" (141). Like Isaiah Berlin's Tolstoy, whose passion for grand, all-encompassing harmonies tugged against his fascination with the defining marks or particulars of particular things and people, Gray looks in opposite directions; Lyn Gardner spoke home when she called him "a curious mixture of mischief and irritability" (2). But Gray's head didn't spin on his shoulders. Instead of immobilizing him, the polarities that gripped him produced some brilliant work.

This stinging tension will always raise questions, particularly about gender confusion. The questions began early. In the stage directions to *Wise Child*, his first London play, Gray calls Jerry "*very pretty*" (73), a term that straight males rarely or never direct to other men. (In *Coda*, Gray called Alan Bates "a famously beautiful man" [148]). Frank Ardolino claims that Ben Butley hates women, using as evidence Ben's rudeness with his student, Miss Heasman, whose name, Ardolino adds, alludes to "Butley's penchant for masculinizing women—'he's a man'" (177). Yet it was Gray who gave Miss Heasman her defeminized last name. And he may have done so because her hind-parts, like those of any woman, or man, for that matter, interested him more than her genitals. This reading chimes with Gray's having chosen the name, Joey, for the woman the hero of *Simple People* gave his virginity to—only to reapply it to Ben Butley's closest male friend.

This all hangs together. The sight of the hind-parts of the wife he's about to murder deters Godboy of *Wise Child* from his dark task. The gay William Booter (whose name is slang for the word, buttocks) in Gray's 1968 novel, *A*

Comeback for Stark, fantasizes about "Nubian boys ... with their slim brown limbs and their *buttocks* like teacups" (51; emphasis mine). Later in the book it's said of a panicked Myra Harkness, "Against her fear she became sticky ... with excitement" (98). Similar female sexual imagery returns in the book's next-to-last chapter when a murder victim "spread[s] across the bed in a dreadful loosening of joints." The book's next paragraph, which also takes place in the victim's death room, reveals a "lean elegant man" (185) holding a revolver. The lean, the firm, and the taut Gray applies to men, whereas women, as in Joe Orton, call forth images of stickiness, breakdown, and sprawl. A fresh female corpse in Chapter 12 of *Comeback* spreads and slackens as it drifts apart. Driving this conceit is a sexual fear and disgust reminiscent of Claud's reaction to Lady Caroline in *Sleeping Dog*. Claud isn't the only male character in Gray's early work to recoil from the female. The foul-smelling marsh Grahame Thwaite falls into in *Little Portia* "clogged him and sucked him [viz., Grahame] down" (17), this after hearing that the marsh would swallow him if he so much as looks at it.

That which is mucky, boggy, and rank is also wet, a derogatory term in Gray. A man in *Otherwise Engaged* remembers calling his wimpish schoolmates drips and plops (39). A boy who insults Grahame Thwaite's aunt is "wet" (27, 46). In response to a disturbing question, Grahame later says, "It's wet.... And dismal" (46). But the question came from the pederastic Lindsay Burnlow, whose face, when he forgets to powder it, looks soft and damp (47). (A woman named Lindsay appears in Iris Murdoch's 1962 novel, *An Unofficial Rose*.) The trope has gained drive and momentum. Grahame, who likes to hunt rats (26), is *called* a rat when he starts to cry (29). This happened as he pulled himself out of the marsh covered with "filth and damp" (17). Rats have been seen prowling this same marsh. Perhaps they have soft, white bellies like the one a friend of Stephen Dedalus "saw plop" (15) into a ditch early in Joyce's *A Portrait* (New York: Viking, 1961, 11). The soft, white face of Lindsay Burnlow also gets wet when he's sexually aroused — by a compliant Grahame.

Gray's rhythmically expanding symbol has charted the boy's fall into sin and corruption. And that's pretty striking — and intellectually stimulating — work coming from a man who'd liken himself 21 years after publishing *Little Portia* to "a plump and degenerate lesbian" (Lady 140).

Three

The Labors of the Thrice-Born

The roles played by Gray's parents in his development invite the oft-posed question: Do families shield us from life's cruelties, or *are* they life's cruelties? As has been seen, the absence of Barbara and James Gray during Simon's crucial formative years stands behind the orphan motif in their son's work. But both the son's handling of the motif in his plays and his discussions of his Montreal childhood in his eight volumes of diaries, or memoirs (1986–2008), suggest that the same separation from his parents that vexed him also honed his mind. The pedophilic teachers who terrified him only burst into his life after his 1945 return to England. Life went better for him in Montreal. The street gang he had joined as a grade-schooler provided the fun of community smoking and theft. Besides, when he left Montreal's cold streets to come indoors, he could always drift into the deep, welcoming arms of his grandmother.

If Gray found this same comfort and protectiveness in his family of origin, he said little about it. Perhaps he was discouraged by the reversal of established parental roles he saw at home. Whereas men usually base their moral decisions on justice, women prize the selflessness, openness, and reciprocity that help relationships flourish. In the Gray family, though, Barbara took on the masculine qualities of aggressiveness and competitiveness. The archetypal mother in Gray is shrill, domineering, and sharp tempered. She can also be tall, in contrast to the loving roly-poly grandmother. The *"very plump hand"* (1SG 322) that passes a personnel executive a cup of coffee in *Caramel Crisis* puts the maternal, or, in Gray's case, grandmaternal, function of nurture into the frame. The title figure of *Caramel Crisis* (1963), Gray's first play, with his love of movie theaters, baths, and taxis that he finds "deep and warm" (1SG 313), seeks the darkness and enveloping safety of the womb.

Gray liked his thick-waisted landlady at Cambridge because she put forth this jolly domestic ambience. She appears in *Little Portia* as a sensual kitchen maid whose wide lap and earthy wisdom get her fired to the chagrin of the Thwaite kids, who, according to their straight-laced guardians, had regrettably fallen under her sway. By contrast, the tall, athletic mother figure in Gray's work shut herself off from her fragile, needy children. Her paradigm — the forceful, self-starting Barbara — ignored the judgmental gaze of (white) male authority figures. Gray says of her in *Jouncer* (2006) that she excelled in hockey and cricket "along with the standing broad jump and high jump" (26).

Barbara, who would later coach women's field hockey at Dalhousie University, Gray said in *Smoking Diaries* (2004), also had the "athletic reflexes" that helped her shine as an ambulance driver during World War II (82). This "tall, vivid woman" (UP 215), who later force-fed her sons on cricket, appears often in the diaries. Rarely deferential or passive, this "zestful slapper and cuffer" (SD 61) practiced an "oaths-and-blows style of parenting" (SD 63) that poisoned the affection she lavished on Simon in the form of stroking, kissing, and fondling, erotic undertones and all (Gray refers to these attentions as "displays of full-bodied passion" [SD 14]).

The term "vivid," which Gray applied to Barbara in *Unnatural Pursuit* (215), he later used to describe Celia Smithers (80) in *The Late Middle Classes*. Though probably not an "athlete at the very highest level" like the Olympian medalist Barbara (SD 231, 80), Celia (who'd be about Barbara's age and build during the play's present-tense action, the early 1950s) loves to play tennis, smokes cigarettes often, and has a philandering pathologist as a husband. Celia might have also resembled Yvonne Thwaite of *Little Portia*, the tennis-playing mother of Grahame and Dianah who "despised everyone she met" (4). But Yvonne dies on the novel's fifth page in a car accident. Her "devastating" (LP 4) digs at her friends look ahead to the intrusiveness of Celia, who forces confrontations and inspects her son Holly's book bag, or satchel, on the sly.

These intrusions have restored Barbara to view. Celia, who also coached women's sports and drove an ambulance in World War II (LMC 56, 63), speaks her mind with a shocking lack of empathy. Bitter and angry, she swipes at other people's weak spots. She routs her less talented tennis partner every time they play, beating her in straight sets without giving up a game. Then she acts surprised, after reminding her that she's too fat, that Myra stops playing with her. (Myra retaliates by having an affair with Celia's husband.) Continuing to live by her own rules, this catastrophically bad mother interrupts son Holly's piano lessons at will to send him on errands. She needs constant reassurances of Holly's love (e.g., LMC 80), which he's supposed to confirm by massaging her legs and feet (just as *Wise Child*'s Jerry did those of Mrs. Artminster). There would be no evidence that Barbara suffocated Simon in these ways if he hadn't called her, in *The Smoking Diaries*, a "middle-aged woman of the middle classes in the middle of the twentieth century" (86). It's a safe bet that her anti–Semitism, homophobia, and racism, prized by her as "mainstream, patriotic" English values (YJ 26), seeped into the offstage conversations between Celia and her husband Charles (LMC 32, 61, 72). These slurs were duly noted. Gray might have been revisiting an unvoiced boyhood wish when he wrote the passage in which Holly welcomes the news from a lying Celia that he's not her child (80).

Being orphaned isn't life's worst blow. Rarely do Gray's women use the accommodating, nonlinear, nonassertive speech often ascribed to their sex. Nor are they adept at comforting or consoling men, a hilarious, but disturbing quasi-exception being a reluctant Mrs. Artminster, who cradles Jerry in *Wise Child*. Celia of *The Late Middle Classes* exemplifies the bullying, hot-tempered Gray matriarch who must have things her way. Slipping a hand between Charles's legs, she tells him, in the play's first act, "We'll go to bed early and play" (34). Perhaps she used this overture to segue to her saying that Holly has started to masturbate. In view of Barbara's "displays of full-bodied passion" (SD 14) with Simon, the discovery might have excited her. It does recall the sexual fear that gripped Grahame Thwaite when he caught sight of a greedy-looking marsh "darkened by ... bushes that ran in a tangle around its slopes, with the water" (LP 16) rising, as if it wants to gulp him down. This clogged vaginal marsh had appeared as a lake full of leeches and water snakes in *Colmain* (163). Though the vagina dentata may retreat, it leaves reminders of itself that must be withstood. Grahame acquires a taste for S&M magazines (LP 213). Why shouldn't he? He needs security, and, in his search for it, over-reacts. Like his author, he goes from feeling stranded to the opposite extreme, feeling engulfed. The images of chained women he finds in S&M magazines screen him from the ravages of the devouring prototype, a figure based on the first woman he ever loved, his mother.

Fear of engulfment by the prototype remained entrenched in Gray's psyche. In *Fat Lady*, he would say that *Dog Days* was about "a man being unmanned by a woman" (140). The fear that prompted this judgment surfaces elsewhere. Men friendly to Penny Newhouse's flirtations in *After Pilkington* get murdered. The implications of a question put to the title character of *A Comeback for Stark*, "You've never been trapped by a lassie, have you, Ronald" (CS 134), foreshadow the gay William Booter's recollections of a woman's mouth that "widened to suck him down into the damp gully" (163) of her throat. Booter has compared kissing a woman to being flushed down a toilet. He's echoing the disgust voiced by the middle-aged gays in Joe Orton's plays who fulminate against the damp, fetid private parts of women.

Despite the baggage heaped on him by Barbara, Gray remembers her with more affection than he does his father, not that he ever wanted to emulate either parent. This son of two avid automobile drivers (curiously, like the major writers Patrick White, Yukio Mishima, and August Wilson, the first two of whom were gay), Gray never learned to drive. Like Grahame Thwaite, he also gave up sports, which he shone in, to spend more time with his books. But he may have also stopped playing soccer and cricket to spite Barbara. His motive? Incredibly, for an Olympian medalist, she bought him a pair of soccer boots without first letting him try them on. Was she conniving at his defeat in order to retain the honor of being the family's top athlete? The question is worth asking. The ill-fitting boots she gave Simon, a "preposterously, not to say fatally, ill-judged gift" (SD 231), hampered his play in an important match.

Yet he cultivated *her* taste for cigarettes rather than smoking a pipe like James (LC 148). In fact, he adds in *Last Cigarette*, "I always see her smoking [Celia smokes often in *The Late Middle Classes*] whenever I think of her" (129). Did her playwright son, the smoker of more than three packs a day, accept her as both kindred spirit and kin despite her faults? And did he express this kinship by distancing himself from his father? He might have been striking out at the womanizing James for hurting Barbara. Nor was James alone on this score. It's more than likely that Gray speaks fondly of Barbara in *Last Cigarette*, which he suspected would be his last word on the subject of his parents, because of the guilt vexing him for having left her alone, despite her entreaties, on what would prove to be her deathbed (LC 148–9).

His coldness toward James surfaces sporadically in his creative work. Both the prologue and the epilogue of *The Late Middle Classes*, which unfolds on Hayling Island about 33 years after the play's continuous action, show Holly Smithers, the Simon James *Holliday* Gray figure (emphasis mine), visiting his former piano teacher (with whom he may have had improper relations as a boy) rather than going to his father on the Isle of Wight, which he could have reached just as easily from his London hotel (LMC 8). (After Barbara's death, James moved to Lyme Regis and then to France [YJ 68]).

Holly needn't visit Charles because of the doggedness with which Charles has been visiting *him*. Having become a psychiatrist (LMC 83), he followed his pathologist father into the healing professions. Having moved to Australia, he, too, lives on an island. His punishing Charles by adopting some of his leading traits follows implacably from his author's inability to shake the influence of James. The painful force of this influence can be tracked. Gray waits until Holly's last speech, where it has the strongest recoil action, to reveal that Holly has "a bit on the side" (88). Sex governed Gray's quarrel with James, which the years had turned into an invisible wrestling match with James's shadow. The different forms the match took always left Gray in a lurch. Natalie Pertwee of *Hidden Laughter* punishes *her* womanizing father by sleeping around. Casting a disapproving eye across a generation, as Gray did with James, her father Harry can only suffer in silence.

As in the work of Joe Orton, the father figure in Gray is cowardly. Ben Butley flees fatherhood, a role that Gray, trying to make sense of his own role as a dad, halves in the two *Japes* plays and *Michael*. Looking with dismay at his ever-ripening wife in *Spoiled* didn't just repel Richard Howarth sexually; in an act of passive aggressiveness, it even sent him to the bed of a male student to prove to Joanna his unreliability and unfitness in the home. So much does it mean to him to distance her that he risks his job to do it. And so worthless would *her* husband be as a father that Margaret Spencer aborts her child in

Close of Play, a work whose patriarchal figure, despite being onstage all through the play, could be dead.

It's a good bet, though, that Barbara Gray never accused James of coldness, as Anita Cartts did *her* husband, the eponym of *Michael* (2004), from whom she hasn't had sex in two years (Four 199). Yes, James, a professional success like Michael Cartts, was a "selfish shit" (Four 199) who rated his fun over his wedding vows. But this "very uxorious philanderer" (J 13) met Barbara's needs, too. What their son condemned, though, was the democratic spirit with which James distributed his seed. In the last section of *Late Middle Classes*, the father's philandering also hurts his son. Gray explains in *Smoking Diaries* that James had an eight-year intrigue with his secretary in London at the same time he was servicing a neighbor (77–78). "Daddy was bonking three women" (87), Gray announces a couple of diary entries later.

Late plays, like the *Japes/Michael* triptych (2000–04) saw Gray re-imagining the marriage bond. If he wanted these plays to exorcise his father's rutting, he failed. In *Old Masters* (2004), that monster of egoism, Bernard Berenson, is bonking three women himself, his Swedish masseuse, his secretary, and his complacent wife. The Charles Dickens of *Little Nell* is a more avid three-women bonker. Gray's 2006 play begins on an August night in 1857, with Dickens performing onstage with the newly met Ellen Ternan. It ends the night of his June 1870 death, again showing him at Nelly's side. During nearly all of the 13 intervening years Nelly, or Ellen, was his mistress. But Dickens was living part of the time with his wife, with whom he had nine surviving children. In the picture, too, was Catherine's younger sister, Georgina, with whom Dickens had fallen in love and, at least according to Peter Carey's 1997 novel, *Jack Maggs*, was bonking regularly. The "sapping logistics of adultery" (LN x) could have been vexing him even before he met Nelly, even if they didn't cause his early death (LN xviii). They also troubled Gray, as is seen in the pattern they etched into his mind. Three pages after applying his witty phrase to Dickens, he tallies the cost of philandering on James: "He ... was prone to bouts of deep depression from spending too much time in the company of ... women not his wife" (xiii).

It has been said that a writer's themes choose the writer rather than the other way around. The resemblance Gray noted between his father and Dickens (the James Gray surrogate in *The Late Middle Classes* is called Charles) goaded him to write, in *Little Nell*, a "psychological and theatrical epic" (LN xii). He had explored intra-family adultery in both *Close of Play* and the *Japes/Michael* trilogy, where Anita probably tupped her brother-in-law both more often and more keenly than she did her husband. Perhaps she even conspired in the two-year-long sexual hiatus she railed against in *Michael* (Four 199). Gray family bonds had already impinged on erotic ones, starting with James's giving up his fiancée to marry, in Barbara, her sister (CODA 7). Then, after Barbara's death, James married her cousin Betty (J 69) and took her to France, from which Dickens was returning about a century earlier with Nell and her mother when they were caught in the Staplehurst train wreck.

Gray's work isn't simple or reassuring. The lives his people lead can be difficult, complicated, and strange, and he takes great risks in describing them honestly. The archetypal mother is both feared and held in awe. His reaction to the father figure cuts much deeper. The persistence of his disapproval, resentment, and admiration of James (whose *Late Middle Classes* stand-in, has, like him, the name of several English kings) reads like an extended, however veiled, confession of inadequacy. It may have also kept him a virgin till age 25; the Hayling Island neighbor Dr. Charles Smithers is bonking in *Late Middle Classes* has an impotent husband. But the shadow of James didn't choke Simon. His plays convey his knowledge that the spark of virtue lies in sinners, just as the wise and mighty can sink to folly, greed, and hypocrisy, like the "overwhelming genius" Dickens (LN xvi) in *Little Nell*. Gray knew the coils of moral ambiguity. He also wrote about scoundrels without condemning their vile actions or trying to apologize for them. On the other hand, virtues like affection, comradeship, and loyalty, though wired into his people, may lack stamina. The English officers who set up camp along a Congo river in *Rear Column* (1978) have come to Africa to help abolish slavery and cannibalism. Yet the actions they take to bring about these ideals are uglier than those of the primitives they had set out to civilize.

This ugliness is rare. Gray's imaginary world is mostly banal and a little sordid rather than evil and oppressive. By blurring the line between victims and aggressors, he, like Chekhov, discloses our secret selves, the ones that lurk beneath those we show on our everyday rounds, i.e., the outward lives of "daily needs in a daily self" (LN xvi). The secret self will burst forth, as it does in Pirandello. Ben Butley coaxes his ex-lover's new boyfriend into hitting him. Helena Twiscombe of *Breaking Hearts* acts up in open view of the authorities at QMC she wants to fire her. Likewise, any number of youngsters in the canon, including Nelly Ternan, will tolerate, if not encourage, the attentions of would-be predators.

The influence of Genet ends in Gray's reluctance either to glorify the transgressive or to sweep his characters into an undertow of dread. The ridiculous and the harrowing often walk together in his work. Some Prufrockian nihilism also leaks through; a comatose patient in a hospital bed remains onstage throughout the entire production of *Life Support*. There's also in the biddable, courteous, and gently self-mocking eponym of *Quartermaine's Terms* the loneliness of an elevated spirit adrift in our unforgiving world. He's not alone. The gentle Devonshire vicar Ronnie Chambers of *Hidden Laughter*, the epigraph of which comes from T.S. Eliot, belongs in this dismal category, together with the badgered, reclusive piano teacher, Thomas Andrew Brownlow of *The Late Middle Classes*.

Gray's treatment of these endearing, if pathetic, souls shows him fending off defeatism. The discovery that life rarely matches our vision of how it should be sensitized him to the open-ended, the evocative, and the absurd. He doesn't brood, knowing that introspection can gag the swift, absorbing stage action he crafts so adroitly. Like good ghost stories, his best work draws on the potency of matters unresolved. Implying that curious things have happened and that others will follow, this potency hangs about like an unearthed static charge. As Clum has observed, Gray puts forth an ambiguous, elusive, and somewhat ominous vision that pulls up short of pessimism:

> Gray's vision focuses on men who find it difficult to muddle on, having found no satisfactory replacements for the lost ideals and passions of their youths. Work offers no fulfillment, love doesn't seem to be a possibility, and sex seems a joyless if necessary activity [Burkman, ed. 62].

Clum has it right. As Robert Simon said of Gray's protagonists in his online *Playbill* obituary, they "seem tragically incapable of emotionally connecting with their fellow beings. Their wives leave them. Their friends abandon them. At the end of the day, they find themselves alone" (2). The publisher called Peter in *Dog Days* (1976) utters witticisms like, "Double divorces are becoming as fashionable as separate holidays" (48) to pad the fear that his wife may be planning to leave him. Also vexing Peter is his inability to say if he'd welcome a parting from Hilary. Nor does he know whether he loves her. All that he does since moving for some unaccountable reason into his own digs is drink, smoke, and let his hair grow; he hasn't even had sex with the woman he has been dating. He's not unique on this score. "Withdrawal from action is the undercurrent of most of Gray's serious characters," said Katherine H. Burkman (Burkman, ed. 162). The terror that builds between expectation and action has led the archetypal male to veer hopelessly between wanting everything to change — now — and wanting everything to stay the same.

Peter's having denied Hilary sex "for months" (DD 36) bespeaks a communication failure, especially between married couples, traceable in Gray to the sudden turns of experience that social interaction of any kind can call forth. In *Late Middle Classes*, the piano teacher Brownlow asks a rhetorical question central to Gray's way of feeling: "Who can say whether the man is playing with the cat or the cat is playing with the man?" (25). Gray blurs guidelines, definitions, and demarcations at many levels, a practice that John Lahr found in Harold Pinter (John Lahr, "Demolition Man: Harold Pinter and 'The Homecoming,'" *New Yorker*, 10 December 2007, 54–69). Pinter's belief that things can be *both* true and false resonates through much of Gray's work. Michael Cartts of the *Japes / Michael* trilogy suspects that he's not Wendy's father. Perhaps he can relax. Fatherhood, according to Gray, goes beyond the blood tie. Michael kept loving Wendy during the decades he also fed, clothed, and helped her with her homework. Ben Butley, conversely, pretends to have forgotten his natural daughter's name and gender.

Dickens's fear of public scandal and humiliation shackled Ellen Ternan during their 13 years together. She had to wait until the aftershocks of his death subsided before she could start a family of her own. But even then, the joys of marriage and motherhood stayed fragile. The frays and snags in the fabric of lies she spun around herself to enter the marriage market could always attract attention. As they eventually did; in her husband and son, the people whose happiness mattered the most to her, this victim created victims. Like other characters in Gray, J.S. Jameson of *Rear Column*, George Blake of *Cell Mates*, and Simon Hench of *Simply Disconnected*, Nelly's heart swings between motives of good intentions and self-deception, generosity and malice — a volatile brew to nourish a marriage that might unravel at any time.

The dark potentialities of our world can also shred all good intentions. The cruelty Burnlow foisted upon Grahame Thwaite began as an expression of maternal love. Richard Howarth of *Spoiled*, another feminized male authority figure, confesses to browbeating young Donald Clenham (SGI 282). Then he steers his rebuke of the shaky, self-deprecating Donald into the region of sex, but not before decrying the evils of cheating on exams; he does this, moreover, in a passage that voices one of the noblest sentiments found in all of Gray's work: "It's cheating. And that's a very serious matter. (*Gently*) I don't mean cheating *me*, about which I care not one damn, but cheating yourself, about which I do care" (1SG 282).

The struggle of toiling against the grain can build anxieties. A woman in *Hidden Laughter* loses her mind tending the flowers in her beloved garden (4SG 11). Another in *Just the Three of Us*, referring to Dickens, says that "real books" "have a way of hurting us as they heal us" (40). She also says that Shakespeare's Sonnet 94, which ends famously, "Lilies that fester smell far worse than weeds," is "full of hatred and very personal" (39). Like the institution of the family elsewhere in Gray, that which sustains and comforts also has sharp claws. The sonnet's next-to-last line, "For sweetest things turn sourest by their deeds," reminds us of those kindhearted acts of ours that wreak destruction.

This line from Shakespeare also evokes the turmoil spread by both the "overwhelming genius" (LN xvi) Dickens and that physician who couldn't heal himself, James Davidson Gray. This turmoil includes but goes beyond the eroticism suggested by both James's womanizing and the name Gray uses to identify Dickens in *Little Nell*, viz., Dick. The bafflement and misery brought by the knowledge that not only the best, but also our nearest and dearest, can damage us the most pervades Gray's work. In the wartime drama, *They Never Slept*, it takes the form of a commanding officer who will commit murder in a flash if it means saving British lives. Intimates find different ways to take each other down, too. A man tries to gas his wife in *Dutch Uncle*, and a wife *does* shoot her husband dead in *Stage Struck*. Gray may have translated

Molière's *Tartuffe* in 1982 because the play's hypocritical eponym betrays for personal gain a man who loves and trusts him.

Gray knew his patch. The English virtues of reserve and restraint hobble the middle class because they thwart the heart. This national inhibition manifests itself as the pressure of things unsaid and the tears held back. But self-control can also serve life. Knowing when to keep up one's guard helps deflect disaster. In one of the most riveting passages in Henry James's *Turn of the Screw*, little Miles tells the governess who suspects him of wrongdoing that he only misbehaves with children he likes. His fingers probing deeply, Burnlow tells Grahame Thwaite, "I must punish you, only because I adore you" (LP 51).

Gray's version of the buried life stems from an instinct for self-preservation. Characters back off from each other to protect themselves, even to their dismay. The failure to live fully inspired Matthew Arnold to write "The Buried Life." Arnold's "Dover Beach, " which is quoted in *Just the Three of Us* (39–40), reckons the cost of this failure, as does most of Henry James and Anita Brookner, whose people will contemplate brave deeds, only to leave them hanging fire. T.S. Eliot, whose picture stays in view throughout the staging of *Butley*, cites "the buried life" in "Portrait of a Lady" (1915). The main event never happens in the life of St. John Quartermaine, who's seen sitting alone in the same place at both start and end of *Quartermaine's Terms*.

This buried life is an Anglicized update of the superfluous man found in Russian writers like Pushkin, Goncharov, and Turgenev. Redundants like Goncharov's Oblomov and Professor Serebryakov in Chekhov's *Uncle Vanya* are often brainy, well schooled, and benevolent, but also incapable of decisive action. This failure runs their fine gifts to waste. The main figure of Dostoyevsky's *Idiot*, which Gray adapted in 1971, takes the prototype to a new level, that of the holy fool, an innocent whose peace of mind, a disavowal of self-importance and self-promotion, defies understanding. Versions of the holy fool, a person always acted on but never blamable despite his miscues, appears in *Sleeping Dog*, *Spoiled*, and *Otherwise Engaged*.

Gray also re-imagines Prince Myshkin's tendency to trip, lurch, and accidentally break things. This is important. Gray's people serve not simply as plotting devices but, rather, as examples of a striving, suffering humanity. For them, slapstick and catastrophe can be two faces of the same coin. Clumsiness comes naturally to them. It also becomes a sign, if not of holiness, then of being out of step with a crass, venal world. In *After Pilkington*, Penny Newhouse rewards the sacrificial love of James Westgate with a fatal bullet. The real-life model for Gray's awkward, accident-prone wimps is a former student, the Swiss Ferdinand Boller, whom Gray called "the most maladroit man I've ever met" (Intro, LP xvi). Like Dostoyevsky's ungainly Prince, Boller spans the rift between our elevated thoughts and their blundering expression.

He also replicates both the mind-body split from Cartesian dualism and the concept of absurdism as the rift between our reasonable expectations and an *un*reasonable world. A good example of the physical world's indifference to our purposes comes in the first scene of *Spoiled*, where Richard Howarth knocks a satchel off a table and breaks a pencil point as he and Donald are supposedly settling down to work. Woody Allen's klutzes and schlemiels may fit the prototype, too. In *The Last Cigarette* (2008), the avid moviegoer Gray states his admiration for Jean Renoir's *Grand Illusion* (1937), which is also a favorite of the Allen role in *Manhattan* (1979).

Most of Gray's people run afoul of the world's intractability. Stubborn physical reality stops Grahame Thwaite at least twice in *Little Portia*, once when some words he deems "impossible to repeat" get lost on his side of a closing door that has suddenly divided him from his interlocutor, his sister Dianah (202). Life's recalcitrance foils him again nearly immediately; reaching out to stroke Dianah's hand, he nudges the prongs of a fork and sends it spinning to the floor (203).

Such moments are revealing. Though known as a comedian of manners, Gray, no one-note writer, alternates a philosophical side, a pragmatic earthbound streak, and the absurdist's flair for the freakish and the offbeat. In the novel *Colmain* (1963), a matron kisses her daughter on the lips and strokes her breasts while talking to her in the dark. The prestige Mrs. Tennant enjoys in Colmain society reminds us that it has chiefly been the novel, not the stage play, that probes the difference (Henry Fielding's *Tom Jones*) or the similarity (Ford Madox Ford's *The Good Soldier*) between appearance and reality. The frequency of cross-dressing and the bondage motif in Gray's work shifts this concern to the theater. The brutality in *Pig in a Poke* (1969) is accompanied by sublime music. In fact, its perpetrator is a yob called Grieg, whose namesake, Edvard Grieg, wrote the music to Ibsen's *Peer Gynt*, a play whose prankster-eponym made one of the worst husbands in European literature.

Peer's returning to Norway to reunite with his long-neglected wife before dying barely tempers his wanderlust. Gray's people misuse their freedom, too. They possess, for better or for worse, a unique and changeless core that remains unaffected not only by the lessons of history but also by everyday existence. The lives led by most of them consist of a succession of small things. With his respect for continuity and closure, Gray will depict this banality. Nor, thanks to his gift for making the ordinary and the prosaic engrossing, does the depiction bore us. Sometimes, he'll disturb the middle-aged everydayness of his people's routines by introducing a figure from the past or disclosing a long-buried scandal, like the incest that shocks the Spencer family in *Close of Play*.

Relevant here is the corpse that's planted, not buried, in Eliot's *The Waste Land*. The tension between surface and depth, the customary and the strange, declares itself in a straightforward idiom that resists analysis. Gray's dialogue makes us feel more like participants than observers. But what are we participating in? Is he describing a culture of malevolence that resembles our own? By suggesting that unseen forces shape everyday events, he's looking into our unconscious while also addressing our minds. This two-pronged approach defies labels. His ability to record, to invoke, and to reveal goes beyond satire. Nor is he subsuming the commonplace inside the metaphysical. Rather than sensing evolving, expanding arcs in his work, we see small details, telling gestures, and revealing sequences. His view of personal relationships stands close to his centrist politics. In both realms, he takes the Burkean line that it's better to accept present flaws than to risk chaos for the sake of a utopian dream. Hewing to the lessons framed by Molière's *Tartuffe* and Jane Austen's *Persuasion*, which find a kindred spirit in another female writer in *Side-Car*, Gray believes that cool-headedness is best. Reason and self-command get things done; impulsiveness wrecks them.

But it's sometimes hard to keep a cool head. Gray depicts characters so deeply mired in what Walker Percy called the malaise of everydayness that their troubles are invisible to them. "I think plays are telling stories about people, that's all" (DiGaetani 101), Gray said somewhat unhelpfully. But help does arrive. Using language that's fixed and denotative while also grazing poetic undercurrents, he defines his characters by the full range of their personalities rather than by their eccentricities and obsessions. This solid foundation moderates his pessimism; the work contains enough moments of warmth and contentment to keep us riveted.

These upbeat riffs add importance by catching us unawares. Life in Gray is often cruel, grim, and doomed; his plays lack both redemptive finales and concluding paeans to love and harmony. He's a dab hand, too, at inserting the well-chosen detail that can turn the ordinary into a nightmare. A fracas in *Quartermaine's Terms* involving Japanese students in a restaurant drops the enrollment the following year at the local language school the students were attending. The ensuing budget constraints and escalation in teaching loads drop faculty morale so far that the school comes close to shutting down.

The back-biting and rumor-mongering sparked by this collective depression sorts with Gray's belief that human nature is the same everywhere and that it's pretty bad. Novelist Michael Cartts of *Michael* (2004) calls the themes of his fiction "love and betrayal ... with an occasional whiff of redemption" (Four 156). Though no mystic, Gray sometimes frames his qualified pessimism in a religious context. Terri Green's protest, regarding her abduction, to a clergyman, no less, in *Just the Three of Us*, "You just can't allow her [Enid Parkhurst] to do this to me, a completely innocent person" (27), makes us ask if anybody can call him/herself innocent. Terri can't, having fucked her boss, Enid's husband, at least once after working late in his office. "Old life itself" (Lady 27) makes its own corrections. School nobodies (drips or plops) panic esteemed ex-classmates who had also enjoyed professional success 20 years after graduation in *Otherwise Engaged*, *Old Flames*, and *Simply Disconnected*.

The imagery of waste intrudes again upon a religious framework when an angry novelist in *Hidden Laughter* grabs a vicar by the throat and calls him a "little shit in a dog collar" (4SG 31). Ben Pertwee, the father of one of the vicar's neighbors, might second this view of Ronnie Chambers. When Ben tells Ronnie that he's an atheist, he's answered, "I don't blame you. I quite understand. Most of my parishioners are like that.... Can't blame them either" (4SG 17). An astonished Ben is left fuming. Though he lacks religious faith himself, he wants others to have it, especially those paid to foster it.

Religion always attracted Gray. A hotel owner in *Wise Child* had an affair with a defrocked priest, and the action of *Dutch Uncle* takes place in a deconsecrated, or defrocked, church. Gray's fiction had already conflated religious faith and sex. A woman's voice sounds "as clear as a church bell" (176) just before having sex in *Colmain*. God enters the erotic transaction again in *Little Portia* when two boys grope each other in a cloister. Despite their fear of getting caught, both boys sense the gravitas the cloister is exuding. "Sin ... in ecclesiastical surroundings. Isn't that what we're after?" says one boy. "I suppose so," his friend agrees, adding, "As long as God's watching" (LP 92). In a scene redolent of Graham Greene, a man holding a switchblade in *Comeback* enters a movie house that was once a church (58). Menace joins hands with religion again four chapters later when a trained field spy's "short, powerful fingers and their shiny nails [drive] priestlike" (100) into the flesh of his murder victim.

Apocalypse is closer than it seems. True, its signs are always small, No one in Gray eats a fellow mountain climber; none grapple with twisted visions of sin and salvation as a way of decoding God's plan. But the signs can *feel* big. A personal tragedy like the probable loss of Howarth's career and marriage in *Spoiled* carries the weight of disaster. But how to avoid the crush of damnation? Gray's answer to this question fuses his intellectual honesty with his recognition of the folly of basing one's belief system, logical-positivist style, on empirical verification. The need for faith voiced in Arnold's "Dover Beach" funnels into Wallace Stevens's appreciation of the urge for immortality and transcendence pervading Christianity. Piers Gray discussed Stevens in his collection, *Stalin on Linguistics and Other Essays* (Colin MacCabe and Victoria Rothschild, eds. [Houndsmill, UK, 1992]). According to Piers, Stevens believes the poet's job is to unify experience in an age of skepticism. All 13 ways of looking at a blackbird check out because they share the common impulse of swathing the looker, or perceiver, with the swarming, jostling particulars being looked at.

Simon Gray mentions Stevens's "Sunday Morning," a work that imbues the everyday with immanence, in *Smoking Diaries*, where he also calls it "a great poem" (186), a judgment he backs by quoting it in *Japes* (12). Piers's commentary, "Our paradise is in the imperfect" (3), finds support in Stevens's building "Peter Quince at the Clavier" around Susannah, from the "Susannah and the Elders" tale in the *Apocrypha*. Even though Susannah's beauty can't relocate from Scripture to our world, where we can savor it directly, it nonetheless merits our attention. The Pertwees in *Hidden Laughter* believe they have found the earthly paradise in the garden adjoining a Devonshire cottage. But the cottage stinks of dry rot, the floorboards have bowed, and the roof has holes in it. Even the garden itself, so enchanting at first glance, is disfigured by a stump filling a place the Pertwees have other uses for. Yet they overcome their misgivings, perhaps intuiting in Wallace Stevens's terms the need to accept the splendors of nature, even if they fall short of divine or Platonic beauty. The mundane offers bounties and blessings. The Pertwees call their property "Little Paradise." The secular, or pagan, joy it offers its London-based owners *will* include some heavenly gleams. Delighting in this radiance qualifies as an act of maturity and common sense. It may be the best that our flawed finite world offers.

Where does this leave the infinite? In *Fat Chance*, Gray speaks of "the totally unexpected maneuvers of … an unidentifiable God" (29). Impulse and instinct trump logic and coherence at all levels of existence for this admirer of D.H. Lawrence. Ronnie Chambers bases his faith upon this outlook. Religious belief for him is an act of supreme inner conviction. It subsumes harsh realities like mass murder, the gulags, and the poisoning of forests and lakes:

> There's no point in believing in Him … because if He existed, and we all knew He existed there'd be no difficulty at all in believing in Him and what would be the point of *that*…. I mean that faith is … a matter of believing what's impossible to believe…. Otherwise it's not faith. It's certainty [4SG 17].

The mystery of unity ratifies this Kierkegaardian leap. A God definable by human processes isn't Godlike. Natural theology uses the order of nature to prove God's existence. Hegelian dialectic describes the world as good rather than something that can be *made* good. To Ronnie, God's incomprehensibility may be the best argument for His existence. The more ugliness and evil Ronnie sees, the sturdier his faith. Kimball King sees this faith permeating his response to Little Paradise. As is consistent with Gray's mind-set, this dynamic is unorthodox:

> Initially, none of the play's adult characters take Ronnie seriously, and he is self-deprecatingly aware of his own inadequacies. By the end of the second act, however, he appears to have influenced the spiritual pilgrimage of every character who appears in the play, all without having induced any of them to attend a single service in his church [Burkman, ed. 175].

If Gray is speaking through Ronnie, he sounds like a man who misses God despite disbelieving in Him. Clum said of Gray's work, "Gray cannot keep homosexuality out, nor can he fully let it in" (Burkman 171). Evoking D.H. Lawrence's practice of sitting sexual encounters in places of worship (e.g., *The*

Plumed Serpent), Clum's sharp insight points to Gray's uneasiness with agnosticism. Even if religion were a con game, Gray wouldn't complain if it were also true. What matters more than his personal idea of God, he suspects, is God's idea of *him*. Ronnie Chambers occupies the same theological turf. Unlucky in love, this shy, awkward vicar who can't help himself helps others, a truth that these others, as King believes, may not recognize, let alone credit. In his maverick way, Ronnie has ministered to his makeshift flock. (He'd be about the age of Mrs. Artminster in *Wise Child*.) His dutiful tending of the garden at Little Paradise signals the spiritual strength he offers his neighbors.

If his faith owes a debt to Graham Greene's belief that God's grace sometimes looks like punishment, it doesn't diminish Ronnie the man, who reminds us of Gray's undervalued wimps. Accommodating and apologetic, Ronnie has either renounced happiness or redefined it. He stands alone among the ambitious, goal-oriented people surrounding him. The quiet self-confidence of this superficially forgettable man rivets Gray without entangling him in mysteries or sending him on guided tours of the soul. Grounded in the everyday, Gray harbors an English dislike of theory, generalizations, and systems. His common-sense preference for clarity of expression over a French weakness for conceptualizing comes across in the pleasing directness of his prose. But he also differs from his fellow English dramatists. He doesn't whine about England's declining educational and cultural standards like the early John Osborne. He lacks the interest in science, politics, and social injustice found in Michael Frayn and David Hare. Nor does he tender the complex angularities and intellectual fireworks of Tom Stoppard.

These differences haven't made him a writer of commercial domestic comedies, viz., "French Window drama," "a totally effete school of drama, aimed solely to flatter and please the rich, idle, mindless stalls public" (Rattigan 7). Gray will shift focus, viz., character types and settings; risk offending his audiences; and dodge audience expectations. All this has a point. Besides challenging himself artistically, he's also denying *us* the smug pleasure of generalizing about his art. In 1978, for instance, this connoisseur of the angst fretting educated, well-to-do middle-aged professionals turned to 19th century Great Britain's smirching of the benevolent imperial self-image it had foisted on its colonial subjects. He did it without straining, feeling at home in the century of invention, adventure, and freebooting capitalism. Combining historical accuracy with a fluent grasp of detail and a strong plot, *Rear Column* re-sites Gray's concern with middle-age angst among the largely successful members of a group that's less select and secure than its members believe.

The play includes in the subjects it treats the collective self-loathing that overtakes the British explorers for having veered, by tiny degrees at first, from moral earnestness to savagery. The influence of H.M. Stanley, the absent leader of this squad of men camped alongside the Congo's Arruwime River, displays Gray's newfound, but vital, ability to steer the action of a play with an offstage character. Stanley *does* appear onstage in the play's last scene, where his weasel words disclaim responsibility for the devastation caused by his wrong-minded executive orders and initiatives.

As will often happen in a Gray play, the recycling of a plotting device, passage of dialogue, or character type from an earlier play shows an improvement from its first occurrence. The off-stage Thomas, co-owner of the Cull-Loomis School of English for Foreigners, drives much of the action of *Quartermaine's Terms* (1981). And he does this job so well for the first half of the play that Gray continues to keep him off stage. Gray did well to trust his aesthetic instincts. Thomas resembles Flaubert's ideal author in being present everywhere but nowhere to be seen. He also helps fuel the argument, endorsed by Lyn Gardner (2–3), that Gray's work improves with the passage of the years.

Gray's poise, clarity of expression, and mastery of background details move the plays along with an easy grace but without calling attention either to themselves or to the authorial judgment that makes them sing. Though nothing seems quotable, little sounds forced, contrived, or flat. His lucid, companionable sentences roll past us without bowling us over, but, in the process, cover more thematic ground than we had thought possible. Be cautioned; turn the pages too fast, and you'll miss some of the richness and subtlety of the writing. If his tone lacks the outrage and anger found in Osborne, its fluid cadences remove all surprise that he and Terence Rattigan, whose prose is also humorously restrained in an English way, should write in *Molly* and *Cause Célèbre* (both 1977), plays about the same murder case.

Idiosyncrasies of inflection and syntax are rare in Gray's work. On occasion, though, his dry, nimble style will reveal some Nabokovian velvet. Take in the visceral rhythms and word choice of a minister who, burning with the heat of belief, laments the apathy of his parishioners in Gray's 1980 adaptation of J.L. Carr's novel, *A Month in the Country*:

> The English are not a deeply religious people. Most of those who attend divine service do so only from habit. Their acceptance of the sacrament is perfunctory. I have yet to meet a man whose hair rose at the nape of his neck because he was about to taste the blood of his dying Lord [3SG 354–55].

On the debit side, Gray may absent-mindedly reach for an adjective when he needs a noun, as when he calls himself, in *Smoking Diaries*, a "chatterbox and disruptive" (107). Finally, Gray will sometimes wrench the reader around by starting two consecutive independent clauses with the word "but." This annoyance comes more often in the diaries (e.g., Lady 65, SD 104); it causes greater regret, though, when it leaks into a stage play. The following passage from *Melon* (1991) shows two straight units, one of them a sentence fragment, beginning with "But": "But possibly his only problem. But I couldn't open myself to discuss his problem with him" (28). A character in *The Rear Column* says, "But he hasn't said no. But he would if you asked him" (RC 13).

Some flaws in dramatic structure also stand out. An odd scene will disclose some cracks and smudges that could have benefited from retouching. Others just lack purpose or payoff. Finally, some defects in plotting have to be fitted into place. But, on bottom line, they're too small and peripheral to detract from a play's value. Mostly, Gray's natural touch with phrasing and design gives his work an integrity, a balance, and an economy that any other playwright would have trouble matching on his/her best day. Gray manages an educated, socially accomplished stance without seeming aloof. A foe of wordiness, he doesn't weight his dialogue with historical detail or other kinds of exposition. Nor do his scenes feel rushed or contrived.

Then there's his knack for getting his audiences back into their seats after intermission, a gift he always possessed. The action of *Otherwise Engaged* (1971) breaks right after Simon Hench, the play's main character, admits to having slept with the beloved of a nervous intruder. In *Little Nell* (2006), the woman whose sexual history is being discussed is the questioner's mother, and he's questioning her lover's son just before intermission. Besides profiting from Gray's immaculate timing, these scenes, written 35 years apart from each other in time, benefit still more from his ear. The supple, polished voice he favors is much harder to achieve than it looks. It also shows, along with the other gems packing his intelligent, richly layered plays, that only a small handful of recent English dramatists have delivered so much value.

Four

Exit Wounds

The four novels Gray wrote before redirecting his imaginative energies to the stage feature young men surrounded by elders who lead hectic, status-driven lives. Regardless of whether they're looking to advance themselves socially, professionally, or financially, these predatory mavens of oneupmanship are often seen trading *bon mots* at trendy parties, usually at the expense of their rivals. In *Colmain* and *Simple People*, the velvet language of politeness veils a scramble for money among people unable to earn it, at least honestly. The most avid scramblers, or scroungers, both of whom resemble Barbara Gray in temperament, have male side-kicks who may also be their lovers—or gigolos. This well-judged move on Gray's part smoothes the way to the male-dominated worlds of academe and espionage which stabilize *Little Portia* and *A Comeback for Stark*, the final two works comprising Gray's debut as a serious writer.

These works also build upon their predecessors. Instead of turning away from *Colmain* and *Simple People*, the two later books carry forward from them. The nurturing grandmother figure who pops mints to mask her drinker's breath returns in *Little Portia* (and also in the early play, *Sleeping Dog* [1967]), after debuting in *Colmain*, as will the headmaster or headmistress who tactfully warns a student with an adolescent crush on a classmate to cool things down. This wise counsel will also improve the youngsters' adult lives, all of which come under risk. The counsel sticks. A believer in the power of early influences, Gray uses the Lawrencean metaphor of electricity — its power to attract, repel, and shock — to limn the difference between heeding a lesson and acting on it.

The attainment of self-knowledge for Gray's protagonists, as for those of Lawrence, is fitful and painful. These men, often fretted by loneliness and loss, brood a good deal, sometimes to the verge of madness. Their troubles are real. What torments them also attracts them, ruling out snap judgments on our parts. Though Gray doesn't sympathize more with evildoers than with their victims, the subtlety with which he matches good and evil keeps us from taking sides. Like Bertolt Brecht, Gray is seeking a rational, not an emotional, response from us. His juveniles realize, too late they fear, that they've become entwined either in plots they've unwisely spun or in somebody else's plots from which they might have fled. In either case, they're soon swamped by forces beyond their control and, sometimes, their comprehension. Nor will comprehension and control come to their aid. Lindsay Burnlow of *Little Portia* only stops abusing Grahame Thwaite when he's caught in the act by another adult. That a rescuer figure must step in to keep Burnlow's hands off of Grahame points the novel's action in the direction of darkness. This darkness spreads. It's a mark of Gray's pessimism that the oldest and most seasoned of the books' four leading figures, the eponym of *A Comeback for Stark*, is also the only one to die.

Death seems eons away from the people in *Colmain* (1963), a satire governed by Gray's wickedly accurate ear for urban pretense and self-promotion. His ear serves him well, his clear, limber style blocking the dandyism often hobbling bright young first-time novelists. Its main target is women, a strategy supported by the novel's setting. Colmain, seaport capital of the Canadian maritime province of New Thumberland, boasts enough civilized amenities and folklore to tempt its inhabitants to lord it over their out-province counterparts. As in Jane Austen, Edith Wharton, and Penelope Fitzgerald, the best practitioners of this class game, and those most likely to turn their fangs on one another to boost their status, are women.

Gray's first swipe at these social climbers comes in a newcomer's observation that most of Colmain's society women "seemed to tower over their men" (29). So pronounced is the domestic power inferred by this height difference that one of Colmain's leading businessmen, though reserved and quiet at home, grows "light-footed and gay" (96) once he sets foot in his men's club. This respite, though, is brief, his wife announcing in the last chapter over tea and cake that her husband has stopped going to the club (194). She means that she has bullied him into staying away. Presumably, she was afraid that that the chess games that took him to the club might have also taught him some gambits he'd bring home with which to check her.

Said gambits would have had to be marvels of ingenuity. In her present state, Mrs. Tennant looks unstoppable. Gray fears her himself. Though he calls her Celia, as he would the dragon mother in *The Late Middle Classes*, she shares none of Celia Smithers's physical agility or love of sports. That he delays mentioning her first name until page 75 of his 199-page novel also suggests that he lacked the nerve at age 26 to confront Barbara Gray head-on. The novel's organization shows him shirking this challenge again. It's another pushy, controlling mother who rifles through her lawyer son's briefcase, just as Celia Smithers would Holly's book-bag in Gray's 1999 play. And even though Celia Tennant provokes her daughter Fairfax erotically, as Barbara did Simon (SD 14), she stands closer to Simon's sexually confrontational grandmother in her coldness to her husband, the mints she pops, and her bosomy softness.

These traits Gray notes often, calling her "positively rotund" (45), referencing her "plump body" (62), and showing her trying to stop a guest from reaching for a slice of cake she had targeted for herself (91).

The menace exuded by this compulsive eater of sweets shows in the book's technique. Just as Gray withholds Celia Tennant's emotionally packed front name till he's a quarter of a way into the book, he never uses this front name at all in narrative; only her fellow characters call her Celia. And even they, like her husband and her author, give her wide berth. Like the squidgy, gelatinous jellyfish who are yearly washed onto Colmain's shore by forces beyond their control, she came to town against her will, her husband having been transferred from the London firm where he was working.

She has learned how to shine in Colmain. Though the town was built by stern hard-working Scots, an effort celebrated annually by a local version of the Highland Games, its social aristocracy draws mostly from its English settlement. This is where Celia, diaphanous and poisonous as a jellyfish, works her wiles. Wily she is. Looking to shed the image of a tenant, i.e., a renter or leasee of someone else's property, she uses her English past to join the social establishment. Gray's satirical descriptions of her efforts to become a stakeholder cut two ways. No, the Kensington flat her family occupied before coming to Colmain probably lacked the elegance to which she has been ascribing it. And the finishing school her daughter attended might not have been the best in Switzerland, as she claims. But she's welcomed heartily into a "sort of *intimate* ladies' club" (60) that meets weekly for the malicious gabfests that pass among its members for refined chat. This malice will fly by Mrs. Tennant. Careful to avoid saying both too much and too little, she has also learned how to snatch those small conversational edges that count so much in the class game.

She fences hardest for advantage at the banquets and receptions to which she finagles invitations. These galas, she knows, besides being traps for the unwary, also empower the verbally gifted to entrench themselves among the select few. What helps her most in these duels of wit she excels in is her background. She's a quick study in appraising her advantages. Nobody in her circle of snobs has the chops to question her belief that one's personal worth is gauged by the amount of time one has spent abroad. And she knows it. But this British passport-holder who has also traveled widely on the Continent overreaches herself. In her zeal to engineer a profitable marriage for Fairfax, she overrates the province's new Lieutenant-Governor and underrates the enigmatic lawyer, Clinton McInley, whom she disdainfully misnames McIsaac (53) and McJoseph (89) to convince Fairfax of his unworthiness.

Ignorant of Clinton's intentions toward Fairfax, or of Fairfax's toward him, she also states her disdain of him in terms consistent with what Celia Smithers and her prototype Barbara Gray accept as mainstream English values. She downplays his good looks as handsomeness "in a Jewish way," adding,

"They are a very deceptive people. They are good at appearing what they are not" (74). This, from an arch-hypocrite and dissembler. When told that Clinton is rich, she answers illogically, "He has made a lot of money because he is Jewish, and he is idle because he is ill" (74). Logic keeps defeating her. Her oft-repeated insistence upon his health problems (e.g., 53) bypasses a dazzling truth that a self-promoter like her should have leaped upon, i.e., that the chronic illness she has fastened upon Clinton could soon make Fairfax a rich widow.

The book's strange, disturbing fifth chapter sends Mrs. Tennant to Fairfax's bedroom, ostensibly to persuade her daughter to attend an upcoming garden party at Freeways, the Lieutenant-Governor's country estate. Her behavior with Fairfax, viz., pressing Fairfax's breast and kissing her lips, again perhaps not by accident, while constantly calling her "my sweet" (e.g., 128–130), implies that she wants Fairfax for herself, not for the L-G. As she lifts her "chubby hand" (129) from her daughter's breast, she calls to mind Gray's bundling Montreal grandmother. But this intra-family sex play also evokes Barbara's unsavory physical attentiveness (SD 14, CODA 7).

And what are we to make of Simon's surrogate in this steamy scene? Fairfax is lying naked in bed, as if awaiting a lover's visit. Her compliance with Celia's attentions suggests that they're neither unwelcome nor new to her. Simon might have reacted in like manner to the encroachments of his mother and grandmother, a possibility underscored by the deep structure these encroachments share with the ritual tiddly-winks games played by same-sex lovers in *Side-Car* (1971). The matter-of-fact tone with which the bedroom scene unfolds shows that, from the outset of his writing career, Gray began discouraging the reader from siding automatically with young victims of predatory sex at his/her predator's expense (Celia never appears in bed with her husband, whom Gray may have deprived of a front name for that reason).

Fairfax will strip again at the garden party, or picnic, Celia wanted her to attend. And again it will be voluntary. This occurs after a long walk with the Lieutenant-Governor, Avril Harris, who's hosting the bash. In this extended scene, her direct, straightforward speech accompanies movements that are physically assured, graceful, and controlled. As her name suggests (Fairfax-fair facts), she believes in openness, candor, and plain dealing. Her rejection — on good grounds—of a marriage proposal from a rich man's son had already riled the matchmaking Celia. She continues to resist her mother's efforts to run her life. Besides skipping the meetings Celia had set up with her socialite friends, Fairfax invites Clinton McInley home to rankle her. Fairfax's "sharp ... gaze" (51) and the sullen, imperious facial expression she wears at social gatherings is no mask. Proud and self-governing, she'd rather turn away a man she loved than see her mother gloat in the supposed wisdom of her choice. "She wants me to do right by her" (172), she says of her mother's fear of Clinton McInley.

Thus she rivets her attention on Avril Harris despite her mother's approval of him. This "young man with energy and possibly a distinguished future" (9) was groomed to prosper. He studied in British Columbia, Oxford, and, because all politically ambitious Canadians must know French, the Sorbonne. Now he's serving, at age 30, as New Thumberland's L-G. This four-year stint, a sinecure really, involves little besides hosting receptions and appearing at semi-official social functions. Gray's practice of referencing him throughout as either the Lieutenant-Governor or the L-G, instead of calling him by name, reflects his belief that there's little to Avril Harris besides his ceremonial job. The L-G will play the role of D.H. Lawrence's sleeping beauty in the novel.

The first test of this sexual innocent comes when he waltzes with Fairfax at a supper dance in Chapter Two. Careful to maintain distance from her, he starts to panic when he finds her moving closer to him. The panic builds. His efforts to hold her off only makes her scold him for squeezing her side. This stripping-away of his defenses has positioned him for a major breakthrough. As Gray will often do, he underscores the power of the breakthrough by describing it in contending terms of attraction and aversion. Bereft of guidelines, the hapless L-G doesn't know what to think or where to turn. His having "never been so close to such large breasts before" (35) leads to the unexpected thrill of inhaling "the slightly sour odor of [the] sweat" (36) that glazes Fairfax's body while waltzing. If it can be called a thrill; so little is known about the under-researched topic of smell that the deep strike it makes on the L-G's psyche leaves him feeling more giddy than enchanted.

Matters crest between these two at another semi-official government function, the picnic the L-G gives at Freeways in Chapter Seven. But first a spot of comedy intrudes. The foot the L-G is rubbing and then pressing against a table leg with his own belongs, not to Fairfax, as he thinks, but to an outraged 70-year-old widow, who later crashes her walking stick against his ankle before bolting the picnic. This scene is not gratuitous. Fairfax, with whom the L-G will later go hiking, has witnessed both Mrs. Wiggs's angry outburst and the cry of pain that leapt from the L-G when the stick came down on his ankle. Prefigured by the emotional gusts that have been rocking him since waltzing with Fairfax, this sudden cry conflates physical suffering with the loss of control. The conflation, which occurs often in Gray, fosters sexual maturity — the kind that mattered the most to the novel's guiding spirit, D.H. Lawrence.

Avril has lost more control and composure than he knows. During their walk in the woods, Fairfax leads the way. maneuvering him into a position where he can't avoid ogling her "plump buttocks" (53, 78), which, she knows, have been mesmerizing him. As in Lawrence's "Horse Dealer's Daughter," a young professional who finds himself alone in the countryside with a woman will stumble into life. Stumble the L-G does (108), as well as stagger and trip. Fairfax has to teach him how to glide sideways between bushes and brambles to avoid getting scratched and stung. And while she holds her poise, his anxiety builds: "He was sweaty, stinging, headachy; she was cool, graceful, and rapid" (167). This would-be political leader has to rely on a woman who's more self-reliant and unruffled than he to avoid getting lost on his own property. Fairfax is even more knowledgeable, steady, and decisive when they reach a clearing. Speaking with a voice "as clear as a church bell" (178), she tells an outclassed and overwhelmed L-G, "If you don't do something soon, I shall scream" (178).

The "terrible sunlit clarity" (181) engulfing him after he's finally coaxed or shamed into having sex shows that lovemaking has sharpened his hold on reality. But this totally new reality terrifies him. He had to be told to take off his clothes, which, she notes, he stacks in "a small careful heap" (180). Fairfax assumes the dominant, or traditionally masculine, role again when she asked a "fumbling and clumsy and uncertain" (181) Avril to lie down beside her. His maladroitness suggests why Gray named him Avril. His age, 30, has put him in the springtime of his life.

But what does this mean? April, a month normally associated with renewal and cheer, is called "the cruelest month" at the start of Eliot's *The Waste Land*. The seasonal changes convulsing the earth in late winter burst forth, too, in the discords and angularities of Stravinsky's *Rite of Spring*. They also call up the turmoil wracking the L-G during *his* rite of passage. But is it a gay man's turmoil? His parents might have called him Avril because they saw him as a font of rebirth and hope for the family. This French name would have also scored him points with the Quebecois, whose help he'd need in the political career they began grooming him for not only early in life but even before his birth. Yet the name's oddness invites the conjecture that they wanted a girl they'd have called April. The equally odd name of Avril Harris's "plump, benign" (109) brother Andor, with its whiff of androgyny, implies that gender confusion might have been harassing the Harris parents during their child-bearing years.

Colmain's deep structure also invokes E.M. Forster, the English language's most respected living novelist at the time of Gray's 1963 fictional debut. This eminence alone merits the various tributes *Colmain* pays to Gray's fellow Cantab. But the frequency of these tributes suggests that Gray might have had Forster's homosexuality in mind along with his prominence and academic pedigree. By setting his first novel in 1936 (20), the year of his birth, Gray called attention early on to its self-referentiality. Nor will readers looking for his footprints in *Colmain* be let down. The same first chapter that gives the book's time setting alludes often to Forster's *A Passage to India*. This master-piece not only includes a character called the Lieutenant Governor; its por-tentous Marabar Caves provide the model for both "the great geological fists" (15) seen along water's edge in Colmain and the symmetry of the book's open-ing chapter. Whereas the first chapter of Forster's 1924 novel both begins and ends with references to India's Marabar Caves, that of *Colmain*, besides identifying the town's "few concrete buildings ... furnished in heavy tasteless comfort" (20) in terms close to those depicting Chandrapore's British Raj, opens and closes by citing Avril Harris's first big challenge, the annual L-G's Ball (9, 23).

The implications set forth by Fairfax Tennant's unusual front name presume, as well, that Gray wasn't thinking only of Forster's novelistic genius while he was smuggling references to the older writer into *Colmain*. Yes, the fair facts alluded to in Fairfax's name do bespeak her direct, no-nonsense talk (during their forest interlude, the L-G wishes that her speech were less "confusingly lucid" [175]). But *Fairfax* is also the name of the ship that sites *Billy Budd*, a novel that torques on the same kind of tragic pedophilic clash that, in milder form, had already shocked Gray. The novel's author, Herman Melville, whom Forster praised in *Aspects of the Novel* (1927), one might add, had strong gay tendencies.

Avril's first reactions to having sex with Fairfax display, if not a gay streak, the same kind of homosexual regret that Gray will return to in *Little Portia* and *Dutch Uncle*. His mind "emptied ... of all muddle (181), Avril recoils from the "squelchy repose" of Fairfax's "gluey body" (182). Sex's afterglow has guttered quickly. Even while basking in "the sweet warmth" and "comfortable darkness" (182) of that body, he has started to worry about the threat Fairfax poses to his career. The threat explodes into life. By some great, unexplained reason, the biggest — and only — supporter of a marriage joining him to Fairfax, Mrs. Tennant, looms in the clearing. Her first question, "I hope you were not disappointed, Lieutenant-Governor?" (185) has a double meaning that puts his future in a harsh glare. Which the title of the book's following chapter, "Mother's Day," heightens: It could refer to Mrs. Tennant, a major player in the previous chapter; it could also be focusing Fairfax, who's not seen in the new chapter, having *already* fulfilled her mother's and perhaps nature's purpose. Avril, Gray has punningly implied, *is* virile. The riot Fairfax has caused in his heart hews to Lawrence's belief that love thrives on the mystery between people, not the sameness. But Lawrence's dark gods have also revealed, working through him, a sense of humor the L-G wouldn't find funny.

He'll fume alone because his male counterparts in the book lack his virility. Or so it seems; when Gray writes about sex, he always muddies the way to clarity. Avril's epicene water-colorist brother Andor lacks fire. He'd not dispute the allegation that the energy he devotes to his creature comforts, however anemic, has left very little for his art (112). In a letter to his brother, he admits that his "weak talent" produces "drab ... dismal" landscapes rendered in "a thin wash of gray" (81). An uncharacteristic burst of energy might have helped him. Andor's "plump legs" (110) have brought him to Colmain together with a Colonel Hamton, a venture capitalist keen to make a land grab, and his partner, Clinton McInley's "delightfully greedy and charming" mother (81). The Italian-born Mrs. McInley uses her veneer of sophistication and old-world charm to hide this greed, an easy enough ruse for her to carry off in raw Colmain.

As Henry James's Daisy Miller did while assessing an American ex-pat's Roman digs, Mrs. Tennant (Mrs. McInley mentions Rome [139]) derides the smallness of the L-G's country mansion (144). The point is worth making because Gray, who knew James's work well (UP 221, 225), may have dipped into *Daisy Miller* more than once while writing *Colmain*. Despite his lack of artistic drive, Andor (whose name sounds like that of Daisy's brother Randolph, also a younger sib), by coming to Colmain to paint its landscapes, is using, if not exploiting, the locale's personality and spirit for personal gain. He may be guilty of far worse. As the courier who took the Miller family from Vevey to Rome was suspected of having done, Andor might have gotten paid to introduce Mrs. McInley and Colonel Hamton to Colmain's mayor.

The impression of rascality overhangs the city. The mayor, Hamton's projected partner in a real-estate swindle the Colonel hopes to perform, has just completed a jail sentence. He's not alone in his legal troubles. Andor and his two traveling companions arrived in Colmain a day earlier than expected. The cause of their hurry comes forth straightaway. The impression given by both Mrs. McInley and Colonel Hamton of wanting to stay in Colmain as long as possible suggests that, if not on the lam, they're nonetheless hiding out. But even Mrs. McInley's son Clinton can't decipher their motives. He does note, however hyperbolically, his widowed mother's "act of grand larceny" (84), an incident that took him from her side in Toronto and brought him to Colmain, allegedly to regain his failing health. He dislikes being with her. Now that she has finagled a place for herself in Colmain society, she's on her own, he reasons. He packs his bags. But he doesn't depart in haste. Guided by the deceit and guile he may have learned from her, he makes sure, before leaving town, to protect his house from any plans she may have for it following the state visit in Ottawa she both managed to wangle and would never consider passing up.

He needn't tell his mother where he's heading any more than he needs to answer her gibe that he'll go anywhere that distances him from her and the Colonel (190). But how much do *we* want to know of his travel plans? A fictional character who's evasive about his movements and motives can entice readers. Clinton McInley's motives, though, go beyond an enticing evasiveness. Like that of Andor Harris, his role in the book is either underwritten or underimagined. Gray's omissions here cause regret because more work on his part might have made Clinton the book's most fascinating character. The tension created by Mrs. Tennant's fear of him and the fun Mr. Tennant has playing chess with him, despite losing every game, have already caught our attention.

Which builds and holds; following the example of Joyce's Stephen Dedalus who wanders Dublin's Dollymount Strand in *Ulysses*, Clinton thinks about coping with the plans of his "high-toned and fastidious mother" (86) while *he* walks, also by himself, along Colmain's seafront. Why, though, after chancing upon Fairfax on the Dingle, is it said lavishly of him, "He had never felt less pleased to see anyone in his life" (88)? Has his mother already given him more than he can handle from her entire gender? Though Gray invites this reading, he shrinks from acting on it. Or perhaps he's implying that watching Fairfax dance with the L-G at the Ball in Chapter Two (36–37) threatened Clinton in some unexplained way.

Clinton next appears alone on the page at the start of Chapter Six. His looking onto Colmain's main street from an office window gives Gray a chance to describe some of the buildings and shops that comprise the town's personality and history. Clinton's thoughtful gaze also calls forth the Biblical scene where Satan and Christ survey, from an elevation, the kingdoms of the earth. If Gray is making a comparison, one of the scriptural figures he has in mind comes to the fore immediately with Mrs. McInley's appearance in Clinton's office. She has come, presumably uninvited, to "settle up" (118), which means convincing her morally indebted son to introduce her and the Colonel to the mayor.

Perhaps Clinton can't deny his charismatic mother any more than Franz Kafka could his father. His coming before us most of the time in a prone position suggests, along with the sickness his mother has assigned to him, that she has drained so much of his vim that his survival depends upon his leaving the nest. This reading sorts with Gray's having made the strongest characters in the novel mothers. If he never mentions Celia Tennant's first name in narration, as if she were a goddess he couldn't name or face directly, he avoids altogether that of the more menacing Mrs. McInley. But this explanation of Clinton's conduct remains unsupported by internal evidence rising from the give-and-take of dramatic interplay.

Elsewhere, Gray scamps little. The puzzling note that begins *Colmain* grips us straightaway. In the L-G's first executive act, he decides to hold the annual Provincial Ball on Christmas Eve, a time the invited guests spend at home with their families. The Ball, which is to take place at Government House, is Colmain's big social event of the year. With a live orchestra playing at the supper dance, it enables mothers to flaunt their marriageable daughters. Gray's high-caliber satire summons up party scenes in Kingsley Amis's *Lucky Jim* (1954), William Gaddis's *Recognitions* (1955), and Anthony Powell's *At Lady Molly's* (1958). Besides displaying their daughters to eligible bachelors, the mothers talk about one another's health and clothing until the booze they've been drinking unleashes their malice.

Their ill-natured sniping soon gives way to *Schadenfreude*. Some of the female guests, for instance, discuss with wicked glee the downfall of the principal of a local college. Two students from the college, the story goes, went to the bad while living with the London family the unlucky principal had recommended. Ugly gossip like this comes easily to the women who have heard about the scandal. As Avril, having been raised in an atmosphere of public service, had to know; his undeclared motive for reducing the Ball's attendance keeps intriguing us as he threads his way through some amusing guests who feel compelled to impress him with their wit or their wallets.

Gray's keen sense of pacing serves him just as well when he's teasing out information as it does when he's withholding it. Credit his genius for narrative selection — which he wastes no time putting on view. Early in the first chapter, he seats the coming action in New Thumberland, whose name evokes those of its neighbors in the Canadian Maritimes, Newfoundland and New Brunswick (which is later mentioned [70]). Using Nova Scotia and its capital city of Halifax as his models (LP xxi), Gray invents and then braids together two sets of economic, social, and geographical histories. He has done his research. Calling forth Sinclair Lewis's American Midwestern state of Winnemac and its capital Zenith in books such as *Babbitt* (1922) and *Arrowsmith* (1925), Gray rehearses the province's geological features, its leading industries, and transport systems.

Once in town, he rehearses with poise and self-composure the levering of subsidies and loans by the municipal government to fund projects like public parks. Various architectural styles, both commercial and residential, come into view, often on the main street of the "shabby little city" (14) that's taking shape before our eyes. Some of these features remind us of Halifax, Nova Scotia. But it's no carbon copy. Sometimes, testing his inventive powers, Gray blurs the resemblance between the two cities. He says, for instance, that Hollington, Colmain's main street, runs parallel to the levee (14); one of Halifax's main streets, Barrington, besides sharing a three-syllable name with its fictional counterpart, also follows a course that roughly parallels the waterfront (*The Green Guide: Canada* [Greenville, S.C.: Michelin Travel Publications, 2003, p. 376]).

Other possible influences besides those of Sinclair Lewis and E.M. Forster emerge. The book's second chapter, entitled "The Ball," reproduces in a minor key the pomp and splendor of the opening scenes of *War and Peace*. As Hélène Kuragina did in Tolstoy's novel, Fairfax displays her "large ... half-exposed" (39) breasts to attract suitors. Nor is Fairfax's opportunistic mother any less ambitious for *her* than Tolstoy's Princess Drubetskaya is for her son, for whom she manages to get a commission in the Russian Guard.

The prose with which Gray develops his satire of the class game, both at the Ball and after it, owes a great deal to Evelyn Waugh. Waugh's bright, glittering syntax and vocabulary, in fact, provide the book's voice. It flashes its stinging, irreverent brightness often. It can also adapt to the same flat, toneless register Waugh favored to unleash some of his most outrageous insights. In a passage that might have otherwise called for some stylistic heightening, Gray says of Colmain's scapegrace mayor that, until recently, he "had spent a year and a half in New Thumberland Penitentiary" (18). He'll apply this deadpan wit to another kind of humor Waugh enjoyed: the ethnic joke. In a paragraph that also sideswipes Dutchmen, Danes, and Italians, a Chinese inventor is blamed for "several horrifying incidents in a New York speakeasy" (13). Selection makes the throwaway tone of the indictment all the more intriguing. Though the "horrifying incidents" stay dark, their easily overlooked source, the bathtub the "sly Chinaman" (18) used to ferment his moonshine (or white lightning) gets a disconcerting, direct look.

Gray continues to exercise his mock-mandarin verbal wit at the expense of non-whites. Using terms that today's readers would reject, he speaks of the "small, squat, ugly, and hopeless" black New Thumberlanders who have interbred with "an unhappy tribe" of Indians, a group both "cowardly in war" and "shiftless and unhygienic in peace" (15). The Waugh-like hauteur and arrogance with which Gray parades these shocking pseudo-stereotypes make us laugh. It's material in this sense that nobody escapes his taunts. As the nonchalant brilliance of the following passage shows, the misanthropy Gray assumes targets so many racial and national types that it mocks political correctness itself; the widow of "a dour, money-making Scot [a.k.a. "that Highland vandal"]who had fallen under a bus in his financial prime ... did not particularly need money, but she did, as she explained frequently, very much need to *make* it" (83).

Quips like this suggest that Gray is ridiculing himself. To sneer at so many ethnic types has a self-canceling effect. Also at stake is his tactic of framing his ethnic slurs in crystalline prose. He has knocked us off our bearings. Certainly, someone who writes with his poise and precision couldn't believe that a ration of "whisky, tobacco, and idleness" has toned down the wrath of some warlike Indian tribesmen into "a mildly spiteful idiocy" (15). Gray has razed those guidelines that anchor both literary and moral judgments. But his razing operations also expose most of these judgments as knee-jerk reactions. By undercutting the facile and the pre-cooked, he has re-aligned our attention. This maneuver helps us. Why spoil our fun? Good teacher that he is, Gray knows that engaging our imaginations trumps solving literary puzzles. He has discouraged lazy reading.

But instead of thanking Evelyn Waugh for showing him how to service readers, he kicks him in the gutter. A reference to the mid-caliber Lancing College in West Sussex in Chapter Three (44) shows him besting Waugh in the same class game that Waugh taught him how to satirize. Waugh, who attended Lancing, would relish the offhand wickedness of Gray's send-off. In a book that came out three years before Waugh's (1903–66) death, Gray, a graduate of Westminster, told the world that, though he borrowed from Waugh, his having attended a better prep school than his mentor also signals his intention to surpass him as a writer.

Colmain reaches out to Gray's writing future in other ways. The great aunt who pays for Fairfax's education without appearing in the book's live action looks ahead to a dead aunt who performs the same service for Logan Bester of *Simple People*. Nor will the school head who discreetly warns Fairfax to temper her adolescent crush on a classmate provide the only other motif that will recur in Gray's later work. The knockabout stemming from the rift between the high drama prompting our acts and the clumsiness of their execution, occurs several times in *Colmain*. Foreshadowing what would become a standby of the Gray canon, Avril Harris's nose collides with Fairfax's forehead when a sudden turn of her head reroutes the "light kiss" (79) he had aimed at her forehead. This "fumbling and clumsy and uncertain" (81) lover has thus become the first of many of Gray's vulnerables whose oafishness certifies their humanity.

The intrusion of the absurd into the plans of others like Avril in *Little Portia*, *Otherwise Engaged*, and *After Pilkington* not only make these men more likable. The spots of physical comedy featuring them also depict, in a way Brecht would have acclaimed, a world that's changeable. And anything that can be changed can also be improved. Chiming with the Marxist writ that inspired Brecht is Gray's faith in a world that thwarts the acts of an Avril Harris. As these disconnects show, the world that sites them offers second and third chances, proving that our efforts can lead to a wider, finer world.

Simon Gray came out swinging in *Colmain*, the prose he uses to describe this world-in-the-making often scoring points rarely attained by first novelist. Twice he'll use the word "snirt" (41, 150) to capture a high-pitched, genteel kind of snort. The fledgling novelist also has both the instinct and the skill to brighten his action with poetic devices. The oxymoron "confusingly lucid" (175) reproduces an overwhelmed Avril Harris's impression of Fairfax's sexual advances to him in Chapter Seven. Gray had already described the Canadian government's indifference to the economic woes vexing Colmain with the synecdoche, "Ottawa didn't express much" (22) interest. Also in the realm of national politics, the metaphor, "New Thumberland ... was a strange province, an empty pocket in a suit stuffed with dollars" (16), captures the breadth of these woes.

Such rhetorical niceties give insight into Gray together with the action he's developing. Style depicts a writer's self-fashioning. It speaks of the places he has been and is colored by what happened there. By forsaking the protective interface of comparison, Gray's preference for metaphor over simile makes *Colmain* a brave book. The preference declares itself in the complex metaphor governing his description of the L-G's lineage: "He came from a rich Ontario family whose roots were sunk deep in the soil and whose branches have spread through the finer atmosphere of Government service and industrial organization" (10). On a smaller but no less revealing scale are his forays into auditory imagery ("the rustle and swish of evening dresses, the clack of voices" [27] overheard at the Ball), assonance ("her gentle dying silence" [47]), and, again, oxymoron (a look of "rosy calculation" [50] on the face of a woman who's pleased with herself). Such linguistic strokes not only improve the novel. Rolling back time, they also invite the claim that, had any of his readers in 1963 predicted that Gray would stop writing fiction to work in another genre, that predictor would have chosen poetry, not drama.

Judged on its own merits, *Colmain* promised so well for Gray's future in fiction that this forecast would have been ignored. Organized around two galas, the nighttime indoors Ball at Government House and the sunlit outdoors garden party, or picnic, at Freeway, which unfold, respectively, in the book's second and penultimate chapters, the book's action confirms Gray's sensitivity to the virtues of balance and symmetry. In no hurry to launch the plot governed by these celebrations, Gray also introduces the L-G a page before bringing him together with the Tennants. The same Ball displays Gray's flair for infusing his comedy of manners with a macabre sense of fun. Here's the L-G greeting a guest at the Ball:

> [The L-G] found Mr. Weatherby's manner odd. "And where is Mrs. Weatherby. I hope she is enjoying it."
> Mr. Weatherby positively loomed. "Mrs. Weatherby is in Holyoke Cemetery," he said very distinctly. "I don't know whether she's enjoying it." He returned to his group [30].

This same surefootedness marks Gray's gift for plotting. After excitement come reflection and evaluation. The following chapter shows Fairfax listening to Mrs. Tennant assess the improvements, if any, the Ball made on her daughter's marriage prospects. The scene deserves a close look. Matching the problems facing a young male writer when he leaves two women alone on the page is that of distributing the plot over a large cast. This challenge, as Tolstoy did in the party scene that opened *War and Peace*, Gray dealt with by introducing several of the book's main players at the Ball and having them reveal traits there that they'd continue to exhibit. By doing this job, moreover, largely from the L-G's point of view, Gray practiced good narrative economy. The perspective of a newcomer to Colmain both puts the invited guests before us without prejudice and tells us how the L-G, who's also preoccupied by the sight of Fairfax's breasts, feels about meeting them.

Narrative economy continues to tighten the book. Gray's knowledge of chess both lends conviction to his account of the game in which Clinton McInley routs Mr. Tennant and foretells Tennant's domestic defeat at the hands of his wife. It also helps launch one of the book's strongest scenes. The fourth chapter of *Colmain*, "Three Invitations," counterpoints two conversations. While Tennant is discussing chess strategy with Clinton, his wife and daughter are reviewing the L-G's marriage credentials. Both conversations treat activities, viz., chess and the marriage market, that include feints and dodges based on the presumed stratagems of others. As in a piece of chamber music, the two conversations split, run alongside each other, and then dovetail. But the music lingers. The chapter ends at the chessboard, where the reckless maneuvers that undo Tennant chime with his wife's haste to marry Fairfax off to the L-G.

Marring this brilliance is editorial laziness. One hotel has "less" (69) rather than fewer floors than another. The troubling combination of "the fact that" appears twice in he same sentence (81). Other flaws come in clusters, too. A sentence in Chapter Four shows Gray calling the same chess piece both a rook and a castle (96). He caused a worse mess by introducing a quarter of the way into the novel (76) the subplot that brings the three visitors from Toronto to Colmain. Credit him, though, for trying to offset the risk he was taking. Mrs. McInley and Andor Harris, two of the visitors, have close family ties to characters he has already committed us to. The third, Colonel Hamton, called a "gigolo" (92) to keep the book's sexual theme in view, shares at a different level the rapacity and greed of Mrs. Tennant in his hope to scam a big profit in real estate. But the introduction of the visitors breaks narrative drive. So knotted are the family ties of both the Harrisses and the McInleys that the time Gray spends on exposition after introducing the visitors from Toronto distracts from the book's main business—Fairfax's bond with the L-G and Mrs. Tennant's efforts to influence it.

He might have avoided the distraction. Though his putting, in Mrs. McInley, a second witch-mother in the book may say a great deal about Gray's psyche, it skews the novel. The roles of the book's two she-devils overlap so much that there's no place for both of them. Knowing that one of them might shove the other out of the plot, Gray keeps them apart. But the damage has been done. Propelled by the visitors from Toronto, the novel's second half founders. Neither Fairfax nor Avril appears in the last chapter, even though a great deal is said about them. Then Fairfaix and her father come home separately without addressing Mrs. Tennant.

The book has trailed off into Celia's recollection of bits of nasty gossip. She eats some cake left over from the party she just gave in silence. Gray has run out of things to say. What can he do now to end matters on a pleasing note? A "softly ticking clock" (199) reminds us that time is running out. But time gobbles everybody. His lame finale gives the impression that he was wishing *Colmain* were a play, not a novel. But what clicks at the end of a play by Ionesco, Beckett, or Pinter falls flat in this novelistic comedy of aggression and unease. Gray has let everybody off—both his characters and his readers—too easily. He needn't have resolved all the issues he introduced. He went wrong in not exploring or developing them more fully.

But enough about these sins of omission. If we extend Gray some charity—which is standard practice for judging first-time novelists—we can confidently give *Colmain* high marks. Even if there's little here to forecast Gray's playwriting future, the book still packed enough promise to send any neophyte writer back to his desk for a second try.

Several of *Colmain*'s benchmark features return in *Simple People*. A sexual innocent is pursued by a self-assured young beauty who will leave him reeling after one go at lovemaking. Nor will the pair be shown together after this lone moment of heat. Also returning from *Colmain* is the intrusion into the plot of two men and a woman, all middle-aged adults; again, one of these intruders has a close blood tie with an important character whom he/she will also try to rip off. The swindle has a history. All three intruders could be hiding from the law. They may even be guilty of crimes worse than those of Mrs. McInley and Colonel Hamton. Though Gray keeps this wrongdoing vague, he does let on that it's serious enough to drive the trio out of England and keep them from their ultimate goal of Vancouver, British Columbia. This careful playing out of background material shows big gains on Gray's part as a structurist. His roguish trio, he made sure, would cause fewer technical problems than their prototypes. Rather than introducing them as a group, he brings in two of them early in the action. The third, a woman, comes in later to speed the action, as women do in his work.

Another difference: *Simple People* is longer, more interior, and less satirical than *Colmain*. Written in richly restrained prose, luxuriously lined but plain to the touch, it provides the same anxious comedy as *Colmain*, but without the cold, appraising authorial eye. Because the 21-year-old Logan Bester is both younger and more carefully drawn than Avril Harris, the stakes also rise in *Simple People*. Much of this consequence builds from the parts of himself that Gray wrote into Logan, a Nova Scotian newly arrived in England, where nothing goes for him as expected. It becomes clear why. Logan was born and bred in Nova Scotia, and, though he lacks siblings, he shares with Gray the plight of feeling like a misfit at home. In a reworking of the Gray family drama, Logan's English-born parents, though Nova Scotians for 30 years, have kept their English ways, few, of which, if any, their son shares with them.

The book's first paragraph links Logan's mother to the mother country. While breakfasting in bed, as usual, Mrs. Bester asks her son to study in Oxford. Her bedsheets "pulled up under her chin" (8), she speaks the first words of the novel. Following her predecessors, Mrs. McInley and Celia Tennant, she's forcing her will upon a resisting child. This coerciveness would be less puzzling coming from a different writer. Would Mrs. Bester have rolled her bedsheets down to her shoulders— or lower — had she already talked Logan into attending Oxford? Characteristically, her husband, Logan's father, says nothing about Logan's education. Replacing him in this regard is the president of McMorris College in Halifax, where Logan took his first degree. But Dr. Dirk's strenuous arguments in favor of the University of Edinburgh fail to dissuade Logan from Cambridge, the best place, he believes, to study English.

Logan's denial of these two authority figures, in their own strongholds, no less, conveys Gray's intention to write, in *Simple People*, a different novel than he did in *Colmain*. His making Logan the later book's central intelligence, a change from the omniscient-narrator technique of *Colmain*, brings this aim into view. A new-world innocent, Logan believes that appearance and reality are one; things in England will be as they seem. No need to worry; he can forget about injury or loneliness because the people he'll meet will resemble those from Nova Scotia. This equation flares out from him. He has omitted something vital from it — his guilt. He feels guilty that his Aunt Agatha's leaving him all her money, less £500 for her brother, Logan's father, cut off her other brother, Logan's Uncle Lionel. His guilt will distract him. Wearing a heavy suit inappropriate to England's weather, he often says "in point of fact" (e.g., 23, 29, 41, 129). This defensive tic, adopted to make him sound authoritative, shows his anxiety. He's playing for time to keep up his side of a conversation, having been distracted by thoughts of his complicity in the disenfranchising of his uncle.

Guilt has nothing to do with his feeling of being stumped nearly immediately after arriving in England. The damp, narrow streets of London, the world's cultural capital for this young Commonwealth citizen, fluster him after leaving Halifax's "clean fresh light" (16) and wide spacious roads. Like the archetypal Jean Rhys heroine, a British West Indian whose introduction to London depresses her, he also feels helpless, adrift, and vaguely cheated. His disquiet grows. The legacy of Scots earnestness and moral stability woven into his upbringing offers as little comfort in Cambridge as it did in London. Joey Romper, a pretty art student he fancies, he judges off limits, as she's living with another man. This judgment is soon tested. Reprising Fairfax's aggressiveness at the Christmas Eve Ball in *Colmain*, Joey holds him close while dancing with him. Then she makes several uninvited visits to his student digs. He's stunned. She'll also sit on his bed, invite him out on dates, and ask him the kinds of questions his home-towners in Worthington, N.S., would deem off limits. To these questions he can only babble non sequiturs in halting sentence fragments. Joey keeps throwing him off stride, not by design, but because her words and acts flout those clear-cut social norms on which he was raised. Like his home-towners, he has always accepted the sequence of pinnings, engagements, and marriages as a natural development of kissing.

Joey has scrambled this logic by making sexual advances to him while she's living with a man to whom she's not married. Like Gray himself (LC 96–98), Logan gets initiated into sex by a woman who's attached to another man. His bafflement builds. Sam Field, Joey's live-in novelist-lover, not only takes Joey's visits to Logan in stride. He even taunts Logan about them: "I imagine you're getting deeper into our customs, exploring them from the inside" (227), he tells Logan the first time the men meet after Logan and Joey sleep together. Nor is Sam's use of calculated backspin his first shock to Logan. Shortly after the two men meet at a gathering of the Wiltshire Society, a Cambridge University literary club, the euphoria flooding Logan, from meeting, in Sam, a published novelist, soon fades. After accepting several of Logan's cigarettes,

Sam drops him to chat with some other guests—but not before inviting Logan to a party at his house the following week. Logan's letdown could have been worse; he has been given a second chance to make new friends. But are they friends worth making? Again, he has to beat back his rising cynicism. Like Lucky Jim (Kingsley Amis's novel of the same name will occur in the text [124]), Sam enjoys railing against English university life and the great composers of classical music. Also, he's barely a novelist, with only one published novel to his credit, *Running Man*, which he spends more time promoting in London than he does writing a second one.

More trials await Logan. After awaiting Sam's party as "a great moment in his personal history" (49), he's bewildered once he arrives there. He's not greeted at the door. Nor does Sam recall inviting him. Then there's the party itself, a spree undreamt of in Worthington. The multicultural guests he finds in a dark room on the second landing have been drinking and dancing to strange native music. He's odd man out amid the "twining, throbbing bodies" (62) on the dance floor. Only Joey, by asking him to dance, overturns his decision to leave. He even sinks his inhibitions while, swaying to the music, he draws her close. In fact, he deliberately leaves his coat at Sam's house to devise an excuse to go back to retrieve it.

Again he's shocked. Even as they're confusing him, matters between Joey and himself *are* speeding forward. She has already returned his coat—along with a written dinner invitation. Back at Sam's house, he's welcomed rather than treated as a rival. His lying to Sam twice, about a scarf he supposedly left with his coat and the note from her he denied seeing, chafes this previously devout truth-teller. His poise has been wrecked. Before going home, he overturns a coffee maker. Whereas Joey can serve tea and sandwiches gracefully, he can't pour coffee, light a match, or undo a knot. As with Avril Harris of *Colmain*, the urgencies of sex have confounded him. Gray planned it this way, having said of these two juveniles, in the introduction to his 1956 reprint of *Little Portia*, "Both of them [are] simultaneously driven by their sexual needs and imprisoned by their fear of the consequences of sex" (xxi). Logan overcomes this fear, but only to see it reinstated in lurid colors when Joey first accepts and then rejects his marriage proposal.

His giddy introduction to Cambridge's literary—and erotic—life followed his disturbing entrance into academic Cambridge. His first letdown is Dr. Andrew Port, who's both his supervisor and tutor. This prolific literary critic who's much admired by the English faculty at McMorris turns out to "the reverse of stylish" (28), a roly-poly in blue jeans and running shoes. His behavior is as disconcerting as his looks. He's standoffish with Logan, and, on those rare occasions when the two do talk, he defects before Logan can say anything of importance. Perhaps, duplicating the waywardness of most of Gray's academics, Port wears running shoes to flee his students. In a related drama, Logan's response typifies *him*. Though he admits that "the meeting with Dr. Port had not gone as he had anticipated" (31), he tries to boost his spirits. He also tries to explain away other discouraging meetings with both fellow students and dons. This job has gotten harder. A leading Rumanian translator he meets at the Wiltshire keeps both breaking into Logan's conversations and luring his interlocutors away. Another don who has supposedly spent the last ten years writing a book on Plato and William Blake is just as rude. A pattern has been set. Sadly, Logan fares just as badly with some fellow students who, when they're not devaluing his undergraduate degree, fault his literary judgment.

Before coming to Cambridge, Logan spent nearly three weeks with his Uncle Lionel in Putney. Originally planning to stay a weekend, he warms to a routine of theatergoing, watching continental films, and browsing book stalls. Every night would mark a tired and happy homecoming to Lionel's antique shop. Surrounded by old maps, books, and furniture, his uncle charms Logan with his old-fashioned courtesy. Belying a wardrobe of floppy old tweeds and cardigans is the "order, coherence, and even formality" (17) of his mind. No toothless lion, he. But how is he surviving? Logan sees very few customers and virtually no sales transacted in the shop. Weighing in on Henry James's international theme, Gray had said earlier of Lionel's business-consultant brother, i.e., Logan's dad, that the same "respect for others" (9) that undid him in London has won him success in Worthington.

Is this passage a foreshadowing? Though aimless-looking, the shambling Lionel has managed to survive in high-octane London without having any apparent source of income. Did Aunt Agatha disinherit him with good reason? Perhaps Logan was wrong connecting appearances to reality. His misgivings mount when Lionel denies hearing the doorbell of his shop put out a clear ring. Continuing to disclaim the presence in his shop of a third person, Lionel later refers for the first time to having "to take ... opportunities" to defuse "some sordid little difficulties" (106) that have inexplicably surfaced. Yes, Lionel has his eye on Logan's money. But he also knows that he'll need help snatching it. Logan has become the target of a conspiracy.

Gray's use of the irony of discrepant awareness has elevated the novel artistically. Both Logan's innocence and his reluctance to believe that his uncle is conspiring against him open a gap between *his* perception of what's happening and the reader's. The gap closes slowly. Lionel's first co-conspirator enters the shop a few days after Logan's arrival. Although his role in the plot resembles that of *Colmain*'s Colonel Hamton, Samuel Chipman gets a closer, sharper look. The more time he spends on the page, the creepier he becomes. His black hair, mustache, and clothes all suggest death, a conjecture supported by his fondness for London's taxis (102), which look like hearses. The link tightens. Logan will mistake the "long black limousine" (196) Chipman later drives to Cambridge *for* a hearse. Though slow to react, Logan began distrusting Chipman when he heard about his extensive "travels and enterprises" (98) in Canada. Logan also learned that Chipman has been using his Fulham-based shop as a conduit for Lionel's goods. If Chipman is Lionel's agent and, by default, his chief source of income, Logan reasons, then both men are probably crooks, given the dearth of cash sales in the shop. Though he never suspects that the shop is a front, he does sense pressure mounting on the two older men. A story overheard about a woman's claim that she was overcharged on an antique she bought in Fulham that was marketed as mahogany rattles Chipman in his presence (233).

But neither Chipman nor Lionel can rob Logan without the help of Maria Hodges, a widow, like Mrs. McInley of *Colmain*, with a flair for the quick kill. Maria's very name spells out the threat she poses. That all-encompassing name blocks all lines of retreat. Just as Maria invokes the world of spirit, so does Hodges imply brute matter, the name Hodge having been applied to callow rustics in the c.1555 play, *Gammer Gurton's Needle* and Thomas Hardy's anti-war poem, "Drummer Hodge." There's the name's unsteadiness, too. Lionel refers to Maria Hodges by both her maiden name, Maria Martle, and her nickname, Gypsy (103). This practice gives Logan cause for worry. Like an alias, multinymity is often a dodge used by those trying to flee the law.

Though the well-traveled Maria Hodges (a hodgepodge of deeds as well as identities) will turn her sexual charms on Logan, she resembles physically neither tall, athletic Barbara Gray nor Barbara's amply framed mother-in-law. Her real-life model is "small and neat and lively" Dolly Hendow, the married woman "with a slight but sturdy figure" (LC 96) who initiated Simon Gray to sex. Wiry, quick, and flamboyant with her scarlet nails and dress, Maria projects a sparkling, unflinching certainty. Both her vibrancy and swift, bird-like manner extend Gray's ongoing distrust of women (Logan's mother miscued by convincing her husband to write to Lionel before Logan's pending arrival in England and again by misjudging Lionel when she said of him, "He doesn't need money. He's quite happy the way he is, with his odds and ends" [15]).

Lionel can whip these oddments into a frightening synergy. Some poodles (French *caniches*) Logan hears about in a song (61) and Lionel's claim that he saw a poodle from his window (109) invoke the legend that Satan first came to Dr. Faustus in the guise of a poodle. As her multinymity suggests, Maria shares this versatility. Using the charm exerted by her "sharp little breasts" (96), she displays her legs to Logan, pushes up against him, and, despite their age difference, kisses him goodbye after their first meeting. And whereas, like Joey, she'll often ask him awkward personal questions (Gray said of Dolly Hendow that he'd "never met a young woman who talked about the things she talked about" [LC 98]), she also keeps dark her own activities and whereabouts (88).

She's her most outrageously triumphant when, having laughed off several attempts by Logan to keep her at bay, she and her two cohorts come to Cambridge bearing hampers of food from Harrods. Lionel has sold his shop. Whatever price it fetched, though, hasn't freed him from problems that "a little help wouldn't put right" (204). He's reaching for Logan's inheritance. Though he, Maria, and Chipman want to go to Vancouver, a destination that will cost more to get to, they'll settle for airfare to eastern Canada (where they can fleece Logan's parents?). Any comfort that Logan is meant to take from this disclosure of purpose melts in Lionel's announcement that "there are a few things Maria would have to settle before being allowed back" (205) in Vancouver. Logan misses his chance to ponder these "few things." Lionel's reference in this exchange to the heretofore unknown and unreferenced Dennis (205) stuns him. Though Dennis never appears, Lionel's mention of him late in the book (Chapter 14 of a 17-chapter work) recalls a similar strategy used in Pinter's *Dumbwaiter* (1957) and *Birthday Party* (1958), where once-mentioned figures called Monty and Wilson are cited in ways that suggest that they're big-time thugs.

Dennis could be running the same kind of crime ring operated by Monty and Wilson, a job that qualifies him as the title character of Sam Field's novel, *Running Man*. Besides noting the impersonality of power, Dennis's putative line of work also infers his ruthlessness. Logan's insistence that he needs Aunt Agatha's money to fund his upcoming marriage leaves Lionel unfazed. He and his friends, having done their homework, perhaps with Dennis's help, already know of Logan's wedding plans. Which won't stop them.; relying on Maria's brilliant sales technique (205), they'll not only persist in their intent to defraud Logan; they'll also do it elegantly. During their evening in Cambridge, they make sure that the topic of money is either sidestepped or addressed only glancingly, in chance references.

Maria, Leonard, or Chipman hold their poise from the moment they usurp the front-row seats saved for faculty members at the Wiltshire Society lecture they have crashed. Logan's passiveness suggests, in customary Simon Gray fashion, that he's conniving at his own defeat. The truth is that he's completely overmatched by Maria, who pretends to delight in all aspects of the Wiltshire evening. So dazzling is she in her clicking high heels and sparkling teeth that, following the lecture, she chats blithely with the lecturer about his own subject. Forget that she knows nothing about the subject other than what she has just heard. Her audacity has crushed her inhibitions. Riding her mojo, she even holds forth to a small but rapt audience of academics on the subject of the English poet Baker (meaning Blake).

Her boldest improvisation, though, takes place out of hearing. Sam Field turns up at the lecture, but without Joey, who, having accepted Logan's marriage proposal, had promised that she'd come. Maria swoops down on Sam and talks to him at length. Presumably, she's persuading him to drive a wedge (while also offering him a bribe?) between Joey and Logan. Joey's absence has given her an advantage upon which she builds. Sam leaves the Wiltshire, but not to collect Joey for a post-lecture dinner party. When it becomes clear that

Joey won't show up, Maria, suppressing her glee, has the gall to throw Logan's grief in his face: "You've hated all this—our coming down and talking to these people and losing your girl" (249). She even claims that she tried to help him recover Joey. But this parting shot, though intended to disable Logan, angers him: "You did it for the money" (250), he accuses her. His accusation jars her composure for the only time in the book. It's in a "shrill" (250) voice that she disclaims all knowledge of money, a sudden flush glazing the false tan that coats her cheeks.

Her calm returns quickly. The person who sets the tone for a battle will win the battle, Logan learns. His small victory imparted but a small touch of color to the Jamesian cloud of fine distinctions, hesitations, and precautions he has been led through. Outgunned from the start, he has lost out to the unspoken, the whispered, and the surmised. Like the dazed heroes of James's *The American*, "The Lesson of the Master," and *The Ambassadors*, he leaves us empty-handed. Gray twists the screws again. Logan will have to pay for the brazenness with which his London visitors annexed the front-row seats at the Wiltshire lecture. Any attempt to resume his studies will run afoul of the spite of those mentors of his forced by the visitors' chutzpah into back-row seats.

The "strains of great music" (254) that peal in the book's last sentence (as they will in the closing moments of *Otherwise Engaged*, *A Pig in a Poke*, and *Hidden Laughter*) clash so stridently with Logan's distress that they resist clear explanations. In their majesty and poise, they comment aptly upon the classic—or simple—tale of experience-crushing innocence we have just read. But these musical strains can also be sounding a version of English post–Colonial blues. Like so many of the book's other components, they have a Jamesian vibe. Losing all has made Logan totally free. What he'll make of this challenge measures his worth.

The other memorable sequence in Gray's 1965 novel, which is also driven by a woman, treats the holy terror of intimacy. Like Maria Hodges, Joey Romper looks more like Donna Hendow than either Gray's mother or grandmother. No fluke, this likeness reinstates the importance of Gray's first lover in his private history. Joey's boyish name and "powerful round buttocks" (180) also reinstate his common practice of matching his juvenile lead to a woman with male characteristics. This backward glance isn't comforting. Tensions rise between Joey and Logan when she visits him in Chapter 11. The twin attempt here on their parts both to reach out to each other and to protect themselves has no counterpart in *Colmain*. The long chapter builds its power and urgency across an ever-widening cultural gap. Shaped temperamentally by the rugged open-air purity of Nova Scotia's Cape Breton and Cabot Trail, an undeterred Logan reaches out linguistically to the sexually casual London art student Joey; but his powerful attraction to her also scrambles his words, making him sound tongue tied.

He's not alone in trying to lessen the gap. Joey, too, coming from the bed of an impulsive creative writer about ten years her senior, wants to understand this provincial academic who has until now built his world around the growing stack of index cards he keeps shuffling. Another obstacle: the budding Wordsworthian Logan worries too much about doing right by her. Yet the fun-loving Joey lacks the moral high ground to pass judgment. Despite her mounting impatience, she's just as guarded as he about declaring her own intentions—which she doesn't know well enough to accept, anyway. Her caution stokes a Jamesian turnabout: Logan's assumption that her physical interest in him clarifies a long-term intention addles, rather than soothes, her. She might have honored his candor and high-mindedness. He has stripped away her defenses. After having made him back-track and over-explain himself, she feels badgered and ashamed when he proposes marriage to her. She fails to see, too, why the monumental task of proposing to her makes him push her away. Over-stimulation has trumped his heart's yearning. But he's governed by more than his heart. A still-stronger impulse rolls his loins against hers; engulfed by this physical closeness, he tells her the same thing (115) she had earlier told him: "It doesn't matter" (160).

Lawrence's love ethic has either shrouded or renewed them. The irrelevance of the "righteous intensity" (160) of Logan's oneness with Joey is an act of faith comprising a category of its own. As in Lawrence, accepting the freedom of not-knowing promotes self-being. Joey's irrelevance confirms her irreducible reality. He needs no reason or excuse to be close with her. That she is, is everything. In another expression of this truth, her telling him, now that he has become to her an object of fear as well as erotic attraction, "I'd better go" (161), bespeaks the desperation of their bond.

This part of the book transcends formula writing. Though much of its brute power stems from Lawrence, it's nevertheless both freshly perceived and admirably sustained. Joey and Logan are both immobilized and driven by the ferocity of impulses they had never felt before, he because of his innocence and she because she has always dabbled in casual sex. They resent each other; they crave each other. But they agree that intercourse can wait. It will have to wait, since the huge emotional distances they have both traveled have frazzled them. They'll spend several hours decompressing and then meet at Sam's, Sam being out of town.

Gray knows the value of decompressing. Having committed us to Joey and Logan, he interposes a chapter between their fraught encounters. Chapter 12 of *Simple People* shows Logan both recovering from his last visit to Joey and preparing himself for the next one. A walk down the College Court takes him out of himself, but not for long. He sees Dr. Port, who, to his surprise, has known about Joey's relationship with Sam Field. Logan is ruffled anew; his studies and private life have collided. He's riled at Joey for keeping him from his work; he's riled at himself for investing so much time and energy in a woman he can't bring to Worthington. He'll tell her goodbye. But, still riveted by her, he shelves these sensible objections. He knocks on her door in an hour or two, shutting it, once inside "as carefully as if it were the lid of a coffin" (171). This simile foreshadows some brilliant moments. A new Logan Bester will struggle crabwise into a form of life that entails death. The farewell speech he had prepared dissolves as he enters her bedroom — which she wisely darkened to derail "those complicated Canadian things" (173) that might impair their lovemaking.

Words, she knows, can douse those urgencies fueled by touch. Comfortable in the realm of feeling, she undresses and climbs into bed. Simpler than Logan, she has also helped him sink his scruples and constraints. "Leave it to the hands, so sensible and inquisitive" (182), he soon reasons, letting matters between him and Joey happen as they were meant to happen. This inevitability surges forward. In a telling post-prandial touch, she excuses him for accidentally destroying a picture of Sam, the best she had ever drawn, which he had stepped on in the dark.

But the body's sovereignty flames out. The thick, heavy darkness of Lawrence gutters into the denial and limitation that always occupied James. Joey misses the Wiltshire. Nor does her phone call to Logan afterward lift his gloom. She says very little. Once she explains that she only slept with him to spite Sam for "his mucking about' (242) with other women, she wants to hang up. She's ashamed of herself for having used Logan. Her reference to the influence on him of "Worthyville," rather than Worthington, shows that she never loved him. Her weasel words, "Things happen" and "it won't matter in the end. Once you get used to it" (243), leave him numb and empty. He's as keen to stop talking as she is.

The other guests at the dinner party following the Wiltshire are celebrating the death of his hopes. Walking away from the telephone, he sees Maria flashing her wit everywhere, smiling and touching everyone she talks to, as she parlays what she learned from earlier conversations into quips of her own; Lionel pockets Logan's money resignedly, as if taking it were the last thing on his mind. Sam held his style too while conveying Joey's regrets over missing dinner. But he did give away a little, answering Logan's dark hint, "I think I'm getting used to things," with the words, "We're very simple, really. Too simple, in a sense" (227).

He's right. Like most men facing the defection of a ladylove, he surrenders to Joey; her having shown him that she's just as adept at "mucking about" as he stops his womanizing. No surprise; men committed to saving love bonds will capitulate. Logan's rite of passage in this coming-of-age story has been both complex and desperately simple. Casanovas will reform to avoid losing their women, above all to other men.

This lesson, along with much else in the novel, represents for Gray, not a rejection of the past, but a change of direction. The novel's voice, though not exactly Jamesian (James is mentioned in the text [11]), does tend to longer sentences that use more subordination than those of *Colmain*. The following one, for instance, shows Jamesian syntax teasing out the kind of cultural distinction in which the Master reveled: "But if Logan wasn't Nova Scotian in the way in which most Nova Scotians were and wasn't English in the way his parents were (whatever way that was) he already had a rich sense of England" (11). Another syntactical sleight-of-hand in the Jamesian mode underscores the import of one of the book's key moments. Gray is describing an outsider's impression of Maria's talk with Sam Field, a critical moment for her because she knows it's her only chance to sabotage Logan's liaison with Joey:

> Whether the writer [viz., Sam] had a lot to say to Maria wasn't clear. That he had a lot to listen to was. Mrs. Hodges had stepped very close to him.... All that Logan could see of Sam ... was half of one grey profile, his jacket and a splash of plum-colored cloth. Mrs. Hodges was speaking in a tone so low that it was almost impossible to hear her; but she was speaking in a tone so intense that it was almost impossible not to try [234].

This brilliant final qualification draws us in. Rarely will even the best writers combine repetition and nuance so effectively. Gray's strategy of giving tantalizing glimpses of Maria's persuasive technique before letting on that she has more to say to Sam has held our attention.

One more distinction that would have pleased James stems from Gray's take on Logan's Canadianness. A Canadian brings to Europe a different value system than an American; as Logan points out several times, Canadians resent being taken for Americans (e.g., 58). These reminders of his countrymen's comparative reticence, reserve, and modesty of expectations are dropped mostly at social gatherings, both the conviviality and competitiveness of which Gray presents smoothly. If anything flows smoothly at a literary or academic social; during several conversations at the two Wiltshires, words that fade into surrounding talk must be repeated.

The point is important because most of Logan's social ties in Cambridge begin at parties. Like *Colmain*, in which two big galas occur in both the second and penultimate chapters, those in *Simple People*, using the same book-ending format, take place in Chapters Four and 15 of this 17-chapter work. Gray also knows how to keep us turning pages. For example, Chapter Six closes with a luncheon invitation Logan gets in the mail, but it's not from Joey, as he had hoped. Joey *will* visit him in Chapter Eight, though without being identified. Both Gray's description of her appearance and her words in this scene could apply as readily to Maria (who invited him to lunch earlier in Chapter Six) as to Joey during the first five pages or so of her conversation with Logan.

Logan's delight in seeing Joey gains from another gradual recounting of information from the previous chapter. Using the device of delayed exposition, Gray confirms in Chapter Seven through Logan's point of view that not only have Maria and Chipman known each other for a long time; these two are also taking turns, along with Lionel, to talk one-to-one with him. That this relay of interviews follows Maria's shocking announcement of the trio's plan to come to Cambridge shows Logan that his would-be visitors have been scouting weaknesses in him that they will review and then attack when they next see him.

Heretofore inclined to give Lionel the benefit of any doubt that rises between them, he also sees now his uncle's complicity in the plot being hatched against him. This expansion of knowledge, together with that of his moral intelligence, stirs the nasty truth that money can cut across family as well as erotic love. Coming to Cambridge did educate him, but not in the expected way. Life's greatest lessons, he now sees, don't come from books. But he's far from acting on this truth. He'll have to decide first how he's going to explain it all to those other Worthington innocents, his parents.

Little Portia gains from being read as the "very personal novel" Gray said it was (Hamilton 41). This story about a self-centered youth gives little sense of the time in which it unfolds. Though it captures the mood of Cambridge in the late 1950s and early '60s, it slights headline developments of the time like nuclear proliferation, drugs, and civil-rights demonstrations. Instead, the book's loose picaresque frame traces the fortunes of the Thwaite orphans—Dianah and, mostly, Grahame—from early childhood to their early twenties. The orphans grow up in Mallows, a Hayling Island estate owned by their great-aunt, Mary Medway. Helping dry, pinched Aunt Mary raise the kids is Colonel Basil Rones, brother of her ex-fiancé, a combat fatality in World War I.

A twofold generation gap between themselves and surrogate parents who are also newcomers to child-rearing tests the kids' powers of self-invention. Specifically, the need to distance themselves from "the most loathed spinster" (8) in her neighborhood and her pukka-sahib consort widened in the kids a split from an adult world already remote from them in both age and attitude. Perhaps this remoteness curbed their interest in political and social change. More significantly, the children's need to shield themselves from adult disapproval taught them that the good manners their elders drilled into them could ward off prying. But, like much else in Gray's 1967 novel, their cultivation of politeness, though useful, will also backfire. Grahame, who resembles Gray with his "round pink cheeks ... [and] mop of moppet's hair" (115), his Nova Scotia and Cambridge schooling, and his losing his virginity to a sexually seasoned woman, discovers that other people find his well-bred airs irksome.

What's still worse, these airs, nurtured to fool others, block his own growth. He learns at college and again at university to feign indifference to those who mean the most to him. Aggravating this self-denial is the habit he picks up, like Pip of Dickens's *Great Expectations*, of wasting emotional energy on people he insists mean nothing to him. He becomes a stranger to his own feelings. He never deals, for instance, with another important early influence he inherited from his author, namely, that of the kindly laundress of the great-aunt who raised him and Dianah. Based on Gray's sexually provocative grandmother, Bella offers Grahame an "easy friendship" that includes putting him on her lap and tickling him to the point that makes him both "desperate to escape" and delirious for more" (20).

The force of Bella's influence stems from her name, which comes from the brothel madam in the Circe, or Ulysses in Night-town, section of *Ulysses* (Homer's Circe turned Odysseus's followers into swine). Bella Cohen exerts such psychosexual force on Joyce's Everyman figure, Leopold Bloom, that, as both dominatrix and the powerful masculine Bello, s/he whips up his masochistic urges—he lets Bella twist his arm and then, sitting on his face, use his ear as an ashtray. At Cambridge, Gray's Grahame falls in love with and is then rejected by the Newnham student he has cast in the role of Bella's replica — the plump-thighed, chesty Sylvie Wasserman. He gravitates to Sylvie despite knowing from the start that he stands no chance with her. A much better choice is Jeannie Haverstock, who's prettier, friendlier, and more approachable. But Jennie loses out; along with her availability, her resemblance in Grahame's eyes to his sister Dianah (150) steers him away from her — and denies him a chance for happiness.

The death of his parents also put conflict, pain, and loss at the core of any love bond for him, a response he never outgrows. He felt safe opening his heart to Sylvie, who not only reminded him of the clam, non-judgmental laundress Bella; he also suspected that Sylvie never felt he was right for her. While still dating him, she began dating the young Jewish doctor she'd soon marry. Both relieved and crestfallen by her defection, Grahame learned that, by choosing her over Jeannie, he had also failed to spot his best chance for happiness, let alone act on it.

He also learned something from the waves of disappointment and relief that overtook him, viz., that strong emotions intersect and collide, rather than running around or alongside each other. The ease with which gain becomes loss and virtue shifts places with vice keeps rattling Grahame. This schooling first declared itself in his parents' death. Gordon and Yvonne Thwaite saw the end of World War II as both a victory and a defeat. Had they lived, they'd have struggled. Being demobbed from the Navy would have left Gordon without a job. It's apt that Yvonne, speaking in the last weeks of a war that killed millions, should say, "we'd better hope for a late rally from Jerry" (5). But even had the war extended another six months, where to find civilian work? Reckless spending had stripped Gordon of the cash to buy into a practice. The evidence suggesting that he and Yvonne were both driving their death car made their end-all as much of a mercy as a catastrophe.

This head-spinning dialectic becomes their main legacy to Grahame. It will take the form of repetition, or cycle, a death sentence in Dante, Nietzsche, and Freud. While attending Windhoven College, Grahame tears up a love letter written to him in the writer's presence. Then he joins the other boys in the dormitory as they swarm Jacobs, the letter writer. Desperation drove him. His suspicion that Jacobs approached him to begin with because he identified with him as a fellow outcast launched Grahame into the faceless midst of Jacobs's attackers. But he also had enough conscience to condemn his spinelessness. To punish himself, he became the outcast Jacobs claimed he was. Spending time alone in the school library, he discovered an annex called the Colluns. Where the ambiguities besetting him multiply; it's here that he meets Michael Cranton, who is "another exile" (66) because his chronic ill health has excused him from all school functions besides going to class.

Cranton soon shows his mettle as "the cleverest boy in the school" (82). His attraction to Shelley and Keats, Lorca and the bullfighter Manolete (1917–47), all of whom died young after achieving dazzling success, impresses Grahame. Serendipity has also graced Grahame, who attains the moral imagination to believe Cranton's claim that he's stronger than his new friend. Cranton had backed this claim by showing him the joys of reading. Thanks to Cranton, Grahame (a natural athlete like Simon Gray) turns his attention from sports to books.

Left to follow his lights in friendly surroundings, this former "leading member of the locker room" (73) discovers a rich, renewable, ever-expanding world. Cranton spoke home when he said that Grahame had outgrown organized team sports (87). But this growth will have a salt edge. Unable to hide from himself, Grahame sees that his prowess in sports was diverting him from important home truths. Cranton tells him that he played cricket and soccer to compensate for his orphan's loss of love; excelling in sports won him cheers and trophies he could hide behind. Hiding stops being an option. While hard to accept, Cranton's words depict him as the "treacherous coward" (80) who persecuted Jacobs for exhibiting traits he loathed in himself.

The karmic pattern that has been morphing loss and gain into new unforeseen shapes has made him its own. Cranton understands the process. He wasn't being playful or malicious when he advised Grahame to read the two gay writers André Gide and Jean Genet. Not only has Grahame fallen in love with Cranton without knowing it; he also writes Cranton a love letter that Cranton destroys in exactly the same way that Grahame had destroyed Jacobs's letter to *him*—in the writer's presence.

Before Grahame gets over this shock, he's stunned by another — Michael Cranton's death. Gray conveys the force of this death upon Grahame by alluding to another tragically early one that continues to haunt a survivor. Grahame grieves in terms that recall those of Gretta Conroy's brooding on the death, years earlier, of her young lover, Michael Fury, another Michael, in James Joyce's "The Dead": "Cranton is dead,' he said experimentally. 'Michael is dead. I would have died for *him*. Dead. Dead'" (99). Gray's description of Grahame's visit to the home of Cranton's mother invokes another great Irish writer's grief on the death of love. Entering the London home, Grahame calls himself "a sixteen-year-old smiling public schoolboy, with excellent manners" (101). His façade is soon smashed by Mrs. Cranton's resentment that Grahame has survived, in Michael, the son he may have also corrupted. By the time she orders Grahame out of her home, giving him the telltale letters he had written to Michael, Grahame feels as shattered as the "sixty-year-old smiling public man" ("Among School Children," l. 8) W.B. Yeats (who's later mentioned in the novel [176]) did when, serving as a school inspector, he spotted a young girl who resembled his forever-gone love, Maud Gonne.

Grahame's superb manners haven't cushioned his shock. The combination of Cranton's death and the wrath of Cranton's mother collapses him. Though his recovery is slow, it moves in a positive direction. As a tribute to his dead friend, he works so hard at his studies that he wins a scholarship to Cambridge. His success builds. The opening of Book Two of *Little Portia* shows him as both a third-year honors student in history and a member of the university's student elite. But, as he had already learned, every blessing he enjoys has a recoil action. His academic and social attainments provide new angles and depths into chafing insights about himself. Cranton had asked him to read Gide and Genet to guide him toward self-knowledge.

Now, four years later, he still needs sorting out. His upstairs neighbor, the epicene mathematician, John Hazings, often poses himself "with one long hand on a slim hip" (130) encased in "white twist trousers" (121) that look like the pair Janice Trullope will wear when she first sees Grahame — in a gay bar, no less. The "white twist trousers" Jan puts on to meet Grahame six weeks after he breaks up with her, like her "extremely short boyish haircut" (285), infer that she knows him better than he does himself. These effects help her regain his love immediately. Occupying a pivotal point in his psyche, Hazings also confirms the grip of Grahame's past. Always looking for male authority figures to bond with, Grahame calls the ace mathematician Hazings "Tops" (127), a term he had applied to the "proper master" (46) of his childhood, the pedophilic Lindsay Burnlow (41). Clinching this affinity are the "magnificent eyes" (135) Hazings turns on Grahame at a crucial moment. Grahame's reunion with Jan later in the book finds him "watching her every movement with the intensity of a blind man whose sight has been restored" (285).

The eye motif gives further insight into him. For the eyes that first "ruled him" were set in the "adored" (44) face of Burnlow. Burnlow's arrival at Hayling Island's Morton School "in the juvenescence of the year" (37) invokes T.S. Eliot's reference in "Gerontian" to Christ the Tiger, who was born "in the juvescence of the year" (ll. 19–20). Burnlow damaged Grahame by showing him that sex was fun. The lesson took hold quickly. When Burnlow's fingers "caught at something" inside Grahame's knickers and then "tweaked it," a compliant Grahame pretended that nothing wrong had happened (47). His question about the school matron who interrupted the fondling ("Why did *she* ... come...?" [53]) implies that he was enjoying Burnlow's attentions. It's indicative of Gray's admiration of Eliot that he adapts in this scene the poet's belief that religious fear ("Christ the Tiger") precedes the acquisition of religious hope. It's also a sign of Gray's gay leanings that he makes Lindsay as much of a redeemer to Grahame as a destroyer, a harsh truth Grahame must accept in order to view himself accurately.

Clouding his view is the elusiveness of freedom. "He was free" (52), Grahame says to himself after Burnlow's dismissal from Morton School, an event that would upset him more than the "lapping closeness" (41) of Burnlow's embraces. Grahame uses the same words to proclaim his autonomy both after his recovery from his nervous breakdown (107) and the loss of his virginity four years later (185). But within an hour of mounting Jan, he's so put off by her table manners that his resolve to stop seeing her leaves him feeling "free as eagles" (190). He hasn't noticed that his assertions of freedom all occur in a sexual context, a region fraught with more strong new forces than he can handle. Addled by the cowardice and dishonesty he'll hide behind when tested, he recants on the marriage proposal he had confidently made at a moment when he was able to stifle his objections to her. His stated reason: lack of funds. Throughout the recantation scene, he answers her simplicity and candor with the same polished evasiveness that had always helped him keep others at bay. The words that end the scene, the chapter, and also the novel's second section, "He knew that he was free at last, absolutely free" (237), describe his dependence upon the quick fix that always rules out honest self-evaluation. Free? He sees right away that he has been cheating himself. In his final act of physical contact with Jan, he clutches at the same stubby fingers he had always found so irksome. He needs to ask himself some hard questions before he sees that she means more to him than he's willing to concede.

She does take him back, but only to sense him wavering between coldness and confused, teary moments of tenderness. His wavering registers the great gulf dividing him from maturity. Other signs in the book argue the same point. Like an autistic child, he both curls up in bed like a foetus (65, 185, 215) and pierces his flesh, driving a wooden table splinter into his finger to distract himself from his mistake of introducing Jan to his sister, Dianah (210). This symbolic retreat into infancy and then the womb tallies with other patterns of recurrence that gauge his lack of progress. He's going around in circles. The name of his Windhoven dormitory, Arnold, revisits him in the first name of Jan's father, whose hometown, Wimbledon, has the same intonation pattern, the same number of letters, some of which recur, and the same number of syllables as Windhoven. Grahame's duties to himself are clear. He has to find the connections between these places and then discover how they chime with his own vital signs.

Gray's 1986 introduction to *Little Portia* calls these vital signs unhealthy. He says too that he used the "recurring motif" of bondage to describe the "the ghastly comedy" (xxi) of Grahame's sexual upbringing. The motif conjures up the sweaty bear-hugs Burnlow put on Grahame while stroking his private parts. It returns with the chained, gagged beauties Grahame dreams about after seeing them on the book jackets in the window of a London smut shop. Gray uses a familiar conceit to show Grahame's own shackling. As in *Colmain* and *Simple People*, the high drama of lovemaking gets muddied in *Little Portia* in the clumsiness of people's efforts to close with each other. Grahame's attempt to kiss Sylvie ends in a collision between his nose and her cheek (161). The necktie that crawls under his ear and the shreds of tobacco that drift into his hair during foreplay blunt the lyricism of sexual abandon as he and Jan approach their first consummation together. But the novel takes the unswerving punctuality of accident beyond sex and into the realm of metaphysical. The smooth, the even-flowing, and the unimpeded denote perfection, a state of being that defines only God. Grahame's Cambridge friend Hazings has put a fragile screen in the entryway of his sitting room, where it can be easily tipped over. His motive? To remind his guests, not merely of their clumsiness, but, rather, of their mortality.

The penalties of being mortal go on. We finite creatures who flop around gracelessly during our time on earth also smell, if not stink. Yvonne Thwaite enjoyed her son more than he did his sister because her smelled nicer (4). Accordingly, the precise cadences of the speech that son will later master are both germ-free and odorless; nothing as human as a solecism can smudge their luster. The same can be said instructively of the artwork looking out at Grahame from the cover of *A History of Human Bondage*:

> On the cover was a lithe blonde girl, her wrists manacled together, and those manacles linked to a chain at her waist.... There was no suffering on her face — painted lips pouted open to admit a metal gag; wide blue eyes ... small neat breasts with nipples around which there were no spots or pimples. Her legs, clamped by the fastenings, conveyed no suggestion of pubic hair. *No smells*. She looked so clean and remote, so pure and loved, in her bondage [218; emphasis added].

It's apt that this manacled girl is a victim of cruelty. Sanitized and spotless, females like her only appear on book covers. They're a literary conceit designed to lure fetishists. Their flawlessness sets them against life to encourage viewers to project their own fantasies onto them (which is why Lawrence hated pornography). And, in another of Gray's reworkings of Shakespeare's Sonnet 130 ("My mistress's eyes"), whereas fantasy divides people, the smell of spotted, oily skin can entice and join them.

Little Portia follows *Colmain* and *Simple People* by building itself around a portrait of the male psyche in extremis. Psychological strips are torn off Grahame as they were off of Avril and Logan. But unlike his two predecessors,

Grahame grows up believing that sex is dirty. This belief begins with the muddy, tangled, rat-breeding marsh he fell into as a boy. Dianah then cleaned him off with fingers, foreshadowing those of Burnlow, that "circled busily between his legs" (18), after which she joined him under an apple tree. The garden symbolism plays on. Di might have been more interested in caressing Grahame than in cleaning him. Once in the house, he still reeks, a truth that amuses Col. Rones, who says with a laugh, "Little boys always smell dirty," adding, "The little fellow ... the little fellow" (19). Note Gray's placement of this repetition — at the end of a chapter. The emphasis created by Gray's rhetorical strategy invites readings that, while different, merge in a powerful unity. The speaker of the repeated phrase, an ex-military officer and battlefield veteran who has seen death at close range, has sited that unity in the great snarling beast of original sin. Did a signal transmitted by Grahame's penis, or little fellow, send him to the mysterious, mud-clotted marsh? Finally, is the bachelor Colonel as intrigued with Grahame's penis as Di?

The vaginal marsh that Grahame may have deliberately slid into focuses these questions, if only because of its persistence. Grahame will throw the "clotted" (103) bundle of letters a distressed Mrs. Cranton forces on him into "a small stagnant pool" (106). The symbolic equation had already been proliferating. Not only did the orgasm Burnlow got from fondling Grahame smell marshy (44); Aunt Mary's face resembled "a bespectacled apple" (53) when she was questioning him about the tender mercies Burnlow had inflicted on him.

Grahame's karma burgeons rhythmically. The office of the House Master in which Grahame hears a lecture on the dangers of masturbation has "a strange smell" (60). The aura emanating from the Master himself has a "dark smell" (60). Gray believes that the more densely human our endeavors are, the stronger the odor they put out. This scrambling of the senses set forth as a poetic ideal by Arthur Rimbaud, viz., synesthesia, imbues the Master's words with the physicality emanating from his person. This dynamism echoes later. A later scene shows Cranton dismissing a love poem Grahame had written him with the words, "You're not Rimbaud.... But you can kiss me if you like" (91).

Dominant, the marsh casts its deepest spell when it evokes its primitive origins as an image of the great sea mother. This spell touches Grahame. Responding to it with a primitivism of his own, he summons up the "malicious snake between his legs" as he smells "the poison of her [Jan's] love" (229). All this happens involuntarily. Though the rankness that's overtaking him is sexual, it's also natural. And, like the apple tree he and Di gravitated to after falling into the marsh, it marks a milestone moment: Eve's giving Adam the apple of Eden was an act of sharing; woman's role since the Fall has been one of sharing, not necessarily one of corrupting. Grahame intuits this ancient truth. Feeling damp and sticky after sex, he says inwardly of Jan, "She had made *him* smell" (230). But his anger blurs. The dissolution of its sharp clarity into confusion joins the smell that "made him sick" with "the smell of desire" (265).

Igniting this juncture is his discovery that he, too, bears the taint of the primeval ooze our forefathers rose from eons ago. Jan tells him that she, too, has been having misgivings about the stench *he* gives off during sex. A second, more important, shock comes in her disclosure that, as strong as the stench is, she can accept it as a natural outgoing of the man she loves. Whether he uses this bombshell of a disclosure as the foundation of a solid love-tie remains unclear. After returning to Hayling Island for Aunt Mary's funeral, he talks of going to Cambridge, not London, where Jan is waiting for him. And he'll go to Cambridge accompanied by the woman he's seen together with in the book's final scene, his sister, Di.

What this actor in a Lawrencean script does gain, like a hero or heroine out of Henry James, is self-knowledge. In another Jamesian stroke, he makes this discovery by rethinking an earlier, all-but-forgotten, event, the Cambridge luncheon where he introduced Jan to Di. The incident began at the start of Book Two, Chapter Three, with Grahame carping inwardly about a bracelet Di was wearing that he finds "extravagantly out of place ... and disturbingly noisy" (198). Lending the incident heft is Gray's strategy of withholding the bracelet-wearer's identity throughout the long paragraph. His cunning accrues artistic capital. A well-placed reference or two in the paragraph suggests that Grahame is faulting Jan, the shoddiness of whose clothes had already annoyed him. Gray has used the art of misdirection to note similarities between the two most important women in Grahame's life that he wants Grahame — and us — to reflect upon. He has primed us for the challenge. We keep looking for clues that will identify the woman in the restaurant.

In the balance, too, are the similarities in feeling Grahame directs to Jan and Di. In an observation that could apply to either woman, he "marvel[s] ... at the transformation" of the "baggy, bowed, and staid" (198) woman he last saw. The agent of this transformation has been love, which can take different forms. Di has reasons of her own for agreeing to the lunch date. She wants to offer Grahame a job in the English language school where she has been chief aide to the school's boss and owner, Ted Spill. Soon after Grahame accepts the generous offer, he's also given a cottage to live in and, most surprisingly, a salary hike to accompany his highly coveted promotion to permanent status. Though pleased, he's too arrogant to see that his elevation has little to do with his teaching skills. Like most of his other windfalls and reprieves, it came from Di.

Who is her brother's keeper. Her giving the impression that Grahame has applied for a teaching job in Kuala Lumpur, where she'd surely join him, helps her bribe her boss to keep Grahame at the Spill Academy. What gave her the power to persuade Ted Spill to flout his professional judgment has to be sex. Ted's compliance adds to Grahame's education. Not only does it burst Grahame's illusions about his market value as a teacher. More fundamentally, it tells him about the give-and-take informing the sexual bond. If Di could sleep with the bewigged, false-toothed Ted Spill and wear in public the tatty bracelet he bought her, mostly to secure her brother's future, then that brother should be content with Jan. But can he be? Gray explains his conflictiveness by calling Jan "perfectly inappropriate, completely desirable" (xxii). Grahame felt unsure about her from the start. Put off by her age (she is 16), her cockney speech, and the slum where she lives while in London, he sees his reason, propriety, and social standards routed by the reek of sex. Gray's withholding her name until page 201 of *Little Portia* after introducing her on page 173 conveys Grahame's resistance to her. This mental cramp will backfire. He knows that his practice of scrutinizing and judging her is tormenting both of them. His cold gaze also misleads him. He congratulates himself for compiling the objective evidence — her lack of education, bad table manners, the tastelessness of her parents' home — to justify her unworthiness. But, to his surprise, breaking off with her leaves him feeling as conflictive as ever. Freedom has eluded him. When he sees her again, six weeks later after having several of his letters to her go unanswered, he recalls Nicholas Urfe of John Fowles's *The Magus* (1965), an educated brat who has to struggle to regain the love and trust a social inferior had previously given him unconditionally.

His underrating his elder sister and only sib, Dianah, whose mother's discounting of her as "pale and thin" as well as "spare and dry" (4) he'd agree with, confirms his ignorance of women. He never saw Di clearly. His boyhood belief that she makes him feel ordinary rather than special (44) has always led him to disregard her. Even as a young man, he would let a year pass without seeing her. What he has been overlooking is her quiet internal strength, her steadiness, and her self-effacing protectiveness. By saying "she's not very bright, but she's gentle" (85), he has missed the truth that her heart his right, an asset that helps her win the presidency of her school's glee club (96). This gifted singer also has the people skills to harmonize with life. The coincidence of her acceptance into "Portsmouth's best secretarial college" (110) and Grahame's Cambridge scholarship rankles him; "Brilliance was brilliance, and sisters were sisters, merely" (110), he growls. He'd be shocked to discover that her secretarial skills will land him a job that his botching of his final paper at Cambridge would have normally denied him.

As with the other major developments in his life (his bonds with Burnlow, Michael Cranton, and Jan Trullope), sex has dictated this career move. Di's sleeping with Ted Spill empowers her to clinch her brother's appointment and promotion. Nor is this the first time that sex stood behind one of her interventions. Sensing something unwholesome behind Burnlow's interest in Grahame, she looked through the keyhole of the room in which Burnlow was fiddling with him. What she saw dictated the only step she could have taken — telling the school matron what was happening to Grahame at that very moment.

This decisiveness typifies her. Any setback or threat to Grahame will bring her to his side. She even does his laundry and cooking during his stay at the language school. This comfort, protectiveness, and support calls to mind his nickname for her: Din; like Rudyard Kipling's regimental bhisti, she's a loyal servant whose moral fiber and dependability vault her over those she serves. Yet the one who gains the most from her benevolence, Grahame, keeps underrating her. Characteristically, he throws a letter on the floor as soon as he sees that it's from her. He has no charity for her, either. His dependence upon her as a confidante makes him resent her. Besides complaining that he can't rise above her, he carps that her life has gone too easily; any prize his gauche hangdog sister wins must be a fluke. He's as startled by her crisp, fresh stylishness when he and Jan meet her for lunch as he is by the solid job she gains.

Yes, the loss of his father at age four or five robbed him of a male role model whose presence in the home might have annulled the mistakes he committed at Mallows School, Windhoven, and Cambridge. But the death of Yvonne Thwaite hit him harder. Lacking a mother, he never learned how women think and feel, a loss that skewed his view not only of women but also of the male-female sexual tie. The torture he will bring upon both himself and Jan Trullope (his true love or a trollop who got more of him than she deserved?) discredits his childhood impression of Pip and Estella "going down the years to their happiness" (21) in *Great Expectations*, a work also mentioned two pages from the end of *Little Portia* (306) to remind us that Eros always foments misunderstandings, clashes, and resentments. Grahame's education peaks in his recognition that he knows very little. Ruled by unconscious archetypal drives, he had lowered himself into the mythic female depths of the marsh at Morton House to compensate for the loss of his mother. Perhaps he knew that unless he did something radical he'd always underrate and distrust women. His absorption into this dark primal source immediately after the banishment of Burnlow from Mallow constituted an effort by his inner intuitive self to connect with the male identity he'd need to later achieve adult maleness.

Janice Trullope's name is but one in the novel with a Dickensian ring, like those of Lindsay Burnlow, Toby Moss, and Francis Meadle. Gray might have also mentioned Dickens's *Pickwick Papers* (21) to dissuade readers from faulting his novel for lacking a plot. But just as Dickens introduced Mr. Pickwick midway through his 1837 novel to unify it, so did Gray take steps to smooth *Little Portia*'s episodic look (the word "pastiche," meaning patchwork or cribbed, appears twice [135, 176] in the book). As in other initiation stories from Fielding's 1749 *Tom Jones* to Ralph Ellison's *Invisible Man* (1952), the book's hero moves from place to place, connecting with different people en route. What he makes of these connections tallies his progress in his fitful education. Fitful indeed; at Cambridge, he overrates John Hazings as he did

Lindsay Burnlow eight or ten years earlier. Other recurring motifs reveal this same muddle. For instance, love always creates a new start for him. His spending time with Jan prompts him to drop his academic career as suddenly as Michael Cranton's influence refocuses his attention from sports to books. In a supporting refrain, Di's discovery of sexual love resonates professionally, creating career changes for both herself and Grahame. And despite her leaving the action for 50 pages at a time, this more stable Thwaite sib always serves as his protector, conscience, and keeper.

Their bond is but one reason to rate *Little Portia* over *Colmain* and *Simple People*, both of which are made of fewer and simpler ingredients. Grahame, for instance, spends considerable time with Jan rather than parting company from her after a one-night stand. Jan's meeting Grahame's sister and her later introducing him to her parents also pose greater artistic challenges than anything attempted in Gray's earlier novels. Finally, the Cambridge Grahame attends has more personality than the one where Logan Bester studied and lived. The organization of *Simple People* limited Logan's university career to a year because the book's organizer didn't feel ready to invest the place with the sharpness and the historical depth that infuse his portrayal of it in *Little Portia*.

This richness surpasses Gray's descriptions of physical setting. The conversations among students, strident and passionate without being shallow, upgrade those in *Simple People*. A new attentiveness is given to conversational style. Engaging in these conversations, Grahame learns, calls for discretion. Even while joining a chorus of praise to D.H. Lawrence, one must avoid the impression of trying too hard. And the other choristers will be high-end achievers, Grahame's having acquired from dormitory life in Windhoven the snobbish practice of ignoring the unfavored. The snobbery persists, to his disadvantage. His Cambridge friends, reminiscent of the Auden Circle at Oxford 30 years before, develop an in-group jargon to discuss, often to boozy excess, films, politics, and jazz. But mastering this jargon has its limits. A dismayed Grahame learns that he lacks either the connections or the smarts to enter the charmed circle within his set of elites. The same Hazings who invites him upstairs for drinks and talk decline similar invitations from *him*.

This regimen slows when he starts dating Sylvie Wasserman, success with whom, he sees, entails feigning indifference. He had ignored the casual anti-Semitism of his friends to date her, but only to face a stiffer test of his democratic principles when he loses her to a Jewish rival. Nathan Hornstein's status as an M.D. stiffens him again. Not only is Nathan a better match for Sylvie than Grahame; he also marries her, a step Grahame couldn't have taken for at least three years. His reaction to Sylvie's prudent choice of Nathan as a husband brings out his worst. With venom, he tells everybody that he broke off with *her*, largely because she was "terrible in bed" (166). Continuing to degrade himself, he acquires a taste for: "Westerns, thrillers, pirate adventures or horror films ... in which girls were victims and captives, bound and gagged, lashed, locked, tethered by leather" (170). This mental and emotional slumming, ruinous enough on its own, ends a long tailspin that puts him in the worst possible mind-set with which to start dating Jan, whom he typecasts at first sight in the role of helpless victim (173).

No disorganized, fragmented test of the reader's patience, *Little Portia* takes a long, brave look at a youth spared only by luck from taking himself down. That youth's addiction to Monopoly, B-movies, and S&M books mirrors Gray's own preferences in *his* early twenties. This tally-sheet of addictions isn't decorative. Gray had spent years sifting, combining, and recombining its parts in search of their meaning. *Little Portia* is one vital result of his efforts. Like Lawrence's *Sons and Lovers* (1913), the book probes issues that its author had to face squarely in order to ripen as both a writer and a man.

Gray resembles C. Day Lewis and Joyce Carol Oates, Julian Barnes and John Banville, by having written, in *A Comeback for Stark*, a thriller under an assumed name. This 1968 novel by one Hamish Reade includes many of the staples of the thriller form — a busy plot driven by characters boldly drawn, if only in black and white, and plenty of violence with global implications. Reade/Gray also leavens the form's usual preoccupation with disruption and displacement with some postmodernist games of hide-and-seek. Balancing ambiguity and actuality, Gray portrays an unstable, dangerous world in which social problems form but one trial. Like Greene's *Our Man in Havana* (1958) and John le Carré's novels of the 1960s, e.g., *The Spy Who Came in from the Cold* (1963) and *A Small Town in Germany* (1968) (one of Gray's spy chiefs has a "smiley mouth" [40]), *Comeback* sets forth a neglected, though important, truth: All societies hire people to do their dirty work, taking care to keep their efforts out of sight, unacknowledged, and deniable. What's left is Gray's description of what ordinary people do when faced by the upshot of these efforts. The collision between the familiar and the unspeakable, Gray believes, brings out the worst traits of both bystanders and pros.

The grief spreads. Wrongness has become commonplace in an atmosphere thick with foreboding. A church that has been turned into a movie house depicts the degradation of standards caused by Cold War politics. Framing the degradation in terms consistent with those of Eliot's *The Waste Land*, a character notes inwardly in the book's next-to-last chapter: "There were no connections between the past and the present" (177). This denial of causality, along with the secrecy and competitiveness of the characters, send the book outside the bounds of narrative convention.

The subgenre most closely attuned to this nihilism is *noir*. *Noir* novels and films usually posit a bleak, immoral world, their scenes unfolding in a moody urban landscape marred by corruption and incontinence. Suspense comes from the hero's efforts to survive the nastiness, a big challenge because his aides have withheld vital information from him, better to clear themselves in case his operation fails. Nor does this betrayal shock him. Spies always lie and expect to be lied to in return. They inhabit a dream world drained of morality, in which their responses pertain only to the execution of their duties. Forget ideals and ideologies. The only loyalty of these technicians is to the jobs they perform.

This absence of a transcendent guiding purpose had already moved them into the realms of nothingness and anti-narrative. The novel's eponym, Ronald Stark, proves that the stripping away of personality can wreck narrative stability. Like many other *noir* heroes, he doesn't know whose script he's acting or what results he's expected to bring about. Gray draws us into his plight before introducing him. The title, *A Comeback for Stark*, wins Stark some sympathy because it describes him as an underdog who's fighting back from loss and defeat. The fight will break him down; the leads and clues he unearths run into dead ends; nobody will help him find new ones. More woe awaits him. The job given him by Department 18 of the British Admiralty offers little chance of survival, let alone success. He never had reason to hope. Destroying suspense, the book's epigraph from Ben Jonson had already belittled his comeback:

> *Spies, you are lights in state,*
> *Who, when you have burnt yourselves down to the stuffe,*
> *Stinke, and are throwne away. End, faire enough.*

This gloom foreshadows Stark's immobilization at book's end, strapped to a bed, his freedom gone. Only the throbbing ache in his loins "that would accompany him to the end" (189) connects him to history and the society he had served. His future in these realms is unclear. But the closing words of *Comeback*, most of which took place in an unseasonably warm week in March, imply that he can expect the worst: "The false summer had ended and … the nip of the cold season was in the air" (190).

But what is Gray trying to prove? If the action comprising *Comeback* is anti-climactic, what's the point of reading it? In keeping with Jonson's epigraph, reminders of the thwarting of Stark come frequently. "All these secrets within secrets and who works for whom" (134), Stark hears from a senior spy who has been trying to make sense of his own days in the service. His words dovetail with those of another spy who told Stark in an earlier chapter: "Listening devices, keyholes…. You watch them, we watch you, and doubtless somebody watches us" (79). The paths of deceit where spies tread can sprout an endless regress of snooping. No spy walks in confidence. After finding himself in a trap, Stark asks his ambusher, "Who do *you* trust?" The answer he gets, "What?" (176) mocks his question. Both men are doing a job that resembles an insane footrace whose contestants keep running longer and faster towards a black hole. When Stark turned a handgun on his fellow spy to back his demand to know the identity of the spy's controller, he was answered, "You're joking, of course. I can't answer that" (175). Nor does Stark shoot the man in his crosshairs. His brother spy, who may also live next door to Stark, given his fondness for Nescafé (103–04, 175), is reminding Stark of a truth he already knows. Deskmen, or spy runners, looking to cover themselves, tell their field workers as little as possible, including their names, if they can get away with it.

Although this treachery could be fatal, it occupies a fog-belt; neither field worker nor runner knows the reason for their meeting. Neither wants to know. The spy inhabits the unseen and the unspoken; like a mystic, he hears voices, has visions, and denies the witness of his senses. Intelligence work has warped his mind. It values surmise over certainty, rumor over fact, and the unsaid over the verified. Appearances count more for him than reality. Often, in fact, an appearance, or even the whisper of one, *becomes* the reality. An agent says of an operation he has been working on, "I couldn't drop it officially because it hasn't started officially. And if I drop it unofficially, it might get started officially" (92).

With an air of insider dash, Gray has dropped us into a maze. Not only have sophistries like the speaker's kept generations of agents afloat in the network; they've also helped the network survive. And the network, like any other organism, has its survival its main business. It discredits anything that threatens it and supports whatever protects or abets it. Because facts must be faced head on, it avoids facts—even the solid one of human existence. As in Kafka, its very being calls for the sacrifice of its apparatchiks, one of whom in *Comeback* is told, "If you are caught by them, there will be trouble. If you are caught by us, you will be killed" (18).

The action of *Comeback* builds from a file that names every undercover agent posted overseas by the British Admiralty. Yet the file's creator says at book's end that the file is bogus—trumped up perhaps to deceive the Eastern Bloc. Whether or not he's telling the truth, the turmoil it has provoked caused four or five deaths already. Which is business as usual in the shadowy realm where it has taken hold. It's impossible to relax when danger is imminent. So nerve-racking is the spy's job of self-preservation that he can fall asleep midday at his office (51)—ironically, a place where he's less safe than many others.

One of the book's smartest scenes features two spymasters at lunch. Acting true to form, each tries to coax information out of the other while offering little in return. Neither loses his poise in this duel of invisible weapons. And when one of them dangles a nibble of chicken-feed, he's seeking gems he suspects are stowed in a different place altogether. To describe the feints, dodges, and maneuvers that shape this world, Gray reproduces the following chat between two of its survivors:

"I see," Hornby made a little sound like a laugh. "And to think I started it all."
"Did you?"

"I presume so."
"But you don't know what we'd been doing before you came to us. Do you?"
"You told me — "
"Whatever I like."
"*Like*? Ah, I see."
"Good."
Hornby rose to his feet. "Well, it's tremendously kind of you to put it all so lucidly" [93–4].

Emblematic of the spy's existence, reasonably enough, is the disguise or mask; only by telling lies or semi-truths through a mask can the spy hope to survive. The name of an important figure in the novel, a treacherous desk man always called "Mr." Openhouse, the deviser of the file that has caused four or five deaths, conjures up that of E[dward]. Phillips Oppenheim (1866–1946), a phenomenally prolific author of some 150 suspense novels and thrillers published between 1895–1944. Like *Comeback*, these works, the most famous of which is *The Great Impersonation* (1920), describe the effect of international intrigue upon everyday life. Following their example, *Comeback* shows a spy, while on assignment, walking down Regent Street to Piccadilly Circus, taking the tube to nearby Leicester Square, and then heading by foot toward Covent Garden. En route, he passes different sorts of Londoners on this busy Saturday afternoon. Even though presumably none of them has any idea of the spy's dark errand, some or all could be bulldozed by it.

Stark, too, his scarecrow face "white and featureless as a fish" (142), also wears a disguise, if only that of a gentleman of leisure (131). Because disguises hide the true behind the false, they help spies. One spy dresses as a beat cop to kill a Soviet agent, soon after which he speeds from the crime site on motorcycle garbed in goggles, helmet, and silk scarf. Masks come easily to him — perhaps too easily. This wide, comforting man "whose strong Scots accent … promised absolutely decent dealing" (134) will not only wear two more disguises; he'll also die clad in one of them. The melting of his make-up in a warm tube train leads to his being spotted and then shot. The mask that's standard issue for spies imperils them as it protects them.

The impersonation, great or otherwise, meant to fool others also smudges the link between the impersonator and his inner core. In another threat to its wearer, it tends to stick, making the spy even more of a stranger to himself. Stark is once accused of impersonating a policeman (73). But what if the accusation were on target? Aren't cops and spies on the same side of the law? To fool anybody, a spy's cover or disguise has to stem from his pastimes, values, and personality; the cover is a possible real-life direction for the spy. Unwatched, though, it can subsume its identity markers and take on a selfhood of its own. A stranger to himself, the agent will merge with his mask or role. That mask, first worn to deceive others, has swallowed his identity. It gets worse. McNab, the Scottish spy, shows what happens when it slides from his face.

Despite these dangers, it remains one of several items in a spy's stock-in-trade. Another consists of mastering the art of armed and unarmed combat. A spy has to protect himself. Suddenly and quickly, an agent pins Stark from behind while pretending to help him out of his coat. Even the out-of-practice Stark shakes off the rust when challenged. He binds and gags the spy Myra Harkness so deftly that only by lying perfectly still can she avoid causing herself horrific pain. Gray's bondage fetish has carried into the pride Stark takes in his handiwork: "He had reduced the woman thus, converted her from a dangerous and mysterious complication into a human bundle whose every physical position depended on his whims" (119). Yet the gloating stops. Within moments, while "shaking with shame" (120), Stark fouls himself.

Because the spy trade invites such wild reversals, it adapts smoothly to Gray's gallows humor. An overweight attacker of Stark in Chapter Six has learned how to convert the mass that usually disservices him into "a terrible weapon" (100). While that mass has immobilized Stark's arms and legs, hands are clawing Stark's groin. Recalling Lindsay Burnlow's hot smothering embraces of Grahame Thwaite in *Portia*, the attacker's arms, which "cuddled around Stark's stomach" (101), have revived the sex-death nexus so central to Gray's work. It takes new shapes in *Comeback*. Because espionage ignores humane values, an ability to spot a weakness or a flaw can gain the spy solid advantages. These outweigh theoretical intelligence work. The list grows. One agent escapes death by ignoring the tradecraft he had learned in spy academy (180). In a related operation, a spy's adherence to the dictates of tradecraft puts him in the right place exactly on cue — to die. He was doomed from the start. The colleague who speaks his epitaph notes the futility of applying standard survival tactics to fieldwork: "He [the freshly murdered spy] was stupid and clumsy. If not, he would have been at the right place at the right time, and you could have killed him. But everything he did was wrong. He followed he wrong person and got killed by the wrong man" (173).

The spy is foiled. And what *Comeback* says about the instability and fragmentation of his profession keeps his prospects dim. Joining the profession certainly won't guarantee anybody's longevity. Gray describes it as a milieu where lives cross and re-cross in a constricting web of inevitability. Spies lack the clout and know-how to pierce this web. They can only be defined in relation to shifting series of differences, which refer, in turn, to other differences in an inscrutable system. Which Gray has scrutinized; if the Special Branch mangles and crushes everything, one of its favorite tools is — the chair. Chairs in *Comeback* can be uncomfortable, fall apart when sat in, or make those sitting in them vulnerable to ambush. This common household item symbolizes Cold War heebie-jeebies. Where to turn? If we're failed by the props and supports our government has devised to protect us, we'd better clasp our handguns, as Stark does in Chapter Twelve, firmly "between his palms, as a priest holds a Bible" (169).

Gray connects the worship of violence to the capriciousness of chairs. Myra Harkness is mugged three times while sitting in a chair. Another chair, built to hold together while supporting a person, comes apart when sat in. Like a slapstick comic, Stark tumbles to the floor while sliding his coat onto the back of a chair, and, in another spot of black humor, the "hottest file of the year" (157) belonging to Department 18 skids across the floor after an agent removes it from his briefcase from a sitting position. A warning to be heeded: the empty chairs in a crowded café that surround a table next to the one at which an agent is told to sit by a colleague.

Gray's taste for the macabre also materializes a glove the slack fingers of which protrude from a coat pocket "like the tongues of dead animals" (73). Karsow, the gold-toothed owner of the coat, continues to prompt bold, disturbing imagery. Soon after leaving Mile End Road, the east London site of QMC, Gray's academic home for 18 years and the setting of *Butley*, Karsow takes a bullet "through his valuable jaw" (182). Gray has reminded us again that spying, though brutal and sordid, can produce laughs at its most lethal moments. Soon before Karsow's death, in a stroke that could have come from Conrad's *Secret Agent* (1907), the spy that Karsow is aiming a weapon at talks him into having tea. Chapter 12 shows Stark falling into a flower bed while preparing to shoot an intruder. These bits of bathos not only show Gray wresting laughter out of terror. They also divulge an absurdist's flair for incongruity. This flair enriches *Comeback*. It tells us, too, that the gun being held by the guy wearing a clown's mask can kill us.

In another incongruity, Ronald Stark evokes those American fictional characters who must get lost before they can find themselves—Ishmael's sea, Huck's river, and Dean Moriarty's open road all spring to mind. This "tall spindly man with thinning hair and long pale cheeks" (38) works for the sinister Department 18, a subsection of the Admiralty. He enters the novel in Chapter Three tailing another spy important enough to warrant both a forward cover and still another watcher to Stark's rear. Note that Stark's quarry is a gay masochist. The associations build. Department 18, where like Stark, that quarry reports, stands above a porno shop near Covent Garden, perhaps the same one whose windows Grahame Thwaite looked into on his way to Jan Trullope's. As it did with Grahame, the smut on show there shakes Stark with sadistic urges.

These urges are new. Stark's life went smash some nine years before the present-tense action of *Comeback*, and it is this wreckage from which he's trying to come back. While investigating in Dorking, a Surrey market town, south of London, he was savaged by three experts. The damage they inflicted on him proves their expertise. His groin, the object of their savagery, has been aching ever since, and his mental anguish has been so keen that he still avoids looking at the wound with which the experts left him. Yet both his battered groin and the resemblance between the nine years since Dorking and the nine months it takes a foetus to develop hint at rebirth. "I've got the nerve back" (171), Stark says. And reborn he is—but into lies and violence, a realm that puts his life expectancy on a par with those of the two men he'll kill. Nor can his partners be trusted to help him prolong this span; each one of them he meets in his daily rounds mentions Dorking within minutes of greeting him.

The vilest of these, sadly for him, is his control, the deceitful, ironically named Openhouse. Even before spending time with Stark on the page, he boasts to another deskman, "I treat him like dirt" (34). True to his words, he taunts Stark relentlessly during their first meeting. The barbs fly immediately. He puts Stark in a low, narrow, uncomfortable chair with arms so thin that an ashtray placed on them will drop to the floor, flinging ashes everywhere. Having thus flustered Stark, Openhouse also mentions his low salary, a corollary of both his unimportance and dispensability in the service. And rather than easing Stark into his new assignment, he keeps pounding him with references to Dorking.

The pounding persists. He'll even document the setting, time, weather, and physical surroundings of Stark's undoing. His aim? To crush Stark's will, to ensure his obedience, and to remind him that the same undoing awaits him if he lets Openhouse down. The message is clear. Openhouse has cast himself in the roles of rescuer, protector, and all-knowing, unforgiving chief. His words of reassurance, "I intend to stick by you to the last ditch, Ronald," (106), ring false. Having frightened Stark, he tricks him into making a mistake, after which he carefully erases from the tape player he operates from his desk the incriminating words *he* spoke to trap Stark into misspeaking himself.

Heavy lashings of sadism from colleagues harrow the book's other main figures, Myra Harkness and William Booter. The latter, holder of a "trifling job in a subsection of the Admiralty" (20) for 19 years, comes to us in the first chapter as the thrice-mentioned "plump man" (9) waiting to watch a movie about "lesbians, or male homosexual prostitutes, or gang rapes" (12). Close in temper and looks to Greene's Mr. K. in *The Confidential Agent* (1939), this "little man with a high feminine voice and protuberant eyes" (24) lacks the swagger and cool paraphernalia of James Bond. In a droll reference to Walter W. Jenkins, a senior staffer for President Lyndon Johnson who was jailed for homosexual solicitation in a public restroom, Gray gives Booter the middle name of Jenkins (15). He's reminding us that the gay Booter's susceptibility to blackmail makes him the last person the Admiralty should trust with a top-secret file—unless as the wily Openhouse implies, the file was meant to be pinched (187). Booter has been pithed. The favorite pastime of this badgered loner consists of riding around town in the womblike security of taxicabs. His favorite reading, apart from fanzines like *Gay Boy* and *He*, comes from a passage in *A Winter's Tale* that invites in his mind a comparison between male lovers to "twinn'd lambs that did frisk in the sun" (25, 188).

But even though he craves a miracle like the one that reunited after many decades of being apart a king and his queen in Shakespeare's play, he's paired off with the Soviet double agent, his co-worker, Myra Harkness. He and Myra, whom he calls "the final nightmare" (47), have been given the document compiled by Openhouse. At the meta-level, Myra represents another chapter in Gray's longstanding quarrel with another "tall, striking brunette " (111) with an athletic frame, his mother. Barbara was certainly on his mind during the writing of *Comeback*; a man in the book marries his brother's fiancée (168), as Barbara did James Gray after stealing him from her dazed sister.

It's notable that Gray made Myra a cryptologist. In a deliberate miscue, he gives her teammate Booter the homosexual preferences of Great Britain's ace decoder and suicide, Alan Turing (1912–54). Myra shrugs off the implications rising from this mismatch. Gray shows her outdoing the wicked mothers in *Colmain* and *The Late Middle Classes*, both of whom rifle through their sons' personal effects in search of covert information. The knowledge and power her decoding efforts win her prompted Gray to give her the same initials as those of the inscrutable powerbroker of *Simple People*, Maria Hodges. Myra has kept her body lean and fit from the sexual bouts she often indulges in, both voluntarily and as part of her job. Oversexed she is. Looking at gay magazines gives her an orgasm (52), and, because her companion Booter can't bonk her, she insults him and fantasizes about tearing him to pieces.

The destruction of men may be part of her deep coding. Two men die soon after bushwhacking her. In what could be a veiled warning to himself, Gray has made it clear that acts of violence against the mother elicit strong, swift punishment. To tighten this a-causal tie, Gray later describes a Baretta that will later kill Myra's would-be murderer as nestling in its owner's hand "like a woman's compact" (144). Meshing with this detail in Gray's ongoing struggles with sexual desire are the homosexuality of Myra's partner and her prospective killers' practice of grabbing her from behind; the thought of "Nubian boys ... with buttocks like teacups" (51) had already inflamed Booter.

Myra's special powers as a decoder and the grace, or luck, that helps her survive danger leap from the book's subtext. Gray has the humanity to show danger joining people. Myra and Booter spend more time together than any two other characters in the book. Yet Gray also knows that the intimacy bred by danger is fragile. His descriptions of Myra and Booter, whether they're alone or together, build to a harrowing vision of the damned. In a different world, these two could be contending for sexual partners. Myra finds Booter repulsive, and the very thought of the "vile smells" (188) beating up from the "damp gully" (163) between her legs disgusts him. It's ironic that her mother's dog is called Mandurung, which sound like Manderley, the setting of Daphne du Maurier's *Rebecca* (1938), the last century's paradigm tale of romantic suspense. No Maxim de Winter, Booter wants to strap Myra to a bed and cut off her nipples (75, 112).

Comeback unfolds in an atmosphere of malaise, a horror of hidden conspiracies that keep taking forms defined by cruelty. At times, the sexually frustrated Myra gives the impression of rushing home to get mugged. One of her abductors, in fact, makes her nipples stand up (97) and her crotch moisten with desire (98). This fusion of job with lasciviousness is typical. By putting similarity at the heart of difference, the book endorses both change and continuity. It has also joined these extremes at the raw subversive level of erotic thraldom. This "sexual thriller," labeled such by Gray in 1986 (LP xxi), slights conventional sex. Like a beheading, the fatal throttling of a spy in Chapter Three bespeaks sexual anger. It also suits the book's bitter logic. The main characters of *Comeback* number a man whose sexual capacity has been clawed out of him, a homosexual whose thrills come from XXX-rated magazines and movies, and a "nymphomasochist" (178) who, to her dismay, remains chaste during the book's week-long time span. The one married spy we meet leaves the plot in Chapter Six together with a wife who did him "a service that ... was ... under an antique law, a criminal offense" (94).

As Greene did in thrillers like *A Gun for Sale* (1936) and *The Ministry of Fear* (1943), Gray equates intimacy with danger. But his partnering Myra and Booter transforms the equation into black comedy. Seizing his chance to develop the joke, he adds a shade of darkness by showing this unlikely pair holding hands as they await their would-be assassin. Whatever promise put forth by the "summer in the air" (38) of the March day on which the action opens has guttered. *Comeback* ends with the words, the "false summer had ended at last and ... the nip of a colder season was in the air" (190).

This chill had already settled in. The book's next-to-last chapter gains speed and drive—but in a rush to the grave. Stark's boast, "I'm back, see, from Dorking" (176), takes on an unplanned meaning. He kills two people here in Chapter 12 and would have died himself had not a colleague from Department 18 materialized suddenly to save him. Such luck can't last. In a small but telling touch, it's said of one of Stark's murder victims, that "he's not official" (175). The wreckage wrought by Cold War politics cuts down those outside the intelligence network. Danger can explode anytime in the roads and streets of countries nominally at peace. No sooner will an information leak occur than word of the leak will reach the security forces of other countries. The self-canceling rhythm created by this clash of surveillance systems chills progress. It also leads to larger, more heavily financed spy networks, creating an unstable climate in which spies spend increasingly more time watching one another.

In a harsh note, the book's last chapter revives the tactic, from those warm, comforting Victorian novels of plot and anecdote, of providing a last glimpse of the major players in the story we have just read. One of these vignettes shows Openhouse and a fellow spy reviewing the case of the top-secret file over an elegant meal. The contrast between the opulence being lavished upon them and the distress of the survivors of the preceding action — Myra, Booter, and Stark — shocks us. The shock waves build when Openhouse, who will also be the last person seen in the book, lets on that the file that shed so much blood was a fraud. Gray's wrenching of the conventional guidelines of the thriller has enhanced *Comeback*. Though he does come up with the surprise ending that typifies the genre, he also puts it on a foundation of bureaucratic bungling, betrayal, and, most of all, erotic perversity. Gray has extended the parameters of the thriller. If the traditional mystery deals with rational crimes and thrillers, sick crimes, the sickness featured in *Comeback* makes the book's transfixed, protesting readers wince. This repulsiveness, it needs saying, was imagined into existence by the same man whose cosmopolitan wit would later charm theater audiences all over the English-speaking world.

Through it all, the technique of intercutting had helped Gray focus a complex pattern of shifting physical settings; the technique keeps freshening our perspective on the characters by showing them at different steps of the developing plot. The pattern itself supplies further variety. *Comeback* takes shape in a rhythm of gray, hard, mazelike streets and interiors that include featureless government offices, cafés, grubby bedsitters, and working-class homes. As he did in *Portia*, Gray will use the furniture, wall hangings, and curtains of these interior spaces to help depict their occupants.

He'll also season the book with diversity whenever his writer's instinct tells him to. In the offices where some of he action builds, his recording only one side of telephone conversation will engage our imaginations. Two notable flaws in his tight, discreetly varied narrative fabric puzzle us by occurring in the area of booze. Any alcoholic should know that the rim of a full brandy snifter, the snifter being convex, can't touch that of a wine glass without wasting the brandy. Perhaps Gray avoided brandy. In the same scene, he shows a hand "wrapped around the stem of a brandy glass" (31), an object too short to accommodate most fingers, let alone a hand.

But this is a quibble. Written mostly in a careful, moderate style, *Comeback* treats its pungent subject matter confidently and unapologetically. As he did in *Colmain* and *Simple People*, Gray stands above his characters. But his tone is less knowing, and he doesn't joke at his people's expense. If *Comeback* plays down the influence of Evelyn Waugh, it also invokes, besides Lawrence and Greene, Henry Green, and le Carré along with Dashiell Hammett and Conan Doyle. The incriminating photo used to snag Booter's cooperation in Department 18's operation (20–21) looks to "A Scandal in Bohemia," while the "gaunt yellow face (170) displayed by Stark summons up that of Sam Spade in the wrenching last chapter of *The Maltese Falcon* (1930).

The rhetoric of *Comeback* yokes this careful planning to a macabre sense of humor. While written in a mid-register prose that contrasts admirably with its corrosive subject matter, the book launches an array of bold conceits. In keeping with the astringency of this busy novel, a passenger in the London tube hangs "from a strap like a neglected fruit" (18). Moving from simile to zeugma, a character's face looks "damp from the heat of Lyons [a diner] and the fear of death" (159). Alliteration can be thematic, as well. The novel's sixth chapter shows two pairs of spies engaged in verbal combat. In line with their snakelike maneuvers, a paragraph that also includes the cluster "so much seemingly simple solidity," describes a "massive man" who's "slow and Scottish in manner" (27). Finally, a ghoulish riff tells of "a bullet [that] burst through ... [the] valuable jaw" (182) of a spy, himself stripped of value save a lifeless mouth full of gold teeth primed for harvesting.

This riff glides smoothly into a novel whose first chapter includes scenes in a porno movie house and a smut shop that includes, besides "pornographic magazines and sexual textbooks" (38), a clergyman ogling "a colored print of a naked girl of some forty-five years bent over a kitchen table for, at a guess, spanking" (39). Adding to this the seductive undies worn by Myra (94–5), the erect position she snaps into with newly moistened lips at the prospect of being raped (54), and the book's many examples of bondage fetish, it makes sense that *Comeback* was written under an alias, or mask. Gray's taking on the identity of Hamish Reade distanced him from the ugliness that clamors through the book.

The alias also screens him from William Booter, whom Gray resembles as a prowler of London's seedy streets and porno shops, an indulger of sadistic fantasies, and, perhaps, the real or imagined lover of a darkly foreign cricket star at college (19; UP 234–9). Gray had other reasons to use a pseudonym. The resemblances swathing Lopez of Westminster School, the Spanish thug who had a bullfighting magazine in his pocket when he tried to kill Stark (101), and Michael Cranton, the admirer of Lorca and Manolete who was also Grahame Thwaite's first love, all identify Gray with *Comeback*. There's more. The striking early deaths of Lepler, Stark's Spanish killer, the Spanish cricketer Lopez, whose name sounds like that of Lepler, Cranton, Lorca, and Manolete form a deathly Iberian pattern from which Gray wanted to move away. This author of a disguise-filled book disguised himself in order to publish it.

As it turned out, Gray also used the pen name of Hamish Reade to help him abandon the practice of novel writing. He might have planned it that way. His 1997 novella, *Breaking Hearts*, though packed with sadistic fantasies, was inspired mostly by his recently deceased brother, Piers. But its main figure, an alcoholic lesbian professor, confirmed Gray's resolve to scale back as subject matter the abduction, mauling, and restraining of young women. Even though these sordid materials would appear in his plays, like *Just the Three of Us* (1997), the constraints of the genre drew much of their sting. Another disincentive: Gray's mother. Myra Harkness resembled Barbara Gray in her height and body build, her sharp temper and her tendency to wear seductive clothing at home (Gray's references to Myra's erect nipples [75, 97, 112] also call to mind the erotic mother). Whatever anger toward Barbara may have smoldering in Gray in 1968 he poured into his closely detailed description of Myra's three sordid abductions. But he also made sure that two of Myra's abductors died soon after mauling her and that the third, Stark, leaves the book lying immobilized, a half-lifer.

Myra's opposite number, Booter, also reflects Gray's inner struggles. Though dead, Booter's mother, who was "sharp-witted" (20) like Barbara, still bedevils her hapless son. He claims, despite evidence to the contrary, that, had she not "deserted him before he had reached his prime," he'd have avoided the "mad and evil" ways that have been oppressing him. Yet the "curse upon her head" (113) that invades his bedtime prayers hasn't poisoned his love for her. Whether or not the homosexuality and fetishism he blames on her has roots in Gray's quarrels with Barbara, these deviations have gridlocked both mother-ridden men. The gridlock will hold. *Quartermaine's Terms* (1981) has in its cast a matricide who loses her mind.

Gray would revive the archetypal mother in *The Late Middle Classes*, which came out two years after *Breaking Hearts*. But she's handled more even-handedly, as is the predatory teacher, whom Gray gave a last name, viz., Brownlow, close to that of Grahame Thwaite's abuser in *Little Portia*, Burnlow. If *Comeback* didn't mark Gray's farewell to obsessions that were convulsing his psyche, writing the book both backed him away from these obsessions and rechanneled his creative impulses. But the process was neither smooth nor decisive. Nietzsche's sick artist, haunted by a sense of the criminal, can't shake off the morbid and shameful impulses that move his art. He wouldn't want to. His art would starve. Thus Gray continued to fuse the repulsive with the attractive. Count the fusion a half victory. No act of purgation, *A Comeback for Stark* won him a bristling page-turner that ended a phase of his career on a promising and inevitable, if not entirely healthy or happy, note. Having swallowed hard, he both knew and accepted the psychic costs of the vocation that awaited him.

Five
Nodes on a Grid

The transgressive vitality of Gray's early plays skewers the prevailing complicity between the British stage and its middle-class patrons. Though these extravagantly imagined works use different techniques and character types than those of Beckett, Osborne, and Pinter, they carry forward the radically subversive and corrosive mode of satire found in these earlier contemporaries of Gray's. Mixing humor and horror, this new theater dismantled the formalism and humanism linked with traditional satire. The erstwhile kitchen-sink school of playwrights used working-class characters, a more demotic English, and a deliberately roughened, less professional-looking acting technique to debunk both the beefy bourgeois defenders of property rights and the hierarchical social order that supported them.

Gray knew that the comedy of manners demands an abundance of ruthlessly precise details that place characters socially, economically, and even temperamentally. Yet the comedy in *Wise Child* and *Dutch Uncle* rips off its courteous masks to show us a surrealistic face. Nor is the whiff of dark absurdity in these plays lost on its fabricator. Gray saw in a 1969 production of *Twelfth Night* he reviewed for the *New Statesman* the same traces of the fury stoking his own drama-in-drag, *Wise Child*, first produced two years earlier. Mindful of the cross-dressing featured in his 1967 play, he calls the comedy spun by Viola's tie with Olivia "intensely erotic and ... dangerous" (286). It's thus no wonder that one outlandish comedy of errors follows another in Gray's play; the danger must be delayed, if not defused. His confused characters are trapped in dreams and desires that have gotten the better of them. Plotting in both *Wise Child* and *Dutch Uncle* indexes Foucault's belief that sex is a discourse forever vying with the social controls thwarting its expression. *Dutch Uncle*, with its keen awareness of the class system, borrows conceits from Joe Orton to develop Foucault's dynamic. In Orton's *What the Butler Saw* (1969), a businessman orders his secretary to undress before he gives her a medical examination. From Orton's *Entertaining Mr. Sloane* (1964) comes the sexual craving directed to a young man by two rival adults. But it's modified in *Dutch Uncle*, where the rivals aren't a brother and sister, but, rather, a husband and a policeman. In a harsh note, the object of their lust, a woman, is sexually shut down, a malaise much more prevalent among Gray's male characters than in his less jittery women.

The malaise vibrates. Portraying a culture both displaced and degraded, Gray's loony obsessions and sardonic street irony also affront social harmony, coherence, and the fixed categories of rationalism and pragmatism on which Great Britain's economic system is built. He needn't strain for the theatrical equivalent of the slit eyeball in Luis Buñuel and Salvador Dali's *Un Chien Andalou* (1929) or Marcel Duchamp's hairy Mona Lisa. His distortions rest on a Brechtian belief in the kinship between the theater and social change; plays should describe the tension between the public and the private, the whole and the part.

At issue is the rift between the world we know and the one revealed in his plays. Scenes of absurdity and cruelty that unfold in familiar, conventional contexts question the security of the world Gray's playgoers will return to after watching one of his plays. He wants to alert these playgoers to the metaphorical wrench between the cozy informality of this world and the alienating scenes they have just witnessed. His works usually begin by soft-focusing love and marriage. But loss, desolation, sorrow, and humiliation intrude quickly. Key here is Gray's sense of timing. His carefully timed intrusions provide the incandescent moments when poetry invests the mundane and deep emotion undercuts the laughter.

The Caramel Crisis, for instance, generates a compulsive vividness within a traditional framework. The action of Gray's telescript opens in a big, paternalistic manufacturing firm of 3,000 workers, several of whom have recently lost their fingers or caught their hair in the firm's loading machines. The firm that's been both dismembering and scalping its employees, ironically called Holman, is now hiring a medical specialist. What Holman should be doing instead is fitting the machines with safety devices to protect its male workers, most of whom perform "highly unskilled ... highly dangerous" (1SG 311) jobs. Manhood stays in the balance. At the outset, a candidate for the medical specialist's job has just been interviewed and rejected. The candidate's name, which is either Peenels or Rennis, may have displayed too much "cockiness" (1SG 311) for the gruffly mannish interviewer who speaks the loudest against him. Other phallic jokes dot the action. The doctor called in to treat a worker who had his thumb (itself a phallic sign) sliced off is called Dr. Leak (1SG 311). This conceit is important. It's commonly thought that Gray's iconoclasm came from Joe Orton, whose plays attack hallowed British institutions like the police, the monarchy, and the Church of England. Yet this influence might have reversed direction. A statue of Winston Churchill that loses its penis in Orton's *What the Butler Saw* suggests that its author knew *Caramel Crisis*, which came out three years earlier.

Destabilizing humor with horror, the grotesque comedies Gray wrote between 1966 and '71 use shock tactics like distortion to dismantle theatrical formalism and humanism. The absence of traditional patterns of family life in these plays portends a loss of origins and cultural roots. Alienation, impermanence and anonymity beat up from the shabby, grimy settings of *Wise Child* and *Dutch Uncle*. As in Arnold Wesker, Shelagh Delany, and Edward Bond, con men, bunko artists, and wannabees of different stripes have replaced the respectable middle class. Fragile bonds of cohesion like the two ill-advised marriages in *Dutch Uncle* and the mother-son bond improvised by a young misfit and Jock Masters, the female-clad crook he's protecting from the police, dispute the steadiness and traction healthy societies need to survive.

The agitation bristling through the traditional family setting of *Spoiled* darkens Gray's satire. The entry of a student into the home of one of his teachers spoils everything of meaning in the home. The speed with which the innocent Donald Clenham catalyzes distrust and anger between the Howarths evokes Freud's belief that civilized man has had a monster lurking inside of him since early childhood. Once awakened, the monster keeps doing its ugly, disruptive work. Donald is disarmed and then shattered by his teacher's smug cleverness and lofty sense of himself, and that teacher's family stands little chance of surviving the stain caused by his wrongdoing.

The depravity that hides behind grand concepts of how to live a good life peaks in *Butley*. When a student at QMC accuses the play's eponym of causing him a great deal of trouble, he's answered, "Trouble for you, fun for me" (B 77). Gray's cynicism often runs this deep despite his agreeing with David Hume, in principle, anyway, that people have "a faculty of sympathy" that counterweights Thomas Hobbes's belief that *"we're composed of greed and fear"* (CODA 152–3). Practice can rout principle quickly. The mad logic governing fixtures from universities to families suggests that each person's satisfaction or well-being hinges on the suffering of someone else. Hobbes has trumped Hume, what Gray portrays having negated what he claims to believe. A fascination with cruelty can seize us at any time. *Sauve qui peut*; survival in Gray basically means self-protection, which can entail putting down a colleague, neighbor, or spouse. The distress that racked Gray's displaced childhood, both at home and at school. gives this ontology both its strong kick and, with it, like Ronald Stark's aching groin, its erotic dread.

Not only do Gray's early plays differ from one another in setting, atmosphere, and emotional tone; the medical background of *Caramel Crisis* also reminds us that, though a veterinarian will appear in *After Pilkington* (1986), the only medical staffer seen at work appears in *Life Support* (1997). This inventive range enhances *Caramel Crisis*, a work whose perspective is from the top down rather than from the bottom up, as it would be in *Wise Child* and *Dutch Uncle*. Gray summarized the action of his teleplay in a 1977 interview with Ian Hamilton:

It [the play] was about this chap who bluffs his way into becoming a medical officer to a large company without any qualifications at all and then does absolutely nothing. He spends most of his time in the bath ... reading thrillers. And they [the personnel experts who hired him] become increasingly desperate as more people need his attention. And he simply refuses to emerge from the company flat he's got himself [1SG 40].

Caramel didn't have to do much bluffing. Though he calls himself Dr. J. D. Caramel, he never qualified medically, having appropriated his doctor-brother's degree along with his wardrobe after his death (1SG 318). He wins the job of medical officer at Holman's even before he says a word because two members of the firm's three-man selection team were threatened by the stronger candidates they interviewed. The team's leader, McWithers, though full of aggressive bluster, is also the most insecure of the three. His more wily, intellectually disposed colleague, Lame, who takes joy in embarrassing him, seconds the idiotic choice of Caramel. Odd man out is the team's remaining member, the quiet, independent-minded Cloon, who differs as much from his two colleagues as they do from each other.

Further proof of the play's economy stems from the way Cloon is deployed. His colleagues block his view of the door they rush to open in order to tell Caramel he has been hired. Then he's squeezed against the wall of a corridor by McWithers and Lame, while, coincidentally, also being shut out of their discussion of hiring policy. In still another meeting, he remains standing while his two colleagues sit (1SG 319). The only time these men heed his words comes after advising him against going public with Caramel's antics. In fact, the more bizarre these antics become, the more determined the men are to defend Caramel: "Indestructible man of mystery" (1SG 324) is what Lame calls Caramel after finding out that he has been ordering candies, cakes, and cigarettes at the firm's expense. When Caramel skips work, McWithers says he needed a vacation (1SG 320).

The colleague they underrate as badly as they overrate the fraudulent Caramel is the only sensible member of their group. He's also the only one who's been given a first name. Though he's decent, humane, and easygoing, this name, Dirk, meaning dagger, conveys his ability to cut through falsehood. His frequent use of the word, No (e.g., 1SG 320, 323, 324, 325) labels him a foe of the pretense, vanity, and fraud peddled by his two colleagues; he wasn't consulted about Caramel's hiring. Yet this man of quiet courage acts decisively, even after being ignored or rebuffed. Besides exposing Caramel's clownishness to the firm's boss, he even pushes Sir Roy's wheelchair to the door of Caramel's apartment.

Sir Roy can't walk. In tune with the play's anti-institutionalism, Gray makes his head of a huge, powerful company that endangers its workers a feeble old man subsisting on gruel. The play's richest, most commanding, and probably most corrupt figure, no whole man despite his kingly name, is a revolting physical wreck. Gray uses him to meet the challenge imposed by a complicated plot whose resolution requires the pinpoint timing of entrances and exits. The action's climax shows Sir Roy "*in a crazed frenzy*" (1SG 328) banging on the door of Caramel's apartment and then, after failing to see that it had been opened, diving through it to his death. Slapstick keeps promoting disaster. Shouldering Cloon aside, McWithers grabs the phone from him and calls central switchboard for a doctor. But in a plot turn that recoils on him, the operator ignores him — he himself, worried about Caramel's foolery, had previously blocked all calls from the medical flat.

If this hilarious development reflects Gray's understanding of the centricity of physical action in drama, the script's four concluding scenes display his knack for cooling down dramatic action without forfeiting excitement. These scenes show the three personnel executives behaving with their wives in a way consistent with their office demeanor. While maintaining this consistency, the scenes also point up the lack of communication between married couples. The communication is physical. His wife gives a fretful Lame some infantile coddling rather than the sex he needs to comfort him. Her harebrained suggestion that he listen to Stravinsky's cacophonous *Rite of Spring* will only intensify the cacophonies shredding his nerves. Going to the opposite extreme, McWithers, his face "*mad with triumph*" (1SG 336) climbs all over his wife, silencing her protests quickly. Cloon, the man of reason and decency, fiddles with an olive. But, belying his dagger-like first name, he's holding a spoondle. Nor does he mention sex to his wife, responding only to her worry that Sir Roy's death might leave him unemployed with the words, "I don't know, my dear" (1SG 331). As Ibsen said in the curtain line of *An Enemy of the People*, the man of purpose and resolve, ignored, devalued, even despised by his neighbors, needs to face the darkness alone.

Holman and Company's impending loss of its best worker is but one passage in the play's satire. In a Marxist note rare in Gray, the firm's 3,000 "highly unskilled" (1SG 311) laborers have been losing their fingers while doing dehumanizing work that has made them prey to "monotonous tension" (1SG 311). Nor does Sir Roy care. Both his indifference to the workers he's morally responsible to and the imminence of Cloon's dismissal from the firm hint at the collapse of British industry (so enticing is the prospect of firing Cloon to McWithers that it whets his lust). The hint has already been duly noted; because an effect has to outpace its cause, a firm run by a puny old rogue who dies within minutes of leaving his private office faces impending collapse. Only a business rotting from within would have undergone a caramel crisis to begin with, one forecast, moreover, by the entropic-sounding name of the factory's chief medical officer, Dr. Leak (1SG 311).

Gray showed his chops as a dramatist at play's opening. Knowing the importance of seizing his audience's attention at once, he borrows a trope from Ibsen's *Hedda Gabler*, Chekhov's *Cherry Orchard*, Strindberg's *Miss Julia*, and

Friedrich Dürenmatt's *The Visit* (1952)—putting on the small screen a clutch of characters who are nervously awaiting the arrival in their midst of the play's major figure. Nifty camera work sustains this apprehensiveness. A conversation between Lame and Caramel negotiated on opposite sides of a closed door (1SG 314–15) takes place with Lame out of the shot. Then a second visitor to the flat, McWithers, holds the screen by himself, again outside the flat, as he tries to get Caramel's attention. Further variety within a unified context comes from the camera's moving between both sides of the flat's door at play's end, a device that brilliantly foreshadows Sir Roy's bursting through the door to his death the second it opens. This sudden blast gathers many of the play's tensions. The mutilation of the workers at Holman has reached its inevitable peak.

Gray's decision to add four scenes to the play after the death of the play's dismemberer, rather than providing a neat, poetically just, finale, shows that the crisis induced by Caramel was one of communication. Last seen preparing to mount his terrified wife, McWithers hasn't yet fired his worthiest aide, Cloon. The opening of the door of Caramel's flat reminds us again that the only alternative to sudden death in our market economy is the slow, piecemeal one induced by the failure to communicate, both at home or on the job. Workers forced to do jobs too mind-numbing to engage their minds will keep losing body parts.

Gray's usual practice of keeping working-class characters offstage abets his satire in *Caramel*. Management's indifference to labor, symbolized at different levels by the Caramel hiring, the dismissal of Lame, and the death of Sir Roy, *could* spur a workers' riot at Holman's. The next step might be the unemployed rampaging louts, vomiting football crowds, and glass-smashing yobs of Alan Sillitoe and David Storey taking the default position given them by their uncaring chiefs and using it to finish the job of tearing down the industrial West as we know it.

Like *The Rear Column* (1978) after it, the 1967 teleplay *Sleeping Dog* shows how the seismic shocks of imperialism throw together races and belief systems and jostle families, while also wrecking long-held certainties and fostering in an obsolete old guard the compulsion to perpetuate prejudice and injustice. It attains this breadth without forfeiting artistic balance. The terrible cost of perpetuating outmoded constructs from the past comes forward in the play's first words, "Whitey, Whitey, Whitey. Here, boy"(1SG 335). The white dog belonging to Sir Hubert, a colonial magistrate, has fled into the African bush. Despite being summoned some 15 times in the play's short opening scene, Whitey remains missing. The jungle has reclaimed the dog, who was less tame and domesticated than his owner had believed. Sir Hubert later says of him, "Almost certain that a snake got him" (1SG 339). The re-emergence of a snake in Gray's other African-set play, *Rear Column* (RC 46), implies our helplessness in the face of sin in a primitive setting. Nor will the frills of civilization always distract the monster lurking within us. Sir Hubert's putative snake and Whitey's canine breed, a poodle, also recall the poodle seen briefly on a London street in *Simple People* (104) and, with it, Satan's visiting Dr. Faustus in the guise of a poodle. In *Sleeping Dog*, the white devil is Sir Hubert. Maddened by the jungle impulses that have swamped his civilized self, he'll later moan, after becoming traumatized by an atavistic mirror meeting with the African bush, "The devil. The devil" (1SG 372).

He has been blindsided by a colonial belief system that portrays natives as cowards, simpletons, and brutes. A comforting stereotype from the Victorian penny-dreadfuls would show a dashing white man rescuing a maiden from a lustful male native. Today, this outdated stereotype lacks credibility. The white meddling that breaks hearts in Conrad's "Heart of Darkness," Greene's *Burnt-Out Case* (1961), and le Carré's *Mission Song* (2006) attains a new level of distress in *Sleeping Dog*, where the native, a Barbadian whose cosmopolitanism has been shuttling him between London and New York, is also gay. His alleged crime: depicting the gin-soaked depravity of the bwana-magistrate's wife and thus pushing the luckless bwana's nose in the same primitivism that charmed Whitey into the bush. Having unconsciously absorbed the worst features of the people and the land he once lorded it over, Hubert has grown fangs. And he can't check his craving for blood.

Mindful of the "slightly Ortonish brand of outrageousness and black humor" undergirding *Sleeping Dog*, John Russell Taylor has summarized the play:

> A retired colonial administrator lures a black barman into the home in England and traps him in the cellar, where he keeps him locked like an animal, thereby recreating in microcosm the old colonial situation [that prevailed] during his career in Africa [160].

This imaginative re-creation has already stung Sir Hubert. A second reference to *Simple People*, which came out (in 1965) two years before *Sleeping Dog*, specifically the Conradian sentence, "From behind, he would have looked like a man in the middle of some unspeakable brutality" (177), portends the swamping of Sir Hubert's psyche by the African jungle. Normal traffic noises on London's streets and roads transmogrify in his mind into the screams of jungle birds. Relief lies nowhere. The ethnic and moral cacophony of Western Europe's madding cities even materializes an African-garbed man in a London office, a black man entering a cab with a white woman, and an interracial gay bar. All this leaves Sir Hubert stunned. Dazed and horrified, as well, the hapless ex-magistrate can't adapt to the codes and norms of a society where blacks have advanced themselves in ways beyond his imagining — or sense of justice.

A big step in the process by which his failure to adapt leads to a loss of self comes in the blackness of a workman who delivers a piano to Greendene, his Sussex estate. This West Indian, who holds his own chatting with Sir

Hubert, marks the invasion of blackness into this bastion of stately white elegance Sir Hubert had bought to fend off the menace of the jungle. He bought Greendene out of necessity. Despite her well-bred cosmopolitan image, his wife, Lady Caroline, has had her own problems adjusting to post-colonial England. These, she has been aggravating by gin. She's being tested more deeply than she knows. The mints she pops can't hide her alcoholic's breath any more than she and her husband of a year's standing can shrug off the omen cast by Greendene's last owner, tellingly, another drinker who kept his dog chained in the cellar of the estate.

Sir Hubert needs to shed a past that's crushing him because it weighs more heavily on him than on his wife. As plausibility decrees, this urgency leaps out quickly. The apparition of a feathered black man on his Sussex lawn tells him that his demons, brought to life by his cruelty to the natives in his charge, have joined him on his trip from Africa. Specifically, he's haunted by the remote contingency that the son of a tribesman he unjustly sentenced to death in Kijarna will know him at a glance in England and take swift, exacting revenge.

His desperation turns his eye to the Trinidadian barman in the South Kensington hotel where he and Lady Caroline put up during renovations at Greendene. Although Claud, who even occupies a basement room in the hotel where he works, rarely goes far, Sir Hubert fancies him a rover. In fact this driver of a Rover (1SG 376) calls him a rover during their first conversation (1SG 353). Belying his nickname, Claud had already become a sitting target for Hubert's madness. He has been serving to Lady Caroline large goes of the gin that has been poisoning both her marriage and her spleen. What snaps her husband's mind and throws his malice into high gear, though, is his discovery of a belittling sketch Claud did of her. In an echo of Sherwood Anderson's *Dark Laughter* (1925), Claud's native wisdom has come forth in his sketch, an act of judgment if not also a source of power, in Sir Hubert's eyes. This power he sees as erotic. A scene later in the telescript, which takes place at Greendene, opens with "*a close-up of an African face, laughing, as much like Claud's as possible*" (1SG 398). In an earlier scene, Sir Hubert had imagined Claud's hands multiplying themselves while darting blackly "*everywhere*" (1SG 371) under Lady Caroline's dress. Sir Hubert's imagination is crushing him. As usual, unchecked power in Gray will take the form of masochism parading as sexual domination. "Did you take her at night, when I was asleep...? Did you *laugh* at me as I kept my watch?" (1SG 388) he will later ask a chained, starving Claud. His cruelty focuses on his obsession, which, like any other, turns inward. When Claud tells him to ask his wife if anything improper went on between him and her, he shocks Sir Hubert into silence, such candor having no place in his private fantasy. (All the major figures in *Sleeping Dog* have something to hide, including the gay Sir Geoffrey, a friend from Sir Hubert's colonial past.)

The abduction motif that drives so much of Gray's work has taken an alarming twist. Light years away from the voluptuous, pristine-looking white virgins on the covers of the Hank Janson paperbacks of Gray's youth, the chained victim in *Sleeping Dog* is a gay black man. Does he deserve his chains? Besides having abetted Lady Caroline's drinking problem, he has also exposed her ugliness with a few pencil strokes, and, with them, the regret that has been piercing Sir Hubert since he married her; the two, though relative newlyweds, sleep in different rooms. Misery wears Sir Hubert. If Claud has taken Lady Caroline's measure so effortlessly, what has he divined about *him*? As a black man, Claud might have discerned the cruelty Sir Hubert inflicted upon his African brothers, reason enough to keep him shackled.

In an allusion to the mints Gray's alcoholic grandmother popped in those days when she'd wrestle a sexually provoked Simon to her breasts, Sir Hubert imagines his wife having been spellbound by Claud's jungle allure. In fact, he'll starve Claud until he recounts in detail his non-existent visits to Lady Caroline's bedroom. He has not only recast Claud in the role of ex-gridiron star Jim Brown's black super-stud: to soothe his heartache, he's also frantically searching for at least one man who finds his wife attractive, even if he has to create him. His sessions in the dungeon with Claud have curbed still more the freedom of both men. At the gala that climaxes the action, Lady Caroline is not drinking. Claud's abduction, which she now participates in, has removed her need for gin. So Claud will stay put, lest she reach for the bottle. The New York where he planned to settle remains more unreachable to him than Moscow did to Chekhov's three sisters.

Sir Hubert has paid too much for his wife's sobriety. He replaced his lost dog Whitey with a black man whom, like Whitey, he calls "sir" (1SG 336, 382). The dog motif doesn't stop here. Sir Hubert keeps Claud in the same cellar where Greendene's last owner chained his Alsatian, or German Shepherd. But Claud's sketches and the expertise with which he plays Lady Caroline's piano before he's lured into the basement both prove that he's neither a dog nor a member of a lowly race. This truth Sir Hubert knows. But, warped by the abuse he heaped upon his former African charges, he lacks the humanity to free Claud and thus himself.

The play's title refers to Whitey, the sleeping or missing dog Sir Hubert should let lie in order to move his life forward. Burying the wrongs and sorrows of the past remains the best way to quash our fascination with cruelty. The symmetry of the play's design tallies Sir Hubert's failure. This wretch who opened the action with the words, "Whitey, Whitey. Here, boy" (1SG 335), will later cry out in the cellar where he has stowed Claud, "Boy, Claud.... Nigger. Blackie, Black-ie" (1SG 380). But the analogy weakens, as most do when the human heart is involved. He hasn't abducted Claud to make up for the loss of Whitey. His obsession, lodged in his psyche, now owns him. It will retain its grip. The many parrot sounds, both realistic and imagined into existence by him (e.g., 1SG 335), convey this rigor. Nor can he wash away his guilt (1SG 386).

His attempts to wash, purge or, shed his torment, though, give *Sleeping Dog* a psychological bite lacking in *Caramel Crisis*. For instance, the pain he suffers knowing that he can't resist the act of cruelty he's about to visit on Claud (1SG 347) has no counterpart in the earlier telescript. "Let madness in and justice out?" (1SG 372) he asks rhetorically, his face wet with tears. Much of the horror of *Sleeping Dog* lies in the speed with which brutality engenders in us the panic of not knowing who we are. Sir Hubert has lost the power of choice. Shredded by his shameful African past, he feels stalked and mocked. He's also carrying this burden in alien ground. The enfranchisement that blacks have won in the social mosaic that has replaced the public-school hierarchy of the past — some of the guests at the party he throws at the end are black — has traumatized him.

It gets worse. He knows that not even an act of the vilest inhumanity can restore his peace. Claud, his dungeon prisoner, invokes the minotaur, whose underground lair in this palace of Knossos bespeaks the corrupt foundation of King Minos's court. No, Claud isn't the beastlike offspring of Lady Caroline, as Minotaurus was that of Queen Pasiphaë. But he needn't be. The play's many mirrors (e.g. 1SB 351), a staple of TV drama since Rod Serling's *Twilight Zone* series (1959–64), often put on view people other than the ones looking into them. This visual trope supplies more than decoration. The array of mirror images in the script helps convey its interdependence theme. In our new post-electronic society (which also happens to be post-colonial), where, said Marshall McLuhan (1911–80), the media theorist whose popularity may have peaked in 1967, everything happens everywhere all at once; we participate in each other. The play's bonding patterns, which include people of different ages, races, and social classes, form a mosaic (another of McLuhan's best-known terms) of the kind that has displaced the old linear hierarchy. Well-mannered scions of established families now depend on people of color for life's essentials. A black man paints and carpenters Greendene before Sir Hubert and Lady Caroline can move in. Another brings her piano into the house. Still another, viz., Claud, serves her the gin she needs to shun the throes of withdrawal anxiety.

This same black man, whose sketches portray the decadence of the old guard, perhaps best understands the malaise plaguing his fast-changing society. The sexual depravity caught in his sketches of Lady Caroline and Sir Geoffrey awoke in Sir Hubert the sexual fear and resentment that prodded him to kidnap Claud. As is always the case in Gray, bondage and domination refer to sex. But even though Claud, who finds truth in distortion, like Stravinsky and Picasso, has mapped this erotic nightmare, his work will lack an audience. The real-estate agent Greatorix, who sold the couple their new home, *does* overhear Sir Hubert talking to Claud. But his calling Lady Caroline Lady

Harriet (1SG 394) shows his salesman's post-sale indifference to life at Greendene.

Herein lies the tragedy that has been developing. The artist has seen the denial of change overriding our scruples regarding sex, race, and politics. But because he has targeted this inconvenient truth, he must suffer, like Joyce's archetypal artist. Meanwhile his work goes ignored. Our interrelatedness makes this loss of his gifts a blow to us all. In this vein, Sir Geoffrey delivers what he calls "his favourite domestic moral": "The dog's the master, the master's the servant" (1SG 399). In a later play that also gauges the social upheavals caused by war, *The Late Middle Classes* (1999), another elderly sexual deviate will say, "Who can say whether the man is playing with the cat or the cat is playing with the man" (25).

Perhaps those out of society's mainstream best understand the global village in which we live; Ralph Ellison's nameless hero in *Invisible Man* (1952) points out that black people already share in a society that has been trying to shut them out. America's disenfranchised blacks also know that this mutuality includes the animals. But like any other social code or set of laws, it can be corrupted. By giving Claud a dog-like name, Rover (1SG 399), and treating him like a dog, Sir Hubert has made himself such a social renegade that cruelty soon overcomes him. He's dying on the inside because, unable to let sleeping dogs lie, he'd like to incarcerate *all* black Africans. In this blanket catch of convicts belongs Claud; no matter that he's Barbadian.

Where will this racist brutality end? Sir Hubert's caving-in to the temptations that came with his colonial magistrate's job makes us imagine the worst, as did the finale of *Caramel Crisis*. Much of the power of *Sleeping Dog* stems from Gray's implication in the mirror imagery so central to the play. Like Claud, he's a transatlantic traveler-cum-artist fixated upon the intensities bred by confinement, beginning with his grandmother's lap, and deviant sexuality. This fixation damaged Gray. But it also helped him master the technical advantages that television has over the stage play. Shrewd camera work in *Sleeping Dog* cooperates with a fine script to link power with sexual domination and control. The long sinister looks Sir Hubert sends Claud while he's mixing drinks (e.g. 1SG 345, 348), for instance, foretells the barman's abduction.

The Simon Gray of *Sleeping Dog* isn't sticking up for those who can't speak for themselves or who wouldn't get a fair hearing if they did. He's hunting bigger game. Even the emerging, or new, democracies can't devise laws that will tame humanity's vilest features. The vileness bound up with our inner beings decrees that one person's welfare feeds on the distress of others. So strong is this impulse that, besides razing neighborhoods and cities, it also poses enticements that very few power brokers of any stripe can resist.

The cancer gains force quickly. The failure or inability of most citizens to know how well or how badly their leaders are performing invites political corruption. These leaders, aware of the gulf between policies needed to cement their power and those that serve the common good, lack incentives to provide good government.

A concern with the primordial roots of politics seeps into *Wise Child*. A down-at-heels Londoner in this, Gray's first stage play (FC 69), calls himself and his countrymen "the beggars of Europe" (1SG 90). He's unconsciously referring to his nation's loss of its colonies, the backwardness of its industrial system, and the fitfulness of both the Butler Education Act of 1946, which opened Britain's universities to working class students, and the National Health Service, implemented since 1948, to vitalize British society. He also has somewhere in mind his society's housing problem, a topic dramatized in Gray's fellow Cantab John Arden's *Live Like Pigs* (1958) and Gray's *Pig in a Poke* (1969). These works showed, respectively, voiceless, disregarded Britons living in poverty and humiliation and, from a different angle, the need to rewrite laws protecting squatters. The efforts of a rich London couple in Gray's play to dislodge their sitting tenant from their home only entrenches him there more firmly.

Wise Child (1969) takes place in Reading, Berkshire. Though 30 miles from London, Reading has recently been attracting derelicts and castaways. Gray shows why. Two crooks on the lam have set down in a seedy Reading hotel. They've lied twice to the hotel's manager: they're waiting for the builders to finish working on their future home, and they mistook the hotel for another, where they had booked rooms, because of the similarity of their names. If the hotel where chance has landed them resembles its surroundings, then Reading bears signs of age, wear, and neglect, making it exactly the kind of place where scavenger birds would light down. This sad phenomenon is not unusual. A black West Indian in the play's cast of four describes both the ethnic and racial cacophony of England's madding cities and towns. Like *Sleeping Dog* before it, *Wise Child* falls short of protesting the plight of the disenfranchised who live in poverty and shame. No spokesman for political or economic change, Gray describes the efforts of his people to survive on the outpost or fringe where fate has dropped them.

Their low expectations in line with their low job qualifications, they meet in the grubby lodgings of a hotel that, if not closed altogether, is under renovation. Robert Gordon, writing in 1992, put both *Wise Child* and the next work Gray wrote for the London stage, *Dutch Uncle* (1969), much closer in spirit to the plays of Joe Orton than to those of Brecht or Pinter when he cited their "black humor, contrived plotting, and ... sensationalistic use of transvestitism" (Burkman, ed. 3–4). Gordon judged well. From Orton's *Entertaining Mr. Sloane* come the hairpiece or wig, the motif of stowing an elder in an old person's home (which also appears in Edward Albee's *American Dream* [1960] and Terrence McNally's *And Things That Go Bump in the Night* [1964]), the rooming house where the action takes place that's also a defrocked or deconsecrated church, and an eponym who lives from hand to mouth. *Wise Child* hums along with the raucous glee of Orton's black comedy. Its bustle is also carefully monitored. Characters both enter and exit from either side of a split stage that puts on view hand-to-hand fighting, a striptease act, and some patchwork rituals evocative of the theater of cruelty.

These motifs jostle any sentimental ideas the play's bourgeois audiences might have been nurturing about healthy suburban family life. But *Wise Child* isn't cheaply cynical. Catalyzed by crisis, fragile bonds are improvised in the play, but, because most of its lonely, badgered people are slow extending trust, the bonds develop warily. Distractions and deviations like gay and intergenerational sex, miscegenation and cross-dressing, make us marvel that they develop at all. Add to this list of disincentives that of multinimity. Someone who uses an alias is hiding, not reaching out to others. Multinimity, like anonymity, also implies rootlessness, a bugbear to the young black West Indian chambermaid, Janice, who's forced into the role of bottomdog amid underdogs, i.e., those whose many setbacks prod them to lash out at their supposed inferiors. Any time is ripe for an assault in this pecking order. Each of the play's three other characters call her "nigger" and "animal" (e.g., 1SG 77, 134). But even an assault is a form of bonding. At final curtain, Janice remains thousands of miles from her tropical home and, locked in a cellar without food, unlikely to see it again.

The action opens several days after the professional thief Jock Masters meets Garfield, or Jerry, Artminster in a *louche* diner. Masters has been hiding out. His younger partner in crime, one Derek Stewbat, was caught and jailed after cudgeling a postman he and Masters had robbed. Masters is now wanted in nine counties. Spotting him immediately as a fugitive, Jerry, who's about 17 or 18, gives him a choice. He can either join Jerry or be turned over to the police. Understanding that he has no choice at all, he accompanies Jerry to his room in a building near Queen Mary College, located "behind the Mile End Tube" (1SG 145). What he finds there rattles him — a closet full of women's clothes, cosmetics, and a wig. He has met, to his astonishment, someone needier than himself.

"It was like he'd been waiting" (1SG 141), Masters recalls of this mirror meeting. And everything that follows the meeting tells him that Jerry, having found him, will fight to keep him. Masters has also assessed accurately the limited freedom imposed on him by Jerry. A week or two later, togged as a woman, he's splayed out on the lobby floor of Reading's Southern Hotel, presumably the victim of a fainting fit, or worse. His con works. The hotel manager, Simon Booker, offers Jerry and his mother a room until she mends.

A month later (1SG 81), which is when the play opens, Booker has made it clear that he wants to sleep with Jerry. His lust builds. Still reeling from the loss of a departed lover, a priest who was defrocked and shipped to Canada, he resembles Claud of *Sleeping Dog* in having a boyfriend in the new world he'll never see again. But the boyfriend's schooling has stuck. Simon Booker, whose age, body build, and eroticism all hark to Simon Booter of *A Comeback for Stark*, has conflated sex and religion. He has even set aside a room in the hotel where, amid a raft of religious paraphernalia and talk, he services his young men.

The person called Mrs. Artminster in Gray's stage directions feels divided about Booker's hotel. Though she frets about being confined, she also needs time to plan her next move. Nor does she mind strategizing in comfortable surroundings while the trail to her cools. Fearing that she and Jerry will soon be kicked into the street, she encourages her "son" to sleep with Booker. Jerry refuses, just as he'll snub the sexual overtures of Janice. The filial love this orphan directs to Mrs. Artminster is the only kind he's capable of. The end of Act Two of *Wise Child* shows him nestling in her arms as he purrs in "*a muffled, contented voice,* 'Mum'" 1SG 126).

As Samuel Beckett did with his two bums in *Godot* (1952), Gray, careful not to trivialize the split, comes up just short of making Jerry and Mrs. Artminster opposite halves of a mind-body dualism. The more physically disposed Mrs. Artminster follows Beckett's Estragon, or Gogo, by grousing early in the play about the pains in her feet (1SG 75). This big eater who takes care with her appearance also complains about the clumsiness of her fingers while trying to remove Janice's earrings. She becomes like a stallion when, minutes later, tipsy with the Scotch she had also tricked Janice into drinking, the housemaid starts to do a striptease.

Gray develops this conceit. Mrs. Artminster later notices that her body is wearing down. At 53, she asks, "Where have my muscles gone ... and why don't I have instincts?" (1SG 118). These worries are genuine. Like any pro whose survival calls for a bygone physical adroitness, she wails, "I'm lost to myself" (1SG 133). The only life she knows, that of a crook, is slipping away from her. Her accomplice has been arrested. Extended confinement looms before *her*, too, either in jail or in Booker's hotel. "I'm dying for my lack of freedom" (1SG 141), she tells Jerry, pondering a bolt. Her words merit attention. In a development as rare in fiction as it is in life, it's the older partner who wants to ditch the younger one.

But can the body exist without the mind or spirit? Jerry, who's barely connected to the physical world, sees Mrs. Artminster falling afoul of the police as soon as she leaves the hotel (1SG 142, 146). His worries make sense. In Artminster, he found the mother he had spent many bleak nights in an East End gangsters' haunt waiting for, a mother he can bond with physically. Having found her, he connives to keep her, buying her liquor, inventing rituals as bonding points, and offering her a first-class train ticket should she let him join her when she decides to flee Reading.

There's evidence to back Artminster's claim that she can outwit the police. Whereas Jerry is never seen eating, Artminster loves her food and, even more dangerously, her drink. A legacy from Dickens, her hearty appetite and gamy language (1SG 39) bespeak a rage for raw, rude vitality found in criminals. But not too rude and raw; posing as a fashion magazine consultant, she dupes Janice into baring her breasts. Though frantic with desire, she rejects rank animal possession. She tells Janice to undress slowly and with a ladylike grace rather than charging her. This restraint typifies her. Having lived by her wits for decades has taught her to avoid impulsiveness. The tradecraft she imparted by slow stages to her young sidekick Derek helped bring about 27 successful heists. And now she's confident that, despite Derek's arrest, she won't be snitched.

She has the savvy to avoid the slammer, unless she fouls it with her alcoholism, a bequest from Gray's grandmother, who'd have been about the same age with the same body-build as Artminster during her bundling heyday with young Simon. But Artminster was sober when, spotting a chance to rest, she faked a fainting spell in the lounge of Reading's Southern Hotel. She extends this period of rest by, Iago-like, encouraging Simon Booker that, appearances to he contrary, Jerry's interest in him is warming. Having also read Jerry's psyche accurately, she builds up the youth's dependence on her, calling him "son" (1SG 99), asking him for a kiss in Booker's presence, and cuddling him when the two are alone (1SG 126).

Gray disallows any simple moral response to her. This racist who accuses "the nigger" (1SG 113) of stealing the whisky bottle she herself nicked from Booker's hoard has learned quickly how to exploit Jerry's dependence upon her. Specifically, she has been using the strategy of intermittent reinforcement. While referring often to Derek's thuggish masculinity, she also tries to convince Jerry of Booker's merits. She has to. Time is shortening for the two frauds, and Booker's lust for Jerry is the sole reason they're still at the hotel. Her sham cuts two ways. Besides pimping Jerry to Booker, she also plays the role of indignant mother, threatening to blackmail Booker for £200, which she'll use to re-boot her life. When Booker dies, Artminster, ever the opportunist, puts on his man's garb and sets about cracking his safe, a job she had already talked about doing several times.

But she still has to deal with Jerry. To defuse Jerry's threat that he'll snitch her to the police if she tries to decamp, Artminster reveals at play's end both her crimes and her identity to Booker. Weary of games and disguises, she has reclaimed her identity as Jock Masters. Or so she thinks. By addressing Booker, she confesses, not to a priest, but to the ex-lover of a priest. She needn't have confessed, to begin with. The purity of Jerry's love, which she hadn't fathomed, would have stopped him from betraying her. Always a force, it resurfaces quickly. No sooner has Artminster togged herself in Booker's clothes than Jerry puts on the dress Janice had left behind after her striptease act.

He transacts the double gender switch without missing a beat. He has reshaped the bogus mother-son bond we've been witnessing into a father-daughter one, no less bogus, but equally heartfelt. This dazzling theatrical trope focuses the tensions leading up to it. Gray had already conveyed the religious intensity of Jerry's need to keep Artminster at his side. Just before the close of Act One, Jerry swabs the same feet the stink of which repulsed him at play's outset (1SG 100, 75).

Any appraisal of the couple's chances to stay together must account for Jerry's accidental killing of Booker. Up to this point, it was clear that Jerry stood for the mind or spirit in an approximate mind-body dualism in which the descendentally disposed Artminster bespoke the body. But to Jerry's dismay, the wish to refine himself out of existence has recoiled on him. Enacting a brilliant conceit on Gray's part, he believes that, unless he moves with the utmost care, his glass-like bones will break, shredding his insides. It's no wonder that, in Artminster's words, he walks "like spiders" (1SG 80). He can't risk falling or stumbling into things. According to Gray's metaphysics, his dread adds up; denoting our imperfection, or distance from God in his work, has always been our inbred tendency to bump or fall into things.

Gray's preoccupation with human contingency has taken a macabre twist. Like a Manichean, the reed-like Jerry has been trying to suppress or deny his physical tie with the world. Not only does the prospect of having sex with Janice repel him as much as that of sleeping with Booker; he has also devised a version of the rock-scissors-paper game that guarantees his loss. The ritual status he has conferred on the game forms a ready bonding point between him and Artminster. Of equal or greater consequence is the pain he absorbs with each of Artminster's whacks across his hands. Thus he achieves two goals by proposing a game at those times when a wrought-up Artminster needs to release her anxieties.

An implied comparison to the detachment with which Joyce's Stephen Dedalus reacts to *his* aching swollen hands after being pandied in *A Portrait* credits Jerry's inventive powers. Which he puts to good use elsewhere: Artminster admires the "brains" (1SG 87) and the "cleverness" (1SG 116) behind his scam to fund their partnership. As a special treat to us, Gray shows Jerry rehearsing the scam both to enforce his compulsion with ritual and to provide a first-hand view of his inventiveness. This denizen of employment offices knows that he can't collect carfare if he rejects any job offered him. This problem he solves by blocking beforehand any possibility of getting hired. He shows up at his job interviews wearing a long black wig. If the wig fails to dissuade the interviewer, Jerry makes himself so obnoxious that he'll have pressed upon him more money than the law entitles him to leave the office. During his week at the Southern alone, he has already scammed £30 (1SG 117). That's all he'll pocket for now. Realizing that the news of his dodge will soon leak to Reading's business community, he'll be taking it elsewhere.

He talked his way out of a job paying a sweet £20 a week because taking it would have also taken Artminster from his view longer than he'd like. He knows that even though her fear of being arrested like Derek has grounded her for now, her growing restlessness might speed her away. Hence the play's title. *Wise Child* doesn't only re-site frail, delicate Jerry as the rough mental equivalent of a mind-body dualism. It also targets his resolve to heal this split by forming a single entity with Artminster, his Jungian other self. Building and sustaining this entity has become a metaphysical necessity for him. If putting on Booker's clothes makes Artminster a man, Janice's forgotten clothes will reverse *his* sexual orientation just as fast.

"A wise son heareth the doctrine of his father," it's said in Proverbs 13: 1. Jerry, lacking a father, must listen to his heart. As his own father, this orphan has reached out to the comforting mother figure whose protectiveness will build his bones. Artminster's words to him in Act One, "It's a wise boy that knows his own," bolster his determination, as his answer to Artminster shows: "Well, I know my own mum all right, don't I, on account of the police of nine counties would help me find her if she was ever lost to me. Wouldn't they?" (81). So great is Jerry's need for the redemption she embodies to him that he'll blackmail her to secure it.

Artminster can shrug off his blackmail threat more easily than Jerry can dismiss her efforts to put him in the bed of Simon Booker, a man with antecedents. Booker's plan to hire Jerry as his desk clerk looks back to another middle-aged gay man who made the title figure of Orton's *Entertaining Mr. Sloane* his chauffeur. Booker's clumsiness also outdoes that of his earlier self, the plump homosexual, William Booter in *Comeback*. It's more costly, too. His inability to avoid walking into things and knocking them over offends the epicene Jerry. An undaunted Booker's lust for Jerry, meanwhile, keeps building suspense. Though Booker has exposed the lie that allegedly brought Jerry and Artminster to his hotel, he's also willing to forgive it if Jerry closes with him. Jerry's continued resistance to his blandishments, though, is wearing down Booker's patience. Even paying Artminster £200 for the boy, he fears, won't get the boy into his bed.

He's right. Gray has all along been equating the bad eyes, or near blindness, that keeps bumping him into things with homosexuality. Artminster insists that Jerry could tolerate Booker's attentions in just these terms: "You could keep your eyes shut" (1SG 118). But his insistence can't quash Jerry's objections, which are couched in the same vein: "Eyes! He [Booker] hasn't any eyes. That's double-glass in those spectacles of his" (1SG 76). Minutes before killing Booker, Jerry, who had earlier turned down his movie invitation by saying of movies that "they hurt my eyes" (1SG 94), calls the hotel manager "homo-blindie" (1SG 140).

The slur hits home, drawing from Booker a mantra of self-pity. At a different level, Booker's poor eyesight lines up thematically with his misjudgment. He overrates his chances to get Jerry into bed, believes Artminster to be a woman, and gets it wrong by calling Janice a "slut" (1SG 141). Of all the blocked characters in the play, he suffers the most. Harking to the mind-body dualism that shapes Gray's portrayal of Artminster and Jerry, his most dangerous failing lies in his practice of fusing sex and religious worship (1SG 106). His calling his priest-lover "one who could stand straighter and pour himself ... fully into those he loved" (1SG 107) registers his fervor to reconcile body and mind, an act of pride that dictates his downfall. God has chosen Jerry as His instrument to punish Booker for trying to usurp the divine prerogative.

His death was prefigured. *Wise Child* bristles with images heartbreaking, nightmarish, even demonic. Tempering this anarchy, though, is a slew of conventions drawn from that most jaunty and agile sub-genre, the well-made play. Moving the complicated plot, building suspense, and keeping the laughs coming in *Wise Child* is a series of precisely timed entrances and exits ordained by the necessity to withhold the secret of Artminster's identity until the end. *Wise Child* also deploys from the school of Eugène Scribe and Victorien Sardou the contrivance of *quid-pro-quo* basic to the genre. The following passage shows Artminster and Booker exchanging witty one-liners with all the aplomb of two people in what is perhaps the best-known example of the well-made play, Georges Feydeau's 1907 *A Flea in His Ear*.

MR BOOKER: Modesty is what I need at the desk.... *She's* no Garfield.
MRS ARTMINSTER: Who?
MR BOOKER: Janice.
MRS ARTMINSTER: Who said she was?
MR BOOKER: I said she *wasn't*.
MRS ARTMINSTER: Why?
MR BOOKER: Well she isn't is she? I was comparing her to Garfield in quietness.
MRS ARTMINSTER: What's he got to do with it?
MR BOOKER: He's quiet.
MRS ARTMINSTER: Who said he wasn't?
MR BOOKER: I didn't.

Matching scenes build from this banter at the end of Act Two when Janice's "*gauchely erotic*" (1SB 125) dance quickens Artminster's lust while in the room next door, which is also in view, Booker is trying to seduce Jerry. Booker's subsequent death provokes a mirror meeting in the stunning reversal that caps the play. Reworking the mistaken-identity trope from the well-made play, Gray shows Jerry and Artminster both clad in gender-based garb opposite to what they had been wearing up to this moment.

Rivaling and then muting the laughter caused by this sartorial switch is our recognition of why it's in the play. As poignant as it is funny, the ending of *Wise Child* rescues it from the artifice and triteness of the sub-genre from which Gray has been borrowing to develop his plot. Jerry and Artminster have been launched into a state of uncertainty that bucks the conventional climax of the well-made play, in which the concluding reversal *improves* the hero's fortunes.

Like *Godot*, Harold Pinter's *Dumb Waiter* (1959), and Sam Shepard's *True West* (1980), *Wise Child* ends at the moment when all the tensions generated by the foregoing action are poised to erupt. Artminster/Masters has been marshaling evidence to justify his leave-taking from Jerry. But after a long silence, he's still onstage, staring at Jerry without moving.

Unwatched and under their own steam, the roles they have been playing now claim a life of their own. Defying traditional guidelines and loyalties, *Wise Child* builds its own sub-text. Only at the end does the identity between what has been said and what has been thought dovetail. The play we had been watching and laughing at, we see for the first time — which is also the right time — *is* the same one that was developing. A real parent-child tie has formed. Hewing to a psychologically realistic rhythm, Jerry and Artminster had gotten fed up with each other, resented, lost their temper, and even threatened each other — within a fabric of forgiveness, acceptance, and protectiveness.

This nurture sometimes reflects their shared understanding that ritual confirms our security both about ourselves and our place in the world. Jerry has read Artminster's psychological needs accurately enough to propose a game of rock-scissors-paper when he needs comforting; at other times, keeping *her* inner demons at bay, he'll bring home a bottle of Scotch. Such acts of kindness touch her heart. As deceitful and scheming as Artminster has been, she has opened up to Jerry. Her immobility at final curtain stems from her appreciation of a co-dependency that has been gaining force for weeks. Appalled, she's facing for the first time the difficulty she'll have walking away from Jerry. We're appalled, too, faced with the question Gray has been priming us to ask: to stay together, can Artminster and Jerry perform the feat of turning their mother-son connection into a father-daughter one?

The play's artistry gives the question bounce. Relying on his knowledge that a stage play needs to use resources besides dialogue, Gray splashes the stage with costumes, an array of synchronized exits and entrances, a fight, and an impromptu striptease act. His stagecraft serves him well. To foreshadow the two-way sartorial switch at the end, he puts Janice onstage in a man's dressing gown. Finally, taking the device of delayed exposition as far as the text permits, he waits until minutes before the close to supply the background data the audience needs to savor the play's finale. It's here that Artminster explains the helplessness she felt during her meeting with Jerry: "It was like he had been waiting" (1SG 145), she says rightly of the aura of decisiveness, resolve, and need he projected while approaching her.

It's vital that Artminster gives this speech, her longest and most thematic in the play, while dressed and coiffed like a woman. This blend of costume and speech underscores Gray's intent that she be responded to as a woman. He had been both inviting and discouraging this response from the start. And even before the start; any audience member could see in the playbill, or program, that the role of Artminster was being played by a man. Readers are given this same information (1SG 72) in addition to seeing Artminster cited in all the stage directions, until the play's final page, with the feminine pronoun. Gray had put us on alert. The very absence of the mystification and misdirection we've been awaiting keeps us riveted. While puzzling over the shock that awaits us, we watch the Artminster simulation with rising amazement.

Unless a director wants the simulation played for laughs, the actor doing it should study the art of the onnagata. In this fixture from Japan's kabuki theater, the male actor distances his female role, taking care to avoid dissolving into it. Tradition demands that we witness onstage a man impersonating a woman. This enactment of the Artminster role not only works best; Jock Masters's long career also makes it the most realistic. His struggles in the criminal underground, including having to elude the police, precludes a feminizing of the role. The daintiness and the fragility of Jerry calls for an offsider with queenly brawn. Nor is there any place for camp. Artminster's words to Jerry grate on us all the more for coming from a man in drag he always calls "mum" (e.g., 1SG 126). The dialogue Gray wrote for Artminster hones this edge, an example being her words of praise for Derek's sexual prowess, which she always voices at Jerry's expense: "He'd have their skirts up and their panties down as soon as look at them" (1SG 81). Finally, the pressure established by Artminster's femininity and garb gives her cigar-smoking and, more astonishingly, her agony of lust as a bare-breasted Janice gyrates in front of him a goofy flamboyance that any actor would prize.

And whom better to grace this gift with than the world-class comic actor Alec Guinness, who had already excelled in drag acting in the movies *Kind Hearts and Coronets* (1949) and *The Comedians* (1966). A sure-fire formula for success had been concocted. Defying expectation, though, this brew of superb acting and a vivid, deftly nuanced script flopped. The 1967 London production of *Wise Child* closed quickly, as did its 1972 New York counterpart, despite Donald Pleasence's dominance as Artminster (<http://www.pleasance.com/theatre/wchild-1.html; 1 April 2009>). Gray knew in 1967 that the English-speaking stage didn't need a revival of *Charley's Aunt* (1892). He slipped up in his guess that audiences on Broadway and London's West End would welcome a brew of frolic and menace stirred up by cross-dressing.

A risk-taker he'd stay. Undeterred by the box-office flop of *Wise Child*, he tested anew in his next stage play, *Dutch Uncle*, the resistance of Anglophone theatergoers to deviant bonding. He did it, too, with his usual attentiveness to nuance and context. The first sentence of his stage directions tells us that *Dutch Uncle* is set in 1952 (1SG 157), the woes of which were still fresh in the minds of many of London's 1969 playgoers. The ending of post-war food rationing in 1952, a long seven years after Nazi Germany's fall, hints at the privation and pain blocking the UK's plod toward pre-war economic prosperity. Vestiges of bomb damage from the Blitz also told of shortages in building materials. Like many of London's bombed-out office blocks, some of its pre-war residential buildings remained holes in cracking, weed-infested pavement. In addition, eyesores that should have been razed years earlier, like the "*decaying house in Shepherd's Bush*" (1SG 151) where *Dutch Uncle* unfolds, disfigured streets all over London.

Popular everywhere, perhaps as means of escape from this ugliness, were murder mysteries. Agatha Christie's *The Mousetrap* began its marathon run at the Ambassador Theatre in 1952, and the notorious Christie murder case (no connection), which later helped abolish capital punishment in the UK, first won public attention the same year. The case might have also stirred in Gray a flair for domestic murder that would surface in *Molly* (1977), *Stage Struck* (1979), and *After Pilkington* (1986). *Dutch Uncle*, which would include in its cast two members of the London police, begins as a foray into this sub-genre. At curtain rise, a man is fitting a gas cylinder with a rubber tube that he then feeds into a hole in a walk-in wardrobe, or clothes chest.

Having snared our attention, Gray uses some creepy plotting to hold it. A few moments of stage action soon supply a motive for the murder-by-asphyxiation trap being devised. It soon becomes clear that two ill-advised marriages are collapsing under the weight of worries caused by drink and sex. Gray's stage directions lend the plot another mystery to temper this harsh, tightly focused clarity. He details closely the physical appearance of the set, noting the grotty furniture and curtains, an old gramophone, and the old newspapers, shoes, and empty cigarette packs scattered about. The documentation gets heavier. Later, he'll mandate the physical features of the play's four lesser characters, their hairstyles, attire, and make-up.

About the appearance of the play's two main figures, he says nothing. What he gives both of them are personae to which he believes good actors can tune their skills. The first of them seen onstage is mincing, paltry Perkin Godboy. The large padlock he brings onto the set portends the abduction motif so vital to *Sleeping Dog* and *Wise Child*. But Godboy, calling his wife May (his prospective murder victim) "dear" (1SG 152–3) the first eight times he addresses her, betrays a lack of the daring a murderer needs. Forget his silken menace. He keeps failing in his several attempts to lure May inside the wardrobe where he intends to gas her.

Despite his mousiness, Godboy holds our interest. His claim that he lives on a government stipend and an annuity from his family (1SG 155) could be true. The more we see of him, the clearer it gets that many families would pay heavily to keep him far from the nest. Nor can he boast of any work history, though his reference to his "professional standing" (1SG 155) could denote the impression he tries to give of being a chiropodist. And he does have a box containing some devices of the trade. But he could just be a foot fetishist, hardly the only one in Gray. A policeman will also stroke a woman's foot later in the play (1SG 235), just as Jerry did that of Mrs. Artminster in *Wise Child*

(1SG 101), a play that opens and closes with some talk of feet (1SG 75, 148); Ellen Ternan of *Little Nell*, who knows what pleases her lover of 13 years, also strokes the feet of a dying Charles Dickens (155). The foot motif builds sinister force. Godboy may be posing as a chiropodist in order to gas a neighbor whose corn he claims should be removed. He tries to gas Doris Hoyden because all of his efforts at play's opening to maneuver May into the cupboard have failed. He's growing edgy. An earlier attempt to smother Doris came apart when her husband, Eric, came calling unannounced.

Emerging from this comedy of errors is the feeling that Godboy would kill one woman as soon as another. The idea gains legs. While confirming his incompetence, his later accidental swallowing of the key to the wardrobe further focuses his sexual impairment. It's revealed at the end of Act One that, in the two years of their marriage, despite her many overtures and entreaties, May has never had sex with him. He does discuss his problem, referring to an old wound his father inflicted on him "in a game with his belt" (1SG 220) that his sister might have joined. He also tells May that, eager as he is to service her, the specialists he has been consulting can't cure him (1SG 163). He's lying. Just moments before he swallows the phallic key, he became so charmed with the sight of May's rump "*sticking out of the cupboard*" (1SG 178) that he misses his best chance to shove her inside.

The inevitable sex-power nexus has emerged. This 52-year-old ne'er-do-well uses the story that he was a constable during the war to hang around the local police station. By associating with men of action, he's compensating for his unmanliness. But more than borrowed glory is driving him. He's also looking for an excuse to spend time with Inspector Mannerly Hawkins, the Alpha male whose efficiency, decisiveness, and daredevil exploits as a crime-stopper he reveres. This reverence has been consuming him. So much in awe is he of what he perceives as Hawkins's pre-eminence that he secretly identifies with it. He knows that he has fallen short of Hawkins's high standard. But he has also found a way to nullify this failure. Lacking a desire for women, he can't match Hawkins's prowess as a Casanova. But he can win the Inspector's attention by assuming the compliant female role. Thus he rhapsodizes at length about the Inspector's prowess. May speaks home when she asks him in Act One, "It's funny to me the way your voice changes with the mention of his name, why didn't you marry him instead?" (1SG 158)

Godboy is too shaken by the question to answer it. But at the end of the act, alone onstage, he flattens himself, his arms spread outward against the door of the same cupboard he intended as May's death space. This striking visual image, enhanced by his anguished curtain line, "Haw-kins" (1SG 195), projects erotic submissiveness upon Christ's passion. His fantasy builds. At the start of Act Two, he's wearing an apron and carrying a feather duster. Although it's the next afternoon, he's still playing the woman's role in his longing to be raped by Hawkins.

When a female cop who has been partnering the *"broad-shouldered ... tough-looking"* Hawkins (1SG 219) says that Hawkins put his hand on her knee, Godboy, not to be outdone in the authority of *his* claim on the Inspector's attention, counters with the words, "He had his hand on my shoulder, twice" (1SG 219). His stakes on this claim rule him. His hero worship of Hawkins leads him to misspeak several more times in ways that label him a would-be murderer. He'll court punishment to glorify Hawkins, the patron saint in his private cruelty fetish. Which is warped and ugly; combining homosexuality and blasphemy, Gray has turned Godboy's passion for Hawkins into an excuse both to murder women and to despise human frailty. Godboy's misanthropy needed little tweaking. He'd have rather battered anew the homeless shell-shock victims he reluctantly tended during the Blitz, insisting that these "bombed-outs" (1SG 187) belonged in jail rather than drinking the tea he served them on Underground platforms.

The voice in which he recalls, or fabricates, this episode, like his conversational style in general, marks an artistic triumph. Recalling the measly Frederick Clegg of John Fowles's *The Collector* (1963), which became a cinematic hit two years later, Godboy is a working-class pawn whose delusions of power go rank, poisonous, and lethal. Again like Clegg, his shabby-genteel speech, a *faux* grandiloquence that both masks and reveals his ultimate coldness, conveys his depravity. What he does *not* say has its own vigor and fluency. He sidesteps any issue of note that May brings up, either pretending not to hear it, such as when she tells him that she's leaving him, or feigning ignorance when she discusses her carnal needs. When she lets him know that she wants sex from him, he'll change the subject or clam up.

Rather than making him an inarticulate, as Fowles did Clegg, Gray gives himself a harder job — that of making Godboy a chatterbox whose words express both his meaning and how he colors it to mislead others. So whereas May's speech is racy, pungent, and shot through with laughter, his pored-over words sound dry, cold, and defensive. Once, when May brings up the topic of bedtime, he replies with diction suitable to a salesman addressing a prospective customer: "Don't forget your night-things in the cupboard, dear. I've left the door open for you to make your selection from" (1SG 176). Bloodless formalized diction is his disguise of choice. He says of his terrified upstairs neighbor, "Doris is thinking in terms of a fatal accident" (1SG 179). He likes such jargon. Later, using the same boilerplate rhetoric of TV news reporting, he lies to Doris's husband, saying, "I regret to inform you that your wife has met a fatal accident" and, "Her release was instantaneous" (1SG 220). Clichés distance him from the violence flooding his soul. The last speech of this believer that a woman's "work is never done" (1SG 184) includes the words "a feather in your cap" (1SG 237). He even cloaks his murderous motives in euphemisms and homey maxims ("Least said, soonest mended" [1SG 200]). This word choice keeps signaling both a dreary conformity and a failure of imagination.

He phrases his urge to gag Doris by telling her, preparatory to removing a corn from her foot, "Probably a mere lotion would do the trick, or I could administer a little whiff" (1SG 167).

The key word in this passage is the inoffensive-looking "mere." Acting on his masochistic wish to go to jail, where he might get cuffed around by Inspector Hawkins, he says of the contents of the cupboard he bought to murder his wife, "There's nothing in there except May's remains," a lie he softens with the self-protective, "I merely mean the bits and pieces of May (*falters*) which she couldn't take with her and had to leave behind" (1SG 201–2). He has blocked out mentally the left-behind clothing of May's. As the action builds, his verbal tics occur with greater frequency to convey the clash between his yearning both to hide and to surrender. He may even be using the word "mere" correctly with Doris. In today's parlance "mere" denotes trifling, small, or insignificant. It had the opposite meaning in Shakespeare's time, which is how Yeats used it in "Leda and the Swan." It's also Ben Butley's sense of the word when he applies Yeats's phrase to a colleague who has had her book accepted for publication: "Mere Edna is loosed upon the world" (B 30). Godboy's ignorance of historical linguistics notwithstanding, he says more than he intends every time he says the word.

His marriage to May is too bland and lackluster to spark any George-and-Martha-style drunken brawls. It's a wonder that the pair communicates at all. Unlike her fussy, finicky husband, May revels in the senses. Living fully in the moment like Artminster before her, she prefers liquor to food. This heavy drinker enters the action popping not mints, but crisps; she'd never worry about having drinker's breath. A stranger to inhibition, she's an all-out sensualist, earthy talker, and lover of her freedom. Invoking Gray's captivity motif, she wants to end the regimen of sexual denial Godboy has imposed on her. The entry of the upstairs neighbor Eric, whose sexual overtures are also being rebuffed at home, raises her spirits, a change she voices, appropriately, in physical terms: "Let's get our hands on something I've got special in the kitchen" (1SG 170), she tells him. And while his wife cringes on the sofa next to Godboy, the kitchen where May has taken Eric sends out gales of laughter punctuated by the noise of things falling (always an emblem of the imperatives of human physicality in Gray). Nor do Eric and May blench when their stout is gone. Grabbing a bottle of gin, she leads him back to the sitting room, where they're soon dancing "*amorously*" (1SG 169).

Counterpointing the movements of the heaving, laughing couple is a different kind of seductiveness taking place on the couch. Within reach of their swaying mates, Doris and Godboy are stock-still. They belong side by side rather than facing each other. Godboy doesn't want to dance with her, as May suggests (1SG 168). Rather, he has been cajoling her to let him remove the corn that, he says, has caused her limp. The sticking point is that preliminary "whiff" (1SG 167) he wants to give her but refuses to describe.

Another thematic strain has entered the counterpoint that emerged when the two married couples shifted partners earlier in the evening. May's pawing and grinding against Eric has quieted her resolve to end her marriage — if a resolve it be. She had made it easy for Godboy to feign deafness when she told him she was leaving him. Instead of looking him in the eye, she waited for him to enter the cupboard before speaking out. And even then, separated from him by a door, she half-sang (1SG 162) her intention to decamp. This muffled exchange took place in Act One, scene one. She's still undecided about staying with Godboy at the end of the next long scene, where she musters all her remaining patience to tempt him into making love: "I'm a warm woman," she tells her "little white corpse" of a husband, using a slew of metaphors: "I'm a warm woman but the fire's going out. There's got to be some hot coals to keep me banked, and you're turning me into embers" (1SG 194).

What happens after these embers cool stirs our fears. May's absence from the stage during most of the second act makes us fear that she's dead. Gray quiets these fears — but only just. Joining the strands of the plot, he restores her to the stage at the very end. Godboy has just stepped inside the cupboard, the door of which she slams behind him, unaware that he's inside. None of the play's hints of looming disaster have led anywhere, everything falling apart in the classic Ealing Studio manner. Though May left, suitcase and all, she didn't go far. Perhaps she should have. Her slamming of the cupboard door implies that she already regrets her homecoming. But, regrets aside, her homecoming infers her intent to stay all along. As was seen in *Godot*, Pinter's *Dumb Waiter* (1959), Albee's *Delicate Balance* (1966) and Gray's own 1967 *Wise Child*, bonds formed in the plays of the era, however unsatisfying, tend to cohere. Accordingly, Godboy's many failures to kill May signal his reluctance to kill her.

An unvoiced, perhaps unrecognized, mutual need that's a face of love will sustain their freakish marriage. Like that of *Wise Child*, the play's finale subverts the industrial West's paradigm of married heterosexual love by showing that love of any kind joins people while also pulling them apart.

This push-pull rhythm defines the chaste marriage of Doris and Eric Hoyden, the upstairs couple half the age of the Godboys. Again, what sustains, also destroys. Like Jerry of *Wild Child*, Doris is a neurasthenic orphan who hates being touched. The limp she walks with shows how her fear of physical contact has put her out of step with life. Symptomatic of her need to stand clear of others is the handbag she always presses to her stomach. This tic developed recently. Her discovery that a policeman was peeking when she was strip-searched at a nearby station house has chilled her sexually. It did worse. The shame that swept through her also made her lose faith in the police's ability to help her should the local thug called the Merrit Street Attacker climb through her window.

What scares her even more is her own helplessness. Despite his promise to protect her, Eric, jobless because illiterate, abandons her for hours every night. His reason? Of course, he's the same thug from whom Doris craves protection. Rather than looking for work, "Between-jobs Eric" (1SG 231) has been ambushing women near bus-stops and snatching their purses. These sorties haven't blunted his love for his wife, whom he refers to frantically as "My Dorrie" (1SG 227) when he thinks she's dead. As orphans, he and Doris need the love they missed as children. The lengths to which she goes to protect him during his grilling by Inspector Hawkins show that the marriage lives in her heart. But it doesn't live vibrantly enough to receive Eric as her lover. Similarly, Eric's tender love for *her* excludes the crucial requirement of honesty; never would he tell her that he's the Merrit Street Attacker.

Both of these orphans must learn how to extend, as well as accept, love. Their marriage runs aground of the police, the implacability of whom is shaped by Inspector Hawkins. As Ionesco and Pinter often did when treating evil characters, Gray tricks us into underrating Hawkins. First, the cultural associations of Hawkins's name reach back a century. Conan Doyle's Sherlock Holmes is remembered as fiction's first hawk-faced sleuth, and his pipe-smoking cartoon offspring, Hawkshaw the Detective, who debuted in the *New York World* in 1913, kept the archetype alive for another 25 years. This legacy having been tallied, Gray's Inspector Hawkins shares fewer qualities with his iconic prototypes than with the irksome Blue Meanies of the 1968 Beatles movie, *Yellow Submarine*, which was probably still fresh in the minds of many viewers of Gray's 1969 play. Also within recall was a police inspector in Orton's *Loot* (1967) who mouths pieties to wrest money from witnesses and suspects. A great talker himself, Gray's Hawkins cadges drinks from Godboy. But his biggest prize is Doris Hoyden, whom he escorts to the police station while locking her husband in jail. Profiting from his cop's eye for human weakness, Hawkins, who liked what he saw while peeking at Doris during her strip-search, uses his coerciveness to break her down. At play's end, she's in the hands of this Dutch Uncle, a stern authority figure who had used the same aggressiveness to subdue Detective Hedderley, his female back-up in the Merrit Street Attacker case.

Hedderley, Doris, and Godboy have all caved into the force of his personality. The archetypal male that enthralls them is always muscular, threatening, and relentless in discipline. Godboy calls Hedderley "sir" (1SG 225) for the same reason that Gray both concealed her first name and omitted her from his list of the play's characters (1SG 150). Her cop's job has replaced her humanity with the power to punish, which she directs to Eric after corralling him as the attacker.

Gender confusion accounted for the play's flying start. Godboy minces about the stage and defers to May as soon as she bursts into his presence with her dole of chips and demotic. This face-off between the brassy and the buttoned-up reminds us that contrast is the heart of drama. Suspense moves to the fore when it becomes clear that both parties are hiding something from each other and that their secrets spring from a shared wish to end their marriage. The suspense holds. Having designed *Dutch Uncle* around the efforts of an ensemble of actors, in contrast to the single-bond focus of *Wise Child*, Gray moves May from the set in favor of developing the "little game of cat and mouse" (1SG 213) that Hawkins plays with the Hoydens.

Already a deft structurist early in his playwriting career, Gray's interlacing of his plot lines fascinates us. The process takes different forms. Characters who come onto the set speak lines that, though undecipherable, both re-route the action and convey a mood (1SG 150, 184, 196). But Gray can also shatter a mood in the interests of reworking a play's texture. Just when their raunchiness is about to take command of Eric and May's erotic clowning on the dance floor, Godboy stops the music, substituting a recording of one of Churchill's war speeches (1SG 168). He also faces away from the audience while fitting a gas mask to a terrified Doris in Act Two, scene one, a step that leads to another radical shift in mood. Following Godboy's statement that Doris looks "as right as rain," Eric surprises everybody by barging in and shouting, "I know" (1SG 210). Rain is looming outside, and he has come back for his raincoat. In a neat dovetailing of form, idea, and wordplay, this thwarting of a dramatic climax also shows the accidental and the spontaneous foiling a carefully planned murder plot.

Dramatic structure continues to show incongruity and accident supporting life. Street noises galore hum and throb during the action of *Dutch Uncle*, like the whistles, shouts, and dog yaps that clamor offstage when the attacker is being cornered and corralled. This din refreshes the action without dominating it. As Godboy already showed in acts of crazed self-confidence that evoke Stalin and Hitler, determinacy can kill. *Dutch Uncle* combines Beckett's preference for a humanity that's famished and scraped with Derrida's aversion to the determinate. Godboy's padlock, an emblem of certainty, discredits the only true sign of the future — the instability of the now. The ontology being debunked includes a complicity with language. Language is a weapon in *Dutch Uncle*. Like the death-dealing words of the Professor in Ionesco's *The Lesson* (1951), the mock-pedantic speech of both Godboy and Hawkins stifles the bald, stumbling rhetoric of the down-and-out Doris and Eric. The logic of the play sends these two ex-orphans to different parts of the same prison at final curtain. But logic doesn't swathe all. May's disregard for future utopias based on ideologies that ignore the marginal and the skewed makes her the play's only character content with the sensual joys provided by present-tense living. And if she doesn't prevail at play's end, she has nonetheless survived the murder-plot aimed at her.

Much of the credit for the play's resourcefulness belongs to its design. Act One, for instance, begins and ends with Godboy and May alone together onstage. Yet perhaps at no time in their marriage have they been more divided than at act's end, where the unpremeditated and the unsponsored have taken charge. The antics prior to May's accidental gassing of the couple's pet guppies, her walking onto the stage and then standing behind Godboy when he believes her to be locked inside the cupboard, and the delayed exposition in Act Two, scene two, in which Godboy describes (or lies about) his life before marrying May (1SH 205, 07)—all celebrate the absurd. Physical comedy had already won Gray a laugh and some gasps in Act One, scene two, when Hawkins's first appearance onstage had frozen Doris. Why the sight of Hawkins shocks her comes clear straightaway. Sensing a conquest for himself and the phallo-centric regime he represents, the virile, assertive Hawkins ignores his host's extended hand to keep his eyes clapped on Doris.

This kind of byplay happens often. As with *Wild Child*, much of the menace as well as the fun of *Dutch Uncle* harks to the well-made play of the turn-of-the-century French stage. Like Feydeau's *Flea in Her Ear*, Gray's inverted pastoral builds a complicated plot with many carefully timed entrances and exits around a sexually blocked husband. A cupboard door both opened and shut by that husband in the first act of the later play occurs "*at almost exactly the same instant*" (1SG 164) as the upstairs neighbors' appearance onstage. Less precision would not only smudge the play's glossy finish; it might also slow the action long enough for audiences to notice that the fun they're having owes so much to contrivance and implausibility.

Gray's knowledge of theater history includes that other staple of the well-made play, the *quid-pro-quo*. In *Dutch Uncle*, the device often operates on the thin line between mirth and fear. Both May and Eric have sexually zipped-up mates. Godboy's being alone at the cupboard at both beginning and end implies that the bedroom woes of both couples have remained unresolved. *Dutch Uncle* raises some disturbing issues without providing comforting answers. Just before May's reappearance at the end, Hawkins announces his intention to give Doris "a Dutch Uncle talking to" (1SG 238) while leading her offstage with his hand on her rump. Having jailed Eric, he has planned a scenario for Doris more terrifying than the misdeeds Eric wrought as the Merrit Street attacker. In fact, both her innocence and her chronic fear of sex restore to the canon in Hawkins the figure of the pedophile. His voraciousness, though, doesn't rule out some amusing wordplay. His having grown up in Ireland's County Mayo evokes a movie starring Virginia Mayo (1SG 211) Eric said he was going to see the night he's brought to boot. This motif peaks, moreover, in an apartment occupied by a woman called May[o].

The offstage development of the Merrit Street horror chimes with the technique governing *Dutch Uncle*, a work with a great deal of movement but little resolution or closure. Like Chekhov's *Three Sisters* and, again, Beckett's *Godot*, the work is very theatrical without being dramatic. Supporting Lyn Gardner's view of Gray as "a chronicler of the unsaid" (10), it moves to a climax that never happens. While Godboy's murder plots against Mae and Doris are losing out to absurdity, Gray sends our attention elsewhere. Godboy's attempt to kill Doris aborts when her husband returns to the flat for his raincoat. But the following occurrence defies what might be expected when a man finds his wife trying to struggle out of a gasmask. Rather than voicing alarm, Eric starts laughing. This absurdity shows sound dramatic instinct, Gray knowing that laughter coming from a stage character usually provokes laughter in the house. Besides blocking the dramatic climax that belongs in the second act, he has also put Eric onstage to stop a murder. But he keeps murder a lively possibility. Both Doris and May, the putative victims, are off the scene during most of Act Two, scene two. When their husbands discuss them in a passage where neither they nor the onlooker knows which wife is being referred to (1SG 227–8), the mounting confusion builds as much anxiety as it does fun.

To keep us alert, Gray syncopates this tension. The descendental thematic drift implied by Godboy's interest in feet as an amateur chiropodist resurfaces from *Wise Child*, specifically Jerry's attentiveness to Artminster's feet 1SG 75, 101). Though Eric is called "foot-loose" (1SG 217), he always stays close to home. Fatigue depicts postwar London, viz., cigarette butts and ashes; the energy May wastes carrying garments from wardrobe to suitcase and back as they drop to the floor; the handbag belonging to a distraught Doris that scatters its contents all over the Godboys' sitting room — all create a pattern of spilling, falling, and leaking compatible with the idea of entropy, or energy loss, the second law of thermodynamics that was fascinating American novelists William Gaddis and Thomas Pynchon at the time.

Perhaps the gas that kills the Godboys' pet guppies has also poisoned the air in the apartment. Evoking the persistence in Gray's mind of the suffocating grandmother who made him laugh so hard that he couldn't breathe, the cupboard that the gas was meant to fill stays in view the whole time the actors are onstage. Its cumbersomeness and its connection with failure make it an effective symbol. By the end of the play's first scene, it has expressed the inner sadness of the people: the regret suffusing the middle-aged marriage and the euphoria that clots into a hangover. The metaphorical gas escaping from Godboy's cylinder has even seeped into London's streets. The perfume Constable Hedderley splashed on herself while dressing as a hooker to attract the Merrit Street Attacker foiled a sniffing dog that was supposed to stop the attacker, not her.

Having an aura of its own, *Dutch Uncle* has a whiff of *The Lavender Hill Mob* (1951). But, like much of the dissident literature coming from the eastern bloc during the Cold War, the play also mixes gritty realism with an absurdist satire that also folds in the music and coarse humor of British music-hall. As is implied by the kitchen sink that stays in view throughout, the flushing toilet (1SG 231, 238), and the many long pauses between speeches, the play's motive impulses are English — and not only the English *stage*. Near the end of the first act, presumably apropos of nothing we have witnessed up to this point, Godboy says "Pierpoint" (1SG 187). Gray is winking at his audience. Albert Pierrepoint (1905–92) was the British hangman who executed one John Reginald Christie in July 1952. It wasn't only Christie's obsession with the morbid and the demonic that riveted Simon James Holliday Gray. He also noticed that the wanton John Reginald Holliday Christie (1898–1953) was born in the same Halifax, Nova Scotia, where *he* attended Dalhousie University between 1953–58 and later used as the setting of his first novel, *Colmain* (1963).

Christie supplies Perkin Godboy's unusual last name because Gray saw Christie's necrophilia and penchant for serial killing as possible directions for Godboy's sexual pathology. He reasoned well. The abuse meted out to Godboy by his father (an ordeal inflicted, as well, on Christie) resonates in Godboy's frigidness with May. It helps to note, in this regard, that Gray's thoughts about Christie may have also inspired his *Molly* (1977). That play's eponym was based on Alma Victoria Rattenbury, who was born in British Columbia, where Gray taught for a year. Alma's marriage to a sexual non-starter led to an affair and a murder trial, which, like the one that would involve Christie and *his* upstairs Welsh-born neighbor, a mirror image of Eric Hoyden, ended in an acquittal.

Ludovic Kennedy's *Ten Rillington Place* (New York: Simon & Schuster, 1961) and its 1971 film adaptation, directed by Richard Fleischer, both ponder the exogamy that explains both Christie's lifelong patronage of whores, whom he tended to savage after getting them in bed. He strangled three prostitutes, in fact, while still dysfunctionally married. He had other maladies. But because the blindness and muteness he suffered during combat in World War I would have caused Gray staging problems, Godboy never served in the military (1SG 186), although he did follow Christie in working for the police.

The Christies also occupied a ground-floor flat underneath that of Beryl and her borderline-retarded husband, Timothy Evans (besides being Welsh, Gray's Eric is also illiterate[1SG 169]). As in *Dutch Uncle*, the two couples were separated in age by nearly 25 years. Godboy's claim in Act Two that Doris died when her corn was being removed has a grislier true-life source. When Tim Evans's Beryl, already the mother of a small girl, told Tim that she was again pregnant, she wrenched an already tense marriage. To buy some domestic peace, she let Reg Christie talk her into aborting the foetus. This plan backfired fatally. Unlike Gray's Doris Hoyden, she — along with her daughter — were strangled to death. What happened next shocked everybody. Christie's claim that he never killed little Geraldine led to her father's conviction and death by hanging in 1950.

In another shock, the case reopened. Michael Eddowes's *The Man on Your Conscience: An Investigation of the Evans Murder Trial* (London: Cassell, 1955) tells how an inquiry mandated by the Home Secretary resulted in a posthumous pardon for Tim Evans, an act that would end capital punishment in the UK. But, along with the stunning artistry that fuels the play, neither this landmark repeal nor the public interest in the courtroom drama leading to it helped sell theater tickets. "Time on Line" for 8 August 2008 reports that Gray's reimagining of the Christie case made for "the worst first night in living memory" (2). This setback forms part of Gray's legacy. Discussing the stage history of *Dutch Uncle*, Oleg Kerensky reports that, despite the prestige the play gained by opening at London's Aldwych Theatre under the direction of Peter Hall, it closed after twelve performances (135). People were tired of the Christie case.

The resilient Gray recovered from the setback. A more damaging blow might have flattened him had he dedicated the play to his wife, Beryl, which was also the name of Tim Evans's wife. Gray's audacity in this regard took two years to surface. The discretion shown in *Dutch Uncle* by this fancier of doubling and mirroring motifs surfaced when, two years later, he dedicated his *next* play, in which a wife is also victimized, to this then-spouse of four years (1SG 239). Another lesson: the box-office letdown of *Dutch Uncle* weaned him away from lower-class characters. Except for *Pig in a Poke* (1969), which he might have finished writing before the production of *Dutch Uncle*, menials and their ilk rarely appear in the canon, those who do playing minor roles and being treated with none of the goofy inventiveness that Gray got from Joe Orton.

Six
The Death of Education

Spoiled (1969) marks a growing tendency in Gray to write about public-school-educated white male professionals who have trouble connecting with others. The man in question can be a writer (*Life Support, Little Nell*), a businessman (*Melon, Otherwise Engaged, Common Pursuit*), or an educator: Ben Butley is a university don in London; Jason Cartts of the Japes trilogy lectures in Guyana; like Grahame Thwaite of *Little Portia*, the eponym of *Quartermaine's Terms* teaches English to foreigners in a Cambridge-based language school. The late-blooming novelist Charles of *Two Sundays* and Richard Howarth of *Spoiled* both teach French, as does as a Mr. Holliday, who, without appearing onstage in *Spoiled*, turns the mind to both Gray's mother and his 1958 lectureship in Clermont-Farraud, France (1SG 251).

Sourced in Gray's playwriting career is the split stage from *Wise Child* that returns in *Spoiled*. Again, the set is functional. The baby wallpaper adorning the bedroom walls comments mutely but sardonically on the play's climax — the seduction of a student by a father-to-be, his French schoolmaster. Richard Howarth has invited Donald Clenham for a weekend visit to learn enough French to get through his O-level exams the following Monday. Like his solo mom, fragile, self-deprecating Donald is nervous about the exam. He has already failed it twice and won't get another try. Gray quickly makes his anxiety a physical fact. Before Donald speaks a word, he accidentally knocks some books to the floor. Howarth is also characterized before speaking. At curtain rise, he's munching some biscuits, as he'll do often. This fidget, like May Godboy's popping of chips in *Dutch Uncle* and Lady Caroline's, of mints in *Sleeping Dog*, resonates deeply. Howarth's wife Joanna calling it a symptom of his self-indulgence (1SG 254, 280, 301) links it to his ongoing practice of ignoring her in favor of his work—e.g., marking exams, directing a student play, and now, with Donald inside the house, devoting the weekend to *him*, rather than her, as he had promised.

The self-indulgence she accuses him of has also fattened him, a recent change that invites several non-exclusionary readings. Knowing that Joanna feels that her pregnancy has made her look bloated and ugly, this closet gay is copying her plumped-up look to ward off sexual demands from her. This strategy is working; according to Joanna, nearly six months have passed since he kissed her "properly" (1SG 301). Ironically, though, the same pregnancy that repels him also entices him, but again in a way that divides him from her. Because a heavily pregnant wife is a gay man's nightmare, Howarth has been stuffing himself in order to look pregnant himself, a wile that shrinks Joanna's identity in the home. If the goal of this ruse is to oust her from the home, it succeeds. The end of the play leaves little doubt that the marriage is over.

Although *Spoiled* isn't driven by self-contempt, its oft-overweight author does scathe the feminized father figure Howarth in terms that apply to himself as both a fat husband (SD 47, CODA 66) and a quondam foreign language teacher. He wastes no time parading Howarth's passion for biscuits. No between-meals snacker himself, Donald comes to his teacher's home still reeling from having lost his runaway father at age three. He discovers early, too, that Howarth isn't the male authority figure he needs to quiet his nerves for the upcoming exam (1SG 255). His practice of saying "um" (e.g., 1SG 295) conveys his anxiety. But Howarth says "um" (e.g., 1SG 252, 267, 274, 281, 298) even more often than Donald, in his own home no less. He's also teaching subject matter he knows stone cold. The dish he drops that Joanna had given him to dry after dinner (1SG 293) evokes the books that a wrong-footed Donald knocked to the floor at curtain rise (1SG 243). Where is Gray taking the teacher-student kinship he has shaped? The Baudelaire poem Howarth recites, "Réversibilité," with its references to shame and remorse (1SG 281), say more about *him* than about his fatherless student.

And he's to blame. The longer he's with Donald, the more predatory he grows. He uses his clout as the boy's teacher-host to stop him from going to church in order to gain more face-time with him. Then he manages this time with brutal efficiency. No advantage escapes him. He steers his reprimand of Donald, after catching him cheating, into the region of sex, a maneuver that shatters the boy's reserves. Finally, in an Iago-like dodge, speaking reluctantly, as if the words have to be wrenched from him, he poisons Donald's friendship with Les Grant, the boy with whom Donald had been planning to visit Paris. (Another ruse smacking of Iago shows Howarth saying later, when asked about what he told Donald about Les, "He asked me my advice about Les and I gave it to him" [1SG 300].)

Howarth claims to have seen in Les Grant the clinging possessiveness common to gays. The bogus indictment hits home, as Howarth knew it would. Innocent, impressionable Donald, sexually insecure himself, jumps at the chance to avoid the taint of homosexuality. Howarth's tactic of trading on Donald's unspoken fears has frightened the boy. It has also shattered his reserve. By saying that the "possessive" Les cares "too intensely" (1SG 271), Howarth transfers Donald's trust and dependence to *him*. This ruse rests on a lie. Les is unusually solid and resolute for his age. By having risked his job security to cover up for a truant Donald at work, he already proved himself the trusty, responsible friend the emotionally shaky Donald needs to shepherd him through France.

Howarth's self-indulgence keeps fouling his judgment. One reason he breaks down Donald's defenses in Act Two, scene one, is to justify his putting a comforting arm around the guilt-raked boy. He's priming Donald for the "basic soothing" (1SG 215) for which his wife has been begging him. Has she been begging in vain? His weekend invitation to Donald exceeded his charter, to begin with. So fixated is Howarth on the boy that he refuses to try on the costume Joanna had sewn for him to wear in a school play. The play is far from his thoughts. Just moments before, while he and Donald were alone together, he broke the precedent, decreed by their professional tie, of addressing Donald as *"vous,"* by calling him *"tu,"* while also speaking of his *"charme"* (1SG 264). His blood is sparkling. He'll later call Donald *"mon enfant,"* again in Joanna's absence (1SG 293).

Joanna needn't hear these words of endearment. His ongoing neglect of her has already smudged the poise and objectivity that served her as a journalist. Testy and easily ruffled even before the play's present-tense action, she recently quarreled with a department-store clerk and a grocer. The empty marriage that induced these rows faces a new hurdle when she sees her mate of two years slighting her in favor of Donald. Donald even sits next to her in Act Two, scene two, to comfort her. In the play's final scene, he needs comforting himself. He's so dazed and demoralized that he can't act. Whatever energy he has he devotes to the restoration of the student-teacher bond between him and Howarth that prevailed until the previous night. He returns the talismanic French-English dictionary Howarth had loaned him, and his last word before leaving the set, addressed to Howarth, is "sir" (1SG 306). His disclaimer comes too late. Everything has come to grief—his church plans, both this cycling date and his holiday in France with Les, and the purpose that brought him into the Howarths' home. Gray has served a warning. The morality governing *Spoiled* is conservative. By tearing down the props supporting Donald's life, Howarth has also torn down his own. And because his wife is pregnant, the dismantling resounds in the next generation, a sign of which is Donald's appalling guilt for having usurped his hostess Joanna's wifely function.

Nothing has escaped the pollution Howarth brought into the home when he invited Donald there for some swot. His pretext answers for both the title of the play he appears in and the damage he has caused. The French word, *perdu*, besides denoting lost, also means hopelessly and terminally stained, i.e., a total write-off. The word targets Howarth's career, his marriage along with his unborn baby's future, Donald's friendship with Les Grant, and the boys' proposed trip to France, which Donald won't go on any more than he'll take the O-level exam that began about 15 minutes before final curtain.

The play's last transaction: Donald's mother had brought the Howarths a cake to thank them for hosting Donald. In and out of view during the preceding action, the box containing the cake stirs dramatic tension. What we've already seen of Gray's flawless timing lets us know that he'd not have displayed an item as conspicuous as a cake box without having first decided where it fits in the action. This place is the play's curtain line, Joanna offering Howarth the box with the corrosive send-off, "To thank you with" (1SG 306). Howarth doesn't reach for the box being held out to him. Why should he? This craver of sweets can eat the whole cake in his good time, because Joanna will soon be walking out on him and the binge-eating she found so rankling. Perhaps her words of thanks come, not from Mrs. Clenham, but, rather, from *her* for being justified to end the marriage.

While he munches his orange cake, if, unlike everything else in the home, it hasn't spoiled or gone rank, he can ponder the cost of his own unconscious wish to end the marriage. He'll have to munch a lot of cake, though, before coming to terms with the prospect that he has spoiled Donald's life for good.

Butley fuses elements of its three predecessors. Besides recycling some of the kitchen-sink rawness of *Wise Child* and *Dutch Uncle*, the play restores the sexual non-starter of *Spoiled* whose sexual avoidance of his wife is also wrecking his teaching career. *Butley* also brings back from *Spoiled* the device of using the verbal skills of the articulate anti-hero as a weapon against himself. Again, the device creates other casualties. But the cut is cleaner and deeper. In *Butley*, Gray has found his stroke. His future drama will portray the trials and crises of England's public-school grads who have refined the tastes they acquired as students. *Close of Play* (1979), which unfolds in the home of a retired professor, stages the psychological fallout of the sins of a doctor, a novelist, and a BBC announcer. Harking to *Godot*, the play's two acts are called "AFTER LUNCH" and "BEFORE TEA" (6).

Common Pursuit (1984), subtitled *Scenes from Literary Life* after the subtitle of Chekhov's *Uncle Vanya*, *Scenes from Country Life*, looks back from the viewpoint provided by the 11 years since their graduation on the careers and private lives of six Cambridge graduates. Their common pursuit? The drive to get ahead, in some cases, at any price. The pitfalls of ambition and success intrigued Gray. The shelves that come into view at the start of *Just the Three of Us* (1997) "*bulge with books (Dickens, Tolstoy, etc.)*" along with "*a cassette player and various tapes and compact disks of classical music*" (7). The woman who filled these shelves also quotes English verse impressively (e.g., 39). Yet neither her cultivated tastes nor the sensibility that has helped her write best-selling novels taught her that kidnapping was wrong. In a reprise of the abduction motif lifted from Hank Janson and used most recently in *Cell Mates* (1995), the writer kidnaps her husband's secretary. Nor did the civilized graces honed by overachievers in *Close of Play* curb their appetite for those standbys of the canon: booze, masochism, and adultery.

Gray has left behind the kitchen-sink iconoclasm of Joe Orton in favor of a darker, more disturbing satire. A professor of classics in *After Pilkington* (1986), most of whose cast members hold graduate degrees, sounds like a barking dog when he laughs (4SG 216). In another reminder of our animal origins, "*animal noises*" (4SG 263) come from the lab of a veterinarian who will soon be murdered. His assassin: the gentle-born wife of an Oxford don. The educated, the successful, and the privileged in the plays of Gray's middle phase outdo their social subordinates in brutishness and savagery.

This truth applies luminously to Ben Butley, an English lecturer in "the Dump," viz., Queen Mary College of the University of London (BH 11). Ben is an avid drinker and chain-smoker in steep decline who's determined in his ruin to drag down everybody in his circle. Harold Pinter's belief that Gray's *Otherwise Engaged* deals with "the demands the weak make on the strong" (Fraser 77) applies even more strictly to *Butley*. John Lahr, reviewing an October 2006 revival of the work in New York, said correctly that "the goal of Butley's wit is to inflict his sense of emptiness on others" (127). He's right. Ben treats everything bright, joyful, and life-giving — like friendship, sexual love, even teaching — with his irony and sarcasm. In the process, he has hit a wall. Sarcasm and irony can critique; they can't nourish or redeem. The 1971 play, featuring his truculent wit, could have been subtitled *Schadenfreude Unbound*. His overwhelming problem? It's easier for him to evade problems with a clever retort than to confront them and (shudder) try to solve them.

The deep layering of this richly nuanced play stops us from loathing Ben as much as he does himself. Attaining a rare intensity of feeling, *Butley* splits our sides with laughter as it tallies the shocking downfall of a man's career (an angry colleague refers to "the days when you still taught" [73]), social life, and viability as both a husband and a father. Lahr has described this loser whose fast mouth and vexed heart keep him riveted on the abyss:

> Bleeding and phlegm ... become Butley. He is ... a bored and unsupportive teacher, an indifferent father, a sad-sack bisexual who, in the course of the play, is dumped by both his wife and his boy-friend.... You'd be hard-pressed, in commercial comedy, to find a more bitter or beleaguered gourmand of grief[126].

There's also his duplicity. While pretending to be hot and wild like fire, Butley knows exactly where to slip in the knife. His gimlet eye for human weakness has made him a sociopath who takes shameless liberties with you, sensing openings you never knew you gave. While waiting for the best time to strike, he masks this menace with an "hail-fellow well met" buoyancy. So quick with words is he that he can make you laugh against your better judgment. And so adept is he at twisting these words that he can trick the victims of his "fierce mockery" (Lahr 127) to apologize to *him* (17, 64).

His two-edged verbal wit takes him even further. For a while, he bids fair to become a new kind of literary hero, one who redefines the norms of his patriarchal state. His erotic bond with his colleague Joey Keyston, which he wants to preserve, goes back to the time when he taught Joey. This bond has recently taken Butley from his duties as a husband and father of a baby daughter. Call him a social rebel who defies both cultural definitions of maleness and proper male behavior while also hacking away at fixed patterns of connecting and networking.

The complex internal life that stokes this rebelliousness invites comparisons with Hegel's archetypal hero—a skeptic who must be punished for breaking bad laws that, thanks to his defiance of them, will improve for posterity's betterment. Other explanations for his comedown cut a broad swathe. He knows that, had he kept to the straight and narrow, he could'a been somebody, but the creeping fear of his irrelevance has turned him to drink. Whenever he can, he gives bourgeois values like independence, initiative, and self-regulation a nasty twist. More committed to whisky than to work, he's preparing to bow out on his own terms. Like Tennessee Williams's Blanche DuBois, another alcoholic with sexual hang-ups, he has concocted what looks like an inevitable and irreversible defeat, a claim supported by his removing a whisky bottle from his briefcase in the play's second act that he keeps swilling.

Hitting rock bottom will keep him sneering at the middle-class work ethic that both built and sustained what he most valued. What boots it that he wrecked several lives on his downward skid? He could coach Richard Howarth in self-indulgence. The same booze that warped his mind has also whetted his dark sense of purpose. Precedents for his moral chaos? Perhaps, like Camus's Mersault in *The Stranger* (1942), he seeks the thrill of rising above the mundane. Gray foreshadows at curtain rise the civilized values he'll try to rout. Taped to a wall of his office is a smeared dog-eared photo of T.S. Eliot, of which Steven S. Cole has said, "The soiled, curled corners of the photograph establish ... that things once important to Butley have ceased to hold his attention" (86).

Cole's insight needs tweaking. The things he refers to vex Ben enough to make him want to smash them. But like many other vengeful people, he suffers more than his intended victims. Ben's messy desk, disheveled clothes, and the *"nasty shaving cut"* (7) on his chin all show him coming apart more quickly than the picture on the wall. Life is bleeding out of him because he has rejected those classic harmonies that nourished Eliot, ironically the subject of his book-in-progress, or -stasis. The stalled book will never get written. His work habits stink. Next, his statements, "Our ends never know our beginnings" (29) and, "Our beginnings never know our ends" (56), clash with the organicity proclaimed in that famous line from Part One of "East Coker," "In my end is my beginning."

Underscoring the importance of Butley's rejection of this quiet confidence and faith in wholeness is the similarity in subject matter between the poem and Gray's play. Both works deal with time, dying, and death. But Ben counters Eliot's faith in the mystery of unity with discord and isolation. When told by his flustered colleague Edna that she works hard at her teaching, he answers hypocritically, "We know you do" (53). Not only has this slacker been degrading hard work; his mitts everywhere, he also stole one of the students in Edna's seminar. Elsewhere, this enemy of peace lets on that, though he doesn't want his wife, Anne, for himself, he resents her having found, in his absence, another man.

Near the end of the first act, she comes to his office to say that she has indeed moved on. Besides having found a job, she has been also been living with Tom, whom she doesn't love. As Ben knows; shifting into the gear of high literature, he fires some Wildean words at her to ridicule her prosaic, serviceable choice of Tom: "You ... said yourself he was the dullest man you'd ever spent an evening with." Without flinching, she throws his mockery back at him: "The dullest man I've ever spent a night with" (39).

But she has come to QMC to reconcile, not to discuss Tom; both she and Ben know that she defected to Tom to save what remained of her sanity after life with Ben. The terms of her peace offer to Ben, "I came to find out whether you wanted *us* back" (38, emphasis mine), posit a wholeness and continuity she has found, however modestly, with Tom but which she's willing to forgo to let Marina grow up in her parents' home. Ben lacks her respect for family cohesion and rootedness. "Frequently.... But not permanently" (39) describes how often he wants to be with his wife and daughter. He's too childish to offer Anne and Marina the fully committed adult love they deserve. He needs to grow up. Like a child, he must have things his own way, in spite of the needs of others.

He forbids her to marry Tom Weatherby. But before he can answer her rejoinder, "Why not?" (41) a distraught Edna bursts into the office, changing the subject of their conversation. This change Ben welcomes, as he has no counter-offer for Anne. Nor does he answer her when asked if he's going to make trouble for her. Trouble is just what he has in store. He uses his first free moment after Anne's departure to disparage Tom in a phone call to the Headmaster of the school where he's teaching. Ben is abasing himself like a Karamazov, rolling in the muck he has made of his life, yet putting on airs to the end. And like those of the narrator of *Notes from Underground*, his assertions of his individuality foil his best interests.

Dostoevsky continues to explain his plight. Ben's failure to make good on his early hopes has filled him with a Karamazov-like self-loathing. He inveighs with good reason. The literal deaths of QMC lecturers in *Old Flames* and *Breaking Hearts* and the moral breakdowns of their colleagues in *Breaking Hearts* and here in *Butley* convey Gray's belief that teaching destroys souls. But, to quote both Ben's and Piers Gray's favorite writer, they leave us groping for an objective correlative. What drives Ben to attack warmth and continuity? A hasty answer lies in the love of Russian literature that led Gray to adapt Dostoevsky's *Idiot* for the English stage in 1971, the year of *Butley*'s debut.

This coincidence backs the claim that Gray was still preoccupied with Russian literature while drafting *Butley*. The echoes are loud. Having nothing better to do, Ben follows Pushkin's Eugene Onegin, the eponym of Lermontov's *Hero of our Time*, and Anatole Kuryagin of Tolstoy's *War and Peace* by disconcerting another man's fiancée. Also like these louts, he sacrifices the happiness of a young woman to boost an ego of little note.

He's infantilizing adult experience. His feigning ignorance of both his baby daughter's name and gender shows him matching or even trying to outdo Marina in babyishness. This reversion delights him. When told that a divorce always hits hardest the children of divorcing parents, he says, "Yes, we do suffer the most" (30). He refers to his Department Head as Cottontail (71). He leaves in his briefcase an unread thesis on Henry James in favor of removing a copy of Beatrix Potter's *Cecily Paisley* (1922), a book of nursery rhymes. His taste in reading prefigures his tactic of seeking refuge in children's verse, doggerel, or word games whenever he feels under pressure. Crawling beneath moral issues helps him deny their existence.

Childish is also his way of retaliating when crossed. Resenting the news that Tom has clicked with Anne, he phones Tom's boss, introducing himself, "Tom's' fiancée's husband" (47). He had already used the telephone as a weapon when he rang Reg Nuttall, the new boyfriend of Joey Keyston. He breaches civility often. Early in the first act, he grabs Joey's briefcase and, unmoved by Joey's rebuke, "All right, all right, let's be infantile" (12), refuses to return it. He's re-imagining Joey as one of Hank Janson's bound and helpless females. Later in the act, he keeps the briefcase for a longer spell, knowing that Joey needs to take it to the library with him to prepare a lecture he's giving that day.

Life's randomness foils Joey. The student demonstrations taking place at QMC have closed the library. But the anger that inspired them also exposes Ben's mean-minded tyranny. Like the South African oppressors the student rebels want stopped, Ben has squelched freedom of choice and movement. The anarchy taking place outside his office windows resembles Ben's byplay with Joey's briefcase. It also evokes Gray's captivity-and-bondage motif. Both stem from immaturity. The student rebels' barricading of the library stops it from being used; the destruction of an ancient document (28) ends the document's life as a source of enlightenment and joy. Mirror images, Ben and the fired-up students half his age dwarf themselves while also depriving others.

This wastefulness helps make *Butley* Gray's best-known, most-often revived play. A more important reason is the spell cast by its most conspicuous perpetrator. The more we see of Ben, the harder it is to say why, callous, brutal, and dangerous as he is, he's also weirdly charismatic. As if to make him stand out more clearly, he has a lineage. Part outlaw, part self-destructive maniac, this trickster-joker descends from Hermes, the son of Zeus and Maia. He loves mischief. As Eshu, his West African name, he steals and lies. But because his nature is plural and thus morally ambiguous, his tricks often have positive outcomes, while his lies disclose higher truths.

We look in vain for this redemption in Ben. Exciting breakthroughs and discoveries can leap from insights stored in the unconscious. But Ben is too calculating in his malice to re-define himself. He refashions Joey in the role of a bound-and-gagged heroine out of Hank Janson. But denying the freedom of other people, he learns, is always self-defeating. Like many of Gray's leading roles, he operates on a narrow track, squeezed on one side by patriarchal expectations and on the other by female competition. He also resembles the protagonists of *Dog Days*, *Common Pursuit*, and *Melon* by running his gifts to waste. These gifts are striking, sad to say. He has, for instance, a terrific memory. Steven H. Gale includes "William Blake, John Donne, Eliot, Gerard Manley Hopkins, D.H. Lawrence, Richard Lovelace, John Milton ... Beatrix Potter, William Shakespeare, and Sir John Suckling" (Burkman, ed. 87) in the roster of authors he either quotes or paraphrases. Ben also has the skills to profit from his fantastic memory. Blaydes cites his "sense of timing ... gift for building suspense and ... delight in playing games" (378).

Overseeing these skills are his devilish powers of calculation. In the play's second act, they serve the infantile goal of having fun. Asked what he'll do now that he has broken with Anne, he says, "Grab my quota of fun, that's all" (49). This fun would include bouncing Anne's Tom out of both his flat and his job. Badgering others is always "fun" (30). He phones Reg at work to talk him into canceling his dinner plans with Joey, who's standing helplessly next to him. Nothing is safe from his zeal to wreck relationships. He even threatens to deflect Reg's attention from Joey to himself.

Forget his lie. "I shall get my fun" (58), he assures Joey. He's right. The pleasure principle continues to rule this "suicidally clever ... man drowning in bad faith" (Brantley 1). Their colleague Edna comes to the office to grouse about an unruly student. When she mentions reporting him to the Dean, Ben's response, "I can see where that might be fun" (54), shows him relishing the prospect of another person's distress. This sadism holds. We wait for some conversion on his part followed by rebirth. But he's so bent on making others squirm that he makes us wait for nothing.

Is he clinically depressed? Though Gray withholds an answer, he raises the question with tremendous brio. Which the name Butley augments and intensifies; the associations called forth with London's storied Big Ben and its longstanding glory clash with both the mediocrity of QMC, or the Dump, where Ben teaches, and the moral collapse of Ben, who's always *called* Ben in the play's stage directions. This was intentional. The first three letters of his last name, But-, label him a contrarian, i.e., one who lives by opposition. The tag fits. Rather than advancing any creative initiative, he looks for ways to thwart the hopes and plans of others. He pelts Joey with personal questions as soon as Joey follows him into the office they share. He has more missiles to fire. He refers to Reg as "Ted" (90), Joey's last lover, in order to make Joey anxious that he'll do it again in Reg's presence. Perhaps he thinks Joey merits the taunt. He accuses Joey of the same selfishness that Joey complains about in *him*. In a reprise of the plotting device from *Spoiled* that sites a nervous younger man on the brink of a watershed moment, Ben trumps up bogus reasons to needle his "protégé" (21) about an upcoming decision on his promotion to full-time lecturer.

It's no wonder that people stand him up. Anne avoided home the past weekend at the time she and Ben had arranged to meet there. Joey, too, skips the dinner date he and Ben had set up for the evening before the play's present-tense action. Ben keeps getting rebuffed. Told that he's not invited to the dinner Joey and Reg had organized, he can watch the ration of lamb kidneys he bought for the dinner spoil and go rank, like Mrs. Clenham's cake in *Spoiled*.

The name, Butley, rings still another bell, invoking that gentleman's gentleman, a butler. Strengthening the invocation is the English tradition of calling butlers by their last name, one that even includes children. The butler in Graham Greene's "The Basement Room" (1949), or *Fallen Idol* (1950), is called Baines by the child who, years later, tells his sad story. Finally, a butler serves his paymaster, another traditional function that the importunate Ben overturns. No Jeeves, he crowds people, usually with the intent of catching them out. He has also disowned his duties as a teacher. (Though he wants to be the only rebel at QMC, he invites any student protester to enroll in his seminar, skip classes, and get full credit, anyway.) Disownment, in fact, is the first quality he displays. Near the outset of Act One, he claims, here on the first day of the new term, that he's too swamped with administrative chores to teach students.

What administrative chores? Four times in the play, he cuts short phone calls from his Department Head. Nor is he busy doing other jobs. When he grudgingly spends time with the student Carol Heasman, he ridicules both her and the essay she wrote for him. Disloyal colleague as well as bogus teacher, he turns away one Mr. Gardner as a tutorial student after driving a wedge between him and Edna, the departmental colleague to whom he was first assigned.

His rejection of Gardner, whom he had earlier cast in Joey's old role, that of protégé-lover, stems from the gender confusion he affects. He tells Anne, whose mother he calls "the mad monk" (14), that her marrying Tom will create a bond of "the two most boring men in London" (40). Even the defenseless and the innocent get swept into his trans-gendered verbal games. Earlier he had said of Anne, "She told me that if I was half a man, I'd leave [her]. But on discovering that *she* was, she left herself. Marina is the odd man out" (29–30). As this heartless reference will soon show, his jests can backfire. Ben doesn't know if he's straight or gay, an enigma that has maimed his sex drive. Virtually dead in the flesh, he offers Anne the same vapid, lackluster love he does Joey.

She wants and deserves more than a part-time, near-celibate husband. But the offer is the best he can make. And the best he wants to make; hiding, as usual, behind a veil of literary conceits, he calls his marriage "an intermission" (68) to his authentic life, the one he shares with Joey. But his bond with Joey, as much as he prizes it, is a literary conceit, too. As he admits, he's married "metaphorically" (65) to Joey.

His practice of interposing literature between himself and life has trounced him, in literary terms, no less. In line with the theatrical trope that labeled his marriage an "intermission," he has unwittingly assumed the role, popular in Renaissance drama, of the biter-bit. His bleeding his ties with both Joey and Anne of any vitality has left him hoisted by his own petard. His two "wives" (66) prefer loveless bonds to the sterile, infantile chaos proffered by Ben, whom they both love but must reject to preserve their sanity. They're acting out of self-preservation. Their knowledge that no intimate adult bond can survive without sex has put Ben out of the game. Their rejection of him is no choice at all. Solid evidence impels them. That neither of them has any illusions about the run-of-the-mill lives that await them with new partners shows how far Ben's value has dropped in the intimacy sweepstakes.

Frank Ardolino's view of Ben as "disheveled, despairing, and misanthropic" (175) covers a lot of ground. Arrogantly, Ben treats others like stage props, possessions, and inconveniences. The mockery he dishes out to them also speeds his own annihilation (Lahr 126). Like Patricia Highsmith's homicidal Tom Ripley, he's a master mimic. The accents he can speak on impulse include cockney, North of England, Scots, Australian, and American (adding, with a grace note from *Gone With the Wind*, "and frankly dear" [51]). But this verbal panache sinks his identity, reinforcing his coward's tendency to hide from people, including himself.

Having ruled out a happy, productive future, he fixates on the past (60). He's being counterproductive. Looking to punish Joey for defecting to Reg, he snaps, "You're going to live with your past.... I'll see to that" (73). Premised on the belief that Joey, like him, lives backward, his threat is empty. Time will waste him as he ponders it, his denial of time's forward flow fretting him as much it does much Dickens's Miss Havisham and Fitzgerald's Gatsby. Some of the offshoots of this childishness have already sprouted. Edna's Byron book will be coming out soon. Vacating both the office *and* the flat he had been sharing with Ben will help Joey move forward with his edition of Robert Herrick. Tellingly, it's Edna who informs Joey about the new office's availability. All the energy Ben has wasted sabotaging others hasn't kept them from both outgrowing and outclassing him. The list grows. Ann has found a job. Her Tom, who was once Ben's student (20), is publishing a novel — with the firm Reg works for, no less.

Ben has boxed himself in. Thanks to Gray's remarkable knowledge of the ways joy and grief intertwine, his portrayal of Ben's psyche in extremis goes unrivaled in 20th-century British drama, John Osborne's Jimmy Porter of *Look Back in Anger* (1956) included. Our emotional investment in Gray's "mad clown" (Weber 2) deepens as the play continues, going from a swipe of contempt to a pang of despair. Very few plays carry this charge. *Butley* doesn't deal with solutions but, rather, in the crushing horror of some people's lives. Both funny and gut-wrenching, its central figure's nihilism feels alive, not glued on or pored over. By depicting it, not *in medias res*, but instead, as a drama of ripe condition, Gray may have even invented a new theatrical form. Bruce Weber has numbered the benefits gained in economy, compression, and drive by Gray's tactic of anatomizing Ben on the verge of his collapse: "Butley is, when we first meet him, already well along in the process of falling apart.... He's drinking heavily, smoking relentlessly, avoiding his students" (66).

Like a Haydn trio, the play built around him uses qualities of refinement, intricacy of design, and formal containment to create a high, almost lacquered, finish. The early scenes don't lay out information in slabs, but, more exactly, release it drop by drop, asking us to work out the truth for ourselves. In short, Gray plays it cool, the right strategy when we weigh the crushing sadness that pelts Ben when he's reminded, by Reg, that he has lost both of his marriages within a couple of hours (66).

Reg has only pointed out to Ben what was projected at curtain rise. A reference to Wordsworth's *Prelude* made by Ben's first visitor (8) will prove thematic. Subtitled *The Growth of a Poet's Mind*, the poem forecasts in reverse the self-loathing and self-destruction that will waste Ben during the coming action. This punishment comes from within, as is shown in the wad of cotton wool covering "*a particularly nasty shaving cut*" (7) Ben brings onto the set. Life keeps draining from him. The first act ends after his episode with Anne. Alone onstage, he's replacing the cotton wool he had used to staunch the cut. But his chin can't heal regardless of how much wadding he uses. He won't let it. Rather than letting it scab, he keeps fidgeting with it (e.g., 57). Advisedly, just before discussing Anne with Joey, he pulls off the cotton wool protecting it. Perhaps he's trying to infect the cut. When it starts bleeding again, Joey dresses it (73), a kindness Ben repays by threatening to pull apart the life Joey hopes to build with Reg.

His having earlier asked Joey to treat his cut conveys two important truths about Ben: he can't, or won't, repair damage he has himself caused, and, left to his own devices, he's a goner. As his shaving cut shows, physical data map this downfall. At play's start, he snapped on a desk light in his office. This apparent trifle reconfirms Gray's outstanding economy of means. The new term has begun, and the lamp of learning will bring light to darkness. But something's wrong. Ben has to turn on the lamp sitting on Joey's desk because his own didn't work.

The play's finale finds Ben once more by himself. After three tries, he can't make his desk lamp go on. He's literally out of touch. A fumbling infant, he has lost his hand-eye coordination. Ardolino calls his failure to light the lamp "an act which represents his dark isolation and essential futility" (176). Having dispelled his support systems, he slouches in moral darkness. Having just banished a student from his office, he may have even short-circuited the light that symbolizes his career.

Thereby hangs the lesson he has been both fearing and craving. The shadows cloaking him remind us how rarely we appreciate the transient joys of daily life—jobs, friendships, family—until it's too late. Gray's treatment gives this commonplace idea power. Besides invoking the mundane beauty that we overlook, the play's closing moments make us ask what Ben will do next. What are his options in the workplace? This question must have been put to Gray many times. As late as 2008, he referred to the "the direction of the rest of Butley's life, the life he's going to lead after the curtain comes down" (LC 214). He never resolved this enigma. Why would he have? Samuel Beckett's claim that he never knew the meaning of the name Godot shifted to his readers the fun of figuring it out for themselves. Gray also doled out some fun. In a waggish moment in *Old Flames* (1990), he had a lawyer identify a man on trial for receiving stolen goods as "our Mr. Butley" (4SG 297). But it's doubtful that Ben, though an outlaw, recovered the motor skills to take up a life of crime after his teaching days ended. The final two letters of his two-syllable last name "-ly" suggest, in line with Gray's having designed the play as a drama of ripe condition, that he has been describing the dregs or lees of a quenched, flamed-out life.

Perhaps he might have included this touch in *Old Flames* to silence those who were still, 19 years after *Butley*'s debut, asking him what happened to Ben. Or he might have been indulging a characteristic fondness for self-referentiality. Ben, a Cambridge man, probably bracketed the Oxonian John Milton's verse among the world's "three most tedious literary subjects" (62) because Gray's academic hero at Cambridge, F.R. Leavis, hated Milton ("Milton's Verse," *Revaluation: Tradition and Development in English Poetry* [New York: Norton, 1963], 42–61). This throwaway note is vintage Gray. At bottom, *Butley* is a tough-minded, morally balanced work, as aware of the serendipity and the knockabout that leavens daily existence as it is of life's betrayals and other woes.

Small touches become telling touches in the play, more thematic than virtuosic. At this point in Gray's career, his work stops being promising. *Butley* is fulfilled, accomplished, and unmistakably his own. Tightly built, crisply figured, and boldly imagined, it marks the emergence of a major playwright.

Also, its blend of artistic refinement and power boosts it to the vanguard of the century's world theater. Though nothing in it is predictable, everything that happens looks inevitable. The play leaves you with the sense of having been grazed by the uncanny, something normally beyond the reach of words. Gray would never again come so close to saying the unsayable.

Both the sayable and the said, in the form of the literary canon that shapes both Ben's career and his downfall, provide a benchmark, too. Speaking of Ben's failure "to piece together meaning and significance" (182), David M. Bergeron sees time harrowing both him and Shakespeare's Hamlet. He develops the comparison at Ben's expense: "Like Hamlet, Butley finds time out of joint; unlike Hamlet, he doesn't know what to do about it" (182). Yes, Ben's losing battle to preserve the past and his denial of the psychological effects of time both nullify him. But it's Shakespeare's romances, not the tragedies, Bergson rightly believes, that meet Ben's calamity head-on: "Gray's use of Shakespeare ... undermines the ironic gap between Butley and Shakespearean characters and the resolution of their actions, particularly in Shakespeare's romances" (179), Bergeron noted shrewdly. The monarch's daughter survives miraculously, for instance, in *Cymbeline*, *A Winter's Tale*, *The Tempest*, and *Pericles*, where she's called Marina. Bergeron contrasts Pericles's discovery of his daughter and wife with the two divorces that hammer Ben in one afternoon — Joey leaving him for Reg and Anne planning to marry Tom. The romances continue to shed light. Like *Pericles*, *A Winter's Tale* treats incest, which grazes *Butley*, too, with Joey's having served as Ben's protégé-lover. But besides including reconciliation, *Winter's Tale* also features forgiveness, a grace that Ben decries.

Hope for him does appear in the form of the student, Miss Carol Heasman, who comes to his office to discuss her paper on *Winter's Tale*. Reading from it, she says promisingly of the play, "The imagery changes from disease to floral, the time from bitterness to joyfulness" (44). But Ben, rather than welcoming this renewal, bridles at what he wrongly perceives as Miss Heasman's hint that he stop spreading venom and bile. Within minutes, he maligns her essay and, with it, the hope that Shakespeare's play holds for *him*. The *Winter's Tale* "of a frozen soul" (43) Miss Heasman cites describes him. Unlike the statue of Hermione that softens and flushes into the beautiful wife of Leontes, Ben remains hard, a stone loser who'll never enjoy a family reunion or spiritual awakening like the one Shakespeare has described.

Accenting the importance of his tutorial with Miss Heasman is its placement, or position. The tutorial, the first scene in Act Two, follows directly Ben's lone exchange with Anne that ended Act One. Though divided by an interval or intermission, these two transactions join. It made sense that Anne, his most vital tie to the world, appears at the key moment when she did. Ben, though, downgrades this vitality by misnaming their daughter Miranda, despite knowing better. He's priming himself to make an offer he knows Anne has to reject — that he re-enter the family part time. Braiding this scene with the next one, the tutorial with Miss Heasman, is the truth that alcoholics like Ben usually squander their families before their jobs. The recurrence of this pattern with Joey at play's end reflects the alcoholic Gray's awareness of this truth. Immediately following Joey's departure from the office he was sharing with Ben is the appearance there of the student Mr. Gardner, whom Ben will attack more relentlessly than he did Miss Heasman.

Soon after first walking onto the set, Ben had produced his copy of *Cecily Parsley's Nursery Rhymes*, a poem from which he'll later recite to Gardner. Ardolino settles for a half-truth when he calls Ben's fondness for nursery rhymes "an indication of his infantilism" (175). Throughout the play, these rhymes also fueled the play's theme at multiple levels, sometimes making Ben's colleagues laugh at themselves, sometimes skewering the vanity and pretense their other colleagues have been using to stand in for the truth. Of one of the works that falls into this second category, Ben's own favorite, Sophia B. Blaydes says, "The poem has the imagery and rhythm of a nursery rhyme, but it has the message of despair" (383). This message has wrenched Ben's life, literature's having already struck back at him when Reg's publishing firm bought Tom's novel.

The ability of a nursery rhyme to pack power inside a brief space gives the lie to the 20 years it took Edna to write her Byron book, the 20 years Ben says he'll need to finish his hopelessly stalled book on Eliot, and Joey's pokiness in preparing his edition of Robert Herrick (1591–1674), ironically the carpe-diemist author of the lines from "To the Virgins, to Make Much of Time," "Gather ye rosebuds while you may./ Old Time is still a-flying;/ And this same flower that smiles today,/ Tomorrow will be dying." Ben cites the power Blaydes found in *Cecily Parsley* (18) when he says of the works comprising the book, "They can still be tongued with fire" (77).

This quip goes out to the student called Gardner. It will also be Ben's last salvo. Credit Rüdiger Imhof for saying that Gardner's entry into Ben's office just before play's end creates a framing effect (231). Ben's fist visitor was also a student who got turned away. But so much havoc was wreaked on Ben between these two visits that the attack he launches on Gardner carries more venom. With Miss Heasman, earlier in Act Two, his rudeness took the form of boredom. Dozing at the start of the tutorial, he drummed his fingers on his desk, recommended finishing their session early, and paced the office to stay awake.

Now Gray didn't bring Gardner into the play five minutes from the end out of desperation; no bearer of a structural flaw, Gardner wasn't smuggled in to resolve the action in a way that the people who had already appeared onstage couldn't plausibly do. His arrival onstage was carefully adumbrated. As Gray said in *The Last Cigarette*, Gardner's carefully timed appearance was crucial:

"He comes on in the last scene, which automatically makes him important, and furthermore we have heard a great deal about him at regular intervals during the play" (214).

A reprise of the optimism found in Miss Heasman's reading of *A Winter's Tale*, Gardner's very name implies the growth and renewal needed to revive Ben's sagging life. Ben has known this himself. He lied to Edna about asking Gardner to cancel her seminar in favor of doing a tutorial with *him*. His motives were not academic. The one-on-one format of tutorials could nudge their professional relationship into a dalliance. This motive was already made clear. In a phone call from James, his Department Head, spurred on by an irate Edna, he referred to Gardner as "she" (36). He's feigning ignorance of Edna's rage. But his mistake with Gardner's gender cuts two ways. Ben already saw Gardner in feminine terms. Just moments earlier, Joey had identified him both as the "boy who complained about Edna's seminar" and "the one you found interesting" (31).

With Joey's defection to Reg a certainty, Ben *has* had his eye on Gardner. He's still thinking of Gardner as Joey's replacement during their short visit. He has him recite a passage from Eliot's "East Coker," to which he counters with another quotation from Eliot. But it's from "The Love Song of J. Alfred Prufrock," and it's spoken by a woman. By telling Gardner, "You're not what I mean at all, not what I mean at all," he's banishing him. "I'm too old for the likes of you" (77), he adds; he has stopped combing the student body for prospective boyfriends. The rejection is blatantly sexual. Moments before, he had recited the following Beatrix Potter nursery rhyme:

Ninny Nanny Netticoat
In a white petticoat,
With a red nose —
The longer he stands
The shorter he grows. (77)

These "uncompromisingly brutal" (LC 231) words have two linked meanings, both of which demean Gardner: the more time Gardner spends in Ben's presence, the more his charm fades; Ben's interest in Gardner sinks in direct ratio to the amount of time spent with him. This "violent insult" (LC 231) is Gardner's send-off. Ben won't teach him, and he can't re-enroll in Edna's seminar. When Gardner cites "all that trouble" he took to sign up for Ben's tutorial he's told, "Trouble for you, fun for me" (77). He's left reeling. His class schedule is blank, while Ben has reverted to his childishness. Since no one else would enjoy the sadistic joke Ben played on him, Gardner's misery will be his private treat, like the cake that stood as an act of judgment on Howarth at the end of *Spoiled*.

Like *Sleeping Dog*, *Wise Child*, and *Dutch Uncle* before it, *Butley* conveys a sense of constricted space and lost options. But this pessimism modifies in

Butley, where everyone but Gardner and Ben looks out to fresh fields. This counterpoint is Gray's most refined and elegant to date. *Butley* unravels both the secrets and wounds within each of its people while steadily shortening Ben's leash, a truth underscored by his remaining onstage during the entire play. The plot opens outward from the office where Ben is confined. Nor do his counterparts languish while he's shredding his life. They're developed as much as the needs of the play demand. Joey, for instance, likes Edna, whereas Ben, who resents the joy of others, greets the news that her book has found a home with the sarcasm, "Now the center cannot hold. Mere Edna is loosed on the world" (80).

Don't bridle. Ben can always muster a quip to smear, sting, or cut someone down. Anne's mother is "the mad monk" (14), and her fiancé Tom, the "most boring man in London" (19). Even Reg's parents, whom Ben has never met, get spattered. But this draft dodger devotes more malice to their son. He has singled out for attack Reg's national service. Asked why he never served himself, he chooses an answer he knows will smart: "I got took for queer" (61).

Reg and his fellow victims of Ben's sour wit have to pause. His wisecracks damage him as much as they do others. He couldn't have invented a worse enemy. His failure to provide sex to both Anne and Joey redirect the sexual innuendoes of the Beatrix Potter poem he recites to Gardner back to *him*. Even though his tactics may change, he never stops scourging himself. Changing his reason for missing military service, he tells Reg that his military board found him suffering from "a touch of T.B." (64). If he's being honest, his chain-smoking stands as one more example of the death wish that has already cut him down to the level of spoiled brat.

Joey, as his last name suggests, could form the keyston(e) that holds his life together. As his childish front name suggests, he has been content to play the roles of protégé, playmate, and lover to his bullying mentor, Ben. His filling of so many of Ben's needs will make his absence a greater loss than Anne's. Was this loss predicted? Another Joey (Romper), this time a woman, occupied the keystone, or apex, of a love triangle whose dissolution in *Simple People* left the novel's hero stranded and dazed. (Outdoing Logan Bester, Ben will become the castaway in two love triangles.) A more conspicuous portent of Ben's expulsion comes early in *Butley*. He hears Joey saying "in point of fact," a phrase Joey will repeat often (e.g., 17), as did Logan (SP 41). When Ben hears it from Reg, though (59), he's shaken; it tells him that Reg and Joey have gotten close.

He has to know that Joey's chance for happiness runs high with Reg. Like Anne's, Joey's casting off of Ben is a responsible adult choice. Joey may have been speaking for himself when he told Ben in Act Two that he could get Anne back if he wanted her (49). Both he and Anne love Ben; neither loves his replacement. But by withholding sex, Ben has denied them the adult love they want and deserve. What's more, Ben can't be counted on to provide either one of them the emotional support coterminous with healthy sex. His one, strategically placed, conversation with Anne conveys his false-heartedness. This pivotal scene does everything Gray asks of it. Having been done correctly, it needed no preambles or sequels. Besides, Gray knew that showing the couple together more than once, in addition to prolonging the play for no reason, would bleed force from their lone stage meeting.

In Joey's case, Ben's barrage was already under way. Joey is facing a major professional hurdle. In two weeks, a panel of his superiors will decide whether he deserves a full-time lectureship or a pink slip. But rather than easing Joey's anxiety, Ben grows evasive and even discouraging whenever the subject of Joey's chances for promotion comes up. He'll invent reasons for Joey to fret. "You're in trouble, " he says. "A member of the department has his knife out" (15). He's taunting Joey to punish him for wanting to leave the office they share to work on a lecture.

Reg would never be this selfish or mean. Solid, practical, and reliable, he has the yeoman virtues of his north-of-England heritage. He did tough duty with the Gurkhas in India when he could have used his homosexuality to skip army service. And since being demobbed, he has been making headway in a London publishing house (Ben calls him a "lucky parvenu" [69]). An over-the-shoulder look back to *Spoiled* tells us that Reg gives Joey the capable mentoring that Les Grant provided the more tentative and indecisive Donald Clenham. Reg leavens this resolve with wit in his conversation with Ben in Act Two, deflecting Ben's insults smoothly and turning Ben's literary education against him. He answers Ben's quip about his metaphorical marriage to Joey in terms more familiar to Ben than to him: "You might say that when he comes to me our Joey will be moving out of figures of speech into matters of fact. Ours will be too much like a marriage to be a metaphor" (66). This candor brought him to Ben's office, to begin with. He wants to include Joey in a three-way meeting to make it clear that he and Joey have become a couple.

Ben reacts to the news of his ouster in typical fashion, seasoning mercurial wit with moral irrelevance. "We're preserving the unities. The use of messengers has been quite skilful" (73). Under the snap and sizzle of his words, though, lies a great sadness. As he did by calling his marriage to Joey "metaphorical," he has interposed a layer of literature between himself and his losses. His skill at word games has clicked into ideal working order, but inside a moral vacuum. His aestheticizing of experience has also failed to staunch his pain. But Gray blocks any impulse we may have for feeling sorry for him. Within a minute, he vows vengeance on Joey for dumping him to be with Reg.

This spurt of malice comes as no shock. All along, literature and its categories have been revealing more about Ben than they have hidden. Two of the three authors he proposed for inclusion in a contemporary fiction course (Burroughs, Genet, and Roth [15]) were gay; besides, Genet is hardly known as a fiction writer. Another exchange in the play's first act also says more about Ben's sexual orientation than he might have intended. It was John Stuart Mill's charwoman (Gopnik 87) who accidentally burned the only copy of Thomas Carlyle's *History of the French Revolution* and not John Ruskin's, as Ben claims (33). And as he might have known? This factual error on his part is so rare that it merits a look. Either his disgust with QMC or sheer cussedness might have led him to pass on this misinformation. But the pride he always displays strutting his knowledge makes this explanation unlikely. Carlyle and Ruskin have meshed in his mind because neither man consummated his marriage.

Ben, a near sexual cipher himself, will later ask Anne, "Tell me, when did we last have it off? Was it that time in the park beneath the trees, or did we have a quick go subsequently, in bed or under the kitchen table" (41). The reference to outdoor sex carries weight. In *Little Nell*, first produced in 2006, 35 years after *Butley*, Charles Dickens deflowers Ellen Ternan in a park (20). These two passages do more than allude to Emma Bovary's fall from virtue in the woods (Gray's purpose in *Colmain*). A virile father of nine, Dickens, though aching with desire for Nell, might have had qualms about introducing her to sex in a bedroom. Better to dispatch it quickly, he probably reasoned, as soon as chance permits. Ben, another victim of sexual anxiety, also might have performed more readily when caught unawares.

His bedroom heebie-jeebies have precedents in the canon. In *Spoiled*, like *Butley* first produced in 1971, Joanna grumbles that her husband (who uses the term "stage fright" [1SG 259]) hasn't "kissed her properly" for five months (1SG 301). He *will* take up her bid for "basic soothing" (1SG 301), but it's with his student, Donald Clenham, who's so un-soothed, or flustered, by his services that he's unable to take the O-level exams for which Howarth had been prepping him.

As if it might tell why Gray dedicated *Spoiled* to his wife Beryl (1SG 241), we might also note that *Dutch Uncle* (1969), the stage play immediately preceding *Butley* in time, featured in Perkin Godboy a husband who, like Carlyle and Ruskin, couldn't consummate his marriage. The tangents where lives, fictional and real, intersect and influence each other always fascinated Gray. They also remind us of the sometimes brutal frankness Gray brought to his work (Pinter 15). Was Gray glad to see Pinter go public with his reminder? To his penchant for self-referentiality may be added Lyn Gardner's disclosure that a scoundrel based on Pinter appeared in a 1993 TV adaptation of *Common Pursuit* (2).

This same effusiveness turns up another of Gray's counterparts, Alan Bennett. Joey tells Ben that Reg's father is a Leeds butcher (22)—like Bennett's father. In fact, Bennett recalls in *Writing Home* (London: Faber, 1994) delivering meat to a Mrs. Fletcher, the mother of Valerie, future wife to T.S. Eliot (ix). This juxtaposition, or coincidence, conveys more than Gray's sense of fun. As if in rebuke, Eliot's photo stays in view during the whole performance of *Butley*. Bennett's homosexuality, aired by him for the first time in print in the autobiographical *Untold Stories* (2005), was no doubt known in London's West End, the nerve center for theater people like Gray, in the early 1970s.

These overlaps and tangents, near parallels and skewed mirror images, combine with earlier observations about eroticism in *Butley* to say something about Gray's gender anxieties in 1971. John Mills groups Miss Heasman, Edna, Anne, and her mother as a quartet of masculine women (420–1). Following suit, Ardolino recasts Miss Heasman as "he's a man" (177). Belonging to this roster is Edna's last name, Shaft, and, for good measure, her recalling to Ben that she began working on Byron while staying "in Ursula's cottage" (74). Gray makes sure we get his point. Asked if she still goes to the cottage, she answers revealingly, "Oh, not in the same way. Ursula got married" (75). The inference is that Ursula changed her sexual preference and, as most other converts to straight sex would do, saw no reason to identify Edna to her husband as her ex-lover.

Together with the sexual pairings in *Wise Child* and *Dutch Uncle*, those in *Butley* bespeak marital anxiety; Mills even conjectures that Marina might have been conceived in "perhaps even the *only* sexual encounter ... Butley and Anne experienced" (419) together. Consistent with Mills's surmise is Gray's having picked Dostoevsky's *Idiot* to adapt for the English stage in 1971 among any number of classic Russian novels because two of its major plot lines dovetailed in his psyche: the invalid Marie's loving but chaste bond with the book's eponym and Natasha's murder on her honeymoon by her lustful husband.

Gray always had the craft to convey a lifetime of futility in a throwaway detail. Also noteworthy is his ability to tune that craft, or technique, to his vision. Our meaning, he agrees with Beckett, lies in our compulsion to narrate our meaninglessness. Most historical or fictional events belong not only to the milieu in which they occur. Like *Godot*, *Butley* shows that the expression of emotional truth needs no words. Alone, pithed, and unable to live or die, Ben silently faces the nightmare of cosmic indifference.

Gray's refusal to hide behind his words neither diminish nor tar him. If moments like the finale of *Butley* reflect his willingness to explore his responses to the world, such moments also give his writing its burn. Whatever of his inmost self he invested in *Butley* makes it his most disturbing, prophetic work.

First shown at London's Queen's Theatre in July 1981, *Quartermaine's Terms* debuted a decade after *Butley* but unfolds nearly a decade earlier, in "the early 1960s" (3SG 4). Harold Pinter directed the work, as he did *Butley*, but, rather than using Alan Bates in the lead role, picked Edward Fox, who'd later star in Gray's telescript, *They Never Slept* (1991) and stage play, the last by Gray that Pinter would direct, *The Old Masters* (2004).

Quartermaine's Terms also follows *Butley* by both peopling its cast with professional educators and unfurling in a single set — the staff room of Cambridge's Cull-Loomis School of English for Foreigners. But whereas the action of *Butley* fills but one afternoon, that of its more leisurely paced successor, like Chekhov's *Three Sisters*, which gets mentioned in the play (3SG 39), both spreads over a period of two-and-a-half or three years and ends with the expulsion of a cultured, refined, low-key figure we have been responding ambiguously to as we did to Ben.

Who could also be dismissed soon after the stage action of *Butley*—a work whose eponym has less charm than Chekhov's Prozorov sibs or Gray's St. John Quartermaine. Why should Ben lose his job? *Quartermaine's Terms* is a sequel or companion piece to the urban-sited *Butley* despite the ten-year gap between the debuts of the two plays. But we shouldn't be surprised. Gray often kept thinking about his plays after production. *Simply Disconnected* (1996) features characters he introduced in *Otherwise Engaged* (1975). *Butley* and *Quartermaine's Terms* both open on a Monday that also marks the launch of a new school term. And besides using academic settings and people, these two plays also build from what Katherine H. Burkman wisely called Gray's "darkly comic treatment of [his] protagonists" (Burkman ed. 14).

These protagonists typify Gray, as well, in reflecting both his technical frugality and his fondness for contrast as a thematic device. All bile and fury, Ben had an animal quickness that included a sinister way of penetrating what someone was up to, a feeling for weakness in friends as well as rivals. St. John Quartermaine, who's even more asexual, benign if also bland and listless, enjoys helping other people rather than tripping them up. Another contrast: in place of the student protests ignited in *Butley* by the government's stand on Apartheid and Vietnam are the mini-scale flare-ups on the cricket grounds of Cull-Loomis and the town-gown friction sparked by complaints from local merchants about the oddities of the school's exotics.

Gordon's reasons for calling *Quartermaine's Terms* Gray's "finest achievement as a stage playwright" (Burkman, ed. 22) frames an issue best approached by looking back to a work Gray wrote even before *Butley*, *Little Portia* (1967), the main figures of which, like St. John, teach at a foreign language school in Cambridge. Harking to Gray's statement about the Spill Academy, "There were French windows everywhere" (LP 248), are the open French windows cited in the stage directions of Act One, scene one of *Quartermaine's Terms* (3SG 8). It's from the other side of these windows, open or closed, that the clamor from the school's cricket pitch enters the quieter, but more clenched, ambiance of the staff room. Finally, French windows play a big role in the climax of both novel and play (LP 262–4; 3SG 69).

Central to both these scenes is a newcomer to the schools' faculties. Derek Meadle shares many of the grievances of his prototype, Francis Meadle. These adjuncts, or part-timers, both teach twice as much for half the pay earned by the permanents. And when school is out of session, they're not paid at all, a hardship that forces them to work as postmen, fearing all the time that they'll be spotted by their colleagues and students during their routes. What's worse, their colleagues keep misnaming them (e.g., LP 261; 3SG 11), implying that, as north-of-Englanders, they'd do well to settle for their lot. They'll remain victims of the class game that, to Gray, has continued to suffuse English life.

But Derek Meadle of Hull (3SG 13) does get his wished-for permanency. He marries, too, creating a bond that rids him of the oafishness that had always caused him embarrassments like breaking glassware and ripping his pants (3SG 60)—though the neck brace he's wearing in the play's last scene (3SG 69) suggests that he's still a klutz. The reason for this brightening of prospects is his function in the plot, that of St. John's foil; as Meadle's fortunes improve, those of St. John drop. Eddie Loomis, the school's co-owner and academic tutor, mirrors St. John, too, but in a more complex way than Meadle does. Though he delights in the school's "growing reputation as one of the best" (3SG 20) of its kind in the country, he also keeps fretting about enrollment figures. So vexed is he at one point, in fact, that he forgets to bring with him the teaching schedules of his staff for the new term (3SG 13–4).

Further anxiety stems from the complaints he has been getting from Cambridge's landladies and restaurateurs about student pranks. Specifically, he has to defuse an incident involving some Japanese at a local eatery (3SG 19, 48) that has already threatened next year's student intake from Japan. Inner peace keeps eluding him. A newly converted teacher who's peddling to her students the Pentecostal creed she has just bought into has him grumbling about students from the Catholic countries (3SG 68) taking offense and quitting the school.

His drive to keep enrollment figures high also means keeping the staff up to speed. And it's to his credit that he'll fault his teachers as gently as he can when he sees them acting out of line. Thus he asks his scruffy "*ghastly*"-looking (3SG 7) junior colleague the first day of the new term, "Mark, is it these fast-fading old eyes of mine, or did you forget to shave this morning, or yesterday morning, even?" (3SG 10) His knowledge that, in student-faculty relationships, appearances have their reality later prompts him to tell Meadle that removing his bicycle clips will offset the impression that he's "just passing through" (3SG 20).

The teacher he has to watch most closely is St. John. In Act One, scene one, he reproves St. John for failing to learn his students' names. Then he notes St. John's failure to return his students' writing assignments. But rather than suggesting that St. John hasn't yet read this work, he tactfully reminds him that the school's reputation depends on its students being able to show friends back home their corrected assignments (3SG 12). Loomis's pragmatic concern over the impression made by the school's departed students runs high.

He singles out, "in spite of this tired old brain of mine" (3SG 56), several postcards addressed to St. John by a former Swiss student named Frederick Boller (e.g., 3SG 11, 56). Unfortunately, these postcards are written in an English so execrable that, in Loomis's view, they must be destroyed before they circulate and smear the school's image. (Boller's place in the plot can be explained quickly. Both he and the postcards he writes St. John "in almost unrecitable English" [LP xvii] come from Gray's own career of teaching foreigners. Gray's self-referentiality also produces in *Quartermaine's Terms* two citations of his birthplace, Hayling Island (3SG 47, 59), which is where Derek Meadle and his bride honeymoon).

Any actor past the age of 40 would relish the chance to play Eddie Loomis. Starting with Act Two, which opens about a year after the curtain falls on the play's first act, he grows frailer and more worn with each onstage appearance. He hasn't been worrying only about the failure of his staffers to pull their weight, even though he might. Having attained his permanency, the once hyper-conscientious Derek Meadle is now dismissing his students early, and St. John, Loomis knows, has skipped one class altogether, causing, in line with the play's sly awareness of national types, his German students to complain about "not getting their money's worth of syllabus" (3SG 68). Also grinding Loomis down is the chronic illness of the school's co-founder, Loomis's business partner and lover, Thomas Cull. When Thomas dies, Loomis abandons the school, finding no meaning in it without his long-time partner.

A brilliant invention, Thomas helps drive the action without showing his face. As his name suggests (Thomas Cull-Thomas Skull), he's associated with the death that will take him at Christmas. He certainly knows about the sacking of St. John, and it's just as likely that he recommended it. From what's said about him, he's a shrewd businessman. The play in which he's an offstage force doesn't satirize a once-vital, but now-exhausted, way of life. St. John is sacked, or culled, because he's the weakest of the herd. By any responsible standard of judgment, his terms, or semesters, at C-L must halt. He deals with students in terms not merely obsolete but, rather, unprofessional. If he's not excusing them before final bell, he'll sit in front of them speechless—that is, if he makes it to class at all. This, as Loomis knows and fears, is distinctly possible; the end of the first scene of Act Two ends with St. John alone onstage — panicking because he doesn't know his teaching schedule here at the start of the school year, even though he has had weeks to think about it. Act Two had opened with him snoozing, his lap full of books and student papers, presumably ungraded and overdue.

Gray had H. Rider Haggard's Allan Quatermain on his mind when he named the eponym of *Quartermaine's Terms*. He would mention Haggard (1856–1925) in *Fat Lady* (1988; 35), and, in St. John, he created a character whose personality, affect, and value system all differ so sharply from those of the stoical hero of novels like *King Solomon's Mines* (1885) and *She and Allan* (1920) that it becomes clear early in the play that he meant us to juxtapose the two men. Both of them, first of all, are out of step with their respective societies, although neither can be called a social critic, rebel, or outcast. But the life of ease and comfort that St. John basks in would repel Allan. Like John Buchan's Richard Hannay, this professional big-game hunter prefers danger to repose. This wizard rifleman also clashes with St. John in both his adaptability and survival skills, or bushmanship. The soft, manually inept, and slow-to-react St. John would die quickly in the same African wild that the twice-widowed Allan continues to patrol into his old age, lacking any other means of self-support.

Having a job, though, beats having none, a plight that faces St. John along perhaps with that other educator, Ben Butley, who, like St. John, misuses the freedom his job permits. We never learn if St. John, like Ben, has his own office because he's such a steady fixture in C-L's staff room, where he's seen alone at both beginning and end of all but one of the play's five scenes. When a colleague, returning from term break at the start of the play's second act, hears that St. John spent the holidays in Cambridge, he thinks "for a moment" (3SG 42) that St. John stayed anchored to the staff room. Credit the colleague's fancy. The play's first act ended with St. John, finding the staff room empty on a late Friday afternoon and stealing into it, as if he had no life outside the place. At play's end, too, after being fired, he remains there, rejecting an invitation to go to the home of C-L's new principal, the man who fired him, for a consoling drink and a family visit. One can see why. The career choice he had made and stood by harks to this famous passage in the "Little Gidding" section of *Four Quartets*:

> We shall not cease from exploration
> And the end of our exploring
> Will be to arrive where we started
> And know the place for the first time.

The familiar for him has greater value than the extraordinary; nay, it's more extraordinary. Home isn't only where the heart is; it's also the only chance of having a heartbeat. Everything else is abstract.

Thus Naomi Siegel, in her review of a performance of the play at Centenary College in Hackettstown, New Jersey, judged well when she called C-L's staff room St. John's "only source of belonging" (2). But how much of a stake can he claim? Just moments after getting fired, he says, "I mean it's no good being all right in the staff room if you're no good in the classroom" (3SG 73). He may have overrated his clubbability. Gray had been questioning all along his fit as a colleague. After being corrected for misnaming Derek Meadle, he's censured for having asked Meadle twice in short order about his holiday (3SG 44). Nor is this gaffe a rarity. His colleagues have already shown impatience with him. He opens the play by misspeaking — on the subject of his colleague Anita Manchip's hair. Early in the next act, his chatter riles Anita, who's trying to work. But so what? Anything like a rebuke or a snub leaves him unfazed. Anita had apologized for the abruptness with which her boyfriend canceled a recent dinner meeting with him on the phone (as with Ben Butley, people are forever canceling their plans with him [e.g., 3SG 25, 27]). Yet he defuses Nigel's rudeness, calling it a blessing as his landlady, he claims, resents the time he spends in telephone talk.

This exaggerated humility fits his character. Gray's Introduction to *Little Portia* notes St. John's "decency, unfailing courtesy, and active but incoherently expressed kindness" (xi). This appraisal is correct. St. John's colleague Mark Sackley asks him to dinner to repay the "companionship" (3SG 61-2, 27) he provided after Mark's wife and children left him. It's also to St. John that Anita confides her heartbreak over a love bond gone sour (3SG 64). And it's St. John's affability and charm that induce Gray, always keen on maintaining dramatic plausibility, to leave him alone with Derek Meadle after the newcomer first reports to C-L. Clumsy and wrong-footed, the accident-prone Meadle tore his pants during his first trip to the school while trying to avoid hitting some students with his bike. The sympathy St. John extends to a dismayed Meadle exceeds politeness. Honest about the torn pants being "a bit of a write-off" (3SG 14), he tells Meadle that he can teach his class without incident by pulling down his jacket to cover the tear. But the comfort he extends Meadle takes him too far. His saying that Meadle looks "rather formidable" (3SG 16) with jacket pulled down to his knees sends the newcomer into a rage.

Bob Rendell slipped up when he said, in his review of the Centenary College revival of *Quartermaine's Terms*, of St. John's colleagues, "They have neither the humanity, patience, or courtesy to include him in their lives" (2). First of all, these lives are full and fast paced. By play's end, Mark Sackley has written a 3,643-page novel (3SG 49), and the family that left him has returned; death has rocked two faculty families, while two others are expecting babies. This flurry has made St. John less of an actor than a stage, one who helps flesh out a space where events occur. As an actor, or agent, he does little. Using a related metaphor, Judith Roof rightly calls St. John, in whom the sap of life has never risen very high, the "immoveable audience of a moveable feast" (Burkman, ed. 38).

Roof's observation squares with Gray's statement, "All the other characters revolve around him [St. John] without making contact with his real nature" (LP xi). Part of the blame for this disconnect lies with St. John. Reactive and passive, he makes little happen. And when he does act, he usually blunders. He breaks a slide projector, for instance. His excuse that the projector broke because of its age fails him, since it was new. He hasn't kept up with technological developments in his field. This failure goes beyond the classroom. His being literally out of touch with his surroundings, a conceit carried over from *Butley*, had already come forth in the previous scene when Mark Sackling faints from the anguish of having lost his family.

This crisis shows once again Gray's talent for defining character through contrast. Henry Windscape, a senior colleague and friend of St. John's, acts straightaway. He reaches the slumping Mark Sackling before St. John does, massages his heart, orders that his head be kept up, and tells someone to chafe his wrists, physically demanding work best done in shirtsleeves. Though reluctant to take off the coat that's hiding the rip in his pants, Derek Meadle does so, anyway, while St. John is still wondering what to do. Elsewhere in the staff room, Eddie Loomis beats him to the phone to call for an ambulance.

St. John's impotence in a crisis is symbolized by bicycle clips. Windscape and Meadle both wear them often onstage (3SG e.g., 13, 16, 18). Sackling has them on, too, for *"the first time in the play"* (3SG 62) after reconnecting with his family. He has livened up, like those men on the go, Meadle, who'll gain his permanency, and Windscape, who'll soon become the school's "sole principal" (3SG 71). As another example, Sackling succeeds Eddie Loomis as "academic tutor" (3SG 71). St. John, having nowhere to go, never wears bicycle clips, lending tang to Windscape's joke about his having spent an entire school break in the staff room.

He has nowhere to go because, regardless of his destination, he'll always be alone. He has an alienating persona. Lacking a self of his own, he takes his cue from others. He needs to learn self-trust. Even though he resists playing the role of voyeur that traps other ineffectual bachelors like him in Gray's work, he tries too hard to please, a mistake that turns his virtues into defects. Gray describes through him, as Henry Fielding did through Tom Jones, the confusion and dismay caused when people fail to temper their goodness with prudence. Agreeable and approving, St. John brings no traction or tension to conversations, even when he's listening to what's being said. As Roof says, his tactlessness corrupts the friendly interest he takes in his colleagues (Burkman, ed. 38). His conversation-ending practice of praising everybody and every*thing* mentioned in his presence, besides impugning his judgment, irks people. Unmediated by tact, it can also deceive him into probing inadvertently the anxieties of his colleagues, *all* of whom, as Gray takes care to show, live on the edge.

Although inadvertent, St. John's Pollyanna ways have recoiled on him. To extend blanket approval everywhere amounts to moral defeatism. Along with his colleague Anita's hair (3SG 5), the school's faculty (3SG 14), its student enrollment (3SG 20), and the discovery on the part of a journal editor connected to the school of a new publisher (3SG 27) are all—"terrific." Then there's the tired adjective "old," that he uses to voice his affection for people. The editor of the magazine with ties to C-L is "old Nigel" (3SG 5), and Henry Windscape "old Henry" (3SG 6). This habit of displaying affection can become unnerving. He commiserates with Sackling when he learns that his wife, called "old Camelia" and son "little Tom," have decamped. But the epithet he uses later—"poor little Tom"—makes Sackling growl that it turns Tom into "something out of the workhouse" (3SG 51). Nor does Sackling share St. John's regret upon learning, after the fact, that they both spent term break in town without meeting for dinner.

Sackling will later object to St. John's failure to "take anything seriously" (3SG 61). He has to tell St. John that, instead of being happy, as St. John believes, their colleague "old Anita" (3SG 26) has spent the last year in misery. Because she distrusts her philandering boyfriend, Nigel, she has had three abortions. Sackling's takedown of St. John in this scene isn't atypical. Others have noted his lazy proclivity to see goodness everywhere. When Anita tells him, "What a nice man you are" (3SG 64), she's not simply extending praise. His failure to engage with life has not only run his goodness to waste. Its way of distorting that goodness also brings out the worst in others.

After Windscape and Sackling ask him to leave the staff room to let them talk privately, they forget about him. Only after a discreet interval does he re-enter the room, countering Windscape's apology by saying that he enjoyed being outdoors. Although nothing in this affable response has registered at the rational level, Windscape knows St. John well enough to recognize that his rudeness will be automatically forgiven. The rub here is his recognition that he can flout decency and even morality in his dealings with St. John. Anita, too, knows that she can break a theater date with St. John, despite his having already bought her a ticket. When she tells him that she has suddenly decided to go to London, he answers predictably, "Oh what a good idea" (3SG 25). He can overlook any slight. When Meadle breaks an unwritten rule not to criticize a colleague—to his face, no less—St. John, the butt of his attack, rather than protesting, shrugs it off (3SG 53).

The play's finale puts him alone onstage with Windscape, the school's new principal. Gathering many of the play's dramatic tensions, their one-on-one exchange wheels in the framework of the family, like the ending of *Wise Child*, Eddie Loomis having recently described his staffers as a family (3SG 68). St. John accepts Windscape's dismissal of him with his trademark decorum. He even helps Windscape through the ordeal. Like Chekhov's Madame Ranevsky of *The Cherry Orchard* and Blanche Du Bois of *Streetcar*, he's determined to bow out becomingly: "I know that I haven't got much to offer—never had, I suppose—and recently it's got even worse—it's a wonder—a wonder people have put up with me for so long, eh?" (3SG 73). He's right about the drop in his classroom performance. He hasn't been earning his keep at C-L, and, either unable or unwilling to spruce up his teaching, knows that it can only get worse. No soft, sweet backward look at a golden age, *Quartermaine's Terms* avoids the elegiac. It's more like a portrait of those who write the elegies—comic, affectionate, regretful, but also dryly aware.

In his decline, St. John offsets Derek Meadle, who, besides winning his permanency, manages to get his wife appointed to the faculty—this, despite what he admits is "quite a serious speech impediment" (3SG 45). This stroke of black humor comes at St. John's expense. He's replaced by two north-country provincials he'd call upstarts were he less kindhearted. It's material that these replacements are husband and wife. St. John's fall is linked to his being single. Meadle enters the play, like him, a bachelor. But his repetition of the phrase "as a matter of fact" (3SG 44), in the second act after closing with Daphne, hints at the strength of their bond, as did the cluster "in point of fact," used by both Joey and Reg in *Butley* index the promise of *theirs*.

St. John is the play's sole character who's not paired off, save Melanie Garth, who perforce lives alone after committing matricide. This same Melanie, the school's Elementary Conversation specialist (3SG 18), comes before us at the Christmas party that closes the play *"nervously smoking a cigarette,"* Gray adding significantly, *"It is the first time in the play she has smoked. She smokes throughout the scene, lighting one after the other"* (3SG 69). Her new addiction recalls the estranged Ben Butley, who smokes his way through the play bearing his name. Given the scourging Gray heaps on himself in his diaries for failing to give up cigarettes, chain-smokers in his work always carry a heavy burden of wrongdoing.

No, St. John doesn't smoke; nor will he start. But his being a bachelor makes him prone to far worse. Windscape asks him to baby-sit his teen-age daughter, who has just come home from hospital, where she was treated for a nervous breakdown. "You're the only person Susan will allow to baby-sit" (3SG 66), he adds. St. John is needed at Susan's side because the Windscapes want to see *La Règle du Jeu* (1929), a film Henry prizes for its decency and humanity (3SG 66), those same traits he values in St. John. Perhaps he also needs to see Jean Renoir's happy farce to purge the distress of watching *M*, the 1931 German classic about a child killer he and his wife walked out on. Conversely, St. John not only finished watching *M*, but even enjoyed it (3SG 66). Now Gray never compares him to the manic child killer in Fritz Lang's movie. But it's worth noting that both men are unassuming and deferential around others, as were Perkin Godboy and Reg Christie, the serial killer upon whom he was based. And, though showing no violent tendencies, the gentle, biddable St. John *has* been unraveling from within, as he admits. As early as the play's second scene, he admits forgetting to give Loomis an "urgent" message (3SG 25) from Thomas Cull. His teaching is faulted twice in Act Two, scene two (3SG 55, 57), a foreshadowing of which came in Act One, scene two, when this butter-fingered man's failure to keep up with scientific advances in his field wrecked a new slide projector.

Gray's interest in Russian literature invests his portrayal of his play's eponym as it did with that of *Butley*. Though called "the perfect outsider" despite having taught at C-L from the school's inception (3SG 62), St. John justifies the label. He pushes no academic or political agenda, and he stands free of factions. But his detachment has foiled him, anyway. In an echo from Tolstoy, his fate is the dramatic unfolding of what's *meant* to happen to him, a step in a process dictated by *him*. His firing stems logically from his behavior. No victim of chance, he has to be fired because he doesn't give value as a teacher. Windscape, whose name is a rush of sibilants, nailed it when he told St. John that "there's no room for you anymore" (3SG 73).

Both the play's comic-ironic tone and muted climax recall Chekhov, like Tolstoy a believer in inevitability. St. John's inertia, irresponsibility, and inability or refusal to resist his sad fate invoke any number of Chekhov's people swept along by a series of events they've put in place. His cool acceptance of Windscape's firing of him echoes the trapped lovers in "The Lady and the Lap Dog," Andrei Prozorov and his wretched marriage in *Three Sisters*, and Mme. Ranevsky's loss of her cherry orchard. And so it goes. St. John's getting four dinner invitations for the same evening in Act Two recalls the hard-luck bachelor protagonists of Gogol's "Overcoat" and Dostoevsky's "Double," minor functionaries both of whom attract heaps of attention before their final defeats. Dostoevsky's Prince Myshkin of *Idiot*, who is much more saintly than idiotic, also resonates here, even though the kindness and charity he bestows upon St. Petersburg's greedy, arrogant big-wigs have the effect of idiocy. The Prince's plight has revived in Cambridge. Despite the truth of Anita's assessment of St. John, "What a nice man you are" (3SG 64), he has to be banished, lest his goodness cause more grief than it already has. This grief runs high. St. John lives and breathes, and he keeps haunting us after his tale ends.

His is the unlived life, an English update of the superfluous man, a character type that pervades 19th-century Russian fiction. The picture of T.S. Eliot that stays in view throughout the entire production of *Butley* brings the archetype up to date. Like Eliot's most famous character, J. Alfred Prufrock, St. John is deferential, polite, and, as the man who can be counted on to comfort a distressed colleague or baby-sit at the last minute, useful. This gallantry has attracted attention. Taking his cue from the idea that Archie Rice, the washed-up music-hall comic in John Osborne's *The Entertainer* (1957), symbolizes Britain's demise as a superpower, Bob Rendell offers St. John as a possible "stand-in for the once powerful British empire" (3).

Rendell's idea has worth. Plays like *Sleeping Dog* (1967) and *Rear Column* (1978) reflect Gray's interest in empire. Britain's dismantling as a colonial power overlapped in time, tellingly, with the publication of Evelyn Waugh's *Brideshead Revisited*, a work that yokes it to the Spenglerian concept (which D.H. Lawrence would have adored) that the mildness and clemency prized by Christianity undercut the ruthlessness so vital to strong political leadership. Here's the best-known passage in Waugh's 1945 novel of upper-class English manners. Its cynicism, accidentally or not, chimes eerily with Spengler's racial mysticism. It shows Anthony Blanche faulting Charles Ryder: "Charm is the great English blight.... It spots and kills anything it touches. It kills love; it kills art; I greatly feel, my dear Charles, that it has killed *you*" (273).

Has it also killed St. John? Waugh's Blanche has aligned charm with the teasing dismissiveness found in Oscar Wilde's mandate that triviality trumps earnestness. The mandate tells us to prize the froth and dismiss what's crucial and imperative. A heavy cold can be worse than a cholera plague; starvation in North Korea becomes a bit of a bore. Ironically, the posh sensibility behind this frivolity builds from a base of dullness, even stupidity. St. John's habit of repeating himself in the staff room *is* dull and stupid, and he bores his students whenever he deigns to teach them. At blame in both cases is his disconnectedness, a flaw that has made him naïve, impressionable, and lazy-minded. Addressing him, his colleague Mark Sackling calls the flaw "both your charm and ... major weakness" (3SG 61). He's right. It's no asset. St. John's colleagues only socialize with him by default.

Gray set the play in the "early 1960s" (3SG 4) because at that time "a courtly tolerance passed out of English life forever" (LP xii). Thus Loomis resignedly keeps St. John on staff at C-L, despite his habit of "forgetting to teach" his students, arguing that, if "we turned him out where would we go, who would have him, one does look after one's own" (3SG 68). The younger Windscape, though, despite his fondness for St. John, reasons more pragmatically. Willing to make tough decisions to improve the school, he fires St. John at great cost to his inner peace. The moment is emotionally wrenching for him. Though he means it when he says that he'll miss St. John, he also knows that C-L can only survive if all of its functionaries function.

Quartermaine's Terms ends at the right time, asking us to imagine how St. John will fare in the jolted, disoriented era of Black Power, the Kennedy assassinations, and the student protests that fueled riots like the one shaking QMC during the present-tense action of *Butley*. The question is important. Though pallid and limp-wristed, St. John isn't bloodless; a heartbeat can be detected behind his excessive decorum. He shocks everybody onstage when, hearing for the first time about Meadle's Daphne, he asks, "What are her legs like?" Like someone out of Chekhov, he has been making his own associations rather than following the conversation flowing around him. He blurted out his shocking question after making Windscape repeat a pleasantry he had uttered a moment before. He's not done talking. Within seconds, another shocker uncoils from his hidden train of thought: "I have a sort of thing about girls' legs" (3SG 45).

Elsewhere, too, he shows that he's more than an absentminded dreamer who tunes in and out of conversations. Less withdrawn than we had thought, he tap-dances his way onstage to open the play's second scene, demonstrating a skill "*at which he's surprisingly adept*" (3SG 20). Nor are all his thoughts idle. In his longest speech in the play, given later in the scene, this virtuoso of rhythm and music talks spontaneously, even mystically, about the terror and beauty of swans. Yet his paean goes ignored; the colleague to whom he directed it was deep in his own thoughts. The paean comes, by the way, a page after the colleague mentions Chekhov's *Cherry Orchard* (32), in which another poetic effusion is uttered but ignored, despite being followed by the sound of a string breaking in the sky.

The faculty at C-L isn't made up of drab, plodding third-raters—though, Windscape, the new principal, will have his hands full maintaining quality control. Windscape mentions being stunned during a recent family vacation by "one amazing ... sunrise" (3SG 55). Similar discernments could be harvested. Earlier, Mark Sackling called his recent bout of novel-writing "the nearest I've come, will probably ever come, to a mystical experience" (3SG 49). Yet how much of this extended epiphany will grace his readers and students? The question carries the weight of Gray's 20 years in academe. The pile of administrative chores facing Sackling as C-L's new academic tutor will leave him too weary to sort out and polish the 3,648-pager he wrote during his brief enforced bachelorhood.

This motif notwithstanding, Gray's satire on education in *Quartermaine's Terms* is mild. Loomis's view of the school as a family reminds us that, after Arthur Miller's *All My Sons* (1944) and Eugene O'Neill's *Long Day's Journey into Night* (1956), family ties no longer stir expectations of gladness and joy in Anglophone theater audiences. An emblematic moment in *Quartermaine's Terms*, which occurs off stage, comes in Meadle's reuniting with, at a Sheffield funeral (Charles Dickens lectured in Sheffield only hours before his death), the woman he'll later wed—and with whom he'll have children. Other signs of renewal? C-L isn't portrayed as a mechanistic system of dead ends meant to symbolize English haplessness. After sagging, the enrollment of the language school has spiked by play's end, reaching a healthy level it bids fair to sustain. Old equipment has given way to new, the faculty has disposed of some dead wood, and the new principal's making that disposal his first order of business implies a more dynamic, innovative leadership than that of the past.

The staffers he and Mark Sackling will have to motivate resemble those found in most corporate structures. If not martyrs or zealots (except for Melanie), neither are they slackers. They also manage to get along with one another, their talk veering between harmless pleasantries and bile, with very little in between. How St. John's absence will affect this alchemy is unclear. But despite the staff's prosaic look, its stability counts as an achievement for having come to pass in a climate of stress and anxiety. Perhaps St. John, feeling the pressures emitted by this ambiance, pitched camp in the staff room to escape it. Others lack this safety. Rain spoils a Windscape family outing to Norfolk. Anita's boyfriend Nigel cancels his long-awaited trip to New York. Sackling misses his half-term visit to his son when Tom comes down with mumps.

Things get worse. Thomas Cull dies, as does Melanie's mother, the first woman at Cambridge University to hold the chair in philosophy. But Professor Garth doesn't die from the stroke that recently felled her. So vile had she become to Melanie in her illness that, to silence her, Melanie pushed her down a flight of stairs, a crime that explains her joining the religious cult run by her mother's erstwhile day helper, Nurse Grimes; Gray said in *Unnatural Pursuit* that Melanie's murder of her mother set off her need for salvation (65). He also provides the motivation behind the murder. Most hateful to the now guilt-racked Anita was her professor-mother's snobbish disdain for her job, that of C–L's specialist in elementary conversation, a post offered her by Windscape, a former student of her mother.

Lives corner tightly in the shadow of C-L. Besides reaching into the future, *Quartermaine's Terms* has a richly entwined back-story. Years earlier, Melanie rejected Windscape's marriage proposal, a decision she has been regretting. And with good reason; Windscape, whom Gray called both "a perfectly fair-minded and honorable man" (LP xii) and "a solid, cheerful dedicated teacher" (Lady 103), deserves his recent promotion. Melanie calls him the school's "only real specialist" (3SG 18), and his quick reaction time quiets the danger caused by Sackling's fainting spell at the end of the play's first scene.

Windscape is fleshed out more fully than his prototype, Geoffrey Winder, Spill Academy's "chief intellectual" in *Little Portia* (244, 255). A dutiful husband and father, he attends weekly therapy sessions with his family (3SG 66). These meetings he values because he's afraid he has been pushing the kids too hard to prime them for the competitive, confrontational age they're soon to enter. He might be right. He talks about encouraging both his daughter Fanny to read serious poetry and his son to perfect the "Chopin piece" he's slated to play at a school concert. That the piece is "rather too advanced" (3SG 39) for Ben might concern his dad more than it does.

That dad's failure to let his children be children has hurt them. The high standard he had set for them shatters the eldest, the putative role model to her two sibs. Though just fourteen, Susan takes her O-level exams two years early, an ordeal that flattens her when she discovers that she only made B's and C's. Despite her father's acclaim for her "six positive passes" (3SG 48), she regrets having let him down. Her failure to score the A's she had aimed for lands her in a hospital, where she later dies. Judith Roof may have diagnosed Susan correctly by saying that she went mad before dying (Burkman, ed. 38).

Ironically, Susan's best chances for recovery lay in the "unconscious moral virtues" (LP xii) of that failed teacher, St. John, which tells why, twice in the play (3SG 43, 61), her father calls him to her bedside. He's good with kids. Windscape's awareness of St. John's healthy, life-giving influence is also running through his mind when, soon after Susan's death, he fires his old friend. Like Joey in *Butley* and Monk Scott in *They Never Slept*, he's a good person forced by circumstances to commit an act of cruelty he loathes. It counts in St. John's favor that he makes this act easy for Windscape to perform. His kindness reverberates. St. John's long, loving history with the Windscape family lends a warm glow to it and, later, to the school's outlook. This is the converse of Greek tragedy, where every change brings a new calamity.

But how reliable is this outlook? The name of Windscape, like that of his prototype from *Little Portia*, Winder, and the college that novel's hero attends, Windhoven, implies the transience of all life's boons—or *wind*falls. Obstacles of different kinds beset St. John's survivors at C-L. A frail, brokenhearted Eddie Loomis, who spoke of his "fast-fading old eyes" (3SG 10) and "old ears" (3SG 22), faces the violence of reinventing himself after being body-slammed by the loss of his vocation and best friend. Daphne Meadle's new adjunct appointment won't rid her of the speech impediment that will make her the laughingstock of her students. The gloomy roster of burdens lengthens—and darkens. Windscape means it when he tells St. John, in the play's last scene, that he'd retain him if "he could see any way" (3SG 73) to do it. Melanie's "once remarkable" (3SG 38) mother deteriorated into a monster that deserves to be murdered. Anita is finally having Nigel's baby, but, after years of enduring his infidelities, has decided she "can't bear him" (3SG 64). Loyalty can also backfire. Susan, the great hope of the Windscape clan, dies at 15 for adhering all too well to the upbeat can-do creed that will drive her country for the next decades. Her efforts, like those of her fellow cast members, rest on a surface no more substantial than wind. It's as if they're all acting out Plato's cave metaphor from *The Republic* or Kant's noumenon-phenomenon split, both of which rob our deeds of vitality or meaning.

No one-man show, *Quartermaine's Terms* raises this vexed issue without moralizing or becoming either formulaic or sentimental. Gray's ability to poeticize material without diffusing its realism helps him render scenes of incredible difficulty with unforced precision. Sustaining it all is his skill in laying out the world in which his people move. Counterpoint, or the art of combining different thematic lines, conveys both the complexity and moral suspense of this world. As St. John shows, our strengths are also our weaknesses, and every human trait carries within itself its opposite sign. This same man whose saintliness shames his colleagues doesn't deserve to work alongside them.

Hard-won insights like this rise from scenes best acted at a leisurely pace. The play's staging needs to convey breadth and range. Whereas *Butley* covers two or three hours in actual time, the more Chekhovian *Quartermaine's Terms*, using the same number of characters (seven), takes that many years to develop. The play's lone moment of crisis comes with Mark Sackling's blackout late in Act One. But the crisis dissolves quickly. Its import came from both what it makes us feel and think about St. John, who's more passive than active during the drama of keeping Sackling alive, little of which is acted out. In *Quartermaine's Terms*, illumination trumps urgency. Nor is the play's unadorned quality just stylistic. It's the same psychological truth of flatness that builds a gentle, bemused intelligence compatible with that of British liberalism at its most open-minded.

The ruin of the play's standard-bearer of this ethic becomes its crowning irony — which emerges at exactly the right time. Gray's assured, shapely plot flows smoothly, using a minimum of materials. Included in this economy is the impressive mileage he gets from offstage characters. Without showing themselves, Nigel, Daphne, Nurse Grimes, Thomas Cull, and Susan Windscape all help build this drama of everyday moments. Unlike *Butley*, its busy, noisy counterpart, *Quartermaine's Terms* proves that, in the right hands, the dailiness of teaching can be retrieved from surfaces composed and calm.

Seven

Coercive Connections

Middle age brought a shift in Gray's theater from a brazenly youthful manner to a more measured, workmanlike one. The shift helped. His phasing out of kitchen-sink aesthetics helped him map the educated middle class as if he were dissecting an etherized patient. This metaphor has a relentless curve. The posh offices that come into view in works like *Dog Days* (1976), *Old Flames* (1990), and *Melon* (1991) all portend the setting of *Life Support* (1997), an ICU room containing a comatose woman. The pattern tightens and vibrates. The woman is the wife of Jeff Golding, a successful travel writer who had roles in both *Otherwise Engaged* (1975) and *Simply Disconnected* (1996). Rather than merely recycling his materials, Gray, during his middle and later phases, continued to mine them for their latent thematic goodness.

It was also Jeff who said of England in *Otherwise Engaged*, that "this sad little country of ours is finished at last" (OE 25). Gray's theater of the 1980s and 1990s justifies this bleak diagnosis. But instead of looking outward to the upheavals caused by Thatcherism, these plays explore the possibilities of finding a deeper, wider life within marriage. Noting this exploratory bent, Philip Fisher's review of a 2005 revival of *Otherwise Engaged* in London refers straightaway to the play's preoccupation with "middle-class freedom among the intelligentsia" (1).

This freedom emphasizes the Lawrencean doctrine of star polarity. Articulated most boldly in Lawrence's *Women in Love* (1920), star polarity maps the freedom permitted to the erotically committed. Gray's take on it is conservative. The restless husbands in his work who fiddle with it sow grief. Mark Melon's decision to have an open marriage costs him his family along with his job, his sanity, and perhaps even his humanity as he slogs across the stage on all fours during those times late in the play when he's not lighting a cigarette or pouring himself a shot. As usual in Gray, alcohol, besides causing problems of its own, worsens others. A man in *Michael* (2000) calls his long drinking spree his "dog days" (Four 177), a direct reference to the title of Gray's 1976 play, which shows drink wrecking both careers and homes.

Even without booze, marriage is always fragile in the plays of Gray's middle period. Most notably, Peter's "oppressive faithfulness" in *Dog Days* (88) makes his wife feel so stifled that she leaves him for a much older bisexual. The confession that Peter failed in his one love tryst kills his wife's interest in him. The fault line is clearly marked. Adultery will demolish marriage in Gray whether it's consummated or not. Unlike their more passionate wives, his halfhearted Casanovas climb into strange beds out of a warped sense of duty to self; sex to them is another commodity to grab if available. They're acting out to their detriment a low-key Oxbridge version of the American success story in which a lonely, misunderstood genius like Melville's Ahab, Fitzgerald's Gatsby, or Orson Welles's Kane clings to a dream of success as it recoils on him.

Thus it's not desire but the commodification of sex that lures men in Gray's *Dog's Day* and *Close of Play* (1979) into disloyalty; the greater the number of bedmates, the glossier the self-image, runs the debilitating mantra. The long speeches that begin *Melon* and its companion piece, *The Holy Terror* (1991), also convey the isolation bred by adherence to the mantra. An undated, unsigned review of a February 2004 production of *Holy Terror* in Richmond ends thus: "*The Holy Terror* ... questions our relationships with those ... closest to us, and why it is often the people that we love the most that we also hurt the most" (2).

To curb the pain, Gray, sadly implying that monogamy is rarely practiced nowadays, recommends forgiveness. A man tells his brother in *Dog Days*, "The great thing is ... to love in spite" (94). The man might have in mind repenting the "sordid combination of sneaking and scrounging" (93) his brother has just confessed to. Though "a bit of an old-fashioned Puritan" (72), he has left his thought hanging because he knows that the goodness of heart it entails falls outside the normal range of human response; damaged people prefer vengeance to forgiveness. But this magnetism, rather than hobbling Gray's inventiveness, quickened it. The womanizing of Bernard Berenson in *Old Masters* (2004) and Dick, or Charles Dickens, in *Little Nell* (2006), the greatest public successes in the canon, both fascinates and repels Gray.

This compulsiveness touches nearly everything he wrote. He didn't topple Dickens and Berenson for fun. These public icons stood for James Gray, the doctor-father whose philandering his son Simon lacked the strength to reject, even after seeing the pain it caused his mother (SD 145-46). That son's ensuing self-hatred created a shift in the Lawrencean paradigm. Whereas the sexual drama in Lawrence always involved him and Frieda, the confrontation in Gray features the playwright and the shadow of his father. This narrative sent him deeply inside himself. Starting with *Otherwise Engaged*, his search for living values had been leading him to the lonely, the mousy, and the despised, a direction made problematical by his having bought into the same class snobbery he loathed; he lacked the humanity to spare from suffering the pathetic Simon Booter of *A Comeback for Stark* and Simon Booker of *Wise Child* if that was his aim. But those two works came out in 1968.

The later *Otherwise Engaged* and the revealingly titled *Old Flames* include underdogs scoring against high-flying ex-schoolmates who have been lodging in their minds and hearts for 20 years as targets for their revenge. Though athletic and popular at school, Gray, no proponent of the easy way out, accepts these long-standing grudges as acts of natural justice. Received standards of success and failure associated with male authority keep failing. *Dog Days*, in which a woman leaves her successful publisher-husband to marry a schoolmaster (a profession that often smacks of failure or weakness in Gray) shows failure intriguing Gray more than success.

In *Hidden Laughter* (1990), the cost of success makes it less preferable than failure. A literary agent helps his wife publish her books, but not because of their intrinsic worth. Her writing brings money into the home and, above all, distracts her from his chronic philandering. At play's end, Louise has lost Henry, their two children, and the house they bought in the first act. Her lone standby is Ronnie, with whom she can implement the sexless intimacy that Ben Butley sought with Joey Keyston. The Simon Gray who disclaimed this bond in *Butley* had ripened in the intervening 19 years. His Louise, a loving mother and a disciplined, conscientious writer, accepts her losses. Gray's pairing her off, however chastely, with Ronnie, whose faith clashes with his society's formula for success, could give her books a metaphysical depth even if they don't make a metaphysician — or best-selling author — of her. In a larger sense, the finale of *Hidden Laughter* imparts a thematic bite that both rescues Gray's "French window" drama from its alleged complacency (Rattigan 7) and sheds light on the intellectual and sociological strengths of the works of his middle phase.

The "*elegant and comfortable*" (OE 9) living room that stands before us at the start of *Otherwise Engaged* opens a big gap with the kitchen-sink school of English playwrights that colored Gray's drama of the 1960s. This gap will hold. The cast members of *Engaged*, a publisher, a journalist, a freelance historian, and two teachers, occupy a different world from that of the denizens of both Simon Booker's grubby Reading hotel in *Wise Child* and the "*decaying house in Shepherd's Bush*" (1SG 151) where *Dutch Uncle* unfolds. Davina Saunders, the historian who turns up in Simon Hench's living room in *Engaged*, for instance, spends her days doing research in the British Museum, a place totally foreign to the people of *Wise Child* and *Dutch Uncle*.

Behind Gray's meticulous scene-setting and bright dialogue lies a knack for pushing tense moments further than we'd have thought possible. For instance, a publisher's living room, like the one in which Simon and Davina face off, with its library of coffee-table books, record player, and liquor cabinet, provides a common staging ground in his work for the clash of primary forces. In this regard, Oleg Kerensky puts *Engaged* at a midpoint between works that feature publishers and writers such as *Common Pursuit* (1984) and *Holy Terror*

(1991) and the earlier *Sleeping Dog* (1967) and *Dutch Uncle* (1969), where any person of letters would be drastically out of place:

> They are essentially about psychological and emotional relationships, about people's attempts to dominate and possess each other, in the case of *Otherwise Engaged*, about efforts to avoid being possessed or involved [134].

Avoidance wasn't a new subject for Gray. He had woven it into his treatments of the captivity motif in *Colmain* (1963), *Little Portia* (1967), and *Dutch Uncle*. Ben Butley had tried to fling nets around Joey and Anne, both of whom he wanted to stay connected with, if only chastely.

Unlike Ben, Simon Hench, the main figure of *Engaged*, likes sex. And audiences have liked *him*. Xandra Gowrie and Jacob Epstein called the play featuring him "probably the most successful … of 1975" (45). The play's popularity supports this verdict. *Engaged* played for two years in London, with Michael Gambon taking over the lead role from Alan Bates midway through its run. Then a cast led by Tom Courtenay performed the work on Broadway to great acclaim. Playing a total of 309 performances from February to October 1977, it was nominated for two Tony Awards and two Drama Desk Awards (<http:www.ibdb.com/production.asp?id=3891>, 20 March 2009).

But what to make of the doggedness with which the work's protagonist keeps other people at bay? Simon's reputation as a monster of non-involvement has stuck. Toby Young, reviewing a 2005 revival of *Engaged*, grounds Simon's "generally aloof, laissez-faire attitude to life" in a contempt for "other people and their problems" (69). Commenting on the same revival of the play at London's Criterion, Philip Fisher notes that the Simon Hench role was played like a "cold fish … absolutely indifferent to human kindness" (1–2).

Well aware that such a brute would repel theater audiences, Gray hides Simon's alienating coldness. His mastery of the art of misdirection helps him hide it as long as is feasible. Simon seems much more decent and supportive than all of his five unannounced visitors in the play's first act. He uses firmness and tact to rebuff the sexual advances of the one woman in his squad of visitors, Davina Saunders, the historian of 24 or 25, who quickly offers him sex to persuade him to publish her book. Whereas he admits that he finds her attractive, he also calls her "possibly the most egotistically unpleasant woman I've ever met" (OE 31). This rebuff hurts her. But when she asks him, looking to salvage some pride from being rejected, if spousal loyalty drove it, Simon replies in controlled cadences, "This is her [his wife Beth's] house as much as mine. It's *our* house, don't you see?" (OE 32). This reply has won our favor. Besides being honest and sincere, it's more than he owes Davina.

His poise in this scene tallies with what looked like the decency and straightforwardness that has been activating him from the start. He's accommodating, agreeable, and upbeat with his first visitor, the student Dave, who has been renting the top floor of his posh London house. His reasons for renting to Dave look fuzzy. Dave raids his fridge, cadges his liquor, and rarely pays the pittance he's charged each month. But Dave is also the son the 39-year-old Simon misses having. In an exchange that looks ahead to the first scene of *Stage Struck* (1979), which also shows a landlord with his tenant, Simon keeps approving of the developments or non-developments that smudged Dave's date with a young woman he had wanted to bed the previous night. Then, in another enigma, despite Dave's lateness with his rent check, Simon not only loans Dave money but also lets him borrow his prized coffee maker.

This last stroke prompts a key insight. The high premium Simon places on the coffee maker signifies a preference for things over people. Placating Dave, a male alter-ego of Davina, gives Simon a moral beachhead. The coffee maker provides him with a useful dodge. By loaning it to his surrogate son, Simon can scotch any other demands Dave might have in mind. So he thinks. As the coffee-maker incident showed, he's likelier to turn down a young woman than a young man. A dangerous tendency; like most sons, biological and otherwise, Dave downgrades Simon's bogus generosity, believing it a ploy to evict him. He lacks the goodness of heart to see, let alone prize, the good-heartedness of the archetypal father, even if it's feigned. Though the right thing happens, the wrong reason behind it should be irrelevant. The communication failure between the men reaches an apt finale. Rather than thanking Simon, Dave retaliates against his alleged deceit, moving two friends into the upstairs flat with him.

A later visitor, Jeff Golding, who'll be together with Simon at final curtain, also tucks into Simon's larder. He follows Dave, too, in having friends. This well-published journalist has been living with Davina, who has followed him to Simon's house to tell him goodbye. The transgressive gusto she displays at Simon's hits upon Gray's belief in the shallowness of human ties. Her grabbing at a chance to get close to Simon follows her discovery of another woman in Jeff's life. A few months before the play's staged action, Jeff accidentally saw his ex-wife in Oxford and soon took her to the empty flat of a friend (this is the same Gwendoline who'll be lying comatose on a hospital bed in *Life Support* [1997]). Plotting dominates this part of the play. Jeff would marry his ex-wife if, during her five years away from him, she hadn't wed a Cambridge don — who has found out about the intrigue and wants his revenge.

Manfred wasn't the first person Jeff angered. As Ben Butley did at a party hosted by Reg Nuttall, Jeff misbehaved so shamelessly at a dinner, practically calling Simon's brother Stephen a pederast (OE 17), that Stephen threatened to hit him. Stephen is seething anew because Jeff claims to have forgotten meeting him, let alone insulting him. What has helped stoke Stephen's rage is a crisis he has been undergoing. Like Butley's Joey, he's an educator who awaits news on a promotion he has been coveting. But he and the young bachelor Joey occupy different crossroads. The Assistant Headmastership Stephen has applied for makes a big difference to him because of the wife and five children he's supporting. At stake, too, is his self-validation. Stephen's lone rival for the job he covets boasts an Oxford degree, a pedigree that outshines by far Stephen's diploma from Reading.

To his amazement, Stephen defeats his rival. His conquest, though, stirs an awakening that dims his joy. He sees that the emotional support Simon has been giving him reflects the same mind-set that prizes an Oxford degree over one from Reading (Simon's Oxford pedigree is mentioned at least twice in the play [OE 15, 60]). Simon hasn't been boosting Stephen's spirits as much as he has been patronizing him. "You've a family to support" (OE 47), he tells his brother after being accused of despising his line of work. Stephen's growing family, Simon has implied, rules out options and blessings like the ones *he* has been enjoying, starting with an elegantly furnished home in swinging London.

Stephen needn't moan. The key difference between the brothers' life styles, it comes out in their last recorded conversation, hinges on children. Whereas Stephen and his wife are happy to let their children be born when they want, even if it means Stephen has to moonlight as manager of his school's football team, Simon and Beth have agreed to remain childless. The demands posed by children would foil their chic life style. Mark Melon, another cultivated urbanite opposed to any demands hostile to *his* chic ways, tells his psychiatrist, "Sheer perfection is routine. And routine is sheer perfection." But this closed circle has come under attack. Melon, citing the shock that brought him to the psychiatrist's office to begin with, ends his speech by saying, "Suddenly ... the ground opens at your feet" (M 1).

As it must — and should. Simon, too, has been using what Anne C. Hall calls "aggressive indifference" (Burkman ed. 113) to preserve his routine. His practice of telling people what he thinks they want to hear, besides making him sound sympathetic, shields him from their emotional needs. Once assured of his support, his petitioners can move happily on. The shell he has built around himself has done its job. But at a cost; by fobbing off the needy, he's also ignoring challenges vital to any close bond. Had Stephen taken his advice about walking away from Teresa when she broke their engagement, he and she would have forgone the hard emotional work that both reunited them and braced up the marriage that has been sustaining them for the past 11 years.

Does this development help make Simon Ben Butley's mirror image? His policy of shunning the emotional demands of others does liken him to Ben, another avoidance artist to whom others bring their problems. Simon resembles Ben, too, by misnaming people he has known for years. Even the plays built around these two men share an important structural similarity. One of their visitors is a wife who reveals an adaptability and decency lacking in her morally inert mate. Detachment in Gray always invites such onslaughts. Whereas Katherine H. Burkman saw Ben as "aggressively cynical," she calls Simon "ostentatiously passive" (Burkman, ed 163). Gray himself bracketed the plays featuring the men. In *Coda* (2008), which came out the year of his death, he said of *Butley* and *Engaged*, that "they seem to be about waste, self-waste, and partly self-disgust" (110).

He reasoned well. Despite using different tactics, the male leads of both plays are in hiding, a strategy implied by their placement in strongholds that, to their chagrin, turn out to lack strength. Ben's babble deflects and stifles the candor of his visitors. The non-confrontational Simon also hides behind words. Tellingly, his longest speech in *Engaged*, which attacks "our zestfully over-explanatory age" (OE 52), comes during a conversation with his wife, Beth, who has been trying to discuss their marital problems. Simon's evasiveness—which he'll show again to Stephen when the subject of Beth comes up in *Simply Disconnected* (SD 42)—has deep roots. The truth scares him. Helping those we love when they're desperate is what most people can do, but Simon can't. It's not that he won't; he can't. He's stymied. Like Ben, Simon is hamstrung by destructive habits of thought, and, unable to sink them, despises himself. He has boxed himself in. Besides being afraid of being found out by others, he can't face the self he loathes.

Gray qualified his reading of *Butley* and *Engaged*, when after calling them plays about waste and self-disgust, he said, "But I may be quite wrong" (CODA 110). Could he have been thinking about St. John Quartermaine? Stephen Hench calls his brother "indifferent. Absolutely indifferent" (OE 48), a term that also applies to St. John. The title of Gray's 1996 play, *Simply Disconnected*, in which Simon returns, conveys the civilized barbarity of both men. Ordinarily a virtue, their joint policy of withholding judgment has backfired on them. They lack moral standards, shutting out ideologies and people who might jar their non-committal poise.

Simon is the worse of the two because, described in greater detail and depth, he gets more of Gray's attention. Besides being a bachelor, St. John has no family that we know of. His fence-straddling causes less damage than does that of Simon, who also gives the term "complacency" new, degraded meaning. Paul Stevens, who reviewed a September 2005 production of *Engaged* in Bath, says rightly that Simon has known about his wife's affair with a colleague for some time (2). The coolness of Simon's response to Beth's confession of infidelity does betoken a calm bordering on the inhuman. Having recently described his routine of playing squash and showering after one of his own sexual bouts, this man of "small pleasures and easy accommodations" (OE 40) acquiesces when Beth says to him, after her supposed day-long academic conference, that she needs a bath herself.

So rankling is his poise in this scene that Beth, despite being the guilty party, wins our approval. The aplomb with which lawless passion collides with the cotton wool of complacency in this scene makes it the play's best. Simon's teasing Beth for recently "becoming a trifle prolix" while explaining her whereabouts and also doubling the number of baths she used to take (OE 53) stokes the reversal of moral positions. His avoidance of the cuckold's high dudgeon has left her dazed and hurt. She feels oppressed by his indifference. The treacherous mate who cornered the innocent one has gotten her comeuppance — but in a way she hadn't expected. Retribution doesn't provoke laughter in this play with a Noël-Cowardlike title. But it snares our attention. Simon is only innocent because he never invested any feeling in his own affairs (in *Simply Disconnected*, he'll tell a young visitor, "You must understand that these were different times.... Sex happened when the mood took one" [35]). By applying this pattern of casual sex, which was less widespread than he claims, to his home, he has cheapened it. His marriage never meant much to him. In his verbal joust with Beth he refers to "*when* you did have an affair" (OE 54, emphasis mine) rather than saying *if*. Spousal cheating was always a given with him — providing that it fell outside of their social set. He has stayed married to Beth not out of need or passion, but to avoid being alone.

The speech in which Simon says that he never saw his marriage as an exclusive sexual bond ends with another cynical stroke — his belittling of Beth's judgment. As Ben said when he learned that Anne had replaced him with Tom Weatherly, Simon calls Ned a loser (OE 54). He was ousted by a nobody. But this nobody has also judged Simon, about whom he has heard plenty in the last couple of months. And the acuity of his judgments means that Simon had misprized him. According to Ned, Simon holds "a deeply contemptuous view of human life," an attitude imposed by a "sanity ... of the kind that causes people to go quietly mad around him" (OE 56).

Ned has spoken home. Except for the care Simon takes washing off the telltale reek of sex after one of his trysts, he doesn't scheme or calculate. He never had to. His good looks, charm, and intelligence have sailed him through life unchallenged. Anything he reached for soon became his. Nor did he hoard his blessings, it can be said on his behalf. This man who never took anything seriously also shared his good luck with others, as when he gave a lunch party to bring together his writer friend Jeff with the Arts Editor of the *Sunday Times* (OE 30).

Yet the name of this paragon of poise evokes that of luckless, self-tormenting Michael Henchard, eponym of *The Mayor of Casterbridge*, whose role in the 1978 BBC telecast of the novel was played by Alan Bates, the Simon Hench figure in *Engaged*'s 1975 stage debut. Near the start of Thomas Hardy's novel, a drunken Henchard sells his wife and daughter to a sailor for five guineas. His counterpart, the daughterless Hench, will tumble a woman young enough to *be* his daughter. He puts little value on the wife he has been taking for granted; what he does prize in her, viz., providing steady companionship and occasional sex, counts more to him than she does.

These services gain nothing special by being provided by her. What had been looking like virtues in Simon turn out to be flaws, even defects and vices.

His failure to commit himself wholeheartedly to Beth has made his marriage as metaphorical as the one Joey Keyston rejected from Ben. Ned was right about the damage caused by Simon's heartless sanity. Beth, for instance, can hardly feel flattered when Simon offers to take her back despite knowing of her preference for Ned. And perhaps Simon was right to discount Ned as a loser. Living with Simon as his wife for nine years could not have given Beth the self-esteem to aim high when faced with the need to replace him.

Simon remains Philip Fisher's "cold fish" (1). He ignores other people's feelings when reaching for what he wants. But we still wonder if Beth chose Ned over him as a way to improve her life or to punish herself. Does Ned's accurate take on Simon's destructiveness lift him morally over Simon? The question cuts deep. To marry Beth, which is supposedly his goal, Ned will have to dump an autistic daughter and a wife who has spent years under psychiatric care. When did running away from such duties become morally preferable to ignoring or even avoiding lesser ones? Was Gray was so distracted by Simon's flaws that he forgot our pledge to help those we love, particularly when they're desperate? Beth's replacement for Simon outdoes him in cold-bloodedness.

But need the point be made? If living with Simon both jaded Beth's taste and scrambled her moral code, then Simon was right to deny Ned stature and consequence. Compared to Simon, most men would look good. Beth recently got pregnant (OE 58) to get his attention. Ned's willingness to ditch his needy family proves that he'd be a terrible father to her child, which she had to know. Simon, besides exposing his own moral darkness, could have judged him correctly, by saying of him, "I can see why he wants to leave home" (OE 56) after he's told about the problems vexing his wife and daughter (the figure of the disturbed daughter will return in *Quartermaine's Terms*).

Moments like this make the inner world of *Engaged* feel intensely raw. By foregrounding grief alongside Simon's moral apathy, Gray is implying that, though wisdom entails caution and patience, being alive means opening oneself to impulse, even chaos. The play opens on a note of anxiety. Dave, Simon's tenant, enters the set complaining that he failed to get sex from the woman he dated the previous night. The anxiety builds. Simon's brother Stephen is agonizing because he's sure that the job he applied for went to his Oxford rival. Oxford, he has always linked with his more favored brother, and it keeps dogging Stephen. He's so upset by its persistence, in fact, that he's ready to carry out an earlier resolve to beat up the ex-Oxonian Jeff Golding for having insulted him years earlier (OE 17).

Violence closes in on Jeff. Manfred, the husband of Gwendoline, with whom he has been sleeping, wants to thrash him, too (OE 29)—as would the author of a book he recently smeared in a review (OE 19). It's no surprise that the prevailing atmosphere of frustration has kept festering. Manfred was also the name of the husband Gray had cuckolded some 15 years before he wrote

Engaged (LC 107). Davina, who has followed Jeff to Simon's to break up with him, has her own heavy pass to Simon rebuffed. Her irritation calls to mind Beth's absence from home, all the more clearly because, when questioned earlier about her whereabouts, Simon had put her in both Salisbury (OE 10) and Canterbury (OE 12). Another pattern that excludes Simon takes hold in Jeff's recollection of throwing a drink at Gwendoline (OE 22). After an irate Davina throws Jeff's house-key at him, Jeff douses her *too* with the remnants of his drink (OE 29).

The ongoing mood of irritation, built in part by the tendency of people to throw, rather than hand things to those who have angered them, holds. Near play's end, Jeff storms back onstage, accusing Simon of having told the police, who just gave him a breathalyzer test, that he was dangerously drunk. This time, though, Jeff is the one who gets splashed with liquor. The trauma seething within Simon needs an outlet, his having just heard about Beth's pregnancy. Marriage's sacramental status has invoked religion. Does Simon's act of throwing his drink at Jeff symbolize his non-redemption? He's not baptized here or elsewhere in the play, symbolically or otherwise, Beth having asked him moments before, "Do you want to live?" to which he could only reply, "What?" (OE 56).

If he's not alive, he couldn't have sired the baby Beth is expecting. This line of thought can be defended. The ten or 15 childless years the couple have spent together imply that he's sterile. Passion would have overcome even the most guarded of lovers during this stretch of time, especially a drinker like Simon. Also relevant here may be the truth that the love rivals of Gray's male leads, like Joey Keyston's Reg, Anne Butley's Tom, and Sam Field of *Simple People* all have one-syllable front names, as do Ben, father to Marina, and Beth's Ned, who's already a father.

The cosmopolitan suavity and wit of the play's characters can't block the rush of blood. A portent of Simon's shadow life came in a story Davina made up in anger about Gwendoline's fretting so much about Jeff's re-emergence in her life that she tried to kill herself. More climactically, a resentful, traumatized Bernard Wood, an ex-schoolmate Simon hasn't seen for 25 years (OE 42), bursts in on him and threatens to kill him. Wood remains desperate. Close to play's end, Simon listens to a message on his answering machine in which Wood claims that he's on the brink of suicide. The moment is critical. Simon's disconnecting the machine before finding out if the threat was carried out masks his fear of the truth that other people are willing to die for love. His having had casual sex with Wood's fiancée had traumatized Wood. But sex of any kind always abhors a vacuum in Gray. The shock waves beating from Wood's trauma shape a countering rhythm that keeps diminishing Simon. Gray also called Gwen's husband Manfred (OE 23), after the Faustian eponym of Byron's dramatic poem (1816–17), to invoke the sexual love that entails risks and agonies beyond the imaginings of the uncommitted Simon.

A work from the nineteenth century greater than *Manfred* frames *Engaged*. At curtain rise, Simon has just brought home a recording of Richard Wagner's *Parsifal*. "*Deeply looking forward to*" spending the next few hours "*listening to it*," (OE 9), he has left a message on his voice mail advising any caller that he's otherwise engaged. Life intervenes. No sooner has he begun to listen to Wagner's last opera than he's interrupted by Jeff, the first of his visitors. It's not until the play's last moments that he settles in to hear *Parsifal*—with Jeff, who had introduced him to Wagner years earlier at Oxford.

Jeff may have acted gratuitously. The sublimity of the music that's swelling as the house lights dim and the stage lights fade to black bypasses Simon. As Duncan Woo says, "Simon remains deaf to what Wagner might tell him; he's otherwise engaged" (69). Gray didn't frame his play within the strains of *Parsifal* to give it elegance or grandeur. Wagner's music is a startling reminder of Simon's lack of imagination; he's numb to experiences not his own. In another fugue-like pattern, his moral distance from others clashes with the unity toward which these others are groping. Wagner's monumental ambition to blend words and instrumental music in an act of mystical hypnosis that will foster social unity leaves the radically self-centered Simon cold.

The elaborate vocal and instrumental orchestration of *Parsifal* also demeans Simon, starting with Wagner's eponym, a subnormal whose compassion makes him saintlike. This righteousness stems from what Dostoevsky in *Brothers Karamazov* calls "active love." Whereas Simon stays physically put during his time onstage, Parsifal goes searching for both the Holy Grail and the Holy Spear, the device that pierced Christ's side. With Wagner's soaring music solemnizing his pain for the benefit of Simon — an apathetic listener — Parsifal continues his quest. The Grail's miraculous healing power, he knows, will deliver humanity from a cycle of birth, suffering, death, and rebirth and into a state of exalted calm, viz., the peace that passeth understanding.

Ironically, Simon has already cultivated this Buddha-like serenity, but it was devoid of the compassion that inspires Parsifal to end suffering in the world. This shortcoming has already bled life from Simon, his moral ignorance thinning his tie to others, including his wife. Nor can the loveless, mechanical sex he knows best rouse urgency in him. He doesn't set out to hurt people emotionally. Yet this very lack of transgressive gusto has a cheapening effect that's diminished further by his unwillingness to reach out to others. Having sex with him would be like wrestling with a mound of cotton wool. Life hasn't caught up with him (OE 41). The ease with which he has reached his goals has dulled him to the suffering that fuels Wagner's two main sources in *Parsifal*—the tranquility of Buddha and Arthur Schopenhauer's belief in the destructiveness of the will. As Lizzie Loveridge said, Simon lacks "emotional intelligence" (1).

The crisis facing him at the end of Act One depicts his inertia. His encounter with Bernard Wood is so vital to his self-understanding that it resumes after the interval dividing the play's two acts. Wood and the injustice the world deals out to his grungy kind had deep roots in Gray's psyche. The appearance of Simon's uninvited and unexpected ex-schoolmate looks ahead to the eruption into the successful London attorney David Davenport's life of *his* ex-schoolmate Nathanael Quass in *Old Flames*. Like the title of the 1990 teleplay in which Daniel and Quass appear, both of these shocks bespeak the "homosexual underpinnings" (Hall 116) of English public-school education that color and sometimes warp the futures of the old boys, or graduates.

This pressure makes the deepest inroads on those despised by their counterparts as losers or "plops" (OE 39). Too sickly to work at a regular job and thus deprived of both a career and a social outlet, Quass waits 20 years after graduation to strike back at his thriving ex-classmate. But what fastened the attention of this underdog upon Daniel is the same festering unrequited love that Gray wrote about in *Little Portia* (1967) and *Two Sundays* (1975). In *Engaged*, Bernard Wood's lingering crush on Simon is more complicated and dangerous. Wood stood out so much in his irrelevance at Wundale School that he's spotted immediately 25 years hence by his ex-classmate, Stephen — a sighting that will recur in *Simply Disconnected* more than a generation later when Stephen identifies Wood's son. Conversely, Simon won distinction at Wundale as "the sexy little boy that all the boys of my [Wood's] year slept with" (OE 34).

This memory has been gnawing at Wood. At a recent performance of Terence Rattigan's *The Winslow Boy*, a teenaged girl in "gray flannel bags, white shirt, and starched collar" (OE 39) who was acting a boy's role immediately evoked Simon. Matters advanced. Still smarting from the knowledge that a "plop" like him could never have lured Simon into his bed, Wood unwisely started courting his female opposite number, the much-younger Joanna. *Winslow Boy* was an inspired choice on Gray's part as a conduit for Simon and Wood. The young hero of Rattigan's 1946 play was accused of committing a serious crime, i.e., stealing a five-shilling postal order, which got him drummed out of college. The idea of deceit flaring out in a school setting recurs in *Engaged* in the intrigue between Beth and Ned. The teacher-teacher bond can be as erotic as the one linking teachers and students. Once again, an educational environment, the language-training center where Beth and Ned teach, has sited damage that rakes at least one family.

Unlike Ronnie Winslow, though, Wood wasn't charged with any specific crime at Wundale, his only failing having been the paltriness that gave him "the pretty rotten future" (OE 41) that might have been forecast for him. Whether he outgrew the homosexuality of his youth, as Simon claims to have done, is unclear. But his watching *The Winslow Boy* together with his allegedly drab "poor old sons" and "poor old wife, the female plop" (OE 39) told him that the world had suckered him again. He tried to cut his losses. But, as often happens when Gray's people opt for the quick fix, the ill-advised bond formed between Wood and Joanna damages both of them. Perhaps Wood chose well to leave the wife and sons who meant so little to him that he never reveals their names or says what has happened to them since his bolt.

But connecting with Joanna was a mistake. So smitten is he that he changed his last name to hers, Strapley, in order to respectably rent a flat with her — where the two of them would live chastely. But as his new name suggests, he has strapped himself to a degrading regimen. Occasionally, Wood will slink into her empty room and sit, lovesick and forlorn, on her bed. In those rare moments when she invites him into her room, she plagues him with stories about having sex with other men. He has no cause to complain. So disoriented is he by love that he cherishes those brutal moments because, painful as they are, they keep her connected to him.

And now she's missing. Wood hasn't seen her since dropping her off at Simon's office two days earlier to display some of her artwork. Though Simon doesn't know her whereabouts either, he does have it coaxed out of him that he slept with the 17-year-old. His confession sharpens the action; the two most radiant objects of Wood's sexual fantasies have gone to bed together. His misery deepens. Not only did Joanna perform an act beyond the imaginings of the measly Wood at Wundale; by bonking Simon, she also granted him the privilege that belonged to Wood, her fiancé. Wood couldn't feel more irrelevant. Or betrayed; the murder threat he directs to Simon is serious. Like Godboy of *Dutch Uncle*, he's the kind of nobody who sees violence as his lone option.

His pawn complex holds. But if he's "incapacitated by devotion" (OE 40), he's also enabled by it. This abject lover will do anything Joanna asks of him to stay by her side. Simon miscued when he first thought him her father. He also failed to grasp the devotion that fuels epithets from Wood like "my girl" (OE 35) and "my Joanna" (OE 37). (Jeff's having called his ex-wife "my Gwendoline" [OE 22] presupposes the love that leads to her remarrying him.) Recalling the religious faith manifested by the vicar Ronnie Chambers in *Hidden Laughter*, Wood's love for Joanna gains strength inversely to its promise of happiness. It feeds on hopelessness, casting Wood in the role of fool-redeemer in *Parsifal*, a work he understands without listening to.

Wagner's titanic art also grazes the heart of Simon. His having intimated its bearing upon Wood urges him to disconnect his answering machine before learning if Wood committed suicide. News of Wood's death would make him feel responsible for it. His dodge fits his character. Beth's wish to marry Ned despite the chance that the baby she's expecting came from Simon provides Simon's biggest shock. Gray removes her from the stage after she makes her statement of intent to let him feel its weight. Feel it he does, against his will. He never knew love so keen and desperate. He has also begun to see that he has reversed roles with Bernard Wood. Even though Wood's new name offers no more promise of rebirth into social or professional success than did his former one, he has made Simon's policy of withdrawal when faced by the pain of others look cheap and shameful.

Betrayal, a major trope in both *Parsifal* and *Otherwise Engaged*, has taken on new urgency. Simon's delayed awakening to the consequences of his choices has reaffirmed his self-image as the unlikely plop of Wundale. He betrayed the gifts that, first, sent him to Oxford after his brother Stephen had to settle for red-brick Reading and, next, landed him both a high-caliber job and wife. Setting aside the jarring note of self-criticism, perhaps he was called Simon, another name for Peter, because his three-time denial of the Christ in him poisoned his commitment to his job, his brother, and his wife. The logical upshot of this looming self-betrayal would be suicide. Killing himself would yoke him to Wood, that father of two who surpassed him in the Brahman virtue of creation and the Christian one of sacrifice.

That's why the Simon Hench of Gray's 1996 play, *Simply Disconnected*, will unplug his phone. Knowing that Wood embraced Shiva the destroyer, the third God of the Hindu trinity, would have put him at a complete loss. He has known that he'll never outlive the cowardice standing between him and the redemptive suicide that awaits him. *Engaged* isn't confined to his selfish pleasures. His generosity in letting his upstairs tenant Dave slide on his rent payments offsets, he hopes, decades of aloofness from others. Suicide is the ultimate sacrifice. But it's also a crime. His refusal to follow Wood to the grave has kept hope alive for him, even though listening with an old friend to music he doesn't understand is unlikely to gorge him with the guilt that can induce contrition and repentance.

Yet killing himself without knowing if Wood reneged on his suicide threat, if poetically just, calls for a faith greater than that of Ned and Beth as they plan their marriage. Doing something either saintly or diabolic in its extremity is what Simon deserves—and needs. His heart fell asleep when he was a boy. But if others closer to Wagner's fool saint than he wouldn't risk suicide, he, too, can be forgiven. Gentler souls than he would also avoid the flames of love, if the scorching of Beth, Ned, and Wood is typical. He has time to repent. Let him live meanwhile with the punishment of knowing that he's a plop. He might also acquire the humility and even the vulnerability to thank the world for what it has given him.

Gray said in his Author's Note to *Dog Days* of his stage work of the early 1970s, when he was nearing the age of 40, "Characters from one play would slip into another ... before either slipping into yet another play or back into the first. The same passages cropped up in different scenes in different plays" (5). He was saying more than he knew. The mismatched couples in *Plaintiffs and Defendants*, *Two Sundays*, and *Dog Days* are all called Peter and Hilary. Their marital woes all stem from their dispositions and temperaments. In *Otherwise Engaged*, *Two Sundays* (1975), and *Dog Days* (1976), an egotist is wed to a high-voltage teacher of English to foreigners. He works as an editor for a London publishing firm, as will the troubled know-it-all, Mark Melon of *Melon* (1990) and *Holy Terror* (1991). He can also have a brother or best friend named Charles. In *Plaintiffs and Defendants* and *Dog Days*, he's offered sex by young freelance artists who've been trying to break up with their gay, or bisexual, boyfriends ("I like sleeping with men, and so does he" [57], says the freelancer in *Dog Days*).

In Gray's case, these repetitions describe stylistic and imaginative consistency rather than haste. The many likenesses between Gray and his male leads tempt us to read his plays as an extended stage memoir. And what he said about himself in his diaries invites parallels between his own personal quandaries and those set forth in his work. The conventions of the stage help him distance these urgencies. For example, the gender confusion that leaps out at the start of *Dog Days* reflects Gray's compulsion to strive for the truth even when it's not flattering or pretty. When told by someone looking at an old photograph of his, "Your Dad's a fine figure of a man," Peter answers, "Actually, that's my mother.... But you're right, she was a fine figure of a man" (11). The revelation moments later that Peter's father died in a car his wife — Peter's mother — was driving, shapes the play's psychological back-story. That Peter never learned how to drive (31) could refer to a fear of death that caused him to marry Hilary, his wife of eight years, a self-sufficient woman whose duties would include driving their son Jeremy to school.

Which might have made Peter feel useless and suicidal? Kerensky's analysis of him provides a good starting point for our own:

> Peter in *Dog Days* is ... in the Butley/Simon mould. Like Butley, he uses and upsets his friends and relations; like Simon, he is a publisher with a schoolteacher brother whom he despises. He is ... outspokenly rude ... and ... obviously unhappy [140].

Guilt rides Peter, his references to homosexuality and gender confusion voicing a desire to escape from himself. There's some objective evidence for this despair. At 31, he might have made himself the envy of all. Like Simon Hench, he matriculated at Oxford. Since that time, though, he has made scant headway at a job he also enjoys demeaning: "We publishers are working hand in hand with the Department of Education. They're making it their job to ensure that our Jeremy won't read when he grows up, and we're making it ours to ensure that if he grows up there are no books around worth his reading" (27).

This protest chimes with his ongoing practice, adapted from Oscar Wilde of treating life's most serious issues with the utmost flippancy His dig at an author whose book his firm is publishing comes straight from *The Importance of Being Earnest*: "Nuzek's reputation depends on nobody reading him. His prose guarantees that nobody will" (29). His habit of reducing everything to a joke might explain why he has stayed a junior editor. He delights in telling how his son has been wiping his bottom with the page proofs of a book he, Peter, brought home (30). Nothing is safe from his wit. This master of the sharp comeback rivals Ben, Simon, and Tommy of *Man in a Side-Car* (1971) in finding ways to ruin dinner parties.

He has also been trying to outdo his five-year-old son Jeremy (Peter's son Jeremy is 16 in *Plaintiffs and Defendants*) in childishness. In this vein, he's failing in his duties to Jeremy because he resents the time the boy spends sleeping alongside Hilary. Yet, as Hilary says, Peter, another of Gray's sexually nonobservant husbands, hasn't made love to her in months (36), providing an intriguing twist on the reference in the play to Wilde's *Lady Windermere's Fan* (31), in which it's suspected that a man is sleeping with his wife's mother. Like Peter's non-observance, his reversion to childhood signals a death wish. Peter says tellingly, during his last staged encounter with Hilary, "I'm too young to leave home" (85). He has been wasting his time if he's trying to force Hilary to choose between him and Jeremy. This battle he has already lost. Hilary has been romancing a colleague. But to what effect? Her choice of a father of three with two failed marriages behind him makes George Green a bad matrimonial risk. But she wants to move on. A contrite Peter's detailing of the wrongs he has committed against her she dismisses as childish, as she does his claim that he and she will always love each other (84, 85).

She has seen through his pose, which, she says, puts him "somewhere between Falstaff and a spiteful woman columnist" (33). A betweener he is. His childishness coexists with his premature aging. Though only 31, he has grown a paunch. He also has dandruff and a smoker's cough, and his boozing has made his eyes red. He has other woes. Like Ben, his quickness with words has recoiled on him. His brother Charles's rebuke, "I'd hoped you'd grown up a little since marrying Hilary" (25), refers to his failure to adapt. Continuing to fight the truth that reality will keep thwarting his expectations, he acts in a way of which only the deluded are capable.

The only false note in the scene where Hilary sends him away comes in her statement that pairing off with George, who's ten years her and Peter's senior, augurs better for her than staying with Peter. In 20 years, she argues, she'll look old, whereas Peter could still attract younger women, if "you [i.e., Peter] watched your eating and drinking" (90). These acts of self-discipline are unlikely to emerge soon, if at all, as she knows. She also knows, as his wife, that he's no Casanova (88). Gray misconceived this scene. Were Hilary a creature of impulse and audacity eager to confront her freedom, she'd have been too caught up with her quest to compile a list of reasons to push Peter out the door. Gray's inclusion of the scene stems from his suspicion of the viability of the George-Hilary intrigue.

He'll omit as well as add data to improve his script. His omission of all his characters' surnames in *Dog Days* foregrounds the truth that Peter has rarely used his own peter, or penis, for fun. The premarital erotic conquests he boasted about to his brother, Charles, were all lies. Hilary's insistence upon having no more kids after Jeremy had stilled his already-weak libido. After having moved into a "*small and depressing bed-sitter in, say, Chalk Farm*" (39), a shanty-town where sordid acts took place in *A Comeback for Stark*, he and the art student Joanna agree to have sex, an act he has to muster the courage to perform — if perform it he does. Following much nervous chatter, he proclaims his freedom (54). An earlier declaration of freedom concluded the play's first scene (39), shortly before it came out that, though still living with Hilary, he's moving out of the conjugal bedroom.

His woes accelerate here. Bolting the family home was just his first mistake. The point is made visually. Though he and Joanna are undressing as Act One ends, they're also standing on opposite sides of his bed. The start of the second act brings no evidence of closure. He's still hiding behind chatter. Joanna answers his vague statement, "We've just been to bed together" with the riposte, "But you can't even bring yourself to look at me." The dialogue ends in bathos. He feels clumsy and inept. After glancing briefly her way, he refers tautly to a "pre-coital depression" he failed to shake (57). They have never been further apart — until the following moments. While being approached by her, he backs away, taunting her about her sex life and claiming that he only climbed into bed with her because he was drunk.

A hint into Peter's vulnerability to a nervous breakdown comes in the way he spends his time. Whereas he's shown twice with both Joanna and Hilary, he holds three conversations with his brother, Charles, including one that ends the play. This scenic distribution hews to Freudian writ. If Freud doesn't reduce every thing to sex, he does base everything, sex above all, in the past. Memory here is key. Gray's memoirs, or diaries, mainly *The Smoking Diaries* (2004) and *The Year of the Jouncer* (2006), describe him getting both closer to his family of origin and as far away as possible.

This difficult maneuver informs the plays. *Dog Days* is so sly and interesting because of its awareness of the difficulty Simon and Nigel Gray had leaving home without their parents when they were evacuated to Montreal. Simon put the phrase "sibling rivalry" (81) into *Dog Days* intentionally. A middle brother, he knew the ruses and the power plays a sib will use to protect or boost his status in the home. He also knew how hateful these ploys could become. Safe, conventional, predictable Charles of *Dog Days* has always ranked lower in the family than the younger, more mercurial Peter. "Oh God, I wish I *were* like him, or even better be him" (70), he tells Hilary soon before confessing that he has always been in love with her (71).

Why shouldn't he love her? And why shouldn't Hilary have taken his confession in stride? Peter has a better wardrobe, a better address, and higher-profile job than Charles to match his superior degree. If all this has put Charles at an odd angle to himself, it also tells why Peter, in Charles's eyes, anyway, should also have a prettier, more accomplished wife. And now Peter has a chance to reconfirm his ascendancy. He can score a point off both Charles and the foursquare Protestant virtues of rational thought, frugality, and respect for hard work Charles has always lived by. Sifting through his arsenal of memories, he tells Charles that he has known for 15 years about his schoolboy practice of masturbating into a sock.

Hearing this news shocks Charles. It also runs his self-esteem so low that he compares himself to the stray dog that has been fouling the lawn of his boss, the Headmaster. It's no wonder that the Author's Note to *Dog Days* says that Gray wrote the play "in an increasing sense of muddle that was eventually like a madness" (5). Madness sounds right. The regrets invoked by *Dog Days* had been troubling him for decades. Charles's response to the news of Peter and Hilary's break-up also probes the depths of Gray's puzzlement over the convolutions of the fraternal tie:

> It's easier for me to bear being what I am [he tells Hilary], a loving family man, an obsequious Assistant Headmaster in a minor Public School, a bit of an old-fashioned Puritan, if *he's* behaving despicably. I want him to live my destructive life for me, while I go on living my decent life for myself [72].

Charles is wrong. Peter wasn't hacking away at the sanity and safety of the humdrum middle class, as his homebody brother claims. But his premarital chastity smashed Charles's morality fantasy, anyway; Charles can't even be wicked by proxy. A counter-rhythm to the permissiveness of an age that made people feel remiss if they didn't grab at prizes they didn't want, society's predatory standards have hurt both brothers. But Peter's wounds cut more deeply. He has one child to show for a sexual history that consists of one woman. And even though but one woman stands between Charles and virginity, too, he'll soon have six kids with that woman who always enjoys making love to him.

Having caught Charles's drift, Peter uses the terms "our joint self" (76) and "brothers under the skin" (77) to shrink the moral distance between himself and his brother. He has inferred the moral from the physical. As he points out, one of them has their mother's hands, while those of the other resembles their father's. The brothers use their hands, moreover, in the same way to achieve their goals. Though they work at different jobs, both men have to scrape and fawn to get ahead (79–80). But humble hands may stay empty. Neither brother has made good on the promise put forth by the hedonism and political activism of the late 1960s.

What applies to one of them keeps describing the other, Charles grudgingly observes. Despite his steady job and, till recently, fixed residence, Peter is as makeshift and provisional as one of Samuel Beckett's bums. Asked if he betrayed Hilary by sleeping with Joanna, he answers unhelpfully, "Oh yes, I betrayed them both.... But incompetently. Neither a successful adulterer nor a faithful husband. Something between the two" (74). Charles, who needed only the slightest prod of encouragement to have sex with Hilary, also defies definitions and categories. The point is made contextually. Charles does gain the Assistant Headmastership at Amplesides, his professional home for 20 years. But the promotion has left him empty. Like Jörgen Tesman of Ibsen's *Hedda Gabler*, he's an educator with housing problems. The announcement that his wife is expecting twins has failed to convince Amplesides's bursar to move Charles's already large family into larger school-owned digs.

This setback causes an inversion. If Charles is stuck in a crowded house he dislikes, Peter faces the threat of rootlessness. After having forsaken the marital bed for a couch, he leaves the family home. This act of protest wins no brotherly support. Charles, who's not above tearing a strip from Peter's hide, walks onstage eating a carrot to mock the pain caused Peter by the loss of his family. Gray is alluding to the carrot-munching Estragon of *Waiting for Godot*, Beckett's embodiment of senile de-sexed homelessness. Each brother is a cross for the other. Their mutual antagonism *could* have fueled a play in its own right, consisting of suffering, forgiveness, and some nods toward redemption.

Charles had told Peter, in the play's next-to-last scene, that "the great thing is, isn't it, to love one another in spite" (94). He may be speaking of the spite that has been impeding their love. Brotherly love, he believes, should conquer spite. The wrath he and Simon sometimes direct to each other, no aberration, informs healthy love of all kinds. The two uxorious brothers drink to this recognition. They see now, perhaps for the first time, that they share many of the traits they dislike in each other. They're much closer than they had thought. Let them shed their personae and cultivate qualities that are inherent and abiding. They'll be casting off the baggage that has made them so self-damning. Withholding judgment will also clear their heads and alert them to the existence of their hearts. They can stop whining about their flaws and deficiencies. These blots have been the point, not the problem. They can now be accepted and forgotten. Both Charles's self-disparagement and Peter's practice of joking about his failings have been preventing the future from singing.

Accepting the "joint self" (76) they have always shared will also help them see through the sham façades of their culture's icons, a huge step toward the attainment of mental health. The play's short final scene, which unfolds some weeks after the brothers' breakthrough dialogue, frames Peter and Joanna. Their agreement to delay a chore they've already been putting off (in order to enjoy each other's company longer) stems from their intimation of the numinous in the ordinary. Soft desires are beckoning Peter. Other options are increasing for him, too. During his first staged meeting with Joanna, she had recoiled from him, saying, "Jesus, what a prick!" His flippant response, "Oh, thank God, I thought you said *prig*" (15), had a rightness that bypassed them both. Sex is the great democratizer. No, he's not ready to sleep with Joanna at play's end. But his long talk with Charles has shown him that trusting his egalitarian instincts in his dealings with her can subdue the disabling priggishness he has been aiming mostly at himself.

Much of this promise is left hanging. Recognition and even resolve, Gray knows, can fail to ignite action; commitments waver and tenacity weakens. Better not to ask too much of people. Nor has he repudiated the deep strain of pessimism informing his body of work. On the other hand, his new attentiveness to the fraternal bond sounds a note of hope that chimes with the play's tone. Because he's better as a describer than a theorist — as a dramatist should be — he makes an important career strike by writing a funny, astute, theatrically compelling play around painful long-standing home truths. His people in *Dog Days* feel more like personalities than object lessons, and they attain life through words that are original, subtly true, and often couched in incisive, memorable one-liners. This stylish elegance imposes itself upon Gray's messy back-story and multiple narratives. Gray has again re-channeled Beckett's *Godot*. Drawing us out of our complacency, the bond (or bone) between Peter and Charles infers the elusive something that validates the self in a post-constructionist climate where identity is becoming so fragile and foggy as to no longer exist.

Self-validation, though, remains elusive. The fraternal bond meets grief in *Simply Disconnected* (1996) along with the other standbys that configured Simon Hench, who returns to the stage (played again by Alan Bates) together with his brother Stephen and old friend Jeff Golding from *Otherwise Engaged*. The Oxford degree that stoked Simon's habit of patronizing his Reading-schooled brother, though unmentioned, still exerts force. Another carryover from *Engaged*: Stephen fails to get the brotherly comfort he seeks in his first-act visit to Simon. His quest looks blocked from the start. As was the case in *Engaged*, Simon has forgotten the names of both Stephen's and Jeff's wives. It gets worse. He ignores an incident in which one of his employees nearly drove a car into his brother. Nothing good can come of the brother's visits to Simon. Whether woe or joy brings Stephen to Simon, all he can count on is indifference — if he can survive the road hazards. Simon, whom he rightly calls "the brother I never had" (40), never deserved his confidence. Nor would Simon cry foul. He has always been indifferent, if not hostile, toward the man he dismisses with the epithet, my "brother by some unnatural law of nature" (43).

The dismissal matches up with his personal history. In the 25 years since we last saw him, Simon has retired from publishing, moved to the country, and become a widower. The collapse of the fierce, desperate love of his wife Beth and Ned, from *Engaged*, though never referred to, still echoes. Beth either miscarried or delivered a baby who died at birth (8, 43). Vagueness also surrounds *her* death. Ned, who might have fathered her baby, presumably parted from her long before she died, some four or five years before the play's staged action.

The calm with which Simon explains Beth's death to Stephen reinstates the indifference that galled everyone close to him in *Engaged*. He has become a more calcified version of his old uncaring self. The afternoon he had set aside to be alone in *Engaged* has grown in time. Rather than leaving a message on his voice mail saying that he's otherwise engaged for an afternoon, he has disconnected his phone. That's not all. More solitary than before, he no longer opens his mail. He hardly knows who he is. Despite having lived the past ten years in the same home, he misnames the only shop in the area (2).

What he calls his problem of "identification" (2) will heap on more grief. His soul has been languishing. The main story of his non-life is that he cares as little about himself as he does his surroundings. At the start of Act Two he says ambiguously and at great personal risk to an angry questioner who's pointing a pistol at him, "Fire away" (30). Coming just after curtain rise, his words give the act a torrid, beguiling start. The audience doesn't know whether to laugh or cringe. What takes over is dismay. If his words convey a startling presence of mind, they also mark the apathy of the nihilist. His brother Stephen has outclassed him by calling himself a coward. The coward believes in something worth saving or protecting, even if it's only his fat skin. He has leagued with life.

Stephen accuses himself of cowardice for coming to Simon with news he should have first shared with his wife (12, 38). His misgivings make sense. Having said in *Engaged* that he was "middle aged" (OE 18), this grandfather must be well past 60. He has been serving as assistant headmaster at Amplesides for the past 25 years after having taught there for the previous 15. And again, as in the first act of *Engaged*, he has come under fire from his superiors—but for having done a deed more outrageous than any for which Simon was ever charged. This oldest character in a play dealing with time's passage finds himself trapped in a looming intergenerational sex scandal.

This understrapper to a female headmaster half his age (10) patted the rump of a student-athlete after a match. Having often been passed over for promotion in favor of younger candidates, Stephen knows humiliation. But now that Helena, his boss, has taken the fondling, or patting, incident to the school's board of governors, she has also made him face the threat of poverty along with disgrace; besides sacking him, the Board could revoke his pension. But what vexes Stephen nearly as much as this foreboding is the identity of his accuser. Looking ahead to a similar incident in Alan Bennett's *History Boys* (2004), Stephen fondled a "fine young cricketer" (10) of 13 who also won an essay prize competing against 17-year-olds.

Luckily, Stephen keeps his job even though his pension will be cut. As an ex-magistrate, he has the legal knowledge to appreciate his good luck. But that luck has limits. Together with the loss of money his retirement will bring goes the distress of being informed on by Toby Winch, his favorite student — as well as a younger alter ego of ex-student-athlete Simon Gray, who loved cricket all his life. Toby delivers this thematic muscle without appearing onstage. Nor does he stand alone in the play as a projection of Gray's many-faceted back-story. Another character who rattles Stephen, as he did in *Engaged*, is Jeff Golding. In the decades that have passed since the action of Gray's 1971 play, Jeff's travel books have made him a "household name" (16) despite their falling short of important literature. No complaints from Jeff; "Signs of small catastrophes" set in places like Portugal, India, and Turkey, and in which, he says, "I tumble into sewers, have rows in restaurants, [and] mistake police cars for taxis" (17), the books target a general readership.

Part of their commercial success comes from Jeff's first-rate memory. At a glance, he recognizes the son of Bernard Wood, or Strapley, even though 50 years have passed since he and Bernard attended Wundale School together. He also remembers calling Stephen "a latent pederast" (OE 20), a slur that redefines itself in *Simply Disconnected*, a script which has claws. In the mode of Ben Butley, he again turns his cruel wit on Stephen, referring to him as the "school pederast" (SD 12), which is, indeed, how he may now be seen at Amplesides (which Jeff uncannily calls "Amplebums" [SD 13]).

Jeff's real victim, though, is Gwendoline, whom he reconnected with in *Engaged* after divorcing. The anxieties that made her suicidal years earlier (OE 25) couldn't have been worse than what's plaguing her now. After reuniting with the alcoholic Jeff, she began drinking to keep him company. But she fell victim to a cruel inversion. Whereas Jeff put down his bottle to write, *she* became an alcoholic, a plight worsened by his loss of sexual interest in her (SD 23). In an echo from *Little Portia*, our last report of her in *Engaged* told of her wrestling with Jeff to gain control of a speeding car. A link between this boozy turmoil and Gray, who didn't drive a car, emerges. The near-fatal car accident in *Engaged* linked Jeff to another pop-culture prodigy, Chekhov's Tregorin, who causes one woman's madness and another's suicide in *The Seagull*. Gwendoline, who left her husband and child in *Engaged* (23–4) to remarry Jeff, has been fuming at him. Their one moment of physical contact in *Simply Disconnected* shows them struggling for a car key, an incident that revives the idea, from works like Shakespeare's *Taming of the Shrew*, Coward's *Private Lives* (1930), and Albee's *Who's Afraid of Virginia Woolf* (1962), that love entails a struggle for power, a point underscored by the key symbolism.

Keeping alive the idea in *Simply Disconnected* is the character called Greg, the odd-jobs man at Simon's country house. Though in his late twenties or early thirties, the "slightly ill-kempt" (1) Greg hasn't made much career headway. Nor are his vocational prospects bright. His fondness for soccer, drink, and his self-admitted verbal cramp (5) all invoke the tongue-tied working-class lout, Arthur Seaton, of Alan Sillitoe's *Saturday Night and Sunday Morning*

(1958). Before curtain rise, Greg had already borrowed £500 to see a soccer match in Amsterdam, where his hooliganism cost him another £500 in fines. He also owes Simon rent money.

But, unlike Dave, Simon's student-tenant in *Engaged*, Greg, besides being older, has a wife, whose importance comes out straightaway. In another reference to *Engaged*, *Simply Disconnected* begins with Simon's engrossment by music—but not by an LP of Wagner's *Parsifal*. He's playing church music on a CD consisting of a duet between Beth—dead now for some four years—and Dave's wife, Mandy, who's also Simon's housemaid. The "beautiful ... sound" made by this "well-matched" (2) vocal pair has another reference point that chimes with music's ability to raze barriers. Simon might have gotten both women pregnant. And now, in the aftermath of the deaths of Beth and her newborn, he's terrified that Mandy will miscarry or die, too. The play's first words, spoken by Greg, "The missus here?" (1) rekindles this fear. Simon, who has usurped Greg's husbandly office, moves about nervously. Nor is he soothed by Greg's next speech: "Yours isn't bad. Flatter than mine, isn't she? Not that I'm a judge" (1–2). Along with breaking thematic ground for Greg's later clash with Simon's brother, a judge, or magistrate, Greg's words trouble Simon anew. They evoke to him the huge difference between the two women. Beth, besides singing flat, has been lying flat in her grave, while Mandy not only lives but also has new life throbbing inside her.

Family ties, their persistence and breakdown both, are the order of the day. Late in the second act of the two-act *Simply Disconnected*, Stephen calls Simon "my brother. The only brother I never had" (40). As has also been seen, he's told in turn, "You're only my brother by some unnatural law of nature.... Go, please" (43). Simon's the unnatural one. He'd rather banish Stephen than discuss with him a desperate issue he himself had raised—the last words Beth spoke before her death. Death has been preoccupying Simon. Hewing to the trope of the thirtyish parents who die in a car crash, from *Little Portia*, *Dog Days*, and *Japes* (2000), he had asked if Jeff was alone in the dangerously swerving car that nearly hit Stephen (40). He kept refilling Gwendoline's drink after Jeff had stormed away from her in Act One, and he's afraid of having helped cause the death of another woman.

Fear keeps nagging him. After Stephen's final departure from the stage, a "*heavily pregnant*" Mandy enters saying "Yo-ho (*dully*) motherfucker" (44) (the word, fuck, in its different forms, is spoken by most of he people in the play, both male and female). This shocking entry, coming just minutes from the end, heightens the agitated tone of the play. Mandy can insult her much older boss because she knows she's risking nothing. Though a skivvy, she's in charge. She has combined the heart knowledge that Gray's women have in greater abundance than his men with whatever she learned about Simon from his wife, her former singing partner.

Above all, she knows that Simon needs her. Along with his recent ejection of Stephen, the deaths in his home have made her his last hard tie to the world. Thus her short, foul-mouthed greeting brings him *"suddenly alive"* (44). He was afraid that her absence from the house for the past hours—Greg had opened the play by asking where she was—meant that a car knocked her into a ditch (people are killed by a car and a bus in *Old Flames* [1990] and *They Never Slept* [1991]). Relieved to find her alive, he asks her to drop Greg and live with him. She laughs at his offer. Why live with someone who's inert, unreal, and only takes up space? "You don't *be*," she says, comparing him unfavorably to Greg, who "is ... and you're not" (45, 44). Again drawing from Archibald MacLeish's "Ars Poetica," she had already said "people are.... Rather than mean" (42).

Simon has been groping toward the moral intelligence that will allow him to confer intrinsic, rather than instrumental, value upon people. Understanding his need to connect with others, he tells Mandy that she and her baby, whose paternity he'll ignore, are "all I've got" (47). But she responds with her trademark working-class truculence. The most she'll give him — after turning down his offer of £500 a month for her, Greg, and the baby—is permission to play with the baby when she brings it with her to clean his room.

Ironically, just when he has begun to intuit the joys and duties of connection, he's foiled. He has also remembered Greg's comparison of Beth's singing to his wife Mandy's, "Flatter than mine" (1). The second and last time the duet sing in our hearing, at the very end, Simon, as deeply moved as he was at the end of *Engaged*, tells Jeff, while sitting *"still and stiff, controlling himself,"* that Beth sounds "a bit flat" (50). Repeating the words that he heard from Greg in the play's first scene disconcerts him. But he sees that he has to speak out. Accepting Beth's fallibility confirms his need of other people; her shortcomings as a singer didn't lessen her intrinsic worth. What he needs is connection, not the cold detachment to judge. He'd gladly trade places with any of the unfortunates who have been passing through his elegant home. Even the dead Beth has a singing partner on the CD that has been engrossing him.

Less caddish than emotionally lazy, Simon could always be kind. And though he enjoys being loved, he also knows that the tenderness he offers in return falls short of what's needed for close, healthy bonding. His sexually touristic life style—a legacy of the 1960s—had brought him together briefly with an array of women he never cared about. He still holds sex as cheap as he did in *Engaged*. Before her pregnancy (and her waddling onto stage clinches the point), Mandy was like a mandolin to him, an instrument he could play and put down. Her duet with Beth has made her less disposable. Stephen had said aptly, if not tactfully, that only the birth of Beth's child could have redeemed the moral defeatism inflicted upon him by his decades of promiscuity. Frittering away his life on casual sex has ransacked his spirit—which a big change is replenishing. But it's far from being full. The imminent birth of Mandy's baby has moved him from a life style governed by sex without love to one of sexless love.

Repetition darkens this inversion. Mandy's pregnancy revives the smudged paternity motif that vexed him with Beth. That Mandy is much younger than Beth during her pregnancy than Beth was during *hers* posits a failure by Simon to keep pace with time. The warning is well judged. He's stagnating. Two younger people call him "old man" (44, 48), making him wonder how long he can keep marking time before it gulps him down.

Which shows why, though based on the superfluous man of 19th-century Russian fiction, he was also reshaped to serve the play's intent. Simon lacks the Byronic glamour that came with superfluity in the people of Pushkin, Lermentov, and Goncharov, even though his nobodiness also stems from moral apathy. Gray establishes this indifference forthwith, noting that, as in *Engaged*, Simon has forgotten the names of the wives of his brother and best friend. What's more, his having unplugged his phone and ignored his correspondence completes the pattern of reclusiveness started in *Engaged*.

The demon of repetition has made him gag. In another echo from *Engaged*, the first act of which ended with Bernard Wood's impromptu visit, the thirty-year-old Julian Wood intrudes on Simon unexpectedly at the end of Act One of *Simply Disconnected* and keeps talking to him after the between-act interval. This overlapping builds a powerful unity. It had to. The fraught interview between the two men alludes to the anxieties gripping Gray, who (in the year of the play's debut, would turn 60) was preparing to both divorce Beryl, his wife of 32 years, and marry Victoria Rothschild the following year (*Who's Who 2007: An Annual Bibliographical Dictionary* [New York: Bloomsbury, 2007, 906]).

The luggage Gray puts in the hands of both Simon and Julian when they meet helps develop their encounter as a mirror meeting between dispossessed souls. Simon couldn't be pleased with what he learns of himself from Julian, who's stammering so much from heroin withdrawal (40) that he can't finish his sentences. On his part, Simon, who had confessed to Bernard that he had slept with Joanna, lies to Julian about having known a Joanna or a Bernard Wood. Julian exposes this lie, saying that Bernard — in at least one more disconnect — did shoot himself as he threatened to do in the phone message at the end of *Engaged* that Simon cut short. Rough justice is about to claim Simon, its certainty enhanced by its tawdriness. The same pistol Bernard had turned on himself is now pointing at Simon, with shabby, trembling Julian both his judge and would-be assassin. An act of recreational sex, Simon sees, can release its offspring slowly.

This news stuns him. Having nothing to lose, the maimed outcast Julian tends toward destructive acts. His having timed his visit to match the 31st anniversary of Joanna — his mother's — first meeting with Simon has also injected into the play the taboo of parricide. The tension builds: Simon gets Julian's name right in spite of having only heard it once (33); Julian's mispronunciations, a function of his stammer, are both funny and disquieting. But he doesn't fumble his words when he takes matters to the next, more dangerous, level, pronouncing to Simon, the epithet, "Your Joanna" (32. 34). Any protective interface that Simon had wanted to hide behind has been ripped away.

The epithet fits; Joanna had fallen in love with Simon, a step he tried to thwart. "A fuck followed by an insult" (36) is Julian's dour summary of an unrequited love that was deflected when Joanna took Simon's £50 in exchange for her promise to leave him alone. So much for the cheap thrill. Simon's insult blighted Julian, who has been subsisting in orphanages, mental hospitals, and prisons, his 17-year-old mother ill-equipped to raise him. But, rather than shooting Simon, he calls him "my father" (36), a title buttressed by the luggage he brought with him. He has come to stay, a sign of which is the silence accompanying his appearance. Whereas the arrivals of all the other visitors came with a cacophony of screaming brakes and slamming doors (e.g., 1, 3, 45), that of Julian emits no sound, Simon's house being more of a destiny to him than a destination.

The play continues to breach stage realism. If Julian is Simon's son, why does he look like Bernard, né Wood (37)? The physical resemblance between the two men defies the laws of genetics. How could Bernard have sired Julian, if, as both he and Joanna claimed (OE 41–41, SD 32), she never slept with him? Gray had a good reason to flout both natural law and stage realism when dealing with this question. He's extending the concept of paternity beyond accepting responsibility, caretaking, and bestowing love, all righteous enough stand-ins for the blood tie. Bernard had said "my girl Joanna" (35, 37) in *Engaged*, and Greg speaks of "my Mandy" (2) here in *Simply Disconnected*. Simon is never this proprietary or assenting—making the play's first scene a dialogue between the two sides of the playwright's personality, the Simon and the Gray, or Greg. The Simon side prevails (The playwright's mother called him "Si" while pleading with him in vain to stay with her at what proved to be her death-bed [LC 148–9]). Found together with Julian by Stephen, Simon demeans his transaction with the younger man, denying anything "of consequence" (57) having passed between them. Reverting to type, he calls Julian Jason (48) after having gotten his name right. He had said of Julian's mother, "She wasn't my Joanna" (34).

Noting this denial of fatherhood, Julian, who needs the ballast conferred by having a parent, identifies with Bernard, the sad lonely plop known at school as the "Wanker of Wundale" (OE 41–2; SD 37). Necessity goads him. Bernard is the same fool who'd later leave his wife and kids to court somebody less than half his age who could barely stomach him. Gray, who has been looking into the problem of self-identification (Simon and Greg), endorses both

Julian's brave search for roots and where it takes him. He refers uniquely to both Julian and Bernard in both works by their surnames. This device marks his approval of Julian's decision to change his mind about living with Simon, if the young man ever had a choice. But the device also tallies Simon's deprivation. If life has been bashing Julian around, it still hasn't caught up with Simon — as Bernard noted 30 years earlier (OE 41). He doesn't deserve a son. The last words Julian speaks, "Julian Strapley, Son of the Wundale Wanker" (48), pack a moral fervor that eludes him. Julian has cast off the same problem with "identification" (2) that has been dogging Simon for decades.

The curtain doesn't drop here. Though bleak, Simon's outlook isn't hopeless. Significantly out of Greg's hearing, he says that he hired his odd-jobs man to ensure that he could retain Mandy, who "means a lot" to him (6), as his housemaid. At issue, too, is his remark that Beth, her singing partner, liked Mandy. Their duets smoothed differences between them in age and social class. Gray contrasts this harmony throughout with the screeching or slamming brakes of cars that contain quarrelling mates and put pedestrians at risk. That *Engaged* and *Simply Disconnected* both end with the childless Jeff and Simon listening to music develops this counterpoint. The music playing at the end of the *Simply Disconnected* has an emotional charge. The hymn Mandy and Beth are singing, though humbler than Wagner's *Parsifal*, which was playing at the end of *Engaged*, represents Simon's last sensuous tie with his wife. It's being played in her honor. For Simon, it has also taken up a shocking life of its own. This usually composed, noncommittal man lets fly "*a terrible howl of grief and rage*" (50) while hearing it because, meager as it may be, it describes her, taken off her guard, as happier and more fulfilled than he ever made her.

The religious nature of the music deepens its effect. Gray gives the vicar who recorded it the same name as that of the one in *Hidden Laughter* who called belief in God a weakness or a form of madness. Religious faith to Ronnie (Chambers) of Gray's 1990 stage play differs from empirical knowledge. It's an embedded structure of feeling that bypasses or transcends what Dostoevsky called Euclidian logic. Beth's having died before she could finish singing her part in the duet fuses in Simon's mind with the wild, lyrical love for Joanna that helped kill Bernard Wood. It gives her music a terrifying power, the meaning of which Simon duly notes: For the wide-awake in spirit, the power of music must be both held close and kept in check.

Souls less tractable than Simon are advised to be wary. Impulsiveness causes trouble, as it did Stephen when he touched his student. Yet Gray, sensitized by upheavals in his own life, believes, too, that the repression of impulse dries the soul. The ending of *Simply Disconnected* evokes that of *Caramel Crisis*, despite the 30 years dividing the works. The repressiveness that haunts the prudent and the temperate fosters a culture where the loudest, most grating voices belong to soccer thugs like Greg. Unlike those of Beth and Mandy, these voices haven't yet merged in our presence. The Jamesian reading that Robert

Gordon gave Gray's *Close of Play* (1979) applies just as strictly to *Simply Disconnected*: "By the end of the play much has been revealed but nothing substantial has taken place" (Burkman, ed. 10).

The play's action bestrides the last third of the last century. Like the Dormobile Simon owns, the buzzword, overcome, spoken five times in as many seconds (22), belongs to the 1960s. Jeff's recollection of the time he threw a drink at Davina Saunders in *Engaged* (OE 29; SD 21), an event Gray included to give her a reason to sashay topless in front of Simon, also invokes the 1968 rock musical, *Hair*, and, with it, the sexual revolution that drew in Simon. Jeff's whimper from *Engaged*, "This sad little country of ours is finished at last" (21), voices a dismay felt elsewhere in *Simply Disconnected*; the policies of Margaret Thatcher, Great Britain's Prime Minister between 1979–90, limited government's role in the economy as a spur to free-market initiatives. Laws should be repealed, not made, Mrs. Thatcher believed, because the welfare state had infantilized the British public.

The weakening of Britain's collective moral fiber she fretted about comes forth in figures as different as Greg, Simon, and Julian. On the far side of the spectrum, Beth's attempt to flee the quagmire brings death — her baby's and then her own. Gumption meets grief elsewhere, as Bernard Wood had already shown. The person in the diptych with the most formal education, Stephen, though lucky to dodge scandal, nonetheless faces the poverty and displacement that go with it. The younger generations are squeezed, too. The boozing and reckless driving of Greg, who has already done jail time, have smudged Mandy's hope to build a family with him.

Should this portent reach the dreadful consummation of turning her baby into another Julian Wood, it might go unnoticed. The people in the play evoke a society full of divisions — between the educated and the unschooled, the rich and the poor, and the rural and the urban; Greg calls Julian "City trash" (47). Yet Gray's 1996 England has grown affluent and more user friendly. Train and telephone service have both improved since 1975, when Simon debuted. The shops are cleaner and more interesting, their wares more abundant and displayed more enticingly. But the speed and hurry of the time also make it likely that many of these wares will stay shelved. They may even go unseen. Ignoring a stop sign while driving Simon's Dormobile at 70 mph on a village road, Greg nearly killed Stephen. Even at a safe 20 mph, a "snarling," Greg missed smacking the rear end of another car "by a whisker" (19).

The odds of surviving a car accident have dropped. Stephen reports having had to maneuver suddenly to dodge a car "swerving all over the place" (39). A struggle for control of that same swerving car reminds us of the husbands and wives who die together in auto wrecks in *Little Portia*, *Dog Days*, and *Japes*. Also surfacing from the deep structure of Gray's life is the drinking involved in both these fatalities and the noisy near misses in *Simply Discon-*

nected. Motifs continue to operate at different levels in the play. The drinks thrown at Gwendoline (OE 21), Davina (OE 29), and Jeff (OE 60; SD 24) call up the alcoholism that cost Gray a yard of intestines and kept him in intensive care for three weeks in the 1990s (Gardner 1).

The pressures that seek relief in alcohol often cause disconnects. Simon has not only never read Jeff's books; he never knew that his oldest friend wrote books, let alone published them with his—Simon's—firm. Gray extends the conceit. The responses or non-responses elicited by writing can cause real harm. According to Gwendoline, Jeff's sexual interest in her lost out to his writing. His "babies" (23), or bestselling books, have all entered the world since he moved to a separate bed. Then, the breach between people and the names they're mistakenly called (e.g., 15, 48) links the Jamesian trope of art's cruelty ("the madness of art") to the divide or communication lapse that overhangs life everywhere. Julian's stammer divides his talk from the meaning it's meant to convey. Simon's making himself unavailable by phone and mail has boxed him in. Greg's turning his back on England and Mandy to watch soccer in Amsterdam both lands him in the slammer and saddles him with debt.

The funneling of too much booze down her gullet stopped Gwendoline from attending Beth's funeral, an event that appalled Stephen, who hadn't even heard that Beth was sick, let alone dying (42). Death itself has been denied the finality of closure. It meets disjuncture again in the angry words Julian sputters at Simon while trying to decide whether to shoot him dead: "You'd make a very civilized corpse" (34). This veiled reference to the next-to-last scene of Pinter's *Birthday Party*, in which a dapper, well-coiffed man seems catatonic, underscores Gray's belief in the need to communicate.

Loss of connection between generations and sexual partners both within and outside of marriage can provoke identity crises and, in the case of Beth and her newborn, death; perhaps this baby of smudged paternity fought its entry into the world. The title of Gray's 1996 play makes this point. *Disconnected*, with its march of glottal and palatal stops, could have stood alone in this regard. It also raises questions. How does the introductory adverb, *Simply*, sharpen our awareness of the play's intent? Though the weakest of qualifiers, adverbs served admirably in the work of Henry James, who was on Gray's mind during the writing of the play; Simon pacifies an irate Stephen, whom he has been keeping at bay for weeks, with the Jamesian idiom: "But here you are. Wonderfully are" (7). Onstage before us is the simply disconnected Simon. That's that. It's a given that needs no discussion. It tells all. Gray's invocation of the great social comedian dovetails with the humor bubbling up from the different word games in the play. The tossing around of the homophones "protégé," "prodigy," and "progeny" isn't the irrelevancy Stephen claims it is (9). And whether he teaches at Amplesides or Amplebums, as Jeff will mockingly say (13), his indiscretion with a student's bum will keep haunting him.

In another example of the play's immersion in theater history, the Renaissance device of the biter-bit enters the picture when a snickering Jeff, having scolded Simon for calling his wife "Gwynyth" in *Engaged* (21), calls her Gwynyth himself (SD 18). Another staple of dramatic tradition has crept onto the set. Its presence rings bells with Gray, whose inability to drive made him count on others to take him places. His *Simply Disconnected*, in which DUI is prominent, disclaims the home as a refuge from hurt. Perhaps a tighter, warmer bond between Beth and Simon could have averted the literal of death of Beth's newborn and the moral death Julian and his mother, Joanna, have been living. This intergenerational tragedy invokes Ibsen's *Ghosts*, a play about syphilis, or what used to be called a social disease, in which the new generation pays for the misdeeds of the old. Similarities between the conceptions of Mandy's child and Beth's casts a dark pall on the future.

Disconnection keeps gaining gravitas. When Simon tells Julian that, while a Cambridge student, he knew a man whose name sounded like that of Bernard Wood, he's lying to protect himself. He had referred in *Engaged* to his student days at Oxford (e.g., 15, 60). But his fellow Oxonian Jeff Golding now speaks of introducing Simon to Wagner when they were both at Cambridge (SD 49), an assertion Simon takes in stride. Another, perhaps more striking, anomaly comes in Julian's disclosure that his arrival at Simon's marks the 31st anniversary of his conception (29). Jeff had set this same time frame, give or take a month or so, at "a quarter of a century ago" (SD 21). Was he lying? If so, his fear of moving cars suggests his implication in the darkness that threatens to engulf his people in the play.

Propulsive, disciplined writing invites the idea that a guilt-racked Simon Gray planned *Simply Disconnected* as a sick joke aimed at himself. Julian's changing his mind about shooting Simon saves Simon's life at the cost of withholding from him the tragic grandeur traditionally extended to parricides. This denial includes the afterlife. The same Simon who throws a drink at Jeff, stands apart from the three people in *Engaged* and *Simply Disconnected* who get splashed, or doused. He's not ready for the anointing that designates movement to a new spiritual level in Christian ceremony.

Mature, complex, and convincing, *Simply Disconnected* is a dreamy, yet tight, play that shows love and need—filial, fraternal and erotic, old and new—driving a search for a self worn down by keeping the Other at bay—even after it has become clear that the Other might be wearing the face of the questing self.

Life Support imbues its charisma in the mysteries of the human condition. Three years have passed since the curtain dropped on the action of *Simply Disconnected* (LS 10), and Jeff's writing career has continued to thrive, with a new readership opening up for him. The bestsellers he has been writing are about to fuel an American TV mini-series. But more precedence belongs, in Gray's 1997 one-act play, to an inner journey he's involuntarily taking. Here he's on alien turf. The success of the journey of this visitor to far-flung Borneo, Portugal, and China depends upon his staying put. His base for the last six weeks has been the ICU unit of a London hospital. His wife Gwendoline, who's now called Gwen, just as he has become J.G., has been staying alive thanks to electrical wires and feeding tubes, the life-support system of the play's title. He's not sure if he wants her to stay attached indefinitely to these wires and tubes. His long speechless hours in the unit have also scrambled time for him. A visitor to the unit who appears on time for her appointment with him is asked whether she came early or late (27).

Life Support enacts Gray's belief in the difficulty of coping with conflicting demands in our multi-tasking, pluralistic world. J.G. is a husband, a brother, a business colleague, and a lover. While the struggle of passive waiting has sent him inside himself, it has also been feeling some effects of these competing claims. Gwen had called him out in *Simply Disconnected* (21) for using information gleaned from maps and guidebooks rather than on-site visits to the exotic places he writes about in his comic adventures. Lately, to silence her, he *has* been getting his materials first hand. A mistake; though it's unclear if on-site immediacy has improved his books, it was on a trip to Guadeloupe that Gwen got the bee sting that put her in a coma. It's symptomatic of the random cruelty of the world that she was stung while squatting and "widdling into the dust" (37). Calamity can strike when least expected. It makes sense that J.G. feels comforted to find her "cocooned ... in complete safety" (8). The world of *Life Support* is unraveling, danger and loss its only fixed points. A radio announcer tells of "a quarter of million people" in Calcutta suffering from an unidentified disease (7). Later, a story in a TV guide about "murder, pillage, and rape" (31) prompts J.G.'s disclaimer, "What a foul world" (31). Why would Gwen, now that she has found peace, want to return to it?

The foulness she's oblivious to takes many forms. A woman recently widowed who'd always cringe at the sound of her husband's singing would "give anything" (11) to hear it again, J.G. learns. He was already rocked by the lesson that values can be situational rather than absolute. In a scene rich in gallows humor, he punched the native soldier who had begun to pee on Gwen's neck, the site of her bee sting, to "neutralize the poison" (38). What price dignity? The television announcer who reported that "the number of dead has now risen to twenty thousand" (7) might have been talking about AIDS (which is mentioned later in the play [14]), a product of physical intimacy. The analogy with both J.G.'s gay brother Jack and the death of Beth's baby in *Simply Disconnected* strikes home. The act of love should beget life, not end it. Accordingly, Gwen's life expectancy in a forest in Guadeloupe hangs upon her degradation. By protecting her honor, J.G., acting like any husband faced by the absurdity of a grinning soldier, "his cock in his hand" (38) aimed at Gwen's neck, caused her death. He was too outraged to understand the meaning of the grinning soldier's partner ordering Gwen at gunpoint to remain silent.

Drawing poison from bee stings was routine "first aid handbook stuff" (30) to the soldiers. But J.G. shouldn't reproach himself, even if his mistake puts him in that hapless crew of self-blamers, the husbands in Simon Gray's theater. Precious few husbands anywhere would have caught the sharp rift between appearance and reality confronting J.G. in this weird episode. No act of retribution or tropical madness felled Gwen; she was taken down by J.G.'s urge to respond immediately to the daylight madness of two young brown-skinned soldiers presumably intent on violating her. Love remains out of joint with its effects. A lower-level example of love inducing hardship comes in a story J.G. hears about a nurse he likes having been switched to another ward for having "tangled up with some married bloke" (40).

Now in his early 50s, J.G. had stopped drinking since his and Gwen's near-fatal drunken struggle for the control of their car, discussed but not described in *Simply Disconnected* (49). Having gained momentum, the conflation of drink and death in *Life Support* will eventually prove lethal. Just before Gwen is stung, she and J.G. drink alcohol together for "the first time" (38) in years. This bizarre, but typical, example of the ravages of drink conveys the self-disdain of the alcoholic Gray. But it bypasses the truth that drinking hasn't killed J.G.'s libido. *Life Support* refutes Gwen's angry charge, from *Simply Disconnected* (21), that J.G. now puts his erotic energy into his writing. Though he may still be ignoring *her* sexual needs, his sap still rises. J.G. has been having an affair with his literary agent, Julia. This fling, though no credit to him morally, shows in him more spark than Gwen and perhaps the audience had credited him with possessing. The trap was carefully baited. Gray's referring to him in the play's stage directions by his initials implies that, like Bernard Berenson, who's cited throughout *Old Masters* (2004) as BB, his work has flattened him into both an industry and an institution.

His appearing to us in an intensive care unit adds to the impression that part of *him* is comatose, like his wife, to whom he is legally joined in both spirit and flesh. Reinforcing this bleak impression is this unsociable man's retort to a visitor's unexpected comment that good support systems, in the form of a network of friends, could speed *his* and maybe even Gwen's recovery. He says that he lacks friends, and he can be believed. His goading of Simon Hench's brother Stephen in both *Otherwise Engaged* and *Simply Disconnected* shows him razing civility with wit.

His heart, though, hasn't chilled. Invoking a proposition perhaps gleaned from E.M. Forster's *Passage to India*, he learns the difference between absence and nonexistence; the counter-pole of absence is presence. This insight is vital. Gray disclosed a soft, wondering side in J.G. by having both his brother (15) and his wife (25) call him by the childish name, Jeffie. Childhood innocence comes into view often in the play. Not only will J.G.'s brother Jack bond with the "frightened boy" (16) who tried to mug him on a dark street. The play's very action, including the scenes that show Jack and J.G. together, unearth J.G.'s own fears and vulnerabilities.

These lie close to the surface; the depths probed in his psyche by Gwen's plight disclose the sensitivity he has been directing to the same literary craft that he has been deriding. Speeding this alchemy is his first visitor, Dr. Pat O'Brien. Pat, as he is known, tells J.G. about two accident victims he had visited in the hospital, both of whom, defying medical science, returned to their normal everyday lives. We've been dropped into a world where daily secular values, like time and its passage, have come under question. This impression builds. Although it's never said, Pat, no M.D., earned his doctorate in some field like pastoral family counseling or hospice-based theology that never existed in J.G.'s university days. During a conversation with him, Pat speaks of "people of your generation" (34).

The impression that we're watching a myth unfold builds with Pat's words that he has come to "keep an eye" (6)—on J.G. Is he a priestly mediator between Gwen's downfall and J.G.'s grief? Has his relative youth made him the symbolic little child who'll lead J.G. to a redemptive spiritual breakthrough? These questions vitalize the play's sagging late-middle aged materials. If Pat's presence in the ICU ward doesn't turn *Life Support* into a play about faith, it does confer upon faith an importance found elsewhere in the canon only in *Hidden Laughter*. Yes, Mr. Rolls, the surgeon, whose name suggests the unstoppable forward movement of time, will decide Gwen's future. When he recommends that she be disconnected from life support, J.G. complies, satisfied that the cruel choice he was given didn't come from a cruel man. Henry Windcape, the man who fired St. John Quartermaine, wasn't cruel, either.

Pat had already put Gwen's—and J.G.'s—best chances beyond the scope of medical science. He's an encourager. The questions he asks J.G. about support systems rise from a belief that a group consisting of friends and family in Gwen's room might form a bulwark of warmth, cheer, and even hope. Above all, J.G. must try to stay upbeat. He learns from Pat that optimism will help him cope with the ordeal that has been grinding him along with Gwen. The optimism kicks in in a way that surprises even him. Defying common sense, he tells a comatose Gwen that a passing need for comfort and acceptance drove him to sleep with Julia, of whom he says, "She meant nothing to me" (29). Shockingly, he says this in Julia's presence. Who protests; as is usual in Gray, the act of sex, both at the time of its occurrence and afterwards, has in *Life Support* different meanings for the principals. The brisk, efficient careerist Julia had to cancel meetings for the same trysts written off by J.G. as "lunch stuff" (29). J.G.'s rudeness has rocked her poise; in a snit, she tells Gwen that she'd have rather gone to bed with *her*.

It's vital that she speaks to Gwen directly. The collapse of Julia's defenses that led her to address a woman unable to hear her prompts other confessions. Faith has taken hold. No mountebank casting spells, J.G. is trying "to love her

[Gwen] back into life" (34). He keeps flouting civility as he does reason. "To hell with all contracts" (32), he tells Julia after refusing to sign the documents that would have sped an agreement to re-script his books for American television. Like a Graham Greene character, he's performing acts that have taken on a meaning beyond their intended ones. Marriage is also a contract. But, rather than banishing it to hell, he amplifies its requirements.

Like Gwen, the marriage is neither dead nor alive. This unclassifiability frees him to find new approaches to her. He takes his cue from Thomas Hardy's poem, "The Self-Unseeing," the last two lines of which he quotes: "Everything glowed with a gleam;/ Yet we were looking away" (39). Both he and Gwen had ignored the "blessings emblazoned" (l. 10) on their marriage. And now, by signing off on Mr. Rolls's warrant to "pull the plug" (44), he'll be killing her a second time. What he has forgotten is that she'll continue living in his heart after the drains are dry.

Some muscle in the back row is protecting her and J.G.'s interests. Pat has been trying to help him handle a love dented by sorrow and guilt. He'll have a lot of work to do. Chance (a major force in Hardy) provides the way. After speaking in Gwen's voice in an imaginary dialogue, mimicking her oft-voiced complaints about him, J.G. hears her say, at the end of scene two, "I'll speak for myself, if you don't mind" (22). The medium of theater has brought her voice to life. He has fused her spirit to his. Though the fusion aches, it's also healthy. Her following his lead by joining with subjects that have hurt their marriage, like their being childless alcoholics, shows him where to direct his efforts. Suffering has matured him — a major breakthrough in light of the *im*maturity of many of Gray's male leads. Rather than silencing her, he accepts the strife he and Gwen have caused each other as a corollary of their marriage; it can't be sugarcoated. Whether he has been listening to her or himself is irrelevant. An awakening has occurred. His validating of complaints he has heard from her many times shows him responding to her with a new attentiveness.

This patience, gentleness, and honesty will also help him cope with the "foul world" (31). Some of this foulness lies in him. And it won't go away. The nearness of Gwen's earthly death stirs in him new feelings of jealousy. Abandoning for good "the lump on the bed" (45) means consigning her to Pat and the hospital's other medical staffers. His uniqueness will be downgraded to a part in a series. He had been protecting it. For instance, his reading of the cricket news (Gray's love of cricket followed that of Rattigan, Pinter, and even Beckett) while being spoken to by Gwen constitutes no act of rudeness, as she says. Knowing that conjuring her into life refutes logic, he has proceeded confidently to myth. The cricket news is helping him avoid the mistakes of both Orpheus and Lot who, disobeying the gods, turned around to see if their wives were following them.

The truth that everything counts in a spiritual transfiguration clarifies the place of J.G.'s hapless brother Jack in the ongoing refinement of J.G.'s mind. Fraternal bonds had resonated in *Engaged*, *Dog Days*, and *Simply Disconnected*. *Life Support*, where they throb more keenly, is dedicated to Simon Gray's brother Piers (1947–1996), who, having died a year before the play's debut, was preoccupying Simon during its composition. Though broke and jobless, Jack has the largesse to bring Gwen flowers. Beth's life-in-death *keeps* helping him surpass himself. Though his stage career has stalled, he's enough of a trouper to address Gwen after being invited to by J.G.

A new player has joined the cast of the resurrection myth, giving it a big lift. Jack sees the moment as a respite from his woes. The play he was acting in has closed, but to reopen in the West End — with another actor doing his role. His sole prospect for work lies in the revival of a musical he was in a decade earlier. But the role he's auditioning for is that of the father of the character he played in the work's debut. This role, which he covets, has smacked him with the truth, a bane to any actor let alone a gay one, that time's forward flow will be making ever-crueler demands on him.

But, rather than extending empathy, J.G. goads and bullies him as brothers did with progressive rancor in *Engaged*, *Dog Days*, and *Simply Disconnected*. His response to Jack's request for £3,000, that he ask Gwen for the money, bewilders Jack. But, a challenge to even finer actors, it conveys more than mockery. Yes, J.G.'s long-term displeasure with Jack has surfaced; J.G. wants to both humiliate and punish Jack for having failed in life. But his barb does more than draw blood. J.G.'s having lured Jack into the resurrection script, all the more powerful for being unwritten, kick-starts Jack's dreams. If the efforts of two people can double Gwen's chances of recovering, Pat would argue, then the theatricality of those efforts might also boost Jack's confidence in reviving his stage career. As in Pinter's *Caretaker*, the brothers in *Life Support* have become each other's keepers. Their joint effort reaps gains. Jack's helping J.G. restore Gwen to life has dignified his plea for money, which, in turn, might have impelled J.G. both to stroke and kiss her for the first time in our presence. In a crescendo to this rising sanguinity, Jack does get his cheque — but only to destroy it and bolt from the ICU in rage. Renunciation has sparked in him the dignity of self-command.

Here is theatrical surrealism without the ornateness of Genet or Peter Weiss. Hacking through inhibition and propriety has cut to Jack's quick, as it did with Julian Wood in *Simply Disconnected*. In their brief chat following his departure, J.G. tells Gwen that Jack did "the manly thing" by prizing his dignity over cash. Her answer, spoken by J.G., "Manly!" (20), dispels more fog. The next time she speaks, it's in her own voice; anger has also revived *her* spirit. The airways keep clearing. Returning to the stage, armed with his new-found manliness, Jack has forgotten his need for money. He reminds J.G. of Gwen's death-bed request that he carry on with his life after her death (as with Gray's parents and those of his stand-in, Holly, in *The Late Middle Classes* [1999], marriage-ending deaths in the oeuvre take the wife). Jack, voicing Gwen's desire, adds that, rather than punishing himself for Gwen's death, J.G. should dismiss it as a "one-in-a million accident" (37).

This appraisal is backed up by Pat, who tells J.G. that guilt has been corrupting his attempt to keep Gwen alive. Rather than moping around the ICU, he should go to Majorca or Bermuda. He needn't worry about betraying Gwen. J.G.'s response: an invitation to play a game of chess. He likes Pat's idea. Chess has been a bonding principle between the two men; its refusal, a rejection of the bond. In an earlier scene, J.G., seeing that Pat's interest in him and Gwen was more professional than personal, bridled. The news that Pat has been coming to Gwen's room to collect material for his research caused an affronted J.G. to scramble the pieces on the chessboard he and Pat were bent over instead of resuming the game.

The finale of *Life Support* recalls those of *Engaged*, *Simply Disconnected*, and *The Late Middle Classes*, which shows two men holding forth in an atmosphere of music. Futility has apparently won out. Just as Pat is smoking a joint, so has J.G. reverted to the bottle. His backsliding, though, doesn't negate a growth in him any more than the growth's surprising form. He follows his brother Jack into manhood by leaguing with other flawed, or broken, people in a splintering world. The doctor who has been healing him is a pothead more mindful of his career than his patients. His indiscretion might have cost Lydia, the beautiful nurse he and J.G. have been ogling, her job in the ICU; a pity because she probably won't like her new one as much. Even though she does it against her will, she enacts a truth common to other characters in the play. Renewal in *Life Support* only sustains itself at a high, often unfair cost. People don't get their first choices. The alcoholic J.G. and Gwen must wait till she's on her deathbed to create new life, an outcome sadly appropriate in a world where the bonds joining people are fragile and shallow. The lesbian Julia probably slept with J.G. to keep her job. Nor does Gray's ending *Life Support*, as he did the other three plays studied in this chapter, with two men onstage, create the promise he'd have won by ending with a man and a woman.

The play's conclusion, though, treads a finer line than do those of the earlier works. Gray sees along with J.G. Gwen's reprieve from our "foul world" as a blessing; supported by the play's reference to Thomas Hardy, her lethal bee sting describes chance as a weapon. Yet, as the title, *Life Support*, implies, good social networking grounded in firm support systems can pad the jolt inflicted by chance. Dramatic structure chimes with this verdict. Each of the five scenes opens with a monologue by J.G. before bringing him alongside other people. Each scene, as well, moves from darkness to light with the chess game about to begin at final curtain signaling the onset of a new life building from the old. Seated on opposite sides of a chess board, the pieces in place, Pat and J.G. are both partners and foes, as were in a different way, generating rhythmic counterpoint, J.G. and Gwen, J.G. and Jack, and perhaps J.G. and Mr. Rolls.

If Gwen's earthly survival depends on being peed on by a young stranger, the faith we need to defuse hardship and grief surpasses by eons the hope and cheer Pat has been trying to rouse in J.G. Yet J.G. comes to terms with this freakishness. And, in her way, perhaps so does Gwen. Following Forster's Mrs. Moore in *Passage to India* and Woolf's Mrs. Ramsay in *To the Lighthouse*, her spirit stirs moral and spiritual growth after her physical death. But, as ambitious as this development is, Gray doesn't stop here. He also suggests a way that Gwen's corpse could have been swept into this growth.

The engine of this transcendence is, once again, music. The symbolism of the Holy Spear and the Grail, both Christian and sexual, makes Wagner's *Parsifal* relevant together with Beth and Mandy's humble duet in *Simply Disconnected*. Still humbler and also more spare and stripped is Gwen's favorite hymn, "Silent Night," which is first heard in the "*desperate and grotesque*" (32) vocal effort J.G. delivers to comfort her spirit. His effort might have succeeded. The last time the carol is heard, it's being sung by Gwen. Having refined his own sensibility, Gray moved from the massive sonorities of *Parsifal* to a duet and, finally, to a voiced solo to show that the truth needs no trimmings or ornaments to touch our hearts. One thinks of Dmitri Karamazov's belief that that the derelict ramshackle church he happens upon in his travels is the kind most favorable for praying.

More than anywhere else in the canon, music in *Life Support* stands for the immanence we can glimpse in fragments but whose full value we lack both the purity and intensity to know directly; an unseen hand led J.G. to look at the sports news rather than face Gwen after hearing her speak. The mortal deaths of two of the three singers in *Simply Disconnected* and *Life Support*, Beth and Gwen, serve notice that those rare glimpses that fuel spiritual growth must suffice for us. J.G.'s bridging of the gulf between life and death describes in little the torment that will greet any further sorties upon the divine. Incitements to belief, the privileged moments that disclose hints of God's purpose don't shrink the difference between the human and the divine. Nor, happily, do they create a dead end. Flexibly and tentatively, the play depicts the operation of divine grace by housing the spiritual in the ordinary. Its family drama conveys this numinousness, Gwen's caroling suggesting spirit grooming itself for salvation.

The caving-in by most of Gray's people to the common pursuit of prizes like money and status blocks the process. On the other hand, the speed with which Gray, who's usually viewed as a French Window dramatist, finds himself warmed by the divine flames implies the speed with which these flames could incinerate both him and us. The spiritual adventure that engulfs J.G. also launches Gray into the ranks of metaphysical playwrights like T.S. Eliot, Christopher Fry, and Jean Genet.

This bruising nascent grandeur surges forth in an age hostile to tragedy by testing the mettle of a posh mollycoddle from the south of England: the absence in the play of semantic obstacles, lexical difficulties, or syntactical challenges bucks the spirit of postmodernism. It is also well judged. *Life Support* is a late 20th-century work that debuted at a time when the fundamentals of the day—free-market dominance, the end of history, and the clash of civilizations—started looking puny and ephemeral. Using postmodernism to question or subvert the play's value system would have lowered the carefully orchestrated intensities that close in on J.G. and even make him perhaps one of the last epic heroes in an unraveling age.

Conclusion

Stranded

Nothing as dogged as a theme explains Simon Gray. Too wily and inventive to be contained by ideologies or-isms, his work lacks a subject or "figure in the carpet" that reveals all. For instance, his canon varies the perennial sad story of social class and its discontents, the story that English writers can never stop telling. Gray both satirized the class resentments of England's professionals and, as his posh holidays to Italy, Greece, and Barbados show, sympathized with them. His lifelong campaign against snobbery and pretense sorts ill with his enjoyment of bourgeois, nay, upper-class, comforts provided by the business-class air tickets and luxury hotels he discusses in his late diaries. Like Scott Fitzgerald, he was seduced by a way of life the seductive allure of which he kept warning us against. And he knew it. The canon takes life from such persistences and even, sometimes, obsessions. Delivered with grace and fluency, these continuities, complex and provocative, highlight the particular and the personal. While crediting "the mystery of his [Charles Dickens's] overwhelming, genius," for instance, Gray announces in his introduction to *Little Nell* his intent to capture in the play his man's "other life, the life of daily needs in a daily self" (xvi) apart from his work.

Gray tempers his ontology with a refusal to ask too much from his people. The reason behind this moral charity comes forth quickly. The festering emotions he exhumes from his characters' psyches gauge the heartbreaking gap between life as it is and ought to be. Any Platonic or Christian ideal that informs everyday reality has bypassed his people. Living in a world accessed mostly through the five senses, they struggle to manage their daily selves. Their exertions tell them to give up searching for the best. Protocols only block our fun. Grahame Thwaite of *Little Portia* kept judging Janice Trullope when he could have been enjoying her. His mistake? We're contingent beings engulfed by contingency. Rejecting what's flawed and faded in the good to hold out for perfection like the real-life communist George Blake did in his pursuit of "the country of the future" (CM 22, 57) will snap one's ties with life and damage one's intimates. Blake's wrong-headedness didn't cost him his author's respect. Like those of Gray's other anti-heroes, Blake's trials depict the joys and frustrations of manliness in what can look like a post-manly age. Like the late fiction of John Updike and Philip Roth, Gray's plays traffic in diminishing male potency, aging, and mortality. A man in *Side-Car* puts the idea of male supremacy "down the flush bowl" (RC 152). Taking a more moderate stand, Gray neither demonizes his male characters nor whitewashes their flaws. Both good and bad, they're always moving back and forth between danger and safety, daring us to judge them. Judgments defy framing. Love even stings couples with self-doubt and resentment during times of harmony. As in the work of D.H. Lawrence, the plays capture the despair, hatred, and incomprehension that drive the sexes both together and apart.

This dynamic Gray describes, like Pinter, with a blend of menace and fun. As was seen in *Simply Disconnected*, some spontaneous word play may deflate a burst of homicidal hysteria. This absurdist deployment of incongruity stands as one influence. Gray's attraction to poetic ambiguities, minimalism, and the lack of common ground between people in Pinter's early plays suggests another. Though he respects the traditional dramatic standbys of plot, scene, and character, his self-referentiality also edges him toward post-modernism, even if he doesn't veer far in this direction. He writes social comedy. While his distrust of absolutes suggests the debunking of objective truth reveled in by post-modernism, he remains an unmagical realist who finds pathos, humor, and conflict in the everyday. No post-modernist irony can derail this commitment. His sometimes dark, quirky plays weave sinewy textures and urbane rhythms into open-ended socially grounded plots.

Which isn't to say that his people don't trip themselves up. The self-trust that Edith Dunlop culls from Jane Austen's *Persuasion* (e.g., RC 156) tells her in *Side-Car* that any success she might enjoy as a novelist entails banishing distractions from her life. But by numbering her husband as a distraction, she's also forfeiting the chance to improve her marriage, which she wants to preserve for the sake of her infant son. Gray has properly weighed and described the problem with which she has to deal. The challenge facing her has more to do with psychology and daily living than symbolism.

Over a broader range, *Common Pursuit* describes several victims of their own callousness, prurience, envy, and deceit. What ramps up the pain are the obstacles that sidetrack the careerism of these four Cambridge chums. During the 20 years following graduation, their efforts build no "creative nucleus" (4SG 148). This loss of both intellectual vigor and literary ambition has, instead, subsided in the philistinism of coffee-table books and hack journalism. The only member of the circle who builds on his undergraduate ideals winds up publishing very little; answering the needs of his "daily self," this gay philosophy don gets murdered by some pick-up he brought home. Nor is this horror the play's dismal last word on the harsh recoil action of sex. A "creative nucleus" that does uncoil from *Common Pursuit* is the baby of the girlfriend of one of the ex-Cantabs and the close friend who stole her from him.

To treat all of Gray's work would both overexpose the subtlety of his approach and make it look mechanical. A play that clarifies the range of his accomplishment is *Stage Struck*. Though branded by Robert Gordon as "an unashamedly commercial thriller" (Burkman, ed. 14), the play belongs in the best tradition of the English stage thriller. Surprises move the plot, some of them clear enough to please the thoughtful reader, others so outrageous that they dash all expectation. Despite the play's debt to Anthony Shaffer's *Sleuth* (1970), the Gray of *Stage Struck* gives no sign of having grown over-productive, repetitive, or shallow. The work reveals a sharp eye for manners, character, and a dramatic style that can deal well with the murderous violence of the attack upon and the dazed recognition of the victim. *Stage Struck* breathes. While keeping the tension high, both the inside-the-theater chatter and the high-voltage excitement of opening night come off superbly. Focusing the charm is the same conflict between work and the quiet desperation of daily living that drove *Side-Car*. Those with jobs have a structure to fit into, a way of staving off anxiety and gloom. There's also the hedge that work provides against the stodge of waiting, as *Life Support* showed. Stage star Anne O'Neill has started to vanish inside her persona. The sad truth this persona depicts is that the skyrocketing of a career also shakes the scaffolding of the careerist's life. Anne wants to dump her mostly out-of-work husband, Robert Simon. That this prize-winning performer of roles like Shakespeare's Portia and Cleopatra and Ibsen's Hedda is also enjoying her third straight hit on London's West End has pushed her sense of entitlement up to the flies.

Gray's sensitivity to intangibles lifts *Stage Struck* above the argument, found in D.H. Lawrence, Christopher Isherwood, and Edward Albee, that women in the past hundred years have gotten strong at the expense of men. Anne's statement to Robert, "I am far more ruthless than you … and I'll do anything however cruel, to get you out of my life," gives full throat to the artist's commitment to her art. But it doesn't flatten Robert into the roles of repressed gay, servant, or gigolo. He has spent seven years nursing, comforting, and indulging his high-maintenance wife as she "whine[s] and snivel[s] and bitch[es]" (3SG 223) while decompressing between rehearsals. And even though he earns so little as a stage manager and sometimes actor that he has become a tax liability to Anne, his stewardship of their home has won him a legitimate claim on it. He has put to good use the time he spent waiting for Anne to come home from the theater. Besides, even though, admittedly, he could spend more time and energy looking for work, he loves the place. The love he extends to Anne, despite her being "vain, boring, not particularly talented and totally selfish" (3SG 224), suggests that being unemployed has kept his heart alive. But how much hurt can that heart bear? The display of a gun and a large knife early in the action recalls Chekhov's dictum that any gun shown early in a story must be fired before story's end. Violence will rip through the home of a famous actress.

Gray refuses to side with that actress or her husband. Instead, he introduces, in Widdicombe, a character who, rather than being the star-quality psychoanalyst he claims to be, has done jail time for crimes like receiving stolen goods, forgery, and burglary (3SG 248). It's apt that the play's fourth figure is writing a dissertation on Henry James. Not only does Herman's research topic pit a Jamesian connoisseurship of nuance and subtlety against the violence that will cause two deaths. It also restores James's oft-dramatized belief that nearly all claimants to titles and honors back their claims with smudged credentials. Just brandish a weapon or two, and these smudges will stand out as clear as murder.

Cell Mates forgoes the compulsiveness of *Stage Struck* while reviving the earlier play's awareness of chasing a dream. Its vivid, convincing realism challenges Ibsen's belief in the sustaining power of the life lie. In 1966, petty Irish crook Sean Bourke sprung from Wormwood Scrubs prison his fellow convict George Blake, a British spy who, having passed secrets to Moscow, had more than 40 years to serve on his jail term. What seizes Gray here is why all of the 20th century's programs based on the perfectibility of man had failed. The best sabotages and disables the good, turning idealists like Stalin and Chairman Mao into life-haters. But Gray keeps the play's action day-by-day and small scale, and thus only suggestive of the suffering caused by inexplicable bureaucratic policies. This Chekhovian approach recreates the daily terms of living under totalitarianism; everyone in power lies to you, forcing you to live on rumors, lies, and naïve hopes.

Like this denial of objective truth, the dishevelment and grunge of day-by-day supervised living in a small Moscow flat turns the play's interest from event to the people's response to it. Gray conveys this responsiveness without exaggerating. Thinking small scale, he shows, discloses pitfalls, as does thinking large. When reality has been displaced, the attempt to get the details right builds an overwhelming and oppressive strangeness. The strangeness is magnified by the ordeal of waiting, if perhaps only for a rumor to cling to despite its flimsiness. The brief speech that opens Act Two, scene three, uses the words "waited" and "waiting" six times along with "patiently" and "very painful" (51). As it did in *Life Support*, waiting makes people tap into resources they never knew they had. What this involuntary self-immersion brings may stun and dishearten. The title *Cell Mates* invokes the truth that both Bourke and Blake have sold out, casually renouncing both their homelands and their marriages during the play's present-tense action.

Their bogus declarations of freedom put an ironic twist on a title Gray had considered using for the play, "Homesick" (FC 20). Other titles he had mulled over, "With a Nod and a Bow" (FC 20) and "I Say, He Says" (FC 15), come closer to the mark. The roles beside those of Bourke and Blake are played by the same actors in both the London and Moscow scenes. Gray's point is clear. Despite the drum rolls heralding the onset of the country of the future, people stay the same. Marx's workers' paradise is a dangerous fiction. States of being repeat themselves, often in a weakened, diluted form. Hopelessness has taken over. All of the cast members of *Cell Mates* are onstage together at play's end. All are troubled by the play's outcome. All have helped bring it about.

What does it mean? Nothing as imposing as a tragedy has occurred, unless the loss of self to pipedreams and booze can be called tragic. The week Bourke was supposed to have spent in Moscow after delivering Blake has stretched into a mandatory five years. Why mandatory? His Soviet handlers fear what he might tell British Intelligence officers back home. He pays heavily for their fears. Only after he has become so degraded by vodka that anything he says in Britain would be laughed off as drivel is he permitted to leave. But instead of accompanying him back to the UK, or at least out of the USSR, Gray ends the play by showing Bourke, who's now called Robert, hunkering down to the same job in Moscow that he did as an inmate at the Scrubs; he's editing, not a newspaper, but a journal, doubtful work for someone so out of touch that he eats breakfast in the afternoon (45).

He's still a captive. A phase of his self-undoing took place when he reversed roles as Blake's protector. This reversal stymied him. After springing Blake from the Scrubs, housing him in a London bed-sitter, and driving him to Moscow, he finds himself betrayed. The KGB officer Blake takes the betrayal in stride; he knew all along that once Bourke set foot in Moscow, he'd be stuck there. The eggs he discusses in the speech that ends Act One (32) overturn their normal symbolic function as agents of rebirth, as does his reference to six weeks (54), the normal time a woman can resume having sex after giving birth. Both Bourke's name and his life have been hijacked. He has a shaky hold on life. Rather than forming part of a dialogue, Blake's disquisition on eggs was spoken into a recording machine.

Even though everybody's tragedy is nobody's tragedy, the erosion of individuality puts selfhood at risk. This threat darkens family life in Gray's oeuvre. A wife in *Japes Too*, speaking about her husband Michael to his brother, says of his renown as a writer, "It depresses him — you'd have loved it, success and fame. Perhaps you should each of you been the other" (Four 147). She's right. The distinction Japes *will* relish as a literary journalist does follow that of Michael as a novelist and talk-show host. More vitally, as Anita's on-and-off lover over a span of decades, Jason or Japes usurps Michael's role as her husband. The blurring of identities between the brothers has also snared Anita, Jason saying of her and Michael, "You are more like each other than either of you recognizes.... Sometimes when I'm with you it's as if I'm with the other, I forget which is which" (Four 144).

Gray isn't talking about physical resemblances that can set in between married couples. The process of Michael's having grown uncannily like Anita accents his likeness to Japes rather than undermining it. This likeness started from within. So much does Michael value Japes's love that he permits him to sleep with Anita. Who also puts a premium on the three-way circuit; she acquiesces when Michael tells his brother, speaking of himself and her, "We need you.... She needs you.... Desperately needs you. As do I" (4SG 157). When she next speaks, she's addressing Michael while looking at Japes. The instability caused by his three-way bond, which has no name, deepens. Anita's jobless daughter Wendy will become a pot-smoking solo mom.

Japes and Michael replicate the alcoholic brothers, the creative writer Simon and the literary scholar Piers Gray. Though some of these continuities defy decoding, Japes teaches in Guyana, where he bloats up while caving in to the same alcohol and "sulky hopelessness" that felled Piers in Hong Kong (MacCabe 2). In *Japes*, he even talks of migrating to Halifax (65), which is also mentioned in Colin MacCabe's obituary of Piers (2). These echoes, like those joining Michael, Japes, Anita, and Wendy, strike a chord with the ones found in *Cell Mates*. Just as Anita's bonds with the Cartts brothers deny her a proper marriage, George Blake rejoices in his ex-wife's second marriage because she "deserves to live under another name" (36). His words hit home. She has moved from a seedy namelessness to the coziness of the named and the socially anchored. She's part of something she can be proud of.

Gray kept trawling the zone between these two realms. The Introduction to his last completed stage work, *Little Nell*, refers to David Copperfield's "heterosexual crush" on the older Steerforth (xxii), a form of love that might resemble Tennyson's friendship with Arthur Hallam, but has still found no name. The complex bond that knits Bourke and Blake during their five years together also defies naming. But the cold-war time setting of *Cell Mates* reminds us that the explorers camped on the Arruwimi River in the Congo some 80 years earlier in *The Rear Column* are also conducting a military operation. This similarity puts forth a truth pertinent to the two plays—military operations cause casualties. But because heat speeds any physical action, those that occur in sub–Saharan Africa look uglier, more disfiguring, and still more evocative of an inborn depravity Gray often gives signs of having bought into. The troubles that wring the explorers probe depths where categories and guidelines taken from the industrial west look flimsy.

Withal, the jungle expedition of 1887 finds Gray on familiar psychological turf. *Rear Column* harks to *Otherwise Engaged* and *Simply Disconnected* along with the Bourke-Blake relationship that fuels *Cell Mates*. The play's all-male speaking roles echo Gray's belief in the firmness and steadiness of male friendship in contrast to the volatility of the man-woman bond. Next, the explorers in *Rear Column* spend much more time waiting than moving. Indeed, their self-explorations will humiliate them; no women need to be dragged onto the set to wreck their peace. Tony Gould calls the play's action "the story of the ... five Englishmen [H.M.] Stanley dumped in the very center of Africa with the bulk of the expedition's slaves and then left them while he went in search of Emin" (xi). Gould is talking about Emin Pasha, the German trader Edouard Schnitzler, a confederate of General Gordon, whom the Mahdi had murdered to publicize his intent to ban all Europeans from the Sudan.

Following Stanley's orders, the men are awaiting the arrival of 600 porters to carry their goods through the bush. They're also waiting for Stanley, whose promised arrival date passes during the play's present-tense action. Continuing to question the authority of the preplanned and the formalized, Gray shows the five travelers faring best when they follow the rule of thumb instead of sets of laws. Best for them is to apply fair play and common sense to the pooling of their resources. Civility both helps their supplies last and promotes their equable distribution, a boon because, like Tolstoy, Gray believes that weather, malnutrition and fever wipe out more expeditions than bullets or bombs.

Hewing to the letter of the law killeth, the stand-fast explorers learn. Jean Colleran judged well to call the play's main issue "the possibility of maintaining in adverse circumstances some fundamentally decent code of behavior" (Burkman ed. 124). Adversity hacks at the explorers from different angles. In William Bonny, the men have but a medical orderly rather than a qualified physician to keep them fit and healthy. And even *he* is hamstrung. The insistence of the group's leader to impose his understanding of Stanley's rules about allocating supplies would deny a victim of yellow fever the quinine he needs. Conversely, a cheerful ability to take things on trust can quiet the inner demons that a place like the Congo, which presses hard on the European psyche, can surface quickly. References to London institutions like Fortnum and Mason's, Lord's Cricket Grounds (RC 26), and, to any East Enders in the group, the Mile End Road (RC 29) form a wall of hominess and civilized certainty around the men as they grope to stave off the horrors of enforced jungle isolation.

A short one-sided battle shatters that wall. Comforting allusions give way to the curse of waiting in "a malignant climate which affects the spleen and liver, which racks the frame with burning or exhausting dysentery, [and] which ... fills the disordered mind with morbid thoughts" (Gould xix). Morbidity soon runs rampant. Grueling enough on its own, the onset of disease and the threat of attack by the natives give the Congo ordeal nightmarish force. Gray understands the inroads that the primitive can make on the civilized. The statement of a French fugitive in *They Never Slept*, "I have not slept for two weeks except with pigs in a ditch" (4SG 387), and the "barking" laughter of a Cambridge don in *After Pilkington* (4SG 216–17) fuse with play titles like *Sleeping Dog*, *Dog Days*, and *Pig in a Poke* to convey the proximity of the animal world to the human. Even the title of an early version of *The Old Masters*, *The Pig Trade*, juxtaposes beautiful artifacts from the Renaissance with the perfidy of those who appraise and deal them.

It befits the desperation of *Rear Column* that two of the explorers are discussing at opening curtain whether to make soup of the turtles they've tied to their kitchen table. The tropical heat is already melting their civility. They and their colleagues have been learning one of Charles Darwin's basic laws: survival means adapting to an environment all of whose inhabitants are competing for limited physical resources. A play about inaction, *Column* unfolds in an age that admires action. The exercise of impulse in the play *will* find resolution — but in madness. How can Europeans relate to the African jungle, a place about which they know nothing? At play's end, the jungle is still unknowable. Recalling Eugene O'Neill's *The Emperor Jones* (1920), its nightly noises mediate upon crimes the explorers have been resorting to in order to survive, like theft, flogging, and the ransoming of natives for food.

Called an "anti-adventure" by Terry Curtis Fox (121), *Column* portrays Gray's vivid response to the pressures of both geography and history. Activating the expedition was a bourgeois mentality seeking release in a heroic struggle based on romantic nationalism. Stanley had agreed to trade with African natives providing that they renounced slavery and cannibalism. This high-minded agenda ignores the darkness lurking in the most civilized heart. Revising the exploration narratives of Britain's imperial heyday, *Column* describes a nation at war with itself. The swampy, fever-rife wilderness of the Congo trumps the optimism and obligation imbuing Victorian earnestness. Following Conrad, Hemingway, and the Saul Bellow of *Henderson the Rain King* (1959), the play shows how writing about Africa has often become a discourse on one's own inherited culture.

Bellow's memorable phrase, "the knife and the wound yearning for each other," stokes the discourse, too. Though tinged with tenderness and fun, *Column* includes some brutality that will scrape at you. What grates the explorers, ironically, is what sent them on their journey to start with. They forgot an important truth: What terrifies us also attracts us and, at some level, even represents our greatest wish. Like Tolstoy, Stravinsky, and the Penelope Fitzgerald of *The Beginning of Spring* (1988), Gray shows in *Column* the folk rhythms rising from a nation's history and geography trumping the decrees framed by its leaders. He does this by infusing the play with Jung's belief that the soul of a conquered people enters and then overtakes the unconsciousness of its conquerors. Though Stanley's rear column hasn't taken legal control of their region of the Congo, they *have* arrogated to themselves the conqueror's right to make rules, which includes killing the local natives who disobey them. But these natives answer to their own gods. They're religious. Disrespect their totems and you'll feel their wrath.

The collective guilt that gnaws the men also makes the Calvinism that supports infant damnation and human depravity look mild. As well it might; during their year at the Yambuya camp, two of the men continue to stab and flog disobedient natives long after their deaths. Nor is sex absent from the cruelty. The medical orderly William Bonny, who's teased by a colleague for consorting with local women (RC 34), will lose weight and become yellow-skinned. Though he probably caught yellow fever, his new skin tone could also stem from Hepatitis B, a disease transmitted by sodomy — an activity suggested by the play's title.

Time strips away civilized restraints throughout the camp. Bonny becomes addicted to the opium he's supposed to dispense. The self-punishing jack-of-all-trades Herbert Ward becomes so fascinated by the flogging he condemned at play's outset that he vanishes in the jungle. Mentally unstable to begin with, Major Edmund Barttelot should never have been named the expedition's commanding officer. Like his counterparts in *Moby-Dick* and Herman Wouk's *Caine Mutiny*, he's crushed by the burdens of leadership. This hater of blacks betrayed his office, his men, and the military family that spawned him by trying to persuade Bonny to declare him unfit for military duty. Then, gorged by self-hatred, he goes on a mad spree of atrocities. The worst of these, an act of cannibalism, costs him his life when he's killed by the husband of the woman whose blood he tried to drink after sinking his teeth into her neck.

His only friend in the group, James Sligo Jameson, condones this cannibalism. Jameson's withholding of moral judgment bespeaks his benevolence; the frenzied Barttelot needs comforting. As will the others at different times, and Jameson will always be ready to furnish it. Thus all of his fellow explorers, Barttelot included, like him. He's a good influence, too. The men, who bring out the worst in one another, stop fighting when he returns to the camp after one of his prowls; Barttelot has good reason to call him "the finest man I've ever met" (RC 19). He'll give his needy mates tea and even quinine from his private store when supplies run out. He also spends a night at the side of a sick mate. But before the end of the scene that shows him comforting the shivering, babbling Ward, he guts a snake he had killed. Jameson paid £1,000 to join the expedition. He's unique in other ways, too. While the others bicker and fume, he's sketching and painting flowers, birds, and other animals. In a crucial plot development, the artwork that most impresses his mates also exposes the anarchy of the creative pulse behind it. Jameson's disinclination to judge Barttelot tallies with the insouciance with which he handles a dead snake. The artist has made an unspoken pact with the devil.

Don't be shocked. In order to extend imaginative frontiers, the artist must flout society's guidelines and boundaries. He must also experience everything, at least imaginatively. Nothing can be off limits to him in his pursuit of the possible. Knowing the value of springing a shock, Gray commits us to Jameson emotionally before making the point that radical freedom like his, though necessary, can lead to conduct that repels and disgusts. He makes the point with élan. Jameson buys a young girl from a local slaver whom he then turns over to a cannibal chief to kill, dismember, and then eat. This violation of one of society's strongest taboos does extend limits, if only for those with the strongest of stomachs. Gray retains his hard focus. Jameson's drawings of the cannibal feast may be "the first ever recorded" (RN 70). But they also fuse as an act of heartbreaking cruelty whose vileness has escaped him. Given the routine flogging deaths inflicted at the camp, he wonders, "What does it matter, one nigger girl?" (RC 71) The "ultimate [act of] horror of intellectual curiosity and emotional detachment" (Stephenson 206) he has performed leaves him unfazed. But why shouldn't it? The artist is a selfish, coldhearted predator in Gray as he is in Freud, Mann, and Patrick White. His inquisitiveness is a public danger. But it also serves the public. El Greco is a greater artist than Velázquez because his imagination was bolder and more anarchic.

An atrocity like Jameson's needn't be staged to vex audiences. "The critics hated the play" (UP 157n) said Gray of the "one [work of mine] I'd want my reputation to stand by" (Berkvist 121). Perhaps he can rest content. Were the horrors in *Column* more subtly noted, Gray's critics would still have moaned. The shocking barbarism that occurs offstage in the play hews to his concept of the artist as a subversive who sometimes pays heavily for the risks he takes.

The deadly accuracy of Gray's take on the historical record supplies other provocations. Like the play's deft fusion of moments weird and tender, bizarre and funny, its rendering of Victorian speech passes historical muster without becoming stiff, fussy, or prolix. Much of this speech describes the ordeal of waiting. Dialogue in this play about human frailty serves what Jeanne Colleran calls "an extraordinarily trenchant, even brutal process of self-scrutiny" (Burkman. ed., 131). The characters don't strip layers of selfhood from themselves to prepare for a defining existential leap. Irving Wardle yoked the ethics pondered in the play to its time setting. "The Victorians were better behaved than we, and so had further to fall" (1), Wardle said in 1978, the year *Column* debuted. He was funneling Plato's concept of the tragic hero into the Victorian twin credos of the call to duty and the white man's burden.

His sharp, luminous reading captures Gray's intent. Yes, the white man's burden usually falls on black shoulders. And as Melville's *Billy Budd* showed, *all* infractions that threaten military governance call for harsh punishment. Swift redress has to follow the theft of British property if order is to be maintained. But the floggings that cause death mostly vent the explorers' frustrations. As the old African hand Sir Hubert says in *Sleeping Dog*, "Let madness in and justice out" (1SG 372). How justice is best served by the Congo's uninvited guests, Gray doesn't say. Why should he? He'd be depriving us of the fun of figuring it out for ourselves. He's more interested in discerning the limits of human endurance. Speaking of the squad of explorers stranded alongside a jungle riverbed for more than a year, he says that *Column* "is not an assertion that the Victorians behaved badly, but an implicit question about whether you or I ... could have behaved better" (1SG 6). Under scrutiny here is the question of whether the explorers were innately wicked or if the rigors of their exile brought out the same savagery in them that the cushions and conveniences of civilization help them — and us — keep at bay.

Our hearts and minds have been stirred. How far do we have to journey into our personal Yambuyas, and how long must we wait there before madness and hysteria gulp us down? These questions matter. Gray took the tormented story of the Aruwami River camp out of history books in order to recreate the slow dismantling of the human psyche by the animal beneath. The play's final scenes, masterpieces of grotesque surreality, strike home. One finishes the play absorbed and exhausted, but not exhilarated or cleansed. *Column* evokes corruption so successfully that it *becomes* corrupting. Credit Gray's risk-taking. Perhaps corruption is a necessary pre-condition of understanding to access the meaning of the play.

The trials of waiting also inform *They Never Slept*, a television movie in which a spy chief yelps, "It's the waiting, the waiting, I can't stand" (4SG 369). Like all military operations, his job includes long spells of waiting that blunt the effectiveness he needs in those moments of hair-raising terror that demand speedy action. Monk Scott's will and grip may already be flagging. The next time he complains about "waiting. Bloody waiting" (4SG 373), his bouncing of a ball harks to Lt. Cmdr. Philip Francis Queeg's fidget with steel balls while breaking down on the witness stand in *The Caine Mutiny* (1951).

The counterintelligence unit he works out of is based in a psychiatric hospital (e.g., 4SG 411). The unit's designation, Section 18, reminds us that the eponym of *A Comeback for Stark* worked for a branch of British security also called Section 18. In view of Stark's betrayal by his chiefs, whatever dread the number may have held for Gray also thickens the murk that World War II has spread over Europe in *They Never Slept*. The murk stays thick and dark. Like other thrillers, the TV movie taps into a collective anxiety, viz., the threat of an enemy invasion. But it's more than a superb thriller. Pulsating with danger and intrigue, it follows *Rear Column* as a disturbing tale of human nature under stress.

The book's wartime setting, London just after the Blitz, resonates with Gray's dark ontology. New government-mandated security measures have given England a stern militarized look. The stifling of free speech by intimidation and violence, for example, is but one of the measures used by the law that curb the rhythm and flow of normal workaday lives. Other Draconian steps have been enacted to protect the public. The awesome professionalism and bravery of the German armed forces calls for an arbitrary system of wartime justice in the UK. Whitehall's policy of meting out swift, hard punishment to Nazi subversives beefed up national security. But it also begot a scuppering of traditions that swathed Whitehall and the general public. The sheer nastiness of what people do to each other when war dismantles civility plays havoc with decency and personal integrity. When an innocent conscript into a big-time spy operation exclaims, "But that must be top-secret info. If I get caught —," she's told flatly, "You'll hang. So don't get caught" (4SG 394). The madness of war *is* best engaged from a psychiatric hospital.

The darkness underlying Gray's other work makes it safe to premise *They Never Slept* on Tolstoy's belief that conflict is embedded in human nature. The last stage direction in *Old Masters*, "*Sounds of war louder and louder*" (69), like that of Gent's *Balcony* (1957), disclaims peace. At every moment, somewhere on earth, people are slaughtering one another. War has shaped the world. The scale of devastation and carnage in World War II razed moral distinctions between "us" and "them." The razing continued. As John le Carré would show in his cold-war novels, there was no high ground left to occupy. *They Never Slept* describes this void. To defend the European tradition of liberal democracy, intellectual curiosity, and duty tempered by tolerance, Great Britain had to use cruel and inhumane tactics—sometimes against its own partisans.

It had to use them constantly. With the enemy on duty around the clock, sleep became just one of the normal human activities dislodged by war. Dropping one's guard while in a nod could be dangerous. The missing arm of Monk's assistant, Bob, refers to the need to match the enemy's attentiveness, not to mention deceit and cruelty, at every turn. It also extends Gray's belief, from *Column*, of making do with what's available. Bob excels as Monk's aide-de-camp. He drives a car as well as playing office squash. Nor is his expertise in these two endeavors a fluke. He'll cultivate whatever skills he needs to function in a world where sudden changes dictate on-the-spot action. What he and Monk also have to ignore, along with going through the chain of command to get things done, is the sight of blood. Warfare rules out squeamishness. Unless we harden our hearts, those less able to outthink the enemy will take our place. Lively instincts, energy, and brutality rule in war together with an eye for both detail and the main point. Monk lies, makes empty promises, and exposes his agents to injury and death to protect his operations. The main point for him means shortening the war and saving lives.

His nemesis: the "most popular woman in England" (4SG 410). Amelia Cleverly, whose last name invokes the traditional English distrust of cleverness or flash, has been using her morale-building radio show, "Afternoon Thoughts in War-Time," to send coded military secrets to Germany. The show provides the benefit of excellent cover for her messages. So soothing and uplifting are her weasel words that her huge listening public depends upon them to stay grounded. These same words send tears down the callous, unrepentant cheeks of Monk. Amelia's cover is nearly perfect. Nobody would expect her to be a spy. Like his fellow countrymen, Monk needs his daily dose of her radio programs. He becomes furious at himself when he finds out that he has been gulled. This fury governs the play's ensuing action. The treachery infusing "the most famous voice in England" (4SG 410) rules out a romantic finale for

They Never Slept; though the opposition of Monk and Amelia forms the play's moral and emotional torque, the two parties never meet.

Amelia's duplicity also yokes the telescript to *Oedipus Rex*. Not only do the soothing native cadences massaging all of England belong to one of the country's worst traitors; the play's closing plot twists are also so relentless that Sophocles might have gladly used them. To atone for having been tricked by Amelia, Monk will now use her to misguide her Nazi friends as long as is feasible before sending her to the gallows.

Where Gray also thought about sending his mother? Amelia's *"horsey"* face and big body (4SG 393) both suggest Barbara, whose athletic five-foot-eight-inch frame included "long legs, a long torso, [and] long shins" (SD 80). But the parallel breaks down. Barbara's driving skills (SD 82) and her coaching of both hockey and cricket (YJ 26) invoke Monk's athletic resourceful driver, Prunella Merriman (4SG 371). Advisedly, Gray limits Pru's feminine charms to the roles of victim, protector and comforter; she has no boyfriend. His purpose: to speed the plot and to keep it on course. He judged well; *They Never Slept* is already thick enough with intrigue and, in its descriptions of the hair-trigger anger and pathos of a wartime leader, paranoia.

Camera work enhances this TV magic. Like *Citizen Kane*, the work opens with archival newsreel footage. The ensuing montage leads to a brilliantly choreographed series of close-ups and jump cuts, dissolves and long-distance shots, that impart authority. Unfortunately, the magic has reached but a small audience. As far as can be determined, this made-for-television film neither aired on BBC Television after its debut nor played in movie theaters. A big disappointment; had it won the attention it deserves, it might have also helped establish Gray as a phenomenon of English television at its best.

The fictional Amelia Cleverly and the actual H.M. Stanley, the man who opened Africa to European trade, both prefigure the "two morally crippled giants" (Four xii) who drive *The Old Masters*, Bernard Berenson and Joseph Duveen, and, later, Charles Dickens, or Dick, of *Little Nell*. Gray's two last plays pinpoint two issues that had appeared sporadically in his earlier work, viz., the cost of public success and the interplay between the achievements and the private daily needs of the achiever. This traffic is handled differently in the late works. Speaking to a women's group in Cheltenham, the high-flying publisher Mark Melon goes mad as soon as he leaves his podium (Four 263). But the same job that has been driving him mad has also kept him out of the madhouse. The material for the bestsellers Enid Parkhurst writes in *Just the Three of Us* comes from the young women she abducts. The rising public success of Michael Cartts of the *Japes* plays stands in inverse ratio to his enjoyment of it.

Gray raided the public sphere in his two last plays not to debunk, but, rather, Fellini-like, to understand superstardom. Colin Simpson said of the two go-getters in *Old Masters*, "Berenson and Duveen ... disliked and distrusted each other from the beginning, but Berenson hated his partner even more than he hated himself" (2). Let's put on the brakes. Why this deep well of hatred that threatened to engulf BB, as he's called in the play? The question goes to the heart of Gray's search for self-understanding. BB had made enough money to buy whatever he wanted. Simpson says that his 30-year tie with Joe Duveen earned him about $150 million, by the dollar value of 1987 (2). Writing 17 years after Simpson, Meryle Secrest agrees that BB always disliked Duveen, whose practices, she adds, as if to explain the hard feelings, were freer and more commercial than BB's and his artistic standards, more relaxed (137). As he did in *The Rear Column*, the Gray of *The Old Masters* is addressing the clash between the claims of protocol and those of pragmatism.

This clash moves to the fore in Gray's re-imagining of the last meeting between the two men, which took place in 1937 in Fiesole, a suburb of Florence, where BB lived mostly with his wife, Mary (who died in 1945), from 1900 to 1959. The "unfinished piece of business" (Simpson 251) that brings the two men together is the painting, "The Adoration of the Shepherds." Secrest calls the work "a wonderful painting of a couple of simply dressed young men kneeling before an infant" (365), which she also displays in her *Duveen: A Life in Art* (363). "The Adoration," which is sometimes called "The Allendale Nativity," after an early owner, now hangs in Washington, D.C.'s National Gallery of Art. Duveen had bought it to sell to steel tycoon Andrew Mellon, who died during the negotiations, but after the staged action of *Old Masters*. Mellon wanted to buy it as a Giorgioni, and BB, the leading authority on Renaissance painting of his day, had helped Duveen clinch the sale on these terms by ascribing the work to Giorgioni. Recently, though, he changed his mind. Despite not having gone public with his about-face, he now attributes the painting to Giorgioni's pupil, Titian. His re-attribution could have big-time financial import. Yes, Titian was the greater artist, but because he was so much more prolific than his teacher, his pictures usually fetched a lower price.

Duveen resisted coming to I Tatti. His junior partner, Edward Fowles, whom he had sent to negotiate on his behalf, had been bullied by Mussolini's border guards before getting rebuffed by BB. In a wild shot that hit its mark, the guards thought Fowles a spy. Calling to mind *They Never Slept*, in which Edward Fox, the BB character, had the play's leading role, former lift operator Fowles was hired by Duveen after telling him what he had overheard from passengers who had just left the art dealer's office. Cunning can help Duveen again now that Mussolini's blackshirts are fouling Italy's great heritage of history and art. But he must come to Italy himself to protect his investment in "The Adoration"—with the help, no less, of BB, another Jew. But the Joe Duveen of 1937 wasn't only Jewish. He's also sharp and tough. Living on borrowed time, his very appearance onstage disproved his doctors' verdict that he'd be dead five years before the action of *Old Masters*.

And with death still an issue, what thrills the play provides. All energy and motion, Duveen flatters, coaxes, and cajoles BB. He even offers him cash on the spot together with a full partnership to deter him from recanting in print his earlier attribution of "The Adoration" to Giorgioni. BB counters Duveen's heartiness, cheer, and munificence with a self-righteous coldness. To Duveen's statement, that "it's good to be talking together again in a way that we used to," he snaps back with the words, "Much of the time we didn't talk, Joe. We ended up shouting into each other's faces. Once or twice I found myself on the verge of hitting you" (39). Nor does Duveen's (1869–1939) forecast of his impending death sweeten BB's memory or warm his heart. He refuses to let Duveen see Mary, and when Mary, whose soon-to-visit children and grandchildren BB had also refused to see (3), comes onstage, he rushes Duveen out of the house, calling his partner's hasty leave-taking *his* idea. This childless crank wants to cuddle up to the pristine aesthetic standards that have been paying the bills for I Tatti.

From the start, he had turned his back on the uninvited Duveen. This intellectual and moral snob wanted to prove to himself that he couldn't be bought. Bought for how much, though? The sex he gets on demand from both his Swedish masseuse and his secretary-bookkeeper Nicky Mariano doesn't only put adultery under the shadow of war as it did in Gray's family of origin; it also sullies BB's moral integrity. The blot stays. Mary is right to call him "a free man" (66) late in the play. But beyond the realm of sex, his freedom counts for little. Breaking with Duveen has put his ownership of I Tatti at risk, threats of war having already squeezed him financially.

What price moral and professional rectitude? The familiar contrast in Gray's work between a person's eminence and the creds supporting it has resurfaced. BB's fame as an art critic has already come under fire. Rumors are buzzing that the "hand that held the pen" that wrote BB's four great books on Renaissance art wasn't always his (52). BB himself cites "the clods of [my] prose you shoveled" (64) during a conversation with Mary. As well he might; Sydney Freedberg (8), Mary Ann Calo (22), and Colin Simpson (62) all agree that Mary had been doctoring BB's labored prose since the 1890s. BB's need of a ghostwriter supplies but one dent in his vaunted righteousness. He sometimes fiddled his attributions, as was seen in the downgrading by other authorities of pictures he had authenticated for money. Even Mary notes his "reputation for dishonesty" (63).

Though more discreet than Duveen about the risks of reworking old masters to boost their market value, BB often knowingly endorsed pictures of doubtful provenance, even fakes. It got uglier. By the time he had become the world's top expert in Italian Renaissance painting, he had been accused of both hiring forgers to restore faded or damaged work and smuggling art out of Italy (Simpson 1). The passage of years smirched the record still more. The "prickly conscience and ... perfectionist expectations" (Secrest 243) he prided himself on kept loosening up in times of financial hardship at I Tatti, which was most of the time.

At his final meeting with Duveen, there isn't much honor left in him to smirch. Simpson may have hit the mark by calling him "probably the most ... unscrupulous art dealer the world has seen" (1). Mary Berenson would have agreed with this verdict. Besides referring to his dishonesty, she also slaps him after hearing him say that "the leaders of the new world" (65), Hitler and Mussolini, will burn all the world's great books and beautiful paintings, as if this impending bonfire sanctioned his nihilistic shrug. This shrug brings a second shock — his confession that "The Adoration" "*was* probably painted by Giorgioni" (67; emphasis mine). He thwarted Joe out of spite.

Did Joe deserve better? Or had life just caught up with him, as it hadn't with Simon Hench? This "most successful art broker of the twentieth century" (Simpson 1) sold tapestries, bronzes, marbles, and terra cotta figures from his auction rooms in London, Paris, and New York. Dozens of paintings by Gainsborough and Rembrandt were also known, called, and marketed as Duveens. This acclaim was justified. Whoever bought an old master was also grabbing a share of art history. Its value transcended its price tag. Collectors of Duveens rarely suffered buyer's remorse. The price of the sublime always kept rising. Joe, as he's called throughout, made sure that it would. Graced with "a boyish earnestness, even effervescence, that captivated everybody" (Secrest 49), he dealt old masters to J.P. Morgan and William Randolph Hearst (Secrest 364). For his efforts, he earned, along with pots of cash, a knighthood, a baronetcy, and a trusteeship in the National Gallery (Simpson 243–4).

His standing dropped. The kudos stopped. His last honor he lost in 1937 while also battling cancer. His sale of the Sassetta panels from his own collection to the National Gallery was denounced by P.M. Neville Chamberlain as barefaced double-dealing (Simpson 249, Secrest 187–8). His claim to BB that he sold the panels for less money than they'd have fetched in the open market (32–3) impressed nobody either at the Gallery or in Whitehall. His trusteeship was lost forever. Still another scandal rocked him in 1939, the year he died of cancer. The over-cleaning of the Elgin Marbles that he ordered disfigured them so badly that they had to be taken from public view.

Yet the conflict between idealism and pragmatism that has been developing takes an unexpected heave. The second half of *Old Masters* shows this skilled manipulator who rewrote art history with a checkbook switching places with BB, the supposed protector of civilized, humane values (Calo 154–7). Joe speaks of this oddity himself when he tells BB that "of the two of us, the scholar and the tradesman, it is you who should be the cynic" (33). Eager to shield high art from the incursions of modernism, BB championed elitist cultural values. At his personal sacrifice, he even agrees to repay the commission he got for authenticating "The Adoration" as a Giorgioni (21). But this reversal of form was shockingly atypical. His cherished culture and tradition usually lost out to commerce. Meyer Schapiro said in *Encounter* in 1961 that BB even confessed that the fame, wealth, and social power garnered by his attributions often compromised his professional standards (57–61). Gray treats this confession with his stock ambiguity. During the course of the play, he has BB talk about having replaced an old master with a fake in order to buy medicine for the Italian troops who were gassed while deployed in Abyssinia (18). Shouldn't professional ethics always give way to life-threatening emergencies?

Joe would have agreed. Yet despite his "drive for attention, money, and control that verged on a kind of mania" (Smith 1), he also displays in *Old Masters* both a tastefulness and a restraint that shame BB. His main client base consisted of American millionaires thirsting for European chic and refinement. But they had to meet the standards of this closet priest of high culture. Some millionaires he wouldn't sell to. And certain paintings in his collection he wouldn't advertise, fearing that they'd fall into the wrong hands, like those of "Mr. Five-and-Dime" (40), Samuel Kress, paradigm of a second wave of robber barons turned art collectors. Joe thus needs BB's compliance on the "Adoration" attribution to preserve his record of dealing at the top tier of America's carriage trade. He had bought the painting to sell as a Giorgioni to Andrew Mellon. Mellon's death, however, forced Joe to flog it at a loss to Kress, who cared little about origins and pedigrees. The nasty letters BB had written to critics and curators after breaking with Joe (Simpson 259) had driven down the price of the work. A further blow to Joe: Kress hung "The Adoration" in the window of one of his Five-and-Ten-Cent Stores (Simpson 267).

Gray's final phase shows him drawn to subjects and ideas in the public domain that lend themselves to dramatic representation. Like *Little Nell* after it, *Old Masters* also displays a softening of mood and a growing curiosity about different ways of being. Imagery in these late works has a gentleness and serenity even as it probes the dark corners of their characters' minds. Gray's ability to choose vivid moments from historical sources and give them life is also quite exceptional. BB betrays those he cares about and knowingly sets into motion scenarios he'd rather avoid. But Gray's prose is so clear, calm, and intelligent that it makes this deceit comprehensible. BB stands close at play's end to the Jamesian heroine who asks for everything but gets nothing — except that he's not sure what he wanted. He definitely stands light years from the eponym of Ibsen's *Enemy of the People*, who finally recognizes that the strong and the independent must often stand alone. He has squandered the financial security of Mary and her progeny to uphold standards he has smirched many times in the past. The gunfire booming outside the walls of I Tatti at the very end suggests the leveling of the same values he invoked to thwart Joe. He stands with the enemy. Though sick, Joe took a boat, a train, and a car to I Tatti to make BB a generous offer. BB's rejection of it, an assault on the civilized practice of compromise, tallies with the looming public danger. Cordite coats the walls of I Tatti.

Conceived as "a sort of psychological and theatrical epic about Dickens" (LN vii), *Little Nell* also describes history-in-the-making. In writing the play, Gray gave himself a hard job, but not one beyond his powers. Historical drama, like historical fiction, imagines the unrecorded — the many yearnings, utterances, and commonplace gestures buried in a dead past — from which they can be reclaimed; because we can't know exactly what happened, let's invent it, as Thomas Pynchon, Don De Lillo, and James Ellroy have been doing with the shards of American history they've unearthed. These writers have succeeded because they know, as Quentin Tarantino showed in his 2009 movie *Inglourious Basterds*, that history needs a charge of imagination to put ways of living on a par with ways of feeling. Any historical setting can be imagined into existence. What counts, as Henry James enjoyed reminding us, is the quality of the imagining.

Though invented, the action of *Little Nell* observes psychological plausibility. The years Gray spent reading and teaching Dickens had equipped him to tune his style to the feelings that drove his people. Like *They Never Slept*, *Little Nell* captures the stop-time drama of the human brain in extremis processing data. But "the sapping logistics of adultery" (LN x) nudge Dick closer to BB than to Lt. Cmdr. Monk Scott. To borrow some descriptions of BB by his lover Nicky and his wife, Mary, Dick is an "unfaithful man with an appetite" and perhaps "like all exceptional men" "a child" (OM 6). He has to have his way, and he hates to admit he's wrong, even if the line of action he has taken has cut off the legs under both him and everyone dear to him.

A complex man with as many flaws as gifts, the Charles Dickens of *Little Nell*, referred to in the play's stage directions as Dick, shows the disorder out of which art is made. Dick struggles to stabilize his inner life while yielding ever more ground to the enticements of money, power, and, chiefly, sex. Always respecting probability, Gray catches both Dick's demons and his tremendous energies. His portrayal of these forces justifies the title Dickens gave himself, "The Inimitable." In 1843, the year *A Christmas Carol* debuted, the book's great warmth and humor fostered more acts of benevolence and family love than most of England's churches combined. Yet Thomas Wright said in a 1934 newspaper article and then, with more thunder, in his biography, *The Life of Charles Dickens* (London: Herbert Jenkins, 1935; e.g., 241–54, 262–6, 280–3), that this man had kept a woman for the last 13 years of his life (LN 21). He was right. At age 45, Dickens had seduced a 17-year-old actress and made her his mistress, while parading in public as a champion of pristine morals.

Gray's treatment of the long affair with Ellen Ternan includes his usual tropes and topics. Which, as usual, he didn't frame to amuse conventional middle-class playgoers; reviewing *Close of Play* in *Spectator*, Peter Jenkins noted in "the course of one Sunday afternoon ... drunkenness, homosexuality, dishonesty, adultery, abortion" (30). Writing with more audacity, Gray called *Common Pursuit* a "play about friendship ... English middle-class friendship"

(UP 21). The play's building blocks—betrayal, impotence, divorce, substance addiction, and murder — he stamps the "routine stuff of English social comedy" (UP 25).

He gives these same materials in *Little Nell* both a gruesome immediacy and an elegant absurdity new to his work. In her *Guardian* obituary, Lyn Gardner said "the final flowering of [Gray's] career" (2) followed his rebound from both terminal prostate cancer and a mandatory stint of three weeks in intensive care after he stopped drinking in 1997. Prominent among what Gardner calls "the finest plays" (3) of this rich last period is *Nell*. The play shows Gray carrying forward with new grace and power an earlier tendency to write like a woman if that means a preference for character, feeling, and motive over physical action. Appalled by the likelihood that Dick may have persuaded Nelly to send to orphanages or even kill the two children he had with her, her grown son asks, eight years after her death, "What manner of man, this Charles Dickens?" (55)

This question stumps Geoffrey Robinson's interlocutor, the author's lawyer-son Henry. Today's prosecuting attorneys would flay Dickens as a sex offender and child abuser. They'd have heaps of evidence with which to flay him. His pathologies in *Nell* include stalking and voyeurism, spousal abuse, substance addiction, and fetishism, as well as statutory rape. The play's opening scene forecasts the effects of these misdeeds. An August 1857 production of Wilkie Collins's *The Frozen Deep*, at Manchester's Free Trade Hall, is ending. Dick is playing the role of the fast-fading Wardour, a member of Sir John Franklin's team of doomed Arctic explorers. Near the end of *Nell*, Dick, who first appeared before us impersonating a dying man, *is* dying. Alongside him at both times stands a helpless Nelly. The girl who had no lines to say onstage can do nothing 13 years later to stave off Dick's literal death. She has remained frozen in the life imposed on her by scripts written by two older men.

That life could have sizzled with challenges and rewards. Nelly had both the presence of mind and the decency to take her lover's dying body from Slough, where she was living with him, to the Dickens family home in Gad's Hill. This self-sacrificing errand was but one of many. Throughout her long relationship with Dick, she had to practice caution, even stealth, to protect the image of "the world's most famous family man" (xvii). The demands of respectability continued to hobble her even after her lover's death. This sad story has been best summarized in Claire Tomlin's *The Invisible Woman: The Story of Nelly Ternan and Charles Dickens*:

> Nelly's involvement with Dickens lasted from 1857 until his death in 1870. During these thirteen years she changed from a girl—poor but petted by her family and pretty, with a good if not brilliant prospect of professional career and doubtless, a husband—into a woman approaching middle age, in delicate health, solitary and inured to dependence on a man who gave her neither an honorable position nor even steady companionship.... She lived the classic role of the Fallen Woman, held in particular public contempt by the Victorians [191].

The anxiety posed by this regimen ground on. To marry George Wharton Robinson, a man ten years her junior, she had to shave a decade from her age and then concoct a story about sickness and convalescence in Italy to explain three more missing years. The sapping logistics of adultery kept flaying her. Prodded by her secret fear of corrupting organized religion with her sin, she made George turn down the offer of a vicarage, a post he was trained to hold, to open a school, one that drained his exchequer and darkened his mind.

It's unclear whether George could have kept his wits had he not also been haunted by suspicions about Nelly. Her girlhood stage career comes into play here. Perhaps a better actress could have calmed his mind. Or did the burden created by her deception blunt her acting skills? It's also possible that hearing the truth of her past from her would have crushed him. These are only a few of the imponderables set forth by *Nell*. At the heart of it all is her long intrigue with Dick. First, Nelly shared fully in the intrigue, her deflowering and all. During her stroll with Dick in Doncaster Park, the "little spade of a beard that could jab through all the softness and roundness and sweetness of things" (15) enflames her. She says she loves it and tugs at it "*gently*" referring to it as "him" (18). Then, after biting it, she "*pulls at it firmly, then savagely*" (20) before sinking to the ground with Dick.

How much urging does a man need? Nor did losing her innocence to such an unlikely swain douse her spark. A remorseful Dick, who tells her she shouldn't be sad, hears her say, "I've never been so happy" (20). Superb stagecraft helps show her rejoicing in the meaning of what she and Dick just did. Distancing himself from the act, Dick got dressed quickly. Then he offered dutiful assurances and, while looking away from her, a towel — which, in her innocence, she uses on her face. She's reveling in the same moment that has been vexing him. She remains on the ground, in no haste to gather the clothes tumbled in disarray about her. Gray has restored the gap in feelings expressed by the first-time lovers in *Colmain*, his first full-length publication, which appeared 40 years before *Nell*'s stage debut — the sexual act in both cases (and perhaps in *Butley*, as well [41]) taking place outdoors in the daytime with at least one of the participants a virgin.

The Doncaster scene in *Nell* supports the claim that no words or definitions can express the vital roles people can play in each other's lives. Because they defy respectability, society has withheld names from some of our most meaningful connections. And, with a Wittgensteinian flourish, Gray also believes that that which is nameless can't be discussed and thus known. When asked by Dick if she regrets the life he gave her, a fortyish Nelly asks in turn, "What other life was there for me? Once you came into it" (29). The questions and answers could have been reversed. The cost of preserving Dick's renown as "the jovial keeper of hearth, house, children, and dogs" (Tomlin 5) label him Nelly's victim. Fear of scandal dogged him with anxiety and guilt before stubbing out his "morphine-and-brandy-dependent" life at 58 (xviii).

Gray has taken us a great distance without straining. Credit his decision-making. Instead of building the action on go-by-the-book Victorian morality, he describes in the last play of his staged in his lifetime the imperatives of sex toppling established social guidelines. Too, he shows the most vital roles in social experience often going *mis*named, if they're named at all. What tag can be put on the bond with Mrs. Artminster that keeps Jerry alive and makes him the wise child of Gray's 1967 play? The canon brims with other examples. Having birthed ten of Dickens's children, Catherine deserved to be called his wife. Yet, vilified and rousted from Gad's Hill, she saw her wifely role stolen from her and then split in two. Dickens spent most of his time with a woman known to the public as a "sort of niece or goddaughter" (37), whom he addressed as both his mouse and his muse. Managing the house at Gad's Hill and taking care of his and Catherine's kids was her sister, Georgiana (27). *Little Nell* discloses in Gray a sharp understanding of the non-classifiable and indefinable. George's misgivings about Nelly's past wreck their marriage despite her assurances of her abiding love of him (38). These assurances were heartfelt. The scenes that show her trying to soothe his nerves have the hypnotic accuracy of the unalterable.

The lurid texts and cover art of Hank Janson's novels have slid into the frame. Women in Gray often take the role of victim. The Old Master BB surrounds himself with women who rub his back, do his bookkeeping, and give him sex. For providing these services, they're either taken for granted or resented. Others share their distress. Pru Merriman is bullyragged and berated throughout *They Never Slept*. Like Janice, the Jamaican housemaid in *Wise Child*, she has booze forced on her. But the vodka she reluctantly drinks is drugged, so she can be stripped and photographed in lewd poses in case her controllers want to blackmail her. Another woman in the telefilm gets run over by a bus, three more die from bullet wounds, and another, a spy, dies from the stress of being pulled out of retirement for another go in the cold. Perhaps the deepest cut will take down Amelia Cleverly, she of "the most famous voice in England" (4SG 407).

This stroke Amelia deserves, just as the real-life model of Gray's *Molly*, the athletic Alma Rattenbury, who also drove an ambulance in WWII, deserved to die for her husband's death. Other women in the canon pay heavily for striking out at their male intimates. Like Anne O'Neill, the female lead in *Stage Struck*, who evicts her husband and murders her lover, that of *After Pilkington* drops a devoted friend after implicating him in a murder she performed. But she dies for her treachery, just as Anne will be caught red-handed by the police soon after final curtain in *Stage Struck*. Gray might have used this melodrama to avenge himself indirectly on his athletic ambulance-driving mother while also dodging his worst dread, the "consequences ... of hurting other people" (LC 14).

Harshly self-critical (Pinter 15, Young 1), he also saw through this dodge, just as he did his pretense to ignore his cheating at cards decades earlier at Cambridge (SD 121). The force of Celia Smothers's Jew-baiting drives her rage against Thomas Andrew Brownlow in *The Late Middle Classes*. Brownlow, with his history of child abuse (51), needed to be stopped. And natural justice needn't be any prettier than its agent. The questions Celia asks after his trip to London with her son Holly made him beat a fast retreat. But not a lengthy one; 45 years after the play's present-tense action, Brownlow is still living on Hayley Island, Celia has died, and her womanizing husband, now remarried, has retired to the Isle of Wight. Holly's visit to Brownlow after a decades-long wait confirms his old piano teacher as a greater influence on him than his parents.

The dynamics of waiting entered Gray's creative bloodstream after he shrugged off a dying Barbara's pleas that he stay at her bedside (LC 148–9). The prominence of waiting in *The Rear Column*, *They Never Slept*, and *Life Support* shows him smarting from his refusal to companion Barbara at the end. This rawness hews to Freud's description of the artist as a battlefield. If it gave the modern English-speaking stage some good scenes, it didn't soothe either Gray's long-standing resentment or the guilt the resentment caused.

The need to quiet his inner strife often redirected Gray's creativity to men and the male-male relationship, which provided creative outlets without the psychological wear-and-tear inflicted on him by the man-woman bond. Reflecting this unconscious preference in *Nell* is his treatment of Geoffrey, the 40-year-old son of George and Nelly Robinson. In terms that Gray could identify with, Tomalin called Geoffrey "the most cruelly damaged" (258) of all those touched by his mother's bond with Dickens. A womanizing son of a womanizing father, Gray snapped to Geoffrey's discovery of Nelly's sexual past. War and peace fuse in Geoffrey, who fought with the British Army in the First World War after being steered into the military by his mother. At the time of the play, 1922, he has returned to civilian life, having retained from his army service a speech impediment and some knowledge of foreign languages.

The tabloid gossip he had been reading about his mother and Dickens will send him to the law offices of the writer's son, Sir Henry. The scenes showing the two men together reveal Gray's keen, resourceful imagination working at top form. Enhancing this brilliance is his placement of the scenes that show the men together. Folded into key moments that show Nelly together with both Dick and George, these scenes provide historical background, comment upon Nelly's two love ties, and sometimes sugarcoat the Nelly-Dick bond — immediately after a time glide revealed the bond's raw, but tender, truth. These displays of the irony of discrepant awareness build tension. Central to their artistry is Henry's lawyerly discretion; he meets all of Geoffrey's painful inquiries with soothing generalities. When it becomes clear to Geoffrey that he knows more than he's saying, suspense sharpens around the question of when or if he will tell all.

Mostly, though, the scenes in Henry's office unleash the psychic energy flying between the two as they either create a bond or acknowledge one already in place. Gray was ready for the challenge. In *Otherwise Engaged* and *Simply Disconnected*, he had already written scenes in which a young unfortunate's bearding of a successful elder changes both men's lives. Alison Vale's phrase, a "steady blurring of the distinctions between [Henry and Geoffrey]" (1) , from her review of *Nell* at Bath's Theatre Royal, captures Gray's ability to apply stagecraft to actuality. Not that the lone interview between the men occurred as it does in the play. It didn't have to. With plausibility and conviction, Gray's invention of it projects a vivid unwritten story upon those great political, social, and cultural events that define history.

Speech conveys the kinship between these two sons of bygone lovers. The "*occasional stutter*" (6) Geoffrey brings to Sir Henry's office will sound an unlikely chord with the lawyer's own verbal tic, the "um" (e.g., 30) that shows nervousness, uneasiness, or the need to pause while groping for a word. Even in the safety of his lair, Henry flusters. As well he might; he's discussing a subject that has been gnawing him for years, and he wants to make the most of his chance to do justice to his words, for both his sake and Geoffrey's. His hour or so with Geoffrey wears heavily on him. Tomalin said that he waited until 1928 before declaring in public that his father and Nelly had a son together (28). In *Nell*, though, thanks to Gray's expertise with the private and the unrecorded, Henry always acts the gentleman, asking Geoffrey about his career and home while also praising Nelly whenever he can.

These outgoings of moral character had to fight big odds to gain voice. At the outset, a fuming Henry threatened to arrest his junior by some 30 years for having come to him to "make fraudulent demands" (6). Countless pretenders to the Dickens bloodline had been badgering him during the 42 years since his father's death. But Geoffrey counters Henry's threat to call the police with words that extract an apology, a handshake, and the drink both men need — along with a reminder to us that Dickens influenced the American thriller more than he did F.R. Leavis's great tradition of English fiction. Sounding like Ross Macdonald's Lew Archer, Geoffrey says, "I'm not here for money. I want information" (7).

Henry does talk gently and diplomatically about subjects like Nelly's age. But Geoffrey's mention of "an outing to [a picnic in] Doncaster" his mother called "the happiest day of her childhood" (11–2) incites a shift in what will be the play's longest scene and denouement. After this face-off, during which private reality vies with the official record, Gray will alternate scenes between the lovers and their children before permitting Henry to confess, to his credit, that Nelly was his father's mistress.

Splendid foreshadowing galvanizes Henry's confession. Though, by telling us something we already know, the confession doesn't add anything new; but it both deepens the men's commitment to each other and speeds the play's action. Having his suspicions confirmed relieves Geoffrey. But it also pelts him with fresh turmoil that dictates a wide-scale on-the-spot overhaul. "All we know about the interview [with Henry]," Gray said, "is that after it Geoffrey cleared all the works of Dickens out of his house, divorced his wife, gave up his bookshop, then became his mother's son and went into acting" (xx). None of this shocks us. Gray's invented exchange between Geoffrey and Henry justifies the tectonic shifts.

Gray's orchestration of mood and tone shows the same inventiveness. Henry had been shaken by a newspaper article about Nelly and his father he had read just hours before Geoffrey's visit. He's still upset when he meets Geoffrey, and late in the play he confides that he still has nightmares about the public readings in which his father "murdered" (53)—using the verb as an intransitive. Dick's description of the never-finished *Edwin Drood*, "It's a love story, with murder in it. And the murder has love in it" (56), probes the dark corners of the next generation. Invoking the love-death interplay in American writers like Poe and Joyce Carol Oates, Henry and Geoffrey face — and share — the truth that their parents discarded their offspring (54–5). In a variation of the bondage motif Gray took from Hank Janson, the unnamable that joined Nelly and Dick had to be kept a secret from the world at large — even as their mutual silence also rendered them bound and helpless.

Nell closes with Henry and Geoffrey shaking hands, as they had done earlier (22). Their handshake symbolizes kinship; the child or children discarded by their parents shared their blood. Meeting on equal footing, the two men are both providing and receiving needed comfort. Henry had just said rightfully that he'll consider Geoffrey as "some sort of relation," the vague "some sort of" coming closer to capturing his meaning than any other word cluster he can find. It's a shining, transcendent moment. The two men have drawn the fangs from their shared legacy of inherited guilt — murder with love in it. Responding both to Henry's touching words and the effort that produced them, Geoffrey, in the play's curtain line, says, "Thank you, sir, thank you" (65). Familiarity hasn't bred contempt. Having received more than he came for, Geoffrey needn't see Sir Henry again. The divisions bred by social class, upbringing, and age have slid silently back into place, leaving *Little Nell* a rich, layered entity that would have closed the career of any playwright on a proud note.

Gray's range is wide and his language, light years more courteous and natural sounding than strained or fussy. Braced by the vividness and immediacy that the best theater provides, his plays also temper their vigor with a well-judged restraint. They're more fun and easier to read than those of Tom Stoppard or Caryl Churchill. As a dramatist, Gray is more relaxed, his talent is more evenly spread, and there's plenty of it, as is shown in his ability to put his people. in a variety of settings historical and contemporary. It's said that he lacks the emotional depth, resonance, and scope of Pinter. If this judgment is correct, it doesn't discredit him. It simply puts his achievement in perspective. We're so hedged in by superlatives today that objectivity is always coming under threat.

Scenes of incredible difficulty in his work come to us with effortless poise. His deceptively straightforward plays hide considerable craftsmanship. Nor does he submit to a weakness that often dogs comic writers—flattening his minor characters, exaggerating their flaws, and playing them for laughs. Writing with fluency and finesse, he handworks his materials with a sure touch and a commendable clarity of purpose. He never acts like a playwright reporting for intellectual duty, bristling with diligence to make explicit and overdetermined what might have been quietly suggested. He uses his lightly carried learning and quiet energy to please an audience, not a seminar of sociologists and dissertation writers. The nuanced dialogue, attention to realistic details, and morally ambiguous relationships distinguishing the plays also frees them from slickness and superficiality. Giving full value, any number of them qualify simultaneously as entertainments, social commentaries, and experiences with unforeseen disturbing entailments. Much of his work won't leave you alone till you've thought a lot about it.

What to ponder? He knows the comforts of communal bonding, both the exercise and cost of curiosity, and the obstacles that thwart us from making the most of life. He also conveys the complexities of a woman's social, professional, and family roles. The women in Gray stand up to modern scrutiny. Indeed, his treatment of the three most familiar female roles—caring for an invalid parent (*Quartermaine's Terms*), rating a career over having kids *(Close of Play, Stage Struck)*, and child-rearing (*Dog Days, Japes, Little Nell*) rings true today. His awareness of the friction caused by convergences between these roles also gives his work a continental flavor. Though sometimes highly plotted, the work describes people on the edge, showing them sliding toward breakdown, probing the fluidity of selfhood without clear guidelines, and ready to conclude that much of life is an absurdity and a cheat.

A wealth of evidence in the canon shows his attraction to the world's pain squaring with this pessimism. Though he'd admit that things do improve for some of us some of the time, this man whose later diaries would keep rubbing our noses in both his physical deterioration and impending death (e.g., YJ 115–6, 168, 206) also believed that for most of us things usually sour. For instance, killings in crime fiction are usually driven by money, passion, and vengeance. *A Comeback for Stark* reminds us that the accidental and the discarded can also turn life into a nightmare.

The deep structure of his work discloses anxieties that both plagued him his whole life and explains his lifelong fascination with the bondage-and-domination themed fiction of Hank Janson. So great was his need of the certainty symbolized by a helpless, bound woman that it darkened his psyche. But he found his stride. His artistry made peace with the dark by facing it honestly. He needed to internalize the fetishism of Perkin Godboy of *Dutch Uncle* in order to make this mousy devoté of poison gas so chilling. His biggest hit, *Butley*, describes the slamming recoil incited by acts of bondage, domination, and coercion. Ben seizes Joey's briefcase to stop him from going to the library to prepare a lecture. Nobody is safe around him. Trying to stir up trouble elsewhere, he phones the boss of his wife's lover. Both of these coercive acts violate Rilke's definition of love. Ben is denying his two closest intimates both the space and security to be themselves. This breach of civility resonates with the student protests taking place at QMC; the freedom Ben is refusing Anne and Joey mirrors in miniature the racist violence of South Africa's Apartheid government. Anyone who controls others against their will, he finds, has also shackled himself to a course of action that must grow progressively brutal and self-defeating.

Gray's writing throngs with that analogue of the certainty fetish, the loss of love. The fiancé of Grahame Thwaite's great aunt Mary Medway in *Little Portia* died in combat (LP 7–8), as did that of *They Never Slept*'s Pru Merriman in a skiing accident (4SG 371). Add to these fatalities the removal of Simon Booker's priest-lover to Canada, Ben Butley's rapid-fire loss of both Joey and Anne and the death of Grahame's close friend Michael Cranton — of a perforated ulcer, like Aunt Mary's fiancé (LP 96). These fictional blows invoke the ulcerations caused by heavy drinking, which Gray, having lost a yard of intestine in the 1990s (Gardner 1), had to know about. But he both knew about and felt rocked by the defections to death of his fellow students Lopez (UP 234–9) and Richard Symonds (YJ 219) and his brother Piers. These shocks prodded him to resurrect the pedophile from *Little Portia* decades later in *The Late Middle Classes*, where he not only gave him a last name close to that of Mr. Brown, one of his teacher-abusers (FL 124), but also planted him in Hayling Island, his own birthplace. Add to these inventions the much gentler treatment Gray gave Thomas Andrew Brownlow than he did his counterpart Lindsay Burnlow in *Little Portia*, and what emerges is the most shining reconciliation between himself and the evil Other in all his work. The middle-aged Holly is last seen playing the piano, the instrument he learned how to play from Brownlow, whom he also calls in the last word spoken in the play, "Lowly" (88), the name he used years earlier when they were alone together. He has accepted the meaning of his own feelings, lowly or subversive as they may be. The withholding of moral judgment has helped him not merely accept but, rather, honor his bond to a disgraced mentor who taught him more than music.

The two men advisedly take leave of each other just before final curtain. They have accepted the tenacity of their bond, one of several like it in the canon. What the members of the long scroll of departed fictional or real-life love interests or abusers share in Gray's work is the spot where they leave both him and those characters he based on himself—i.e., playing the abandoned lover, an anxious role that also motivated his restoring his stand-in, Holly Smithers to Hayling Island and Brownlow in the final scene of *The Late Middle Classes*. Any squaring of psychological accounts or interweaving of loose threads from a troubled past lends comfort.

That comfort, though, has limits. Being human means living in darkness and dread. Yes, Holly sought the outcast Brownlow, just as the rich man's son Ivan Karamazov did the despised Smerdyakov. But Holly's last goodbye to his old teacher leaves some big questions unanswered; any living soul is a work in progress that rules out definitive reports. Both the musical context of the last scene of the play and the play's denial of closure invoke another writer of jarring adult scripts who wasn't brought up by his parents: Stephen Sondheim. In this regard, believers in coincidence will note that the 1979 debut of Sondheim's musical extravaganza about cannibalism, *Sweeney Todd*, occurred a year after that of *Rear Column*. And the failure of Sondheim's Bobby, like so many of Gray's anti-heroes a member of the professional middle class, to bond emotionally in *Company* (1970) identifies a fear of intimacy characteristic of both writers. The penalties assessed by this fear shape our humanity.

This avoidance mind-set aligns Gray with the means-oriented approach to life traditionally associated with women. It has long been accepted that women favor process over product. A preference for relationships over justice has led them to trust imagination, intuition and impulse, an attitude that clashes with the ends-oriented living that men have been linking to a penchant for justice, trophies, and material proofs. The ease with which Ben Butley's wife adapts to Ben's bolt from the nest points to a belief in Gray in the superiority of woman's coping power. Anne is flexible. While having found both a job and a live-in boyfriend since Ben's departure, she's still keeping alive the option of taking him back; Ben's friend Joey says that she *wants* him back. But Anne's intuitive grasp of process, which translates to food on the table and love in the heart, is a rarity in the Gray canon. The fox that slips nightly into Gray's garden in order to kill Gray's dog, symbol of domestic love and loyalty, is Gray himself. We've been stopped again from taking his measure. Women in the novels *Colmain* and *Simple People* and the plays *Otherwise Engaged* and *Dog Days* outdo their male counterparts as schemers, opportunists, and bottom-liners. Women can also rob people of their freedom. *Just the Three of Us* dismantles the narrative that had cast men in the tyrant's role in *Sleeping Dog* and *Dutch Uncle*. In Gray's 1999 play, a failure in imagination, which is usually seen as a male failing, prompts a female novelist to abduct young women so she can tell *their* stories.

Like Dostoevsky, Gray equated certainty with denial and even death.

When he wasn't chewing over its benefits, he yoked it with the straps and ropes that bound Hank Janson's heroines. His malaise fits the profile of the self-punishing addict whose tobacco, drink, and womanizing had long since stopped providing relief.

The psychological upshot of his desperation reconfirms the gender confusion in his psychological Gestalt. Gray kept reprising the role of the forlorn lover in his work. His resemblance to deserted fictional heroines ranging from Ariadne and Dido to Miss Saigon also accounts for his overdue resignation from the faculty of QMC after 18 years and, more significantly, his divorcing Beryl after 32. The separation anxiety caused by his evacuation to Montreal at age four sunk deep, stubborn roots. He needed the security provided by the eight years of intimacy that backed Victoria's promise to marry him and a long run of stage hits to shed the prototype of the stranded female. He wrote so astutely about the feminized Jerry's fears of being marooned in *Wise Child* because he shared them.

The warm assurances of love suffered their first icy stab with his evacuation from his parents' home. What followed made him feel like a victim in a conspiracy plot. The upheaval that stuck him in the home of his bundling grandmother in French-speaking Montreal primed him to equate love with the physical suffering that crested in the words of a sweating, panting Lindsay Burnlow to Grahame Thwaite in *Little Portia*: "I must punish you, but only because I adore you" (51). Gray's childhood loss of faith in the transformative possibilities of courtesy, kindness, and love shook him. Yet, rather than wilting into furtiveness or exploding into fury, he found an outlet for his anxieties in creative writing. He'd redeem the cruelty that by stages had seeped into him.

This step brought anxieties. His having stayed in the rank of lecturer during his 18 years at QMC (because he hadn't published any scholarly research) barely worried this already-successful playwright. As he already showed in his portrayals of Edith in *Side-Car* and Anne in *Stage Struck*, the rigors of artistic endeavor that he had already survived outweigh those of academe. It's revealing that these committed artists are both women. His dramas of thwarted desire impinge upon accepting blame for losing things, like a child or parent (*Quartermaine's Terms*), a love-partner (*Butley*), or a home and career (*Spoiled*). Recounting such crises of the heart usually come easier to women writers (Emily Dickinson, Elizabeth Bowen, Jean Rhys, and Anita Brookner spring to mind) than to men.

No escape or denial, Gray's writing entailed a brave leap into the murk and anarchy of his psyche. Gray agreed with Thomas Mann and Tennessee Williams that all artists are monsters. This recognition helped him fight off the paranoia he ascribed to himself in the subtitle of *Enter the Fox*. His efforts hark to Shakespeare. "This thing of darkness," viz., Caliban, that Prospero acknowledged and made inner peace with in the finale of *The Tempest*, also helps frame Gray's sometimes monstrous inner turmoil. But Gray stood up to both the physical self-disgust of his last years and the ghosts of his earlier ones. The astonishingly precise, relaxed method he sustained in plays as powerful as *Butley*, *The Rear Column*, and *Little Nell* describes his career as an extended master class in the art of distilling pain into art. In his modesty, he'd have downplayed this feat. He'd have been misprizing his gifts. We've seen why. Mostly, he's an unfussy, but supremely confident writer who attains his near-invisible effects by listening to his characters while keeping his virtuosity to himself. The completion of his revels finds him, though uneasy with his grandeur, dominant and dazzling.

His imagination distilled his technique, too. The predominance of plot in works like *Butley*, *They Never Slept*, and *Simply Disconnected* brings more joy than worry. Plot juices conflict, the heartbeat of drama. Those of Gray are complicated but well-oiled and -timed, their points binding neatly without dwarfing character. In the interests of realism, his people will speak over each other or begin a speech off camera or while walking onto the set. These devices claim our attention. Gray is a fine storyteller. His strength lies not only in a lively, sometimes extravagant imagination but also in his ability both to modulate pace and to layer physical action into scenes dominated by talk — scenes where his knowledge of when to release information and when to hold it back leaves us half a step behind and eager to catch up.

Feeling and craft have dovetailed. Combining cutting observation, dramatic warmth, and black humor, his plays excel in both scene-framing and evocative dialogue. Gray has the writer's full tool kit — empathy, curiosity, a skinned eye, and a well-tuned ear — which helps him write plays at once intimate and expansive, plausible and bold. His sentences, bright but not showy, are sophisticated without sounding bookish or self-conscious. These gifts depict him, in a 40-year career that spanned 35 plays, five novels, and eight non-fictional books, as a provocative, diligent artist who steadily refined his craft while also scouring both his psyche and the world at large for challenging new subjects and ideas. Lyn Gardner was right when she saw a major artistic breakthrough in the works of his last decade (1). Facing his inner Caliban flooded his hiding place with sunlight. Vital here is the compulsion that sends his fictional stand-in Grahame Thwaite against all good sense into the mucky, rat-infested pond near his childhood home.

This immersion in fear set a direction for Gray. He could say eventually that, even though Butley and Simon Hench were both him, he was neither man. He had subsumed them, as he did his other creations, inside his art. The embrace of darkness found at the end of *The Late Middle Classes* (1999) signals the self-acceptance that helped him deep-probe the addled mainsprings of that art, viz., social class, homosexuality, and adultery. Gray never shed the coerciveness he found so riveting in the Hank Janson books. But he redirected it to healthy goals. The attainment of full psychic growth for him entailed immersing himself in Grahame's sinister pond, camping out along the banks of the Arruwimi, and watching and waiting alongside a comatose wife. All of these challenges rest upon a full acceptance of the archetypal female that had made him the "toy boy" "she loved to fondle" (SD14). Her excesses are typical.

Celia Smithers is another overly attentive mother who belongs in the same category as Gray's bundling grandmother and Grahame's sister Dianah, whose "fingers circled busily between his legs" (LP 11) while she was cleaning him after his ordeal in the pond. A boy growing up in a home surrounded by female predators has good reason to distrust life. But without defusing this threat, Gray locates it inside a blueprint of engagement with life that, for all its dangers, includes a warm, outgoing attitude toward sex and parenting found in Anne Butley and Simon Hench's fecund sister-in-law, Teresa. The sexual eagerness of ingénues like Janice Trullope of *Little Portia*, Davina Saunders of *Otherwise Engaged*, and, as Gray describes her, Nelly Ternan of *Little Nell* offers healthy, life-giving outlets missing from the voyeurism, fetishism, gender confusion, and dishonesty that cramps any number of Gray's male figures. The members of this hapless group face long odds. Rejecting the anger, self-pity, or the dazzle of instant gratification that leads men to these indulgences is daunting work. But shirking it invokes the false gods of closure and conclusiveness, a fantasy system held in place by the same ropes and chains that fetter Hank Janson's carefully posed cover girls.

This scenario adds another coat of darkness to Gray's tense velvet comedy. What follows is a moral mismatch with Gray's perception and appreciation of human worth. His confrontation with our deep indeterminacy links freedom to the confusion and pain that rise from our contingency. Freedom came to him when he redefined the link between the sacred and the profane. Symbolizing the liturgical form of the chorale, the music played at the end of the two Simon Tench plays represents his submission to the universal.

Gray was always intrigued by pockets of experience that, rather than being faced directly, must be courted obliquely. Approach is key. To forget the self meant no longer being a slave to its limitations. The attainment of power and transcendence, he saw, meant leaving the self behind; being must be understood in relation to *it*self, not *one*self. This wisdom about our potential for growth puts deliverance, not in resolution, but in the ambiguity and incongruity into which figures like Jeremy and Artminster of *Wise Child*, *Butley*'s Anne and Joey, and J.G. of *Life Support* are seen stumbling as they take their leave of us.

Standing with firmer feet in the same frame with them is Simon Gray, on the lookout for the good laugh line that will also blindside us with its thematic bite. Though brought up on a tradition that prized pedigree, provenance, and heritage, he spent his life fighting disruption and waste. Yet, true to his playwright's gift for sympathy and emotional insight, his fractured autobiography draws attention to the way we process time and give it meaning. That he's more about continuity than about change counts as a triumph over the irreparable and the inescapable. Though his efforts might not have redeemed this obduracy, they do temper it while often shaking the rafters with our applause.

Bibliography

Fiction

Colmain. London: Faber and Faber, 1963.
Simple People. 1965; rpt. London: Sphere, 1968.
Little Portia. 1967; rpt. London and Boston: Faber and Faber, 1986; "Introduction" by Simon Gray, ix–xxiii.
A Comeback for Stark ["A Novel of Espionage by Hamish Reade"]. New York: Putnam's, 1968. London: Faber and Faber, 1969.
Breaking Hearts. London: Faber and Faber, 1997.

Nonfiction

An Unnatural Pursuit and Other Pieces. London: Faber and Faber, 1985; New York: St. Martin's, 1985.
How's That for Telling 'Em, Fat Lady? London: Faber and Faber, 1988.
Fat Chance. London: Faber and Faber, 1995.
Enter a Fox: Further Adventures of a Paranoid. London: Faber and Faber, 2001.
The Smoking Diaries. London: Granta, 2004.
The Year of the Jouncer. London: Granta, 2006.
The Last Cigarette. London: Granta, 2008.
Coda. London: Granta, 2008.

Play Collections

Otherwise Engaged and Other Plays. London: Eyre Methuen, 1975.
The Rear Column and Other Plays. London: Eyre Methuen, 1978.
The Definitive Simon Gray I. London: Faber and Faber, 1992.
The Definitive Simon Gray II. London: Faber and Faber, 1992.
The Definitive Simon Gray III. London: Faber and Faber, 1993.
The Definitive Simon Gray IV. London: Faber and Faber, 1993.
Four Plays. London: Faber and Faber, 2004.

Stage Plays/ Debut Dates and Sources

Wise Child. 1967, SG1.
Dutch Uncle. 1969, SG1.
Spoiled. 1971, SG1.
Butley. 1971, SG1. Simon Gray, *Butley.* New York: Viking, 1972.
Otherwise Engaged. 1975, OE.
Dog Days. London: Eyre Methuen, 1976; "Author's Note" by Simon Gray, 5–8.
Molly. 1977, RC.
The Rear Column. 1978, RC.
Close of Play. 1979, Simon Gray, *Close of Play.* New York: Dramatists Play Service, 1982.
Stage Struck. 1979, SG3.
Quartermaine's Terms. 1981, SG3.
The Common Pursuit: Scenes from the Literary Life. 1984, SG4.
Melon. London: Methuen, 1987.
Hidden Laughter. 1990, SG4.
The Holy Terror. 1991, Four.
Cell Mates. London: Faber and Faber, 1995.
Simply Disconnected. London: Faber and Faber, 1996.
Life Support. London: Faber and Faber, 1997.

Just the Three of Us. London: Nick Hern, 1997.
The Late Middle Classes. London: Nick Hern, 1999.
Japes. London: Nick Hern, 2000.
Japes Too. Four.
Michael. Four.
The Pig Trade. Four.
The Old Masters. London: Faber and Faber, 2004.
Little Nell. London: Faber and Faber, 2006.
The Last Cigarette. 2009.

Television Plays and Movies

The Caramel Crisis. 1966. SG1
Sleeping Dog. 1967. SG1
Pig in a Poke. 1969. SG2
Man in a Side-Car. 1971, RC.
Plaintiffs and Defendants. 1975, OE.
Two Sundays. 1975, OE.
After Pilkington. 1987, SG4.
Old Flames. 1990, SG4
They Never Slept. 1991, SG4.

Adaptations

The Idiot (Dostoevsky), 1970. London: Methuen, 1971.
Tartuffe: An Adaptation (Molière), 1982, SG3.

Film Adaptation

A Month in the Country (J. L. Carr), 1987, SG3.

Play Review

"Mostly Superior." *New Statesman*, 29 August 1969: 285–6; review of Shakespeare's *Twelfth Night*.

Interviews

DiGaetani, John Louis. "Simon Gray." *A Search for Postmodern Theater.* New York: Greenwood, 1991, 97–104.
Fort, Viola. "Simon Gray." <http://www.untitledbooks.com/features/interviews/simongray>, 30 April 2009.
Hamilton, Ian. "Simon Gray." *New Review* 3 (January–February 1977): 39–46.
Hattenstone, Simon. "Interview: Simon Gray: The Butt End of His Days." *Guardian* <http//www.guardian.uk/uk//july28/theatrearts>, 1 December 2008.

Criticism and Commentary

Ardolino, Frank. "The Denial of the Feminine and Shakespeare's Lost Daughters in Simon Gray's *Butley*." *Journal of Evolutionary Psychology* 25 (August 2004): 175–9.
Bainbridge, Beryl. "Life, Death, and Cigarettes." *New Statesman* 133, 3 May 2004: 40.
Bergeron, David M. "Simon Gray's 'Butley' and Shakespeare." *Rocky Mountain Review of Language and Literature* 38 (1984), 4: 179–88.
Berkvist, Robert. "Simon Gray Explores the Roots of Atrocity." *New York Times* 10 November 1978, 5, 30; review of *The Rear Column*.
Blaydes, Sophia B. "Literary Allusions as Satire in Simon Gray's *Butley*." *Midwest Quarterly* (1977): 374–91.
Brantley, Ben. "Zingers Shoot Forth from Inside a Toxic Fog." *New York Times* <http://www.theater.nytimes.com/2006/10/26/theater/reviews/26butl.html> 29 February 2008.
Burkman, Katherine H. "The Fool as Hero: Simon Gray's *Butley* and *Otherwise Engaged*." *Theatre Journal* 33, May 1981, 2: 163–72.
_____. "Hedda's Children: Simon Gray's Anti-Heroes." in Burkman, ed., 155–64.
_____, ed. *Simon Gray: A Casebook.* New York: Garland, 1992.
Clum, John. "'Being Took Queer': Homosexuality in Simon Gray's Plays." In Burkman, ed., 61–83.
_____. "*Hidden Laughter* and Middle-Aged Complacency." In Burkman, ed., 167–72.
Colleran, Jeanne. "The Power of Detachment: Inside and out of *The Rear Column*." In Burkman, ed., 123–35.
Fisher, Philip. "Otherwise Engaged." *The British Theatre Guide* <http://www.britishtheatreguide.info/reviews/otherwiseengaged-rev.htm>, 29 February 2008; review of *Otherwise Engaged*.

Fox, Terry Curtis. "Heart of Grayness." *Village Voice*, 4 December 1978, 121–2; review of *The Rear Column*.

Gale, Steven H. "Simon Gray's *Butley*: From Stage to Screen." In Burkman, ed., 85–99.

Gardner, Lyn. "Obituary: Simon Gray: Playwright, Diarist, and Novelist Who Bridged the Gulf Between Intellectual and Popular Drama." *Guardian* <http//:www.guardian.co.uk/culture/2008/aug/10/simongray.theatre>, 11 September 2008.

Gordon, Robert. "'Experimental Drama and the Well-Made Play': Simon Gray and Harold Pinter as Collaborators." In Burkman, ed., 3–24.

Gould, Tony. "Appreciation: Simon Gray, 1936–2008." *Guardian* <http://www.guardian.co.uk/culture/2008/aug10/simongray.theatre>, 16 October 2008.

Gowrie, Xandra, and Jacob Epstein. "BBC TV: The 'Lost Plays' of Simon Gray, David Mercer, Peter Nichols, Alun Owen, Harold Pinter, and Many Others." *The New Review* 3, June 1976, 27: 45–9.

Hall, Ann C. "Deceit, Desire, and Simon Gray's *Otherwise Engaged*." In Burkman, ed., 109–22.

―――. "Theatre Review of Simon Gray's *Hidden Laughter*." In Burkman, ed., 179–82.

Imhof, Rüdiger. "Simon Gray." In Hedwig Bock and Albert Wertheim, eds., *Contemporary British Drama*. Munich: Hueber, 1981, 223–52.

JCh. "Film: *Old Flames*." Timeout.com <http://www.timeout.com/film/reviews/65976/old-flames.html>; review of *Old Flames*, 29 February 2008.

Jenkins, Peter. "Tea for Two." *Spectator*, 9 June 1979, 30; review of Simon Gray, *Close of Play*.

Kerensky, Oleg. *The New British Drama: Fourteen Playwrights Since Osborne and Pinter*. New York: Taplinger, 1977.

King, Kimball. "*Hidden Laughter*: A Review." In Burkman, ed., 173–7.

―――. "The Unraveling of Melon." In Burkman, ed., 149–64.

Lahr, John. "The Grief Game." *New Yorker*, 6 Nov 2006, 126–38; review of *Butley*.

"Little Nell by Simon Gray, directed by Sir Peter Hall." 7 July 2007. Notes from the Panopticon <http://www.thinkhard.org/2007/07/little-nell-by-.html>, 29 February 2008.

Loveridge, Lizzie. "A Curtain Up: London Review of *Otherwise Engaged*." *Curtain Up: The Internet Theater Magazine of Reviews, Features, Annotated Listings* <http://www.curtainup.com/otherwiseengaged.html>, 23 October 2009.

Mills, John. "'Old Mr. Prickle-pin': Simon Gray's *Butley*." *American Imago* 45 (1987): 411–29.

MW. "Theatre Review: Never Judge a Book by Its Cover." *BA Education* <http://www.ba-education.com/for/entertainment/rtl/theholyterror.html>, 16 April 2007; undated review of *The Holy Terror*.

Pinter, Harold. "Foreword." *Simon Gray, An Unnatural Pursuit and Other Pieces*. New York: St. Martin's, 1985.

Rendell, Bob. "*Quartermaine's Terms*: Affecting Revival of Simon Gray's Bleak Comedy Drama." *Talkingbroadway.com* <http://www.talkingbroadway.com/regional/nj/nj 206.html>, 7 September 2008.

Roof, Judith. "Simon Gray and the Pedagogical Erotics of Theatre." In Burkman, ed., 25–39.

Shaw, Peter. "Staging England's Decline." *Commentary* 65 (April 1978): 88; review of *Butley*.

Siegel, Naomi. "Behind Ivy-Covered Walls, Where Life Begins and Ends." *New York Times* <http://theater2.nytimes.com/2007/03/04/nyregionspecial2/04NJtheat.html>, 29 February 2008; review of *Quartermaine's Terms*.

"Simon Gray: Rakish and Versatile Playwright." *Times* <http://www.timesonline.co.uk/tol/commentobituaries/article 4480324.ecc?token=null&print>, 1–3, 18 August 2008.

Simon, Robert. "Simon Gray, British Playwright of Wit and Intelligence, Dies at 71." *Playbill.com* <http://playbill.com/news/article/print/120203.html>, 13 September 2008.

Stephenson, Anthony. "Simon Gray." In *Dictionary of Literary Biography: British Dramatists Since World War II*, ed. Stanley Weintraub. Detroit: Gale, 1982, 199–208.

Stevens, Paul. "Theatre and Dance; Review: *Otherwise Engaged*." *BBC.co.uk* <http//

www.bbc.co.uk/somerset/content/articles/2005/09/22otherwise-engaged-review-fe...>, 1–3, 29 February 2008.
Taylor, John Russell. *The Second Wave: British Drama of the Sixties*. London: Eyre Methuen, 1971.
Vale, Alison. "*Little Nell.*" *The British Theatre Guide* <http://www.britishtheatreguide.info/reviews/littlenell-rev.htm>, 8 March 2008.
Walsh, John. "*The Year of the Jouncer*, by Simon Gray." *Independent* <http://www.independent.co.uk/arts-entertainment/books/reviews/the-year-of-the-jouncer-by Simon-Gray.html>, 1–2, 29 February 2008.
Wardle, Irving. "Review of *The Rear Column*." *Simongray.org* <http:www//simongray.org.uk/RCtimesreview.html>, 18 January 2009.
Weber, Bruce. "So Sad It's Funny, and Getting Sadder." *New York Times* <http://www.theater.nytimes.com/mem/theater/review.html?r=&res=9905EFDA143AF93BA2>, 9 February 2008.
Wu, Duncan. "Simon Gray: Numbness of the Heart." *Six Contemporary Dramatists: Bennett, Potter, Gray, Branton, Hare, Ayckbourn*. New York: St. Martin's, 1995, 65–80.
Young, Josa. "The Late Great Simon Gray." <http://www.huffingtonpost.com/josa-young/the-late-great-simon-gray-b-176306.html>, 7 February 2010.
Young, Toby. "Thrilled by Ibsen." *Spectator*, 12 November 205, 68–9; review of *Otherwise Engaged*.

Other Relevant Works

Calo, Mary Ann. *Bernard Berenson and the Twentieth Century*. Philadelphia: Temple University Press, 1994.
Conant, Eve. "A Death in the Family." *New York Times Book Review*, 1 April 2007, 21; review of Maggie Nelson, *The Red Parts*.
Fraser, Antonia. *Must You Go? My Life with Harold Pinter*. London: Weidenfield and Nicholson, 2010.
Freedberg, Sydney. "Berenson, Connoisseurship, and the History of Art." *New Criterion*, February 1989, 7–16.
Gopnik, Adam. "A Critic at Large: Right Again: The Passions of John Stuart Mill." *New Yorker*, 6 October 2007, 85–90; review of Richard Reeves, *John Stuart Mill; Victorian Firebrand*.
Gould, Tony. *In Limbo: The Story of Stanley's Rear Column*. London: Hamish Hamilton, 1979.
Gray, Piers. *Stalin on Linguistics and Other Essays*. Ed. Colin MacCabe and Victoria Rothschild. 1992; New York: Palgrave Macmillan, 2002.
Holland, Steven. *The Trials of Hank Janson*. Tolworth, Surrey, UK: Telos, 2004.
Janson, Hank [pseud. for Stephen D. Frances]. *Kill Her if You Can*. 1952; Tolworth, Surrey, UK, 2005.
Leavis, F.R., *D.H. Lawrence: Novelist*. 1955; New York: Simon & Schuster/Clarion, 1969.
MacCabe, Colin. "Obituary: Piers Gray." *Independent* <http://Independent.co.uk/news/people/obituary-piers-gray-1326909.html>, 17 January 2009.
Massie, Allan. "Life and Letters: Passionate Friendships." *The Spectator*, 4 April 2009, 76.
Peppiatt, Michael. "The Art of the Deal." *New York Times* <http://query.nytimes.com/gst/fullpage.html?res=9404E4DB1530F93AA2575ACOA9628>, 7 March 2008; review of Meryle Secrest, *Duveen*.
Porter, Bernard. "Did He Puff Up His Crimes to Please a Bloodthirsty Readership?" *London Review of Books*, 5 April 2007, 9–10; review of Tim Jeal, *Stanley: The Impossible Life of Africa's Greatest Explorer*.
Rattigan, Terence. *The Collected Plays of Terence Rattigan: Volume Two: The Later Plays, 1953–77*. Cresskill, NJ: Paper Tiger, 2001.
Schapiro, Meyer. "Mr. Berenson's Values." *Encounter* 6, January 1961, 57–61.
Secrest, Meryle. *Duveen: A Life in Art*. New York: Knopf, 2004.
Simpson, Colin. *The Partnership: The Secret Association of Bernard Berenson and Joseph Duveen*. London: The Bodley Head, 1987.
Smith, Roberta. "The Art of the Art Deal: A Portrait of the Old Master." *New York Times* <http://www.query,nytimes.com/gst/fullpage.html?res=9406ED9103FF93AA2575ZCIA9629CB87>, 7 March 2008; review of Meryle Secrest, *Duveen: A Life in Art*.

Sutherland, N.S. *Breakdown*. New York: Stein and Day, 1977.
Tomalin, Claire. *The Invisible Woman: The Story of Nelly Ternan and Charles Dickens*. New York: Knopf, 1991.
Waugh, Evelyn. *Brideshead Revisited*. Boston: Little, Brown, 1945.
Wright, Thomas. *The Life of Charles Dickens*. London: Herbert Jenkins, 1935.

Official Memorial Website

<http://www.simongray.org.uk/>

Index

Albee, Edward 210; *The American Dream* 116; *A Delicate Balance* 129; *Who's Afraid of Virginia Woolf?* 12, 191
Aldington, Ricard 31
Alfie (movie) 20
Allen, Woody: *Manhattan* 51
Amis, Kingsley: *Lucky Jim* 66, 74
Anderson, Lindsay: *If...* 24
Arden, John: *Live Like Pigs* 116
Ardolino, Frank 40, 146, 155
Arnold, Matthew: "The Buried Life" 50; "Dover Beach" 50, 53
Austen, Jane 35, 59; *Persuasion* 52, 209

Banville, John 93
Barnes, Julian 93
Barry, Philip 19
Bates, Alan 3, 35, 40, 155, 173, 177
Baudelaire, Charles 17; "Reversibilité" 137
The Beatles 20; *The Yellow Submarine* 130
Beckett, Samuel 71, 105, 187, 203; *Waiting for Godot* 118, 129, 132, 139, 148, 155, 188
Bellow, Saul 201; *Henderson the Rain King* 215
Bennett, Alan 1; *Forty Years On* 23, *The History Boys* 24, 190; *Untold Stories* 155; *Writing Home* 154
Berenson, Bernard 8, 9, 220
Bergeron, David M. 11, 149
Berlin, Isaiah 40
Best, Georgie 20
Blake, George 19, 32–3, 208, 211, 213
Blaydes, Sophia B. 1, 11, 150
Blood Diamond (movie) 6
Boller, Frederick 50, 158
Bond, Edward 107
Bourke, Robert 32, 211, 213
Bowen, Elizabeth 235
Brecht, Betolt 12, 58, 69, 116
Brookner, Anita 50, 235
Brown, Mr. 34–5, 39, 233
Buchan, John: *The Thirty-Nine Steps* 159
Buñuel, Luis 106

Burkman, Katherine M. 14, 48; 156, 175; *Simon Gray: A Casebook* 1, 10
Burn, John 33, 35, 39
Burroughs, William S. 154
Byron, Lord: *Manfred* 179–80, 194

Caine, Michael 20
Callow, Simon 13
Calo, Mary Ann 222
Camus, Albert: *The Stranger* 141
Carey, Peter: *Jack Maggs* 46
Carlyle, Thomas: *History of the French Revolution* 154
Carr, J.L.: *A Month in the Country* 56
Chamberlain, Neville 223
Chandler, Raymond 37
Charley's Aunt 124
Chekhov, Anton 5, 34, 47, 164–5, 210–1; *The Cherry Orchard* 109, 162; 166; "The Lady and the Lap Dog" 164; *The Sea Gull* 28, 191; *The Three Sisters* 1, 35, 132; 156, 164; *Uncle Vanya* 50, 139
Christie, Agatha: *The Mousetrap* 125
Christie, Beryl 134
Christie, John Reginald 134–5, 163
Churchill, Caryl 232
Clum, John M. 18, 34, 48, 54–5
Cole, Steven S. 141
Colleran, Jeanne 217
Collins, Wilkie 9; *The Frozen Deep* 226
The Comedians (movie) 124
Conan Doyle, Sir Arthur 102, 130
Conrad, Joseph 33, 215; *Heart of Darkness* 111; *The Secret Agent* 98
Courtenay, Tom 173
Coward, Noël 177; *Private Lives* 191

Dalí, Salvador: *Un Chien Andalou* 106
Dante 83
Darwin, Charles 215
Day Lewis, C[ecil]. 93
De Gaetaini, John 30
de la Mare, Walter 4

245

246 Index

Delany, Shelagh 107
De Lillo, Don 225
Derrida, Jacques 131
Descartes, René 51
Dickens, Catherine 227
Dickens, Charles 9, 10, 11, 14, 34, 40, 46–7, 49, 119, 166, 208, 220; *Bleak House* 22; *A Christmas Carol* 225; *David Copperfield* 32, 213; *Great Expectations*, 10, 11, 36, 82, 91, 146; *The Mystery of Edwin Drood* 22, 231; *Oliver Twist* 9, 22; *The Pickwick Papers* 91
Dickinson, Emily 235
Dostoevsky, Fyodor 196, 235; *The Brothers Karamazov* 142, 180, 234, 206; "The Double" 164; *The Idiot* 5, 50, 164; *Notes from Underground* 142
Duchamp, Marcel 106
du Maurier, Daphne: *Rebecca* 100
Dürenmatt, Friedrich: *The Visit* 110
Duveen, Joseph 220–1, 223

Eddowes, Michael: *The Man on Your Conscience* 134
El Greco 217
Eliot, T.S. 6, 11, 141, 154, 206; "The Buried Life" 50; *Four Quartets* ("East Coker") 8, 141, 151, 159; "Gerontion" 85–6; "The Love Song of J. Alfred Prufrock" 8, 47, 151, 164; *The Waste Land* 51, 63
Eliot, Valerie 154
Ellison, Ralph: *Invisible Man* 91, 115
Ellroy, James 225
Epstein, Jacob 173
Evans, Beryl 134
Evans, Geraldine 134
Evans, Timothy 134–5

Feydeau, Georges: *A Flea in Her Ear* 122, 132
Fielding, Henry: *Tom Jones* 51, 91, 161
Fisher, Philip 173, 178
Fitzgerald, F. Scott 208; *The Great Gatsby* 146, 171
Fitzgerald, Penelope 59; *The Beginning of Spring* 15
The Flame and the Arrow (movie) 37
Flaubert, Gustave 56; *Madame Bovary* 154
Fleischer, Richard 134
Ford, Ford Madox: *The Good Soldier* 51
Forster, E.M.: *Aspects of the Novel* 64; *A Passage to India* 63–4, 201, 206
Forster, John 9
Foucault, Michel 105
Fowles, John: *The Collector* 127; *The Magus* 90
Fox, Edward 3, 155
Frances, Stephen *see* Janson, Hank
Frayn, Michael 55
Freedberg, Sydney 222

Freud, Sigmund 3, 21, 26, 33, 84, 107, 186, 217
Fry, Christopher 206

Gaddis, William 133; *The Recognitions* 66
Gale, Steven H 144
Gambon, Michael 3, 173
Gammer Gurton's Needle 76
Gardner, Lyn 3, 14, 40, 132, 226, 236
Genet, Jean, 47, 84, 85, 154, 204, 206; *The Balcony* 30, 218
Gide, André 84, 85
Gogol, Nikolai: "The Overcoat" 164
Goncharov, Ivan 50, 194
Gone with the Wind (movie) 146
Gordon, Gen. Charles George (Gordon of Khartoum) 214
Gordon, Robert 35, 156, 196–7, 210
Gould, Tony 18, 214
Gowrie, Xandra 173
Gray, Barbara (playwright's mother) 15, 20–1, 42–6, 59–61, 103–4, 136, 220, 229
Gray, Ben (playwright's son) 13
Gray, Beryl (playwright's first wife) 135, 154, 194, 235
Gray, James Davidson, M.D. (playwright's father) 5, 8, 15, 42, 45–7, 49, 171
Gray, Lucy (playwright's daughter) 13
Gray, Nigel (playwright's elder brother) 13, 186
Gray, Piers (playwright's younger brother) 11, 13, 103, 142, 204, 213, 233; *Stalin on Linguistics and Other Essays* 53; *T.S. Eliot's Intellectual and Poetic Development* 8
Gray, Simon: academia 24–6, 30; *After Pilkington* 8, 14, 15, 18, 22, 25, 44, 50, 69, 107, 125, 140, 214, 228; autobiographical elements in the work 13–14, 41–5, 194; *Breaking Hearts* 10, 11, 25–6, 30, 47, 103–4, 142; *Butley* 1, 2, 3, 5, 8, 11, 12, 17–8, 22, 25, 30, 33, 40, 47–8, 50, 98, 107, 139–55, 156, 159–60, 163, 164–5, 167–9, 172–9, 185, 227, 233–7; *The Caramel Crisis* 15, 106, 107–10, 114–5, 196; *Cell Mates* 10, 13, 19, 32, 42, 49, 139, 211–3; childhood 4–5, 11, 14–5, 235; *Close of Play* 4, 11, 12, 13, 15, 29, 45–6, 51, 139–40, 171, 197, 225, 232; *Coda* 4, 7, 19, 23, 40, 46, 176; Colmain 21, 23, 32, 44, 51, 53, 58, 59–71, 72–6, 78, 81, 87, 92, 100, 102, 134, 154, 173, 227, 234; *A Comeback for Stark* 13, 16, 17, 40–1, 44, 53, 58–9, 93–104, 118, 171, 186, 218, 232; *Common Pursuit* 4, 5, 11, 12, 13, 14, 16–8, 20, 31, 34, 36–7, 136, 139, 144, 154, 172, 209, 225–6; *Dog Days* 9, 12–8, 29, 44, 48, 144, 170–2, 183–9, 192, 197, 204, 214, 232, 234; *Dutch Uncle* 11, 29, 37, 49, 53, 64, 105, 107, 116, 123–35, 136, 139, 151, 154–5, 172–3, 182, 233–4; *Enter a Fox* 3, 10, 20–1, 30, 235; *Fat Chance* 32, 54; *Hidden Laughter* 1, 6–7, 12, 13, 26–7, 35, 45, 47, 49, 53–4, 78, 172,

183, 196; *Holy Terror* 12, 13, 171–2, 184; homosexuality 16, 31–3, 39–41, 64, 100, 104; *How's That for Telling 'Em, Fat Lady* 34, 44, 158; *The Idiot* (Gray's adaptation) 14, 143, 155; "In Memory of Lopez" 25, 233; *Japes* 10, 14, 45–6, 48, 53, 136, 192, 197, 213, 232; *Japes Too* 13, 14, 45–6, 48, 136, 212–3; *Just the Three of Us* 9, 10, 13, 14, 28, 30, 35, 49–50, 52, 103, 220, 234; *The Last Cigarette* 4, 6, 8, 20, 45, 51, 150; *The Late Middle Classes* 7, 9, 20, 34, 43–8, 59, 100, 104, 115, 204–5, 229, 233–4, 236–7; *Life Support* 3, 10, 12, 26, 28, 36, 47, 107, 136, 170, 174, 199–207, 210–1, 229, 237; literary influences 6–12, 50–1; *Little Nell* 2, 8–10, 16, 22, 26, 32, 40, 42, 46–7, 49, 57, 126, 139, 208, 213, 224, 225–31, 232, 236–7; *Little Portia* 13, 14, 15, 18–20, 24–5, 32–4, 38, 41–4, 49–51, 53, 58–9, 69, 74, 82–93, 97, 102–4, 136, 156, 160, 167–8, 173, 181, 191–2, 197, 208, 233, 235–7; *Man in a Side-Car* 9, 12, 13, 15, 18, 26–8, 35, 39, 52, 61, 185, 209, 235; *Melon* 6, 12, 13, 21, 56, 136, 144, 170–1, 175, 184, 220; *Michael* 9, 11, 45–6, 48, 52, 136, 170; *Molly* 29, 56, 125, 134, 228; *A Month in the Country* (Gray's adaptation) 56; Montreal grandmother 17, 33–4, 39, 42, 61, 83, 236; *Old Flames* 4, 13, 15, 17, 24–5, 36, 52, 132, 148, 170, 172, 180, 192; *The Old Masters* 3, 8, 9, 28, 46, 155, 201, 214, 218, 220–4; *Otherwise Engaged* 1, 3, 7, 8, 9, 13, 15, 17–8, 21, 24, 28, 35, 41, 50, 52, 57, 69, 78, 136, 140, 156, 170–1, 172–83, 185, 189–91, 193–4, 196–7, 199, 201, 204–5, 213, 230, 234, 237; pedophilia 33–5, 61, 64, 136–9; *Pig in a Poke* 8, 37–39, 40, 51, 78, 116, 135, 214; *The Pig Trade* 214; *Plaintiffs and Defendants* 13, 17–8, 28, 183–5; *Quartermaine's Terms* 3, 7, 13, 14, 27, 34, 47, 50, 52, 56, 104, 136, 155–69, 176, 178, 202, 232, 235; *The Rear Column* 1, 5, 6, 47, 49, 55–6, 110, 164, 213–8, 219, 221, 229, 234, 236; religion 53–5, 120, 183, 196; sadism and bondage 34–7, 51, 100–1, 107; *Simple People* 6, 7, 19, 21, 23, 30, 40, 58, 69, 72–82, 87, 92, 102, 111, 179, 234; *Simply Disconnected* 11, 13, 17, 29, 38, 49, 52, 156, 170, 176–7, 180, 183, 189–99, 200–1, 204–6, 209, 213, 230, 236–7; *Sleeping Dog* 5, 26–7, 41, 50, 58, 110–16, 117, 125, 136, 151, 164, 173, 214, 217; smokers and smoking 163; *The Smoking Diaries* 1, 4, 7, 19, 23, 35–6, 43, 46, 53, 56, 186; social attitudes 10–21, 51–2; *Spoiled* 15, 17, 29–30, 32–3, 35–6, 45, 49–51, 53, 107, 136–9, 145, 153–4, 235; *Stage Struck* 8, 13, 14, 15, 18, 26, 30, 49, 125, 210–11, 228, 232, 235; style and dramatic technique 17–9, 55–7, 69–71, 98, 102–3, 105–7, 110, 124, 133–4, 172–3, 236; *They Never Slept* 3, 49,

155, 167, 192, 214, 218–20, 221, 225, 228–9, 235–6; *Two Sundays* 15, 18, 20, 24, 28–9, 31, 35, 136, 181, 183; *An Unnatural Pursuit* 3, 13, 14, 18, 20, 23, 31, 43, 167; *Wise Child* 3, 13, 39, 40, 43, 53, 105, 107, 116–24, 125, 129, 131–3, 136, 139, 151, 155, 162, 171–2, 228, 235, 237; *The Year of the Jouncer* 1, 4, 8, 10, 30–2, 43, 186
Greco, El 217
Green, Henry 102
The Green Guide: Canada (Michelin) 67
Greene, Graham 10, 11, 55, 102, 203; "The Basement Room" 145; "The Burden of Childhood 40; *A Burnt-Out Case* 9, 111; *Collected Essays* 10, 40; *The Comedians* 124; *The Confidential Agent* 99; *The End of the Affair* 9, 10; *The Fallen Idol* 145; *A Gun for Sale* 101; *The Heart of the Matter* 10; *The Ministry of Fear* 101; *Monsignor Quixote* 10; *Our Man in Havana* 93; "The Young Dickens" 10
Grieg, Edvard: *Peer Gynt* 51
Guinness, Alec 3, 124

Haggard, H. Rider 158; *King Solomon's Mines* 159; *She and Alan* 159
Halifax, Nova Scotia 5, 67, 134, 213
Hall, Anne C. 175
Hall, Peter 135
Hallam, Arthur Henry 213
Hamilton Ian 7, 19, 107
Hammett, Dashiell: *The Maltese Falcon* 102
Handel, Georg Friedrich: "Paradise Duet" 12
Hardy, Thomas 36–7, 205; "After a Journey" 7; "Drummer Hodge" 76; *The Mayor of Casterbridge* 177; "The Self-Unseeing" 203
Hare, David 55
Hawthorne, Nigel 3
Haydn, Joseph 147
Hayling Island 5, 20, 24, 158, 233
Hearst, William Randolph 223
Hemingway, Ernest 215
Herrick, Robert 146; "To the Virgins, to Make Much of Time" 150
Highsmith, Patricia 146
Hitchcock, Alfred 36
Hitler, Adolf 131
Hobbes, Thomas 107
Hotel Rwanda (movie) 6
Hough, Graham: *The Dark Sun* 7
Housman, A.E. 25
Hume, David 107

Ibsen, Henrik 213; *An Enemy of the People* 109, 224; *Hedda Gabler* 12, 109, 188; *Peer Gynt* 51; *The Pillars of Society* 9
Imhof, Rüdiger 1, 32, 35, 150
Ionesco, Eugene 71; *The Lesson* 30, 131
The Ipcress File (movie) 20

Irons, Jeremy 3
Isherwood, Christopher 210

James, Henry 14, 50, 79, 81, 196–8, 225; *The Ambassadors* 78; *The American* 78; *Daisy Miller* 65; "The Lesson of the Master" 78; *The Turn of the Screw* 50
Janson, Hank 40, 139, 143–4, 231, 233, 235–7; *Kill Her If You Can* 36; *Skirts Bring Me Sorrow* 35; *Torment for Trixie* 35
Jenkins, Peter 225
Jonson Ben 94
Joyce, James 29; "The Dead" 84; *A Portrait of the Artist as a Young Man* 27, 41, 120; *Ulysses* 65, 83

Kafka, Franz 66, 95
Kant, Emmanuel 168
Keats, John 84
Kennedy, Ludovic: *Ten Rillington Place* 134
Kerensky, Oleg 135, 172, 184
Kind Hearts and Coronets (movie) 124
King, Kimball 54
Kipling, Rudyard 25, 40
Kress, Samuel 22

Lahr, John 48, 140
Lancaster, Burt 37
Lane, Nathan 3
Lang, Fritz: *M* 163
The Lavender Hill Mob (movie) 133
Lawrence, D.H. 7, 8, 31–2, 34, 40, 54, 58, 62, 64, 79–80, 87, 92, 102, 164, 171, 209–10; *Aaron's Rod* 31 "The Daughters of the Vicar" 8; *The Fox* 38; "The Horse Dealer's Daughter" 62; *Lady Chatterley's Lover* 38; *The Plumed Serpent* 55; *Sons and Lovers* 16; "The Virgin and the Gypsy" 38; *Women in Love* 31, 170
Leavis, F.R. 8, 16, 26, 219, 230; *D.H. Lawrence: Novelist* 7; "Revaluation" 148
le Carré, John 102; *The Constant Gardener* 6; *The Mission Song* 6, 111; *A Small Town in Germany* 93; *The Spy Who Came In from the Cold* 93
Lermontov, Mikhail 194; *A Hero of Our Time* 143
Lewis, Sinclair: *Arrowsmith* 67; *Babbitt* 67
Lorca, Frederico Garcia 84, 103
Loveridge, Lizzie 180

Macdonald, Ross 230
MacLeish, Archibald: "Ars Poetica" 192
The Mahdi 214
Mamet, David: *Oleanna* 30
Mann, Thomas 29, 217, 235
Manolete 84, 103
Mao Zedong, Chairman 211
Massie, Allan 32
Mayo, Virginia 37, 132

McCabe, Colin 53
McLuhan, Marshall 114
McNally, Terrence: *And Things That Go Bump in the Night* 116
Melville, Herman: *Billy Budd* 64, 217; *Moby-Dick* 171, 216
Mill, John Stuart 154
Miller, Arthur: *All My Sons* 166
Mills, John 155
Mishma, Yukio 44
Molière: *Tartuffe* 50, 52
Montreal, Canada 1, 4, 5, 14, 42, 186, 235
Morgan. J.P. 223
Murdoch, Iris: *An Unofficial Rose* 41

Nietzsche, Friedrich 27, 83, 104
Nixon, Cynthia: *Lawrence's Leadership Politics and the Turn Against Women* 31

Oates, Joyce Carol 231
O'Neill, Eugene: *The Emperor Jones* 215; *The Iceman Cometh* 1; *Long Day's Journey into Night* 166
Oppenheim, E. Phillips: *The Great Impersonation* 96
Orton, Joe 41, 44–5, 135; *Entertaining Mr. Sloane* 105, 116, 121; *Loot* 130; *What the Butler Saw* 105–6
Orwell, George 10
Osborne, John 1, 55, 105; *The Entertainer* 164; *Look Back in Anger* 147

Paltrow, Gwyneth 20
Pasha, Emin 214
Percy, Walker 52
Pierrepoint, Albert 134
Pinter, Harold 1, 3, 4, 11, 19, 48, 71, 105, 116, 140, 154, 169, 203, 209, 232; *The Birthday Party* 77, 198; *The Caretaker* 204; *The Dumbwaiter* 77, 129
Pirandello, Luigi 47
Plato 217; *The Republic* 168
Pleasence, Donald 124
Poe, Edgar Allan 231
Potter, Beatrix 11; *Cecily Paisley* 143, 150–1
Powell, Anthony: *At Lady Molly's* 66
Pushkin, Alexander 50, 194; *Eugene Onegin* 143
Pynchon, Thomas 133, 225

Queen Mary College, University of London 25–6, 98, 117, 140, 144, 235

Rattenbury, Alma Victoria 134, 228
Rattigan, Terence 203; *Cause Célèbre* 56; *The Winslow Boy* 181
Raven, Simon 13
Reade, Hamish (pen name for Simon Gray) 93, 103
Rendell, Bob 160, 164

Renoir, Jean: *Grand Illusion* 51; *La Règle du Jeu* 163
Rhys, Jean 73, 235
Rilke, Rainer Maria 233
Rimbaud, Arthur 88
Robinson, George Wharton 227
Roof, Judith 160–1, 167
Roth, Philip 154, 209
Rothschild, Victoria Katherine (playwright's second wife) 4, 53, 194
Ruskin, John 154

Sardou, Victorien 122
Schapiro, Meter 224
Schopenhauer, Arthur 180
Scott, Sir Walter 32
Scribe, Eugène 122
Secrest, Meryl 221
Serling, Rod: *The Twilight Zone* 114
Shaffer, Anthony: *Sleuth* 210
Shakespeare, William: *Cymbeline* 149; *Hamlet* 149; *Othello* 137, 128; *Pericles* 149; Sonnet 94, 149; *The Taming of the Shrew* 191; *The Tempest* 149, 235; *Twelfth Night* 105; *A Winter's Tale* 99, 149, 151
Shaw, Peter 5
Shelley, Percy 84
Siegel, Naomi 159
Sillitoe, Alan 110; *Saturday Night and Sunday Morning* 191
Simon, Robert 48
Simpson, Colin 220-2
Sondheim, Stephen: *Company* 234; *Sweeney Todd* 234
Sophocles: *Oedipus Rex* 220
Spengler, Oswald 164
Stalin, Josef 131, 211
Stanley, H.M. 6, 55, 220
Staunton, Imelda 3
Stevens, Paul 176
Stevens, Wallace: "Peter Quince at the Clavier" 54; "Sunday Morning" 53
Stevenson, Robert Louis 32
Stoppard, Tom 55, 231–2
Storey, David 110
Stravinsky, Igor 215; *Rite of Spring* 63, 109
Strindberg, August: *Miss Julia* 33, 37, 109
Summer Days: Writers on Cricket 20
Sutherland. N.S.: *Breakdown* 21
Symonds, Robert 31–2, 233

Tarantino, Quentin: *Inglourious Basterds* 225

Taylor, John Russell 111
Tennyson, Alfred Lord 213
Ternan, Ellen 9, 49, 225
Thatcher, Margaret 197
"Time on Line" 135
Tolstoy, Leo 40, 164, 214–5, 218; *War and Peace* 67, 70, 143
Tomlin, Claire: *The Invisible Woman: The Story of Ellen Ternan* 9, 226–7
Turgenev, Ivan 50
Turing, Alan 100

Updike, John 34, 209

Vale, Alison 230
Velázquez, Diego 217

Wagner, Richard 199; *Parsifal* 12, 180, 182–3, 192, 196, 206
Wardle, Irving 217
Waugh, Evelyn 25, 67–8, 102; *Brideshead Revisited* 164–5
Weber, Bruce 147
Weiss, Peter 204
Welles, Orson: *Citizen Kane* 71, 220
Wesker, Arnold 107
Wharton, Edith 59
White, Patrick 29, 44, 217
Wilde, Oscar 19, 142, 165; *The Importance of Being Earnest* 184; *Lady Windermere's Fan* 185
Williams, Simon 13
Williams, Tennessee 5, 140, 35; *A Streetcar Named Desire* 162
Wilson, August 4
Wisden Cricket Monthly 20
Wittgenstein, Ludwig 227
Woo, Duncan 180
Woolf, Virginia: *To the Lighthouse* 206
Wordsworth, William: "I Traveled Among Unknown Men" 7; "The Intimations Ode" 6; *The Prelude* 147; "A Slumber Did My Spirit Seal" 7; "Strange Fits of Passion Have I Known" 7; "Tintern Abbey" 6
Wouk, Herman: *The Caine Mutiny* 216, 218
Wright, Thomas: *The Life of Charles Dickens* 225

Yeats, W.B.: "Among School Children" 85; "Leda an the Swan" 128
Young, Toby 173

www.ingramcontent.com/pod-product-compliance
Lightning Source LLC
Chambersburg PA
CBHW051217300426
44116CB00006B/605